POLITICAL DYNAMICS
IN CONTEMPORARY JAPAN

The papers in this volume grew out of a conference sponsored by the Joint Committee on Japanese Studies of the Social Science Research Council and the American Council of Learned Societies and by the Japan Society for the Promotion of Science, with additional funding provided by the Japan-U.S. Friendship Commission.

POLITICAL DYNAMICS IN CONTEMPORARY JAPAN

Edited by
GARY D. ALLINSON
and
YASUNORI SONE

Cornell University Press

Ithaca and London

Cornell University Press gratefully acknowledges
a grant from the Suntory Foundation that
aided in bringing this book to publication.

The costs of publishing this book have been defrayed in part by the 1992
Hiromi Arisawa Memorial Award from the Books on Japan Fund with respect
to *Crested Kimono: Power and Love in the Japanese Business Family* by
Matthews Masayuki Hamabata, published by Cornell University Press. The
award is financed by The Japan Foundation from generous donations
contributed by Japanese individuals and companies.

First published 1993 by Cornell University Press.

International Standard Book Number 0-8014-2852-1 (cloth)
International Standard Book Number 0-8014-8096-5 (paper)
Library of Congress Catalog Card Number 92-56777
Printed in the United States of America
*Librarians: Library of Congress cataloging information appears
on the last page of the book.*

∞ The paper in this book meets the minimum requirements of the
American National Standard for Information Sciences—Permanence
of Paper for Printed Library Materials, ANSI Z39.48-1984.

CONTENTS

TABLES AND FIGURES

Tables

Figures

CONTRIBUTORS

GARY D. ALLINSON is the Ellen Bayard Weedon Professor of East Asian Studies in the Department of History at the University of Virginia.

IKUO KUME is an Associate Professor on the Faculty of Law at Kobe University.

MASARU MABUCHI is an Associate Professor on the Faculty of Law at Osaka University.

MARGARET A. McKEAN is an Associate Professor in the Department of Political Science at Duke University.

MIKE MOCHIZUKI is an Associate Professor in the School of International Relations at the University of Southern California.

MICHIO MURAMATSU is a Professor on the Faculty of Law at Kyoto University.

HIDEO OTAKE, a member of the faculty at Tōhoku University during the course of this project, joined the Faculty of Law at Kyoto University as a Professor in late 1992.

FRANCES McCALL ROSENBLUTH is an Assistant Professor in the Department of Political Science at the University of California at Los Angeles.

FRANK SCHWARTZ is the Assistant Director of the U.S.-Japan Relations Program at the Japan Society in New York City.

YASUNORI SONE is a Professor on the Faculty of Law at the Mita Campus of Keio University; he is also a Professor on the Faculty of Policy Management, as well as an Associate Dean, at Keio's Fujisawa Campus.

YUTAKA TSUJINAKA is an Associate Professor in the Department of Political Science and in the Institute of Social Sciences at the University of Tsukuba.

FRANK UPHAM is a Professor at the Boston College Law School.

ACKNOWLEDGMENTS

THIS VOLUME IS THE PRODUCT OF A LONG-TERM PROJECT IN BINA-
tional scholarship conducted under the auspices of the U.S.-Japan Cooperative Program in the Humanities and Social Sciences. The program is administered jointly through the Japan Society for the Promotion of Science
in Tokyo and the Joint Committee on Japanese Studies of the Social Science Research Council (in New York) and the American Council of
Learned Societies. The first step in our undertaking occurred in 1987
when a group of one Japanese and six American scholars met for a planning workshop in New York City. A second meeting was held in June
1989 at Airlie House (Warrenton, Virginia), where six Japanese and five
American scholars met to discuss preliminary findings. A third and final
meeting took place in August 1990 on Maui, Hawaii, where all of the current authors were in attendance to present penultimate versions of their
chapters. English was the language used at all three meetings, and the participants from Japan all submitted essays written in English. This project
thus offers a perhaps modest, but nonetheless striking, example of the success of Japanese internationalization.

During our work, we have incurred debts and obligations to many organizations and individuals, and it is our pleasure to acknowledge them
here. In the United States, we offer our appreciation to the Social Science
Research Council for its financial assistance. We also extend our joint
thanks to the many staff members at the council who facilitated our work.
They include Ted Bestor, Yasmine Ergas, Mary McDonnell, Elizabeth
O'Brien, Blair Ruble, and Stefan Tanaka. The Japan-U.S. Friendship Commission underwrote the costs of the American participants at the Maui

conference and also provided funds to defer many of the expenses of producing this volume. To the organization we extend our heartfelt appreciation. We also value the highly professional assistance that Linley Sloan, former executive director of the commission, and Eric Gangloff, its current director, extended to us. Richard Samuels and Michael Reich attended the first planning workshop. They made stimulating contributions to our proceedings as did Deborah Millie at our Airlie House meeting. Gary Allinson thanks Mary Brown of the Asia Program at the Wilson Center (Washington, D.C.) and Richard J. Smethurst and the Asian Studies Program of the University of Pittsburgh for lecture invitations that enabled him to present and reflect on the ideas for this project. Mark Tilton offered incisive editorial counsel at a critical juncture.

In Japan we thank the Japan Society for the Promotion of Science, which underwrote the costs of the Japanese participants in the last two conferences. We also extend our appreciation to the Suntory Foundation for its support of research activities undertaken by the Japan team.

Finally, we all owe a debt of gratitude to T. J. Pempel in his role as a reader for Cornell University Press. With his inimitably low-key style, he has made this a better book in many ways.

A Note on the Usage of Japanese Names

It is customary in Japan to place the family name before the given name. We honor this customary usage when referring to Japanese authors who have published in Japanese. We thus cite the author of *Sengo Nihon no kanryōsei* as Muramatsu Michio. Japanese authors, however, usually employ English-language conventions when they publish in English by placing their given names before their family names (e.g., Michio Muramatsu). Therefore, when citing English-language publications by Japanese authors, we do likewise. We also refer to the Japanese authors in this volume according to the same convention, placing their given names first.

G. D. A.
Y. S.

POLITICAL DYNAMICS
IN CONTEMPORARY JAPAN

ANALYZING POLITICAL CHANGE:

TOPICS, FINDINGS, AND IMPLICATIONS

Gary D. Allinson

OUR PURPOSE IN THIS VOLUME IS TO CAST EMPIRICAL LIGHT ON JAPANESE politics since the 1970s in order to illuminate salient changes and to interpret their significance. Rather than dwell on topics that have attracted wide attention, such as industrial policy and trade disputes, we treat previously unexamined issues that became controversial after 1970. We adopt a broad perspective on the social context of political action while emphasizing political change and process as well as actors and institutions. And we illuminate how both the shifting contours of political space and the constant fluidity of political alignments accentuate the importance of competitive negotiation in Japanese politics.

We were drawn to this undertaking by a desire to understand the interplay between public and private interests from both a general and a particular perspective. On the general level, we sensed a distinctive quality about the relationships among public institutions, private groups, and the public interest. Japan was a society in which cooperative relations between big business and the government seemed unusually salubrious. Moreover, the boundaries between public and private domains seemed to be rather permeable as the use of industrial policy and retail trade regulation both suggested. Finally, government policies had for three decades apparently satisfied the great majority of the Japanese populace, in part, surely, because public and private interests had meshed. For all these reasons, we thought it valuable to study how individuals, groups, and institutions negotiated their interests, especially in areas not previously subject to scholarly inquiry.

The importance of public and private interests in the contemporary era takes on heightened significance when considered against the background of Japan's modern history. Since the Meiji Restoration of 1868, public authority has shaped private interests in many ways. Especially in the years between the Restoration and the 1950s, the state played an intrusive role in education, culture, security, policing, and social welfare. We are primarily concerned, however, with broad issues of wealth and power, so we focus our remarks briefly on the role of public authorities in nurturing economic development and on their relationships with the private groups that have assisted and benefited from the policies of state.

A strong drive to catch up with the West compelled the newly unified nation after 1868 to promote forced modernization at state initiative. Bureaucratic directives, public funding, and government provision of infrastructure were just three devices employed to nurture a private economy based on large-scale industrial firms. These efforts fostered a modern textile industry after the 1880s and a diversified heavy industrial sector by the 1910s. A brief respite from intrusive government control occurred during the 1920s. But, thereafter, the twin forces of imperial expansion and global war swept private interests into a tight embrace with governments whose policies led ultimately to destruction.

After Japan's defeat in 1945, private business interests were severely weakened in their ability to provide a counterbalance to the public authority of the Japanese state. The Occupation purged several thousand executives who had been leading figures in the private sector. Their successors faced overwhelming challenges in managing reconstruction, and most of them were preoccupied with events at the firm level for the ensuing decade. Occupation policies also restrained the former financial conglomerates (*zaibatsu*) and peak business associations from resuming the authority they had exerted before the war. Not until the late 1950s, therefore, did big business regain some of its influence in national affairs. That influence blossomed during the 1960s when business became a major political partner in driving Japan's "economic miracle." But unpopular acts of environmental pollution and *kinken seiji* (money politics) forced business to retreat from its political salient in the 1970s.

While private interests in the business sector concentrated on reconstruction, public authority under the Allied Occupation drifted into the hands of the national bureaucracy. The bureaucracy had been an important force before the war. It had, however, always had to contend with other institutions and elites in a multivocal constitutional order. An autonomous military, a privy council, a formal aristocracy, an imperial household ministry, and informal coteries of prominent former officeholders (*genrō* and *jūshin*) were among the groups that had restrained bureaucratic influence before 1945. The purge conducted under the Occupation and the new postwar constitution effectively removed all of these groups as claimants to power while the bureaucracy assumed a new lease on life as the instrument through which the Occupation was administered. Under these circumstances, a powerful public institution found itself in a unique position to shape private interests.

By the late 1950s economic growth assumed the highest priority as a national policy. Political, academic, and bureaucratic elites formulated and articulated the policy. Business elites saw fit to support it. And the populace, hungry for the material rewards it promised, quickly endorsed the policy, too. During the 1960s and early 1970s Japan engaged in a concerted effort toward economic expansion that brought public and private interests into close conjunction. Central ministries used a wide repertoire of policy tools to encourage private interests to conform with public policies. In most (but not all) cases private business went along with these policies, and they eventually produced rewards for nearly everyone as I illustrate in Chapter 1.

Owing to the rapidity of economic growth and to its thoroughgoing social consequences, Japanese society experienced a shift in the balance of power by the late 1960s. It was a gradual and subtle shift, but a fundamental one, nonetheless. One small, but telling, indication appeared in changing patterns of the "descent from heaven," or *amakudari*. This term refers to the actions of former bureaucrats who leave national ministries and undertake new careers. Since the late nineteenth century former national bureaucrats had been able to command prestigious positions upon their retirement, a practice that denoted the relatively greater influence of public authority embodied in national civil servants. They commonly assumed high-ranking posts in private firms and, both before and after the Pacific war, they often ran for election to the national legislature and frequently became cabinet ministers. The ability of former bureaucrats to command position and place reached a crescendo in the 1950s and 1960s when they dominated the prime ministership, key cabinet posts, and major leadership positions in the private sector. By the early 1970s, however, both the ruling party and private corporations had developed enough talent and expertise in their own ranks that amakudari officials were almost shut out of top positions thereafter in favor of men groomed from within. This was one way in which the balance of skills, talents, and, therefore, influence shifted between the public and private sector at the beginning of the third postwar decade.

The same shift in power manifested itself in other ways, too. For nearly one century, Japan had relied on government support, public funding, and bureaucratic inducements to generate wealth through private corporations for public ends in the form of a national commitment to economic development. This pattern of wealth generation was not, of course, the only one that appeared during that epoch, but it was a dominant tendency. By the late 1960s the very success of Japan's economic policies, exemplified by consistently high rates of growth for more than one decade, began to alter perceptibly this pattern of wealth generation. More and more wealth was being created under private auspices, at private initiative, for private ends as higher profits for corporations and higher incomes for families and individuals. These private ends marked the realization of a public interest, economic growth, but they also embodied undertones of selfishness and some loss of public-spiritedness.

The shift in power eventually fostered new ideological tendencies that manifested themselves most clearly during the prime ministership of Nakasone Yasuhiro between 1982 and 1987. At the same time the shift emboldened a resurgent business community to take a leading role in the political life of the nation. And it prepared a more affluent populace, described at greater length in Chapter 1, to respond to calls for lower taxes and reduced government. During the 1980s these phenomena—a conservative ideology, a bolder business community, and a concerned public— joined to create the environment in which a movement for administrative reform (gyōsei kaikaku) took place. It is this movement that provided the particular reason for our studies of public and private interests.

The specific features of administrative reform are discussed in greater detail in Chapters 1, 2, 7, 9, and 10. In light of the historical discussion we are pursuing here, this movement was important for three reasons. First, it represented an explicit effort by the private business sector to roll back the state. The movement was a direct challenge to the bureaucracy to put its house in order and to limit its interference in private-sector activities. Second, the movement included an effort to enhance the private sector at the expense of the public by privatizing key government monopolies, especially rail transport and telecommunications. In this regard Japan's administrative reform echoed changes occurring at the same time in England and the United States, but it can also be regarded as an unprecedented sign of private influence over public institutions. Third, conservative interests in Japan exploited the administrative reform movement in order to reduce the oppositionary political influence of organized workers in public enterprises. They did this by dividing those enterprises into smaller units and by making them private, thereby diffusing the influence of such workers and creating a work environment conducive to moderate political behavior.

Administrative reform thus provided an inviting laboratory in which to study contests over public and private interests. We proceeded by examining many topical issues important to the politics of the 1970s and 1980s; they are treated in Parts 2, 3, and 4 of the volume. Part 1 precedes them with three chapters in which we set the topical studies in context. In Chapter 1, I analyze the socioeconomic changes that emerged after the early 1970s to shape altering patterns of political behavior. Michio Muramatsu adopts a pluralist perspective to survey major policies and how they change, in Chapter 2. And Margaret McKean, in Chapter 3, presents a critical review of recent literature on Japanese politics in order to pursue a theoretical analysis of the state and its relationship to public interests.

Two issues prominent during the period under study were the regulation of financial policy and the privatization of government monopolies. In Part 2 we explore the processes and consequences of reforms in the financial system. Frances Rosenbluth concentrates in Chapter 4 on the politics of financial deregulation while Masaru Mabuchi analyzes in Chapter 5 the complex countercurrents set in motion by simultaneous efforts to deregulate and to reregulate financial policy. Privatization was a complex process with wide-ranging effects, but its consequences bore most heavily on organized labor. In Part 3 we illustrate how privatization enhanced already strong tendencies toward moderation among Japan's unionized workers. Ikuo Kume examines private sector labor unions; Mike Mochizuki studies the response of public sector employees to privatization; and Yutaka Tsujinaka offers a tentative assessment of the new labor federation (Rengō) that emerged in the late 1980s.

During the 1960s and 1970s many crucial political decisions in Japan were made in the councils of the ruling party or the offices of the national bureaucracy. That continued to be true during the 1980s as well, but the increasing complexity and controversy surrounding many issues forced more bargaining into a wider variety of political spaces. Three chapters in Part 4 illustrate this tendency by examining heretofore only partly studied sites and modes of political negotiation. The administrative reform movement of the 1980s relied frequently on advisory commissions (*shingikai*) as a vehicle for shaping consensus, promoting political agendas, and inducing reforms. Frank Schwartz studies the roles, functions, operations, and achievements of such bodies both before and during the 1980s in Chapter 9 while Hideo Otake analyzes, in Chapter 10, the complex political peregrinations of one such body established to consider land use policy. Another controversial issue that was played out in a variety of sites under shifting patterns of political alliance was regulation of retail trade. Frank Upham explores this issue in Chapter 11. The volume closes with a chapter by Yasunori Sone in which he uses the notion of *gyōkai* or "policy clienteles" to depict the structure of political bargaining in Japan's negotiated polity.

Our purposes here are to identify and to interpret the changes that seem to underlie an increasing complexity in Japanese politics. Our findings collectively reveal three significant changes that have arisen since the early 1970s. One is an increase in the scope, frequency, and intensity of political bargains negotiated through organized and institutionalized groups. In general this finding underscores what many advocates of a pluralist polity have been asserting. An incremental growth in affluence and in the capacity of groups to organize, marshal resources, develop expertise, and articulate demands has heightened the incidence of political negotiation, not only at the national level but at other levels of the political system as well. In Chapter 1, I illuminate the socioeconomic context that has shaped these developments and in many succeeding chapters we describe more concretely how such negotiation has expanded.

Many different types of organized interest groups appear in the following chapters. Some are broad, industrywide bodies, such as the construction trades mentioned in Chapter 2. Others are narrower in scope and represent more homogeneous interests, such as the banking association examined in Chapter 4, the trade associations for steel and coal discussed in Chapter 6, and the real estate developers treated in Chapter 10. We also devote considerable attention to labor as an organized interest group. In Chapters 6, 7, and 8 we explore how organized labor works both at the enterprise and the federation levels to achieve its political objectives, and in Chapters 9 and 10 we illuminate the roles that labor has played on shingikai. Ample finances, educated staff, political expertise, and strategic knowledge are four important resources that have enabled groups like these to assume an apparently heightened capacity for political participation in the contemporary polity.

We also detect a second change that we find quite important, however conceptually elusive it might seem. We believe that in recent years disorganized or unorganized groups in Japanese society have increased their ability to realize political ends that in some measure meet their needs. Even to raise this issue is to provoke a host of analytical problems. How can we determine what unorganized and, possibly, inarticulate groups really need? Are apparently salutary outcomes not just the unintended consequences of elite behavior? Or could they not be the logical results of a perfectly operating political "market?" Our task in this volume is to unveil, not solve, this problem of interpretation in Japanese politics for almost the first time. We suggest that Japanese political processes do operate to favor disorganized, unorganized, inarticulate, or otherwise inchoate political forces, at least sometimes and in general ways. In Chapter 1, I show how socioeconomic changes have facilitated the emergence of such outcomes while Margaret McKean in Chapter 3 provides a theoretical explanation for them. Two specific groups that have benefited from such processes are financial consumers, whom Frances Rosenbluth discusses in Chapter 4, and small retailers, whom Frank Upham examines in Chapter 11.

Consumers and small retailers are only two among many unorganized, disorganized, or partially organized social groups that have become the focus of political attention in recent years. Two other groups are the chronically ill elderly and school children returning from lengthy residence abroad. These are groups with definable social characteristics, but they would be difficult, if not impossible, to organize as institutionalized interests. Nonetheless, problems associated with these groups have become objects of political policy in recent years. Such problems may first be articulated through extrapolitical avenues, such as letters to editors, discussions on TV talk shows, commentary among business people, and research reports from think tanks and universities. Concerns arise about the elderly and the school children themselves and, also, about beleaguered family members as caretakers for the elderly and parents worried about their children's mobility prospects. In due course public institutions use public funds to seek resolutions to the problems. On occasion such responses occur because political elites themselves perceive the problems and strive to resolve them; in other cases inchoate pressures emanating from many social sources oblige political elites to take action, possibly against their will. We want to highlight this qualitatively new type of political interaction, which we believe is a product of the steadily increasing diversity and affluence of Japanese society, because this admittedly elusive phenomenon of unorganized political pressure is illustrative of how extensive and differentiated political negotiation has become in contemporary Japan.

The third and final change that we identify is the increasing importance of international influences on Japanese politics. These take two forms. Some international influences arise owing to Japan's increased participation in the external world. Membership in multinational banking consortia, investments abroad, international trade, borrowing on external markets, and foreign residence by Japanese nationals are just some of the international activities that have become far more apparent since the early 1970s. In one degree or another, all of these activities have consequences for domestic politics. The second type of international influence is direct foreign pressure on the Japanese political system. This kind of pressure is referred to somewhat pejoratively in Japanese as *gaiatsu*. Its principal source in the 1980s was an increasingly frustrated United States, although European nations also brought gaiatsu to bear on Japan.

In many chapters we address the political implications of international forces on Japan in the years since 1970. One example of influences arising from increased participation in the international economy appears in Chapter 4. When Japanese corporations gain access to foreign capital, they acquire political leverage that enhances their power in contests with the bureaucracy. Frances Rosenbluth explains the evolution of this process in her discussion of financial deregulation. The vigorous prodding that characterizes American gaiatsu had an increasing impact on a range of political issues by the late 1980s. Michio Muramatsu, Masaru Mabuchi, Hideo Otake, and Frank Upham delineate how such pressure affected political practice in construction, finance, land use, and retail distribution, respectively.

The consequences of expanded international participation and of intensifying international pressure are difficult to discern, and even more difficult to generalize about, because they are recent. They, nonetheless, suggest one cautionary note concerning current fashions in the interpretation of Japanese politics. When foreign interests bring pressure on the Japanese government, they sometimes align themselves with a coalition of domestic producer groups, a bureaucratic section, and a party faction. At first glance, this kind of pressure is reminiscent of the politics of iron triangles or subgovernments. The presence of foreign interests, however, injects an entirely new set of ingredients into Japan's political practices. It is important to be sensitive to the new constellations of power that may emerge from political contests like these, and we urge caution in leaping too quickly to embrace what may have become overly rigid concepts that do not capture the full complexity of political change in the dynamic contemporary polity. To understand better the implications of international participation and pressure, the first step is to produce sensitive empirical studies, and we strive to do so in the chapters mentioned.

These changes are three principal signs of subtle, but significant, alterations in the practice of politics in contemporary Japan. They denote modes of political interaction that are discernibly different from those that prevailed through the late 1960s. Until then, bureaucratic elites, operating both as incumbent officeholders in the central ministries and—in their roles as former bureaucrats—as key leaders in the ruling party and the business world, dominated Japanese politics with a technocratic style of governance. If the populace complied with their policies, it was, in part, out of a sense of duty and, in part, out of a sense of gratitude for the benefits of the policies they pursued.

By the 1970s, however, this pattern of interaction had begun to change. As indicated in many of the following chapters, the bureaucracy found it increasingly difficult to work its will on the polity after the 1970s. Bureaucrats became more defensive in many ways, and they had difficulty pursuing their technocratic, directive style of governance. Richer and more autonomous business firms accounted in some measure for a relative reduction in bureaucratic power. They no longer required the kind of resources and guidance that bureaucrats had provided during the 1950s and the 1960s, and their growing confidence and success in domestic and international markets enabled them to set a more independent course. A more affluent society also tilted power balances between the bureaucracy and other groups in Japan. An earlier pattern of diffident and dependent behavior gave way to one in which citizens with a consciousness of their rights began to press their demands in the voting booth, through interest groups, in celebrated court cases, and in direct bargaining with officials. We are in broad agreement that changes like these, described in greater detail in all of the chapters to follow, have lent a new tenor to Japanese political life since the 1970s. It is too early to make conclusive claims about the significance of these changes, but we hope that our work begins at least to outline what is significant about Japan's changing political order.

The changes noted, and the findings from our empirical studies as well, have persuaded us to suggest some conceptual alternatives for the study of Japanese politics. From the outset we wanted to ask more than the classical question, Who holds power in Japan? We also wanted to know, How is power exercised? And on whose behalf is it wielded? We have tried to do more than map the locations of power and the interactions of power-holders. We have also tried to understand the process of political bargaining, the relations between political elites and societal interests, and the consequences of political negotiations for groups and individuals in Japanese society.

To address such issues properly, it is necessary to advance conceptual alternatives that alleviate the anomalies inherent in some models of the Japanese polity. For this purpose we define politics as a field of action in which the pursuit of interests is the primary objective. According to this definition, conventional sites of political behavior at the national level continue as objects of inquiry and studies of bureaucratic and party roles in the formulation and passage of laws remain a major part of political research. More important, this definition validates the significance of a broader range of political spaces, some of them new and distinctive. Quasi-formal fields of action (such as shingikai) and wholly informal political spaces (such as those created when small retailers battle with invading department stores) also become legitimate subjects for political investigation. The novelty, scope, and multiplicity of recent changes in Japan make this more capacious view of politics imperative if we are to appreciate fully how the Japanese polity is changing.

Some hypothetical examples help specify our definition. The field of political action widens or narrows depending on the significance of the interests being pursued and the number of interested participants. A narrow field of action would be created by a specialized interest attracting the attention of only a few participants. For example, a manufacturing firm might impose on a Diet member to intercede with a ministry to expedite imports of licensed technology. Or a small group of local residents might press a municipality to honor right-to-sunlight guidelines abused by a private developer.

In contrast, issues of broad social and economic significance are more likely to attract a range of participants and to be played out on a wider field of action. This could be the case with a major tax reform. Pressures for such a reform might generate beyond the boundaries of the formal political arena, through widespread tax evasion, for example. The aggregated effects of many anonymous, individual choices could in time oblige bureaucrats or politicians to take action, either against their own inclinations or out of a necessity they had long failed to recognize. In the early stages of bargaining, negotiations in pursuit of tax reform might occur in many forums. In Japan, shingikai are one forum in which such preliminary bargaining often occurs, but it can occur in other, more informal settings as well. Political issues eventually wend their way through party and bureaucratic fields of action before they finally arrive at the national legislature to be passed into law. Even after laws have been passed, however, bargaining can persist over implementation on a political field as wide as that which brought the issue to the agenda in the first place.

Implicit in this view of politics as a field of action is the claim that groups and individuals can, and do, pursue political interests outside the formal settings of national policy-making. Certainly, major national issues are finally resolved with the passage of laws in the Diet. But it seems increasingly clear that many political bargains are negotiated in Japan without ever going near the Diet. For example, the Ministry of International Trade and Industry (MITI) has often sought to achieve its political ends through informal negotiations. In pursuit of such ends, it may implement the spirit of laws passed in cursory form by the Diet. But in other cases it may rely on broad authority—generously self-delegated—to pursue objectives never specified in law. Frank Upham's study of retail trade regulation delineates how the task of striking political bargains can essentially be delegated to private parties working under the loosest regulatory supervision. In these ways, participants in Japanese politics engage in negotiations well outside the party and legislature arena to achieve interests of significant value to them.

Labor often pursues its interests outside formal national institutions as we make clear in the chapters in Part 3. The predominance of enterprise unions creates a setting for the pursuit of worker interests that brings labor and management together in small units at the factory or enterprise level. In this way organized workers, most of whom are employees of large firms, have been able to pursue the economic security that seems to assume highest priority for them. The findings advanced by Ikuo Kume, Mike Mochizuki, and Yutaka Tsujinaka all confirm that organized labor has achieved handsome gains by complying with management in a spirit of cooperation to increase productivity, to ensure employment, and to enhance compensation and benefits. The aggregate effect of many salutary bargains struck in separate enterprises has been a marked achievement, at least for organized workers who remain employed.

Another tendency, however, runs counter to this one and diminishes labor's collective influence. As both Ikuo Kume and Mike Mochizuki affirm, material gains for continuing workers are often purchased at the expense of other workers who are fired or terminated. They form a pool of discharged workers who do not realize the benefits of their employed brethren in union firms. Such individuals are joined by legions of nonunionized workers in small and medium-sized enterprises. This tendency segments the work force politically and dilutes the influence of organized labor as a collective force in national politics. Segmentation, in turn, jeopardizes the well-being of many workers. The relatively low wages, the inferior benefits, and the poor job conditions of nonunion workers all imply that they have suffered from labor's inability to sustain itself as a unified force in national political life.

Labor's power in the contemporary polity is, thus, exercised more effectively across a diffuse array of firms and enterprises than as a unified collective force at the national level. In a society with a viable national health system and low rates of unemployment, workers have given highest priority to material compensation and longer tenures of employment. By pursuing these objectives at the enterprise level, organized workers in large firms have been politically able to achieve their main goals. Because public sector compensation is linked directly to that of workers in private firms, organized workers in the public sector have also reaped benefits from this strategy. In the process, however, organized workers have been willing to abandon some of their fellow employees, and they have overlooked the political needs of unorganized and part-time workers, especially those in small and medium-sized firms. In an economy in which much job growth has occurred in just such firms, as I reveal in Chapter 1, the strategy of organized labor has ensured a steady decline in unionization rates. Consequently, labor's collective influence as an opposition force in national politics has declined because such trends have eroded support for the socialist parties that compete against the ruling Liberal Democratic party (LDP).

Worker emphasis on economic security was one manifestation of the pragmatic and materialist values that animated political participation during an era of growing affluence. As I explain in Chapter 1 at greater length, steady economic growth conferred a measure of economic citizenship on nearly everyone in Japanese society. At the same time, it fostered a wide variety of fragmentation among groups and institutions. These tendencies provoked a more contentious and competitive polity, especially in the face of constraints posed by governmental debt problems. Domestic pressures on the national government were severe enough, and the intrusive role of gaiatsu only exacerbated them. By the late 1970s political institutions seemed overwhelmed with the need to control and contain demands, needs, and aspirations.

It appears that one consequence of these changes has been a serious challenge to the capacities of formal political institutions to process all of the demands imposed on them. In the following chapters we trace the nature of such challenges in a variety of ways. Masaru Mabuchi demonstrates how a once-strong ministry came under considerable pressure from domestic interest groups and foreign governments at a time when its own ability to act was severely hampered by governmental debt problems. Hideo Otake describes a ministry that wanted to pursue a consistent set of land-planning policies but was faced with a prime minister, ruling party, and conservative interests intent on achieving other ends. And Frank Upham explains how a ministry too short of resources and personnel had to cede regulatory authority to private parties to implement one set of laws it monitored.

We have found that the response to capacity constraints led to negotiations in a variety of political spaces. Sometimes political participants strived to contain conflict within the confines of formal, national institutions. Thus, the bureaucracy sought to maintain its power or to strike direct bargains that won at least a temporary solution to problems it confronted. Evidence confirming this kind of response appears in the chapters by Frances Rosenbluth, Masaru Mabuchi, Hideo Otake, and Frank Upham. In other cases the ruling party played a role as a mediator among ministries or between constituent groups and the bureaucracy, striving also to contain conflict within national institutions. Michio Muramatsu and Frances Rosenbluth cite examples to describe how.

A second response to the threat of an overloaded capacity was to shunt potential conflict toward quasi-formal political spaces. The shingikai is a classic example of a political forum employed for the purpose of channeling conflict, ameliorating differences, and promoting integration in Japanese politics. Frank Schwartz traces how such bodies have been used since 1945 and how, in the 1980s, Prime Minister Nakasone exploited analogous quasi-formal shingikai to promote his personal political agenda. While such bodies carry out their mandates, they engage in complicated political peregrinations. In a unique study, Hideo Otake explains how one of Nakasone's advisory bodies hammered out a position on land-use policy in the face of sharp ideological cleavages among its members as they worked amid a rapidly shifting political climate.

Finally, we have discovered one extreme response to the challenge to capacity. As Frank Upham indicates in his chapter, when MITI simply was not capable of dealing with political interests that were too numerous, too geographically dispersed, and too controversial to control, it actually ceded its authority (temporarily) to the disputants themselves. To understand the frequency of this response and its viability, we need more studies that are as detailed and authoritative as Frank Upham's. But whatever we learn, his findings strongly confirm the importance of examining, first, the implementation (as well as the formulation and passage) of laws in Japan, and, second, the informal spaces in which the implementation of laws can be negotiated.

In the following chapters we explore a number of controversial, but previously unexamined, issues in Japanese politics. These issues include the reregulation of financial practices, privatization's effects on the labor movement, the politics of public works spending, the formulation of land-use policies, and the regulation of retail trade. Our studies illuminate many, complex political problems that are resistant to uniform solutions readily applicable nationwide. These problems are of immediate concern to many individuals and groups in the private sector and to influential participants in the ruling party and the bureaucracy. The problems themselves generate persisting dissension that fosters nearly continuous negotiation in a context in which relative political strength among fluid coalitions seems to shift constantly. As a consequence, the interests of one group may prevail momentarily only to be overwhelmed later by those of other groups. All political participants must be prepared to win and lose as well as to compromise and to wait for a better day. Nonetheless, out of these fitful, contradictory processes emerge political decisions that do seem, as Margaret McKean contends in Chapter 3, to serve public interests in the broadest sense.

We have tried to capture some sense of these dynamic processes by defining politics as a field of action in which the pursuit of interests is the most important objective of political participants. This expansive view of politics helps to direct attention to events and changes that sometimes take place outside the formal institutions of national politics, and it creates the opportunity for developing a more nuanced view of the Japanese polity that depicts both how power is exercised and on whose behalf it is wielded. We would be the first to concede that party politicians and bureaucrats play a major role in shaping policies in contemporary Japan. But we also believe that societal interests, whether organized or not, have come to impose increasing constraints on the untrammeled authority of political elites. One stunning example of the increasing significance of such behavior occurred in late 1992 when public outrage over tainted campaign contributions forced the resignation of Kanemaru Shin, leader of the LDP's largest faction. Societal interests constrain political elites both wittingly and unwittingly and in roles as promoters, opponents, victims, and beneficiaries of policies. Moreover, constraints operate not only in central institutions of state but in a myriad of political spaces from farmsteads to factory sites and shopping districts. We believe that an approach that is sensitive to the shifting contours of political space and the fluidity of political alignments promises to enrich our understanding of contemporary Japan and to deepen our appreciation for the increasing complexity of Japanese politics.

We advance this conceptual alternative, and the empirical and interpretive findings contained in the chapters, to engage current academic debates. We recognize, however, that the controversies now surrounding this subject in academic circles alone resist easy solution. It is even less possible to resolve controversies spawned by new contingents of instant experts who seem to be making increasingly more inchoate claims about Japanese political intentions. At most, we hope to clarify the debates and to restore some sense of balance and civility by offering the results of careful empirical research in a moderate, illuminating manner.

We must also stress that we are not trying to construct a new orthodoxy for the interpretation of Japanese politics. Ours is an initial attempt to understand the broad significance of political change since the early 1970s. Inevitably, we can only proffer tentative conclusions. Furthermore, we do not claim to be in complete agreement on all issues. It would be difficult to secure such consensus in any group of twelve academics and even more difficult to do so in a binational group that represents a wide range of partisan positions. We have, thus, tolerated, even encouraged, interpretive variety. We hope that readers will find this approach both provocative and informative.

Part 1 of this volume is the most general in its topical and chronological coverage and in Chapter 1 we provide the historical and socioeconomic context for the subsequent chapters. Readers will want to approach the volume by reading Part 1 first. Parts 2 and 3 can be read interchangeably. They both deal with processes of negotiation over specific issues and institutions, finance and labor, respectively. Part 4 also examines processes of negotiation but in specific sites called shingikai and in a specific mode labeled "privatized regulation." In the concluding chapter we analyze the implications of our findings from the perspective of government and market relations at the gyōkai level.

PART ONE

STRUCTURAL FEATURES OF JAPAN'S DYNAMIC POLITY

Defining the boundary between what is political and what is not has been a long-standing analytical challenge for political scientists. In recent years powerful voices within the discipline have addressed the challenge by identifying a state on one hand and a society on the other—with varying degrees of success. Whether one enlists the terminology of state and society or other concepts and language, it is certain that to appreciate contemporary Japanese politics one must recognize how deeply and persistently socioeconomic change impinges on political attitudes and behavior.

The first two chapters in Part 1 adopt complementary, but slightly different, perspectives to address this interpretive challenge. In Chapter 1 Gary Allinson casts direct light on societal realms beyond the purely political. He illustrates how continued economic growth and the affluence it has promoted have conferred an unprecedented measure of economic citizenship on many groups and institutions in Japan and have also fostered widespread but subtle structural transformations. In the last half of his chapter, he demonstrates how economic citizenship and structural changes have facilitated the emergence of a more extensively and strenuously negotiated polity. By providing both a historical context and a substantive analysis of Japan's negotiated polity, he intends his chapter to serve as a general introduction to the other chapters in the volume.

Michio Muramatsu, in Chapter 2, focuses more intently on the political realm to assess how events of the 1980s affected what he has defined as "patterned pluralism." He finds a continuing retreat of bureaucratic power that enhances the already strong influence of the Liberal Democratic party (LDP) in a one-party dominant regime. Like Allinson, he stresses the importance of mass attitudes and behavior in shaping political change whether manifested through the electoral system or through interest group activity. Muramatsu and Allinson both agree that democratic participation by the Japanese citizenry and its consequences for the diffusion of power in contemporary Japan are very important.

If they appear to disagree, it is because they adopt somewhat different perspectives and concepts when striving to capture effectively the significance of the increased influence of the Japanese populace. Looking outward from the formal political arena, Muramatsu uses the concept of pluralism to contend that the political arena itself is expanding to absorb this growing popular influence. Increased interest group activity, attentive politicians, and defensive bureaucrats are three signs of the changing political realm in Muramatsu's view. Looking toward the formal political arena from its socioeconomic periphery, Allinson uses the term *economic citizenship* to suggest how the concerns, needs, and demands of an affluent populace—whether articulated or unarticulated—shape attitudes and behavior in the formal political arena. In his view politicians and bureaucrats are obliged to negotiate constantly as they strive to keep pace with socioeconomic changes that are often beyond their capacity to control or absorb. For both Allinson and Muramatsu, therefore, the inherent dynamism of Japanese society fosters, out of necessity, a more broadly negotiated polity.

Margaret McKean, in Chapter 3, deftly confronts two difficult questions that are directly related to these issues: How does the "state" arrive at its decisions? And how do its policies affect public interests? Measuring the strength of the state has never been easy, and it is complicated in contemporary Japan by the rapidity of change. After conducting a comprehensive review of current literature, McKean concludes that the state (in her definition, the bureaucracy and the LDP) is not the powerful monolith it has long appeared to be. It has become vulnerable and reactive in many ways, following and coordinating as often as leading. Nonetheless, it retains a great deal of "skill" that preserves far more than a vestige of power. Using its skill essentially for the purpose of self-preservation, the state, in McKean's view, is obliged to pursue policies that—perhaps paradoxically—do serve public interests.

CHAPTER ONE

CITIZENSHIP, FRAGMENTATION,

AND THE NEGOTIATED POLITY

Gary D. Allinson

THE AFFLUENCE THAT MANY JAPANESE CAME TO ENJOY AFTER THE 1970S was the culmination of long, hard efforts. In the first part of this chapter I sketch briefly how those efforts produced sustained economic growth that caused new lines of structural fragmentation while conferring economic citizenship on a scale unprecedented in Japan's history. I direct attention to social groups and institutions that are central to an understanding of socioeconomic change and its implications for Japanese politics after 1970: large corporations, the small business sector, families, women, interest groups, the labor movement, and political and business elites. In the second and third parts of the chapter I analyze how widespread economic citizenship attained under conditions of structural fragmentation shaped political attitudes and behavior in a negotiated polity.

Citizenship and Fragmentation in a Growing Economy

Japan's postwar economy is often characterized as a phoenix risen from the ashes, but this metaphor is inaccurate and misleading. Japan's economic position today is attributable to a long, slow accumulation of material gains that were first set in motion during the Tokugawa period (1600–1868). An increase in output and productivity brought a slight but perceptible quickening in rates of economic growth. Urban and rural entrepreneurs accumulated enough wealth to provide the resources for sustained development in some regions and industries, and a small, but indeterminate, portion of society enjoyed an increase in living standards before 1868.[1]

The economic growth of the late Tokugawa period, however slight it may have been in quantitative terms, did offer a foundation on which to build. Between 1868, when a new state turned in earnest to the promotion of economic growth, and 1945, when the Meiji constitutional order fell, Japan employed a wide variety of public policies, personnel, and institutions to advance the nation's economy. It also unleashed the talents and energies of many private-sector interests. Although this potent combination of state and private ventures spurred a volatile economy that evolved in fits and starts, Japan did grow at increasingly more rapid rates between the 1870s and the late 1930s.[2]

The benefits from these developments were unevenly distributed. At the top of society a thin stratum of business owners and managers reaped massive fortunes. Below them, a relatively well-off group of middling status emerged, consisting of white collar workers in new urban professions and small-town elites in both new and old callings. At the bottom of society, however, massive numbers of landless tenants in the countryside and casually employed, poorly paid workers in the cities often struggled on the brink of survival. The first burst of military expansion in the early 1930s prompted a momentary improvement in living standards for many, but by the late 1930s all strata began to suffer the decline in living standards caused by war and destruction. When the war ended in 1945, most Japanese faced dire conditions of economic deprivation. One year later, per capita consumption in Japan was equal to only 14 percent of the American average. For many Japanese, such deprivation continued well into the 1950s.[3]

This course of economic development had three implications that are of immediate concern. First, in a society in which material inequities were widespread, many adult males were deprived of full economic citizenship before 1945.[4] This disability impeded their interest in, knowledge of, and participation in formal politics. (Women, of course, were barred from par-

1. The classic statement of these changes is Thomas C. Smith, *The Agrarian Origins of Modern Japan* (Stanford: Stanford University Press, 1959).

2. Kazushi Ohkawa and Henry Rosovsky, *Japanese Economic Growth: Trend Acceleration in the Twentieth Century* (Stanford: Stanford University Press, 1973), 19–43.

3. Alan H. Gleason, "The Level of Living in Japan and the United States: A Long-term International Comparison," *Economic Development and Cultural Change* 37 (January 1989): 267.

4. My use of the term *economic citizenship* is suggested by, but does not derive directly from, T. H. Marshall's chapter "Citizenship and Social Class," in Seymour M. Lipset, ed., *Class, Citizenship, and Social Development* (Westport, Conn.: Greenwood Press, 1976), 65–122. I define economic citizenship to mean the possession of constantly enhanced economic resources that make it possible to exercise full political rights and influence whether among individuals, groups, or institutions.

ticipation for legal reasons.) Second, these same material inequities facilitated the conduct of a form of politics in which elites predominated. Landlords in rural areas and new urban professionals in the cities exercised what little power the court, the military, the aristocracy, the bureaucracy, and party politicians were willing to disperse away from the political center. Third, children from families that had suffered as many as two decades of deprivation were, in many cases, the adults who toiled on factory floors and labored over office desks during the years of rapid growth after 1955. Deprivation had accustomed them to work hard, to comply, and to save. In light of these observations, it is not surprising that many in Japan (although, of course, not all) diffidently acquiesced before the 1970s to policies of economic growth determined largely by party, bureaucratic, academic, and business elites.

The performance of Japan's economy in the postwar era has been quite salubrious in comparison with the prewar period. A difficult decade of reconstruction returned the economy to its prewar peak by the mid-1950s. Thereafter, the economy began to expand at a rate of 10 percent per annum in real terms for nearly two full decades. This sustained, rapid expansion was unprecedented for Japan, and it visibly outstripped Japan's counterparts in North America and Western Europe as well. In the early 1970s, however, declining investment rates and the shock of an oil crisis brought rapid expansion to a halt.[5] Henceforth, annual rates of real growth dropped to about the 5 percent level. Although modest in comparison with earlier achievements, such growth still nearly always surpassed Japan's major competitors, fomenting envy, trade dilemmas, and diplomatic problems that have been well examined elsewhere. Our purpose here is to understand how Japan's continued economic expansion in the 1970s and 1980s conferred broader economic citizenship and caused subtle structural fragmentation.

Consistent economic growth spread affluence throughout Japanese society. To the naked eye, some institutions benefited handsomely, especially large financial organizations and manufacturing firms producing for export markets. Their extravagant new headquarter buildings, their well-dressed executives enjoying lavish perquisites, and their costly purchases on the international art market were all signs of their growing affluence. More prosaic profit statements and cash reserves offered compelling testimony to just how wealthy many large corporations had become. High earnings bestowed a kind of autonomy on private enterprise. Cash reserves and overseas business successes made it possible for large firms to reduce their reliance on city bank financing and, thus, indirectly,

5. Edward J. Lincoln, *Japan: Facing Economic Maturity* (Washington, D.C.: Brookings Institution, 1988).

on bureaucratic control over their operations.[6] Greater corporate resources also made it possible for private firms to circumvent government control in other ways.[7] Such autonomy reinforced a fragmentation of power among politicians, bureaucrats, and the business community that was occurring for other reasons, as later comments reveal.

Large firms did not monopolize the distribution of wealth, however. After the early 1970s, most of the new business establishments opened in Japan and a large percentage of new jobs arose in the small and medium-sized enterprise sector.[8] Some of the most vibrant entrepreneurial activity in the economy occurred in this arena.[9] Although it produced quick fortunes for some, it also led to rapid failure or recurring bankruptcy for others. Nonetheless, many small firms, as well as their owners and workers, reaped significant material benefits and enjoyed a visible increase in their political resources as a result of continued affluence after 1970.[10]

Rural Japan and agrarian households had been among the most materially disadvantaged in Japan before the mid-1950s. As postwar development progressed, country cousins drew abreast of their urban relatives in many ways. A generous program of rice price supports was one policy that helped to elevate farm incomes. A conscious effort to disperse manufacturing jobs to rural areas was another. And government policies that redistributed tax revenues to agrarian regions was a third.[11] Taking advantage of jobs outside agriculture to supplement farm income, many families witnessed a steady increase in wealth. Their gains offer a critical explanation for the oft-remarked equality in the distribution of incomes among families in postwar Japan.[12] By the 1970s a kind of rural "middle class" had emerged that in its living standards and social aspirations was nearly indistinguishable from its urban counterpart.[13]

6. See especially Chapter 4 by Frances Rosenbluth.

7. John Haley, "Government by Negotiation: A Reappraisal of Bureaucratic Power in Japan," *Journal of Japanese Studies* 13 (Summer 1987): 343–357.

8. Sōmu-chō, Tōkei-kyoku, ed., *Nihon tōkei nenkan (1990)* [Japan statistical yearbook] (Tokyo: Ōkura shō, 1990), 137 (hereafter cited as *Ntn*).

9. Hugh T. Patrick and Thomas P. Rohlen, "Small-scale Family Enterprises," in Kozo Yamamura and Yasukichi Yasuba, eds., *The Political Economy of Japan, vol. 1: The Domestic Transformation* (Stanford: Stanford University Press, 1988), 331–384 (hereafter cited as *PEJ* 1).

10. Takashi Yokokura, "Small and Medium Enterprises," in Ryutaro Komiya, Masahiro Okuno, and Kotaro Suzumura, eds., *Industrial Policy of Japan* (San Diego: Academic Press, 1988), 513–539.

11. Kent E. Calder, *Crisis and Compensation: Public Policy and Political Stability in Japan, 1949–1986* (Princeton: Princeton University Press, 1988), 231–273.

12. See Martin Bronfenbrenner and Yasukichi Yasuba, "Economic Welfare," in *PEJ* 1:93–136.

13. One suggestive description is William W. Kelly, "Rationalization and Nostalgia: Cultural Dynamics of New Middle-class Japan," *American Ethnologist* 13 (1986): 603–618.

Sample surveys of household incomes conducted in the mid-1970s and the late 1980s offer especially compelling evidence that nearly everyone in Japan benefited in some way from increased affluence, even after rates of growth slowed. Changes in income, savings, and liabilities indicate how. The surveys evidence that average household income rose in every income quintile by about 70 percent in nominal terms. This increase was more than enough to outpace the rate of inflation. It, thus, provided many households with the opportunity to spend more and save more at the same time. On average, households in all quintiles increased their savings during this era, and those in the two lowest strata increased theirs at a higher rate than the other three. Surprisingly, perhaps, debt rose in every stratum. Across all groups liabilities increased from about one-fourth of annual earnings to about one-half by the late 1980s. Middle-income groups were the most avid debtors, whereas the poorest and wealthiest households acted with more restraint. Although the income gap between the poorest and richest families did widen slightly after the mid-1970s, the net savings gap actually narrowed. And, after four decades of economic expansion, even the poorest households had a financial cushion equivalent to two years' income.[14]

The use of household income as an index of affluence demands caution. First, the data derive from self-reports by a sample of only ten thousand households. Problems with accuracy, honesty, and disclosure inevitably arise. Second, these figures reveal only changes in current income, savings, and liabilities. They say almost nothing about possession of tangible assets. During decades when land, housing, and commercial property values were rising at often dramatic rates, those who owned such assets won significant increases in wealth in comparison with those who did not.[15] Third, household incomes were clearly a product of household composition. The families with the highest incomes were also the largest and those with the most income earners. Households in the lowest income categories were, on average, the smallest and had the fewest income earners; they consisted either of young, unmarried persons or of elderly couples in semiretirement. One found an array of household types in the middle rank, but those consisting of middle-aged parents with one or two children going heavily into debt to purchase housing were common.

Despite these caveats, the surveys still confirm that, after the highly inflationary years of the early 1970s and through the late 1980s, income, savings, and net savings rose among all strata in Japanese society.[16] These

14. Ntn (1990), 542–543; Ntn (1978), 420–421.
15. Haruo Shimada, "Structural Policies in Japan," in Samuel Kernell, ed., *Parallel Politics* (Washington, D.C.: Brookings Institution, 1991), 281–321.
16. See Bronfenbrenner and Yasuba, "Economic Welfare."

changes were instrumental in conferring an unprecedented measure of economic citizenship on families of all social ranks. They began by fostering a highly materialistic consumer society that grew to maturity after 1970. By 1985 Japanese consumption per capita had increased ten times since 1946.[17] Such rapid material gains spurred a desire for more but also provoked anxieties about securing present earnings and assuring future income. These concerns drew many to consider, for example, how economic policies fostered financial stability and influenced interest rates. Worried about the future, too, families had to reflect on the relationships between high government debt and retirement and welfare programs. Ready access to a print and visual media that were themselves democracy-promoting phenomena heightened public concerns about these kinds of issues. Thus, by default—if not by conscious choice—enhanced economic citizenship obliged many Japanese families to participate in a polity that often unevenly, unpredictably, and arbitrarily did, nonetheless, respond to their demands. In Chapter 3 Margaret McKean offers an ingenious theoretical explanation for why their demands were met.

To appreciate fully the importance of the structural changes taking place in this affluent society, we need to examine more closely some of its institutional features. Owing partly to the limits of prewar economic development and partly to the destruction of cities and industrial plants, Japan in the early postwar period was still a society in which tiny family farms and small family shops predominated. As late as 1955, 25 percent of the labor force was self-employed and another 31 percent consisted of unpaid family workers. The shift to a society in which urban, white-collar, salaried workers predominated transpired in the 1960s, when large numbers of persons were drawn off the farms of rural Japan and lured to new jobs in the nation's cities.[18]

The trends set in motion during the 1960s continued at a reduced pace after the 1970s. By the end of the 1980s unpaid family workers comprised only 9 percent of the labor force and the self-employed had shrunk to 15 percent. Fully three-fourths of the labor force had achieved the status of employee.[19] Most of them resided in small family units in urban and suburban areas. They changed housing with some frequency, owing to job transfers, school considerations, and residential preferences. These families also lived, far more than their ancestors had, physically separated from parents, siblings, and kin. More isolated socially than ever before, many families, nonetheless, could—and did—take pride in thinking of themselves as members of a bona fide "middle" class.

17. Gleason, "Level of Living."
18. *Ntn* (1990), 72–73.
19. Ibid.

The origins of Japan's national income offer another perspective on the significance of shifts in employment status.[20] In 1970 individual proprietors (both agricultural and nonagricultural) generated 21 percent of the national income and corporations another 16 percent. Rent, interest, and dividends accounted for 8 percent, and the remaining 55 percent of national income appeared as wages. In the next two decades, with the shrinkage in the size of the farm populace and some reduction in the number of small retail establishments, individual proprietors found themselves accounting for only 10 percent of national income. Corporate income had shrunk to 11 percent of the total, while rent, interest, and dividends had risen to 12 percent. Because interest on savings comprised nearly 80 percent of the last category, it would be an exaggeration to say that Japan was becoming a nation of rentiers. But the size of this figure does signify the growing importance of earnings accruing to millions of small savers (a point to which we will return). Finally, nearly 70 percent of national income appeared in the form of workers' wages by the late 1980s. The growing relative importance of wages, in conjunction with the rising incomes already noted, further nudged Japan in the direction of a consumption-oriented society.[21]

Contrary to common notions about the Japanese employment system, the country's swelling contingent of wage earners did not find jobs in large enterprises. Instead, the 1970s and 1980s witnessed a shrinkage of about 10 percent in the number of large establishments (with more than one thousand workers), and a commensurate reduction of nearly four hundred thousand jobs. Conversely, nearly all new jobs created during the period were in small firms (employing less than one hundred workers). Such firms comprised 99.2 percent of all private business establishments on the brink of the 1970s, and they employed 71 percent of the private-sector labor force. Twenty years later those figures were 99.3 percent and 77 percent, respectively.[22] The growing importance of small firms was driven by expansion in the service sector and by the diffusion of flexible production in small enterprises.[23] Both of these tendencies militated against the emphasis on concentration and economies of scale that had characterized the high-growth years. They fostered instead a kind of fragmentation in the economic arena that paralleled developments in other parts of Japanese society.

Relative stasis in big enterprises and the commensurately greater importance of small firms had direct consequences for a major social institution,

20. *Ntn* (1988), 560.
21. Gleason, "Level of Living," 271–276.
22. *Ntn* (1988), 120–124.
23. See David Friedman, *The Misunderstood Miracle* (Ithaca: Cornell University Press, 1988); Patrick and Rohlen, "Small-scale Family Enterprises."

the labor union. From its postwar inception in the late 1940s, the Japanese labor movement had always been most successful in organizing large firms in the private sector, not small ones. In 1970, 58 percent of workers in large firms (employing more than one thousand) joined unions, whereas fewer than 5 percent of workers in small firms (less than one hundred) joined. Precisely the same ratios still obtained twenty years later. Labor had managed to organize an additional six hundred thousand workers during the intervening years, most of them in the public sector. But it had failed to keep pace with overall expansion. As a consequence, the national unionization rate fell from 35 to only 25 percent, and unionized workers comprised less than 20 percent of the total labor force as the 1990s began. Other dilemmas contributed to labor's demise, as subsequent comments illustrate, but structural transformations amid a rapidly evolving economy were crucial to its retreat from power.[24]

The institutional shifts under discussion affected not just organized labor but all members of the work force, men and women alike. Women, for example, entered the labor force in much larger numbers. One might, therefore, assume that—as in other countries during this era—the social and economic roles of women as a group changed significantly. This was not the case. Although more women assumed a variety of new jobs in an expanding labor force, their socioeconomic status seems to have changed relatively little as a consequence. To explain this inertia amid a dynamic economy, one must examine more closely women's roles in society and the labor force.

After 1970 the number of working women in Japan increased steadily. For the next two decades, however, they continued to comprise a nearly unchanging 40 percent of the nation's labor force. The portion of all women working also changed very little. About one-half of Japan's adult women were employed at the start of the seventies. That portion dropped slightly during the difficult years of the mid-seventies, but it returned to one-half by the end of the eighties. Before the seventies unpaid jobs on a family farm or in a family shop occupied most working women. Thereafter, many won new positions as salaried employees in manufacturing firms, service establishments, and retail stores.[25]

The pattern of female employment across the life cycle remained largely unchanged during these two decades. A large majority of women (over 70 percent in 1989) took jobs after completing their educations and worked for several years between their late teens and midtwenties. When they married, and especially when they had children, most women left the labor force—but not all of them. Even among women of child-bearing

24. Ōhara shakai kenkyūjo, *Nihon rōdō nenkan* [Yearbook of Japanese Labor] (Tokyo: Ōhara Shakai Kenkyū, 1990).

25. *Ntn* (1990), 72–73.

and child-rearing age (those between twenty-five and thirty-five), about one-third continued to work.[26] Once child-rearing duties lightened and children began to enter school, mothers often returned to the labor force until their late fifties. Thereafter, as children left home and the high costs of raising them receded, many women retired from the labor force. This pattern of lifetime employment strongly suggests that women worked primarily to supplement family incomes, and many surveys substantiate this claim.[27]

Although Japanese women realized expanded opportunities for employment after 1970, most working women did not find that wealth or power followed in train. To improve working conditions and compensation for women, Japan enacted a new Equal Opportunity Employment Law in 1986. Early surveys of the law's effects, however, indicate that it may have worsened, rather than improved, the position of women.[28] Wage data also confirm only the smallest gains for women when compared with men. It is notoriously difficult to conduct such comparisons, owing to disparities in age, seniority, skills, and work classifications. In cases in which these attributes are roughly equivalent, as among pharmacists of the same age and experience, women do better than average, earning 78 percent of a man's salary. Women, however, were generally paid only 60 percent of the wages of men with comparable education throughout the two decades after 1970.[29] A new practice of "channeling" women in noncareer tracks holds every promise of keeping their salaries distinct from, and lower than, those of their male counterparts. Thus, women continue to earn significantly less than men and they have won only the most marginal earnings gains in the past two decades.

Women also seem to have realized minimal gains in status and influence at their jobs. Part-time work attracted a growing portion of employed women, whose status often remained low.[30] Firms hired part-timers to economize on wages and benefits, and they simply did not extend full privileges to workers in such positions.[31] Other women may actually have suffered a loss in job status when they ceased to be self-monitored

26. Machiko Osawa, "Working Mothers: Changing Patterns of Employment and Fertility in Japan," *Economic Development and Cultural Change* 36 (1988): 623–650. Osawa's findings strongly suggest that those who continued to work between ages twenty-five and thirty-five were women of lower educational levels who suffered low socioeconomic status (644).

27. Mary Saso, *Women in the Japanese Workplace* (London: Hilary Shipman, 1990), 92–102.

28. Ibid., 15–21, 64–66.

29. *Ntn* (1990), 104–105.

30. Saso, *Women in the Japanese Workplace*, 143–170.

31. For a fascinating account of how women in such positions, nonetheless, fought to maintain power and self-esteem, see Dorinne Kondo, *Crafting Selves: Power, Gender, and Discourses of Identity in a Japanese Workplace* (Chicago: University of Chicago Press, 1990).

workers on the family farm and were forced into rugged day labor on construction crews. Still other women, the vast majority, pursued the kinds of jobs that had been common for them since the 1960s. They worked on assembly lines, did clerical tasks, or served customers in retail establishments.

In only two ways does it seem that a portion of employed women have won higher status and influence. First, the number of women in professional and technical occupations rose from about one million in 1970 to nearly three million in 1989.[32] Having more women in highly skilled jobs could bespeak increasing status, if not influence. Second, the number of women in managerial positions rose from about 50,000 to 190,000 in this two-decade period. Nonetheless, women still held only 8 percent of all managerial positions (up from 4 percent).[33] They, thus, wielded commensurately less influence than their male counterparts. In sum, although women found new jobs that were often more secure and sometimes of higher status, work itself was not a dramatically liberating or empowering experience for most women. They undertook it to supplement family income, and it tended to subordinate women and their jobs to family—not broader societal—considerations.

Beside the large contingent of women who struggled throughout their lives to balance family and job duties stood another group, about one-third of all adult women. The women in this group consisted mainly of full-time homemakers who enjoyed a kind of upper middle-class status and resided in urban and suburban areas.[34] The presence of such women, and the values they espoused and exemplified, may well have impeded the ability of other women to achieve full equality in the workplace.[35] Moreover, this bifurcated pattern of life and work that divided women into two discernibly different subgroups was another form of structural fragmentation. It led to markedly different patterns of political participation, too, as later comments suggest.

Examining the more formal political realm and how it was influenced by postwar affluence, one finds that interest groups expanded in close conjunction with economic growth through at least the late 1960s. There were already many interest groups in Japan before 1945. Often they had been organized by elites for elites. Such bodies included business associations, administrative organizations, and landlord groups. In the postwar period additional groups of these types continued to form. But they were joined by a panoply of new groups organizing different societal interests, such as workers, welfare recipients, small enterprises, citizens' groups, and

32. *Ntn* (1990), 73.
33. Ibid.
34. Ibid., 71.
35. Saso, *Women in the Japanese Workplace*, 97.

professionals in a variety of new fields. Growth in the numbers of all interest groups rose at increasingly higher rates from 1945 through 1967 before it began to taper off (at least among the sample studied in the 1980 survey).[36]

Although the nature of the evidence makes it impossible to delineate fully how the political capabilities of these organizations have changed over time, one can demonstrate what kind of resources they possessed in 1980. Nearly one-half of the 252 groups surveyed had annual budgets that exceeded one million U.S. dollars. This enabled nearly three-fourths of the groups to employ five or more staff members; 36 percent employed twenty-five or more. The leaders of these bodies included proportionately almost as many college graduates as did the national Diet and, in fact, included proportionately more graduates of Tokyo University (Tōdai). Many groups, labor unions, in particular, still relied on people with modest levels of education for their leadership in the 1980s, but even labor unions counted among their staffs at central headquarters men with Tōdai degrees. Nearly 60 percent of the sample had been in existence for twenty-five years or more, so many had accumulated long experience at representing the interests of their constituents.[37]

Interest groups are one further indication of structural fragmentation in Japanese society and an attendant dispersal of power. When a narrow stratum of elites organized groups before the war to promote their interests, they, too, had begun to fragment the political arena.[38] But they often shared broad goals with the other elites in the parties and bureaucracy whom they were trying to influence. In the postwar era the eruption of many diverse groups that often represent interests in opposition to the mainstream has promoted a steadily more competitive polity. Educated leaders with long experience, trained staffs with political expertise, and expanding budgets all enable pressure groups to represent the interests of more people, in more forums, and with greater impact. Interest groups have also deepened the potential exercise of power in a negotiated polity because they act as surrogate agencies of economic citizenship. They mediate the interests of affluent, and sometimes not so affluent, constituents who delegate to them a measure of their own political influence.

Sustained economic growth and the stability that ensued fostered one last set of structural transformations that influenced patterns of political power in Japan after the early 1970s. An extended period of gradual

36. Muramatsu Michio, Itō Mitsutoshi, and Tsujinaka Yutaka, eds., *Sengo Nihon no atsuryoku dantai* [Postwar Japan's pressure groups] (Tokyo: Tōyō Keizaishinpōha, 1986), 72–76 (hereafter cited as *SNAD*).

37. Ibid., 26–41.

38. Bernard Silberman, "The Bureaucratic State in Japan: The Problem of Authority and Legitimacy," in Tetsuo Najita and J. Victor Koschmann, eds., *Conflict in Modern Japanese History* (Princeton: Princeton University Press, 1982), 226–257.

growth made it possible for many organizations in Japanese society to routinize patterns of recruitment and promotion of personnel. Organizations in different spheres of activity—private enterprises, labor unions, and political parties—all began to adopt an essentially bureaucratic paradigm of operation reminiscent of that employed by the ministries of the central government after the 1890s. Individuals won entry to business firms, union positions, and elective office when young. As their careers in an organization lengthened, they assumed progressively more important duties. Having proved their mettle in a range of responsible positions, they could in due course expect to be promoted to higher positions. Top posts went to those individuals who had provided the longest, least-damaging service to the organization and usually only after they had reached their fifties and accumulated two decades or more of service.

This paradigmatic pattern of recruitment and promotion was institutionalized in large private concerns during the 1950s and 1960s. Previously, and especially during the prewar era, Japan's highest-ranking business executives experienced significant job mobility.[39] Such mobility was attributable to many factors: the constant creation of new firms requiring leadership, the demise of old firms that put leaders out of work, and frequent transfers of personnel between the public and private sectors. The economic instability of the early postwar years perpetuated this pattern as did the effects of the political purge on wartime business leaders. The purge created a vacuum of experienced leadership that drew many government officials into private firms, and the widespread instability also fostered continued movement among firms. By the late 1950s, however, many of the most important large enterprises found themselves able to recruit new talent in an orderly, systematic manner and to promote incumbent personnel on a steady basis. As a result, more companies began to groom their leaders from among the ranks of long-serving personnel, and fewer hired outsiders from other firms or retirees leaving government service.[40]

The early 1970s marked a watershed in these developments that had important consequences both within firms and within the broader business community. An index to this transition is available in the career backgrounds of the men who held the highest-ranking positions at Keidanren, or the Federation of Economic Organizations, Japan's most important business association. Before the early 1970s, most of the chairmen and

39. Morikawa Hidemasa describes how slowly a professional managerial class emerged in Hidemasa, "The Increasing Power of Salaried Managers in Japan's Large Corporations," in William Wray, ed., *Managing Industrial Enterprise* (Cambridge: Harvard University Press, 1989), 27–52. For fuller treatment, see Hidemasa, *Nihon keiei shi* [A history of Japanese management] (Tokyo: Nihon keizai shinbunsha, 1981).

40. The ideas addressed here are elaborated at greater length in Gary D. Allinson, "Japan's Keidanren and Its New Leadership," *Pacific Affairs* 60(Fall 1987): 385–407.

vice-chairmen at Keidanren, along with its executive director, were former national bureaucrats who had entered the private sector late in life. After the early 1970s, the majority of Keidanren's leaders consisted of business managers who had served their entire careers in the private sector. This shift in the background characteristics of key business leaders manifested a new pattern of recruitment and promotion that took place within a closed hierarchy confined to the private sector.[41]

At the same time these changes were occurring in the private sector, a similar pattern of recruitment and promotion was emerging within the conservative ruling party. In this case, the appearance of a bureaucratic paradigm was the product of a long period of institutional stability during which former bureaucrats dominated the upper reaches of the party and bureaucratized its personnel practices in the bargain. Seniority within the party came to be defined in terms of the number of elections won. New legislators were welcomed into the fold and assigned seats on parliamentary committees, party divisions, and research bodies. As they won reelection, developed expertise, and nurtured a constituency base, legislators assumed more demanding duties as committee and division chairs. Success at the polls five or six times running usually resulted in appointment to a minor cabinet post. And for the most successful, those with ten legislative victories to their credit and a long record of competent service in party and parliamentary offices, the highest cabinet posts and ultimately the prime ministership came into reach.[42]

The principal effect of this pattern of promotion in the LDP was to accentuate service to the party as the fundamental criterion for highest office. As a result, it became more difficult for retired bureaucrats to enter politics and win high party positions quickly, and, as a corollary, professional, lifelong politicians came to dominate the highest ranks of the party. Such men had educational and occupational backgrounds, professional skills, and personal attributes that all distinguished them sharply from bureaucrats on one hand and business leaders on the other.

Recruitment to leadership positions within closed professional hierarchies fostered a crucial alteration in patterns of elite interaction, leading to another instance of structural fragmentation. Previously, former bureaucrats had played leading roles both in key private-sector organizations and in the ruling party. Long personal association and common backgrounds fostered a shared outlook that helped immensely in cultivating the consensus that characterized policy-making in the 1950s and 1960s. Certainly differences of views existed, but they could often be ironed out through a

41. Ibid.
42. Gary D. Allinson, "The Structure and Transformation of Conservative Rule," in Andrew Gordon, ed., *Postwar Japan as History* (Berkeley: University of California Press, forthcoming).

process of "amicable negotiation."[43] After the 1970s, subtle barriers arose among elite groups that were nearly obliged by experience and responsibility to represent separate spheres of Japanese society. The need to represent separate and often private interests, coupled with the disappearance of the common ground on which former bureaucratic leaders had once stood, provoked more competitive negotiation in elite politics. In place of the transcendental and selfless politics that former bureaucratic elites had (at least in part, sincerely) epitomized, Japanese politics began to carry a far more private, self-interested tonality after the early 1970s. One symbol redolent of this change was the demise of Prime Minister Tanaka amid accusations of avarice and power grabbing.

An extended period of economic growth, continuing at slower rates after the 1970s, conferred a broader measure of economic citizenship on important groups and institutions in Japanese society. The wealth accumulated in the hands of large corporations enhanced their autonomy from bureaucratic control and heightened their independence. Many firms in the bustling small business sector also realized gains in wealth that they translated into political influence in numerous ways. Families across all social ranks seem to have enjoyed a higher measure of affluence, giving them an inherent interest in a range of political issues many had never confronted before. Many women found work that might have conferred a greater measure of economic citizenship on them. It appears, however, that their roles as supplementary income earners subordinated their political interests to those of the family itself and did not direct them toward other women or other workers. Labor unions benefited from increased dues and income, giving them the opportunity to enhance their expertise and influence. The same was true of interest groups in general. Many possessed substantial resources that underscored their expanding importance in the political process. Finally, the institutional stability that steady growth brought nurtured the appearance of two distinctive bodies of corporate leaders and professional politicians. The economic citizenship of such elites had never been in doubt, but changing values and perceptions in the early 1970s lent a new tenor to relations between them.

These same groups and institutions also experienced subtle changes in their structural relationships after the early 1970s. Large corporations and their leaders found themselves in a position to challenge bureaucratic authority and to resist the embrace of the state. The small business sector witnessed a structural fragmentation caused by technological and organizational changes. People in this segment of Japanese society often responded by organizing more aggressively to promote fragmented and

43. See Allinson, "Japan's Keidanren," 403–407.

specialized, but, nonetheless, collective, interests. The growing affluence of families, occurring as it did in a highly mobile society, seems to have promoted a deeper measure of family-centeredness, symbolized by the slogan of *maihomuizumu* (My-homism) and by the appearance of a panoply of consumer micromarkets. This tendency may have persuaded more families to delegate their political influence to surrogates in the form of interest groups. In general, the growth in numbers and resources of interest groups dispersed political influence over a broader field. Trends in the union movement, however, offer a paradoxical spectacle. On one hand, Rengō did represent an organizational effort to centralize, and, thus, concentrate, union influence. On the other hand, as Yutaka Tsujinaka suggests in Chapter 8, the center governed with a very light hand so that much union influence continued to be diffused at the local level. How the effects of broader economic citizenship and social fragmentation played themselves out in the political arena will be examined in the next two sections.

Conservative Hegemony and the Electoral Context

Social fragmentation has, perhaps, caused, and, certainly, been reflected in, a segmentation in the polity, especially among political parties. The clearest party divisions of the postwar period appeared momentarily just as the era of rapid growth began. In the late 1950s newly united parties, the LDP on the right and the Japan Socialist party (JSP) on the left, between them captured 98 percent of the seats in the lower house of the Diet.[44] Thereafter, two-party domination steadily eroded. First, the JSP split in 1960, with a moderate wing leaving to form the Democratic Socialist party (DSP). In 1965 a new party, drawing support from the adherents of an evangelical Buddhist sect, appeared calling itself the Clean Government party (CGP). At about the same time, the Japan Communist party (JCP) adopted a policy of responsible parliamentary government and began to win increased electoral support. Other minor parties formed, too, representing the interests of salaried workers and consumers. This segmentation of the party spectrum offered opportunities for individuals in a more diversified society to tailor their political tastes to a much wider array of choices.

Taste, however, is inherently fickle, and that proved to be the case with many Japanese voters. At first the DSP, CGP, and JCP began to attract

44. T. J. Pempel, "The Unbundling of 'Japan, Inc.': The Changing Dynamics of Japanese Policy Formation," *Journal of Japanese Studies* 13(Summer 1987): 271–306.

voters in rising numbers. But the increases quickly tapered off, and a kind of equilibrium developed between the segmented opposition parties and the ruling LDP. Beneath the surface of formal electoral behavior, another significant tendency began to manifest itself. More and more voters declared themselves independents. Claiming no hard and fast party identity, they shifted their votes among parties and candidates according to personal whim, current issues, candidate personality, party platforms, and other considerations.[45] By the late 1970s such voters comprised more than one-third of the electorate and were the largest identifiable bloc of voters, along with a contingent of nearly equal size that claimed to support the LDP.[46] Many of these independents were young, geographically mobile voters with weak ties to political parties and residential communities and strong susceptibility to momentary political appeals. They were essential to the growing political support that underwrote the progressives' gains in the late 1970s.

Fitful developments among opposition parties and momentary electoral victories by progressives have sometimes obscured the more important fact about electoral trends after 1970: the LDP maintained a broad, solid base of support for the next two decades. Because the lower house holds slightly greater constitutional powers than the upper and because postwar prime ministers have preferred to hold seats there, lower house election results are a sound gauge of electoral sentiment. In table 1.1 I delineate the division of the vote by party for the seven elections held between 1972 and 1990 and in table 1.2 describe how votes were translated into seats among parties in the lower house. The figures do reveal that for a majority party the LDP did not attract overwhelming popular support. Its share of the total vote ranged from a low of 42 percent to a high of 49 percent. These figures understate its actual strength, however, because many unaffiliated candidates were actually LDP members running without party endorsement. The ballots that went to the New Liberal Club between 1976 and 1986 can in retrospect be seen as LDP, or at least quasi-LDP, votes.

Owing to its organizational prowess, its loyal supporters, and its ability to exploit the advantages of a malapportioned legislature the LDP was able to translate its modest electoral margin into secure legislative majorities. Sometimes this meant accepting unaffiliated candidates into the party's embrace, and, sometimes, as in the late 1970s and early 1980s, it required the party to engage in deft coalitional politics. But its opponents never offered a plausible threat to LDP domination of the lower house be-

45. Gary D. Allinson, "Japan's Independent Voters," *The Japan Interpreter* 11(Spring 1976): 36–55.
46. Tōkei sūri kenkyūjo, ed., *Daiyon Nihonjin no kokuminsei* [The fourth Japanese national character study] (Tokyo: Shiseidō, 1982), 137.

Table 1.1. Votes by party in House of Representatives elections, 1972–1990

	LDP	NLC	JSP	CGP	DSP	JCP	Other[a]
1972	24,563 (47)[b]	—	11,479 (22)	4,437 (8)	3,661 (7)	5,497 (10)	2,789 (5)
1976	23,654 (42)	2,364 (4)	11,713 (21)	6,177 (11)	3,554 (6)	5,878 (10)	3,273 (6)
1979	24,084 (45)	1,632 (3)	10,643 (20)	5,283 (10)	3,664 (7)	5,626 (10)	3,079 (6)
1980	28,262 (48)	1,766 (3)	11,401 (19)	5,330 (9)	3,897 (7)	5,804 (10)	2,569 (4)
1983	25,983 (46)	1,342 (2)	11,065 (19)	5,746 (10)	4,130 (7)	5,302 (9)	3,212 (6)
1986	29,876 (49)	1,115 (2)	10,413 (17)	5,701 (9)	3,896 (6)	5,313 (9)	4,136 (7)
1990	30,315 (46)	—	16,025 (24)	5,243 (8)	3,179 (5)	5,227 (8)	5,715 (8)

Source: Miyakawa Takayoshi, *Seiji handobukku* [Politics handbook] (Tokyo: Seiji Kōhō Sentaa, various dates and editions).
[a]Very small parties and candidates running without party affiliation (*mushozoku*).
[b]Votes and percentage of votes (in parentheses) in thousands.

Table 1.2. Party segmentation in House of Representatives elections, 1972–1990

	LDP	NLC	JSP	CGP	DSP	JCP	Other[a]	Total
1972	271 (55)[b]	—	118 (24)	29 (6)	19 (4)	38 (8)	16 (3)	491 (100)
1976	249 (49)	17 (3)	123 (24)	55 (11)	29 (6)	17 (3)	21 (4)	511 (100)
1979	248 (49)	4 (1)	107 (21)	57 (11)	35 (7)	39 (6)	21 (4)	511 (99)
1980	284 (56)	12 (3)	107 (21)	33 (6)	32 (6)	29 (5)	14 (3)	511 (100)
1983	250 (49)	8 (2)	112 (22)	58 (11)	38 (7)	26 (5)	19 (4)	511 (100)
1986	300 (59)	6 (1)	85 (17)	56 (11)	26 (5)	26 (5)	13 (2)	512 (100)
1990	275 (54)	—	136 (27)	45 (9)	14 (3)	16 (3)	26 (5)	512 (101)

Source: Same as table 1.1.
[a]Members from minor parties and members without party affiliation.
[b]Number of seats and percentage of seats (in parentheses).

cause they were too fractured by party divisions and too riven by ideological differences. Events of the late 1970s did seriously disturb the LDP, but it took heed of the dissent and recouped many of its losses in the 1980s.

Two of the most dramatic exceptions to stable dominance arose in an upper house election in 1989 and a lower house contest in 1990. On these occasions scandal and unpopular policy-making threw a deep scare into the LDP, which seems precisely what a populace eager to chastise the ruling party intended. Scandal took two forms. Bribe-taking from an advertising and real estate conglomerate called Recruit tainted nearly every faction leader and other high figures in the party during 1988 and 1989. In a desperate effort to find someone with a clean reputation, the party installed Uno Sōsuke as prime minister in mid-1989, only to discover that he was guilty of buying the silence of a former mistress.[47]

Unpopular policy-making took the form of a consumption tax implemented in 1989. A visible cost that was a nuisance to pay, this tax quickly caused deep distress among consumers in general and women in particular. Uno's sexual peccadilloes only exacerbated displeasure with the LDP. The electorate found an easy opportunity to express its unrest in the upper house election during summer 1989. Shifting support in massive numbers to the opposition parties, voters dealt the LDP one of its worst defeats in a postwar election and drove it into a minority in the upper house.

The lure of the opposition continued into the following year. Attracted in part by the strong feminine image that Doi Takako projected as leader of the JSP, a wave of new voters resuscitated that party by giving it 24 percent of the returns. In spite of its troubles the LDP still managed to increase its support slightly, and it was able to continue governing with a comfortable margin. After severe JSP losses in spring 1991 local elections, Doi Takako resigned the party's presidency, and it appeared that the LDP had weathered yet another short-term challenge from the opposition parties.

The electoral behavior of Japanese women had a great deal to do both with the challenge to LDP dominance and with the quick demise of that challenge. Women voters were important because they turned out at slightly higher rates than men and, thus, comprised a majority of the electorate in national contests.[48] Two special characteristics of the female vote had implications for the LDP hegemony in the seventies and eighties. First, many women felt loyal attachments to centrist and progressive parties that adopted strong positions on domestic welfare issues, parties such as the CGP, JCP, and JSP. Such women were likely to be of lower socioeconomic

47. Kent E. Calder, "Japan in 1990: Limits to Change," *Asian Survey* 31(January 1991): 21–35.
48. Watanuki Jōji, "Yūkensha to shite no Nihon josei" [Japanese women as voters], *Revaiasan*, no. 8 (1991): 23–40.

status and to work throughout their lives. Some belonged to households in which the male household drew a low income or worked intermittently; others were female households trying to rear families on low incomes. These women needed public services they could not afford on the private market, such as nursery and child care facilities, unemployment compensation, and health and welfare programs for themselves, their children, and elderly dependents. Women facing these needs seem to have supported the progressive parties in disproportionate numbers on many occasions.

The second characteristic arose particularly among women who thought of themselves as independents or who had only weak ties to the LDP. These women participated in sporadic outbursts of chastening votes. Such outbursts occurred during times of crisis or scandal, when women were so directly affected by political policies or the behavior of politicians that they were obliged to speak out. This happened in the late sixties and early seventies during the environmental crisis. Confronting pollution and safety problems daily in their communities, women mobilized to vote against the LDP. It happened again in the late eighties. The consumption tax and the sex and corruption scandals in the LDP forced women to overcome their customary diffidence and to express their political views more assertively.[49]

Women's political activities were not confined to voting. Women discernibly increased their levels of political participation in many ways during the 1970s and 1980s. In an eleven-year period after 1976 they doubled their participation in election campaign activities, they increased their attendance at political gatherings, they engaged more in citizens' movements, and they also contacted more frequently local—and even national—politicians. Although their rates of participation rose during this period, women still engaged in politics only half as frequently as men. It also appears that the women drawn into greater activism were members of the second group identified earlier. They were better-educated women of upper status living in cities and suburbs who did not have to work to supplement family incomes. They had the time to pursue political activities and the knowledge required to do so effectively.[50]

These findings strongly suggest that the social fragmentation that divided working women from nonworking women was reflected in fragmented forms of political behavior. Poorer working women channeled their political energies into electoral support for parties that advocated social policies responsive to their needs. Wealthier, nonworking women voted for the parties of their choice and also participated in a variety of political activities. The hallmark of those activities, however, was their own fragmentation. Women activists were far more likely to concern

49. Ibid.
50. Ibid, 33–36.

themselves with local than national issues.[51] Finally, many women were provoked to cast chastening ballots during periods when political trends offended their sensibilities or threatened their direct interests. But having done so, they often returned to earlier habits of behavior and forswore engagement in sustained opposition.

The one thing that women in Japan did not do during this period was to organize effectively in a single, large body to pursue systematically their interests at the national level. The fragmented, sporadic quality of their political behavior thus served in the end to minimize the importance of women's issues on the national political agenda and to preserve the formal arena of politics as a nearly male bastion.[52] Many politicians, especially those in the LDP, found this a natural and congenial outcome. As well they might—it was an essential adjunct to LDP domination.

Outside the lower house LDP dominance was even greater in other electoral settings. Until 1989 it enjoyed a sometimes slender but always workable majority in the upper house. In prefectural assemblies, the LDP could not parry challenges in some of the most urban areas, such as Tokyo and Ōsaka, but its adherents dominated assemblies in the rest of the country. After facing a brisk challenge in the early 1970s to its hold over executive offices in prefectures and municipalities, the LDP managed to reduce the strength of its opponents and to deflect or co-opt the rising tide of progressive governors and mayors. The symbol of its success was the victory in 1979 of Suzuki Shun'ichi as governor of Tokyo Metropolitan Prefecture. Although Tokyo was one of the country's strongest bases of support for the opposition parties, Suzuki continued to be reelected as governor throughout the eighties. In 1991, already past ninety, he won reelection for a fourth time. His victories were like jabbing a stick in the eye of the opposition.

Despite some shaky moments, the LDP was able to maintain enough of a majority to select the prime minister and to form every cabinet during the seventies and eighties. A list of the prime ministers who led those governments follows:

Satō Eisaku	November 9, 1964–July 6, 1972
Tanaka Kakuei	July 6, 1972–December 9, 1974
Miki Takeo	December 9, 1974–December 24, 1976
Fukuda Takeo	December 24, 1976–December 7, 1978
Ōhira Masayoshi	December 7, 1978–June 11, 1980
Suzuki Zenkō	July 17, 1980–November 27, 1982
Nakasone Yasuhiro	November 27, 1982–November 6, 1987
Takeshita Noboru	November 6, 1987–June 3, 1989

51. Ibid.
52. Susan Pharr, *Political Women in Japan* (Berkeley: University of California Press, 1981).

Uno Sōsuke   June 3, 1989–August 10, 1989
Kaifu Toshiki   August 10, 1989–November 5, 1991
Miyazawa Kiichi   November 5, 1991–

At the risk of simplification, one can divide the ten leaders after 1972 into three groups: the constrained, the strong, and the weak. Beginning in 1972, five men held the prime minister's office for only about two years each. During this era, factional bargaining was complicated by Tanaka's anomalous position as a party leader and an indicted criminal; it shaped political opportunities by constraining both prime ministers and the party from taking decisive leadership on many issues.[53] At the outset of his tenure, it appeared that Nakasone Yasuhiro—derided as Tanaka's pawn—would be as constrained as his predecessors. But a stroke in 1985 effectively diminished Tanaka's power and opened a vacuum that Nakasone moved energetically to fill. His strong "presidential" style and his ambitious reform efforts invigorated the LDP's hegemony during the mid-1980s.[54] His successors, however, all suffered weaknesses. Takeshita and Uno immediately ran afoul of scandal. The party then turned in desperation to the Miki faction, as it had following Tanaka's departure in 1974, and placed Kaifu Toshiki in office. Buffeted by insoluble international problems and difficult domestic ones, he managed to cling to office for two years even though he faced more constraints than his counterparts of the 1970s.

The conservative hegemony was, thus, both precarious and durable. Its durability was attributable to the LDP's skill at translating a minority of lower house votes into a consistent majority of lower house seats. This enabled the party to form governments and to rule under prime ministers primarily beholden only to the LDP. In addition, LDP strength in the upper house (until 1989), in gubernatorial and mayoralty posts and in prefectural and municipal assemblies, gave it an extensive political authority throughout the nation that it adroitly exploited.

Nonetheless, with the exception of three years during the late 1980s, the LDP always enjoyed a rather precarious dominance. During this two-decade period Japanese voters seem collectively to have struck what we can call a "tacit covenant." The covenant was based on a partly reluctant vow to keep the LDP in power. At the same time the covenant sustained

53. An especially acute analysis of this epoch is Chalmers Johnson, "Tanaka Kakuei, Structural Corruption, and the Advent of Machine Politics in Japan," *Journal of Japanese Studies* 12 (Winter 1986): 1–28.

54. For thorough analyses of the Nakasone administration, see Kenneth Pyle, "In Pursuit of a Grand Design: Nakasone betwixt the Past and the Future," and Michio Muramatsu, "In Search of National Identity: The Politics and Policies of the Nakasone Administration," both in *Journal of Japanese Studies* 13(Summer 1987): 243–270, and 307–342, respectively; and Otake Hideo, "Nakasone seiji no ideorogi to sono kokunai seijiteki haikei" [The ideology of Nakasone's politics and the domestic political background], *Revaiasan*, no. 1 (1987): 11–30.

an opposition that was, although badly segmented, just strong enough to pose a standing threat to LDP hegemony. When the party betrayed the public trust too egregiously, as it did during the scandals of the late 1980s, voters quickly chastened it. Or when its policies seemed too ill-suited to society's needs, as they did during the environmental crisis of the 1970s, voters again chastised the LDP by shifting more support to the opposition. Contradictory findings from opinion surveys confirm precisely this kind of ambivalence on the part of many voters, especially independents who were numerous enough to constitute a swing vote in every election. They did not like the LDP and would rather have seen an alternative, but they were unwilling to accept the risks and uncertainties the alternatives posed.[55]

Underlying this risky, tacit, collective strategy of ambivalently supporting the LDP while working to hold it in check was a strong current of popular pragmatism. Japan's version of pork-barrel politics draws its sustenance from this pragmatism and its essentially materialistic character. Distributing governmental largesse to constituents has been a basic task for Japan's political parties since the 1910s.[56] Under the LDP, however, the task was elevated to a technically proficient, hallowed duty.[57] Voters, especially those in rural areas, expected the largesse, and they were not disappointed. During the seventies and eighties, they came to expect it even more. Survey research by Miyake Ichiro illustrates clearly that voters prize local politicians who can "deliver the goods," not men of vision and reputation who are politically clean.[58] Some corruption can, thus, be tolerated to justify the pursuit of local interests as the postindictment career of Tanaka Kakuei in Niigata Prefecture so convincingly attests.[59] Quite unapologetically many voters emphasized the importance of political exchange—votes for government payoffs—by the 1980s.

In recent decades the materialistic bent of millions of small savers mentioned earlier has forced onto the political agenda some controversial financial issues. The interests of these families and individuals demonstrate how the field of political action was extended into seemingly apolitical arenas by the purely economic behavior of many thrifty, pragmatic households. Historically, Japan has had two forms of deposit-taking institutions, the postal savings system and banks. The former is a public

55. Allinson, "Japan's Independent Voters."

56. Tetsuo Najita, *Hara Kei in the Politics of Compromise* (Cambridge: Harvard University Press, 1967).

57. Kent Calder in *Crisis and Compensation* substantiates this claim in copious detail.

58. Miyake Ichirō, "Jimoto rieki shikō to hoshuka [Tendencies toward local interests and conservatism]," *Revaiasan*, no. 1 (1987): 31–46.

59. Fukuoka Masayuki, *Nihon no seiji fūdo: Niigata sanku ni miru Nihon seiji no genkei* [Japan's political culture: A paradigm of Japanese politics as seen in Niigata's third district] (Tokyo: Gakuyō shobō, 1985). See also Johnson, "Tanaka Kakuei."

institution and the latter are private. After 1955 the best interest rates offered by the two types of institutions were nearly the same, except for one thing.[60] Interest paid on bank deposits was taxable, but interest earned on postal savings accounts was tax free up to a certain amount. Thus, by saving through the postal system and by opening multiple accounts after reaching the taxable limit, small savers could effectively reap a higher return because their earnings went untaxed.

In the two decades after 1965 a dramatic shift in the allocation of savings between institutions took place. Bank deposits continued to grow; they rose twelve times over between 1965 and 1985.[61] But during the same period the value of deposits in the postal savings system increased thirty-eight times. Those deposits had equaled 14 percent of the value of all bank deposits in 1965, but by 1985 they equaled more than 45 percent. The sums involved in this reallocation of savings had critical implications for the Ministry of Finance (MOF) and for the Ministry of Posts and Telecommunications (MPT), which operated the postal savings system but did not enjoy control over the use of its funds. That control remained in the hands of the MOF, which employed the funds for a valuable off-budget account called the Fiscal Investment and Loan Program (FILP) that financed many public expenditures. Both ministries had a strong interest in regulation of the postal savings system and the use of its funds, and a bureaucratic squabble predictably ensued. In addition, private banks also entered the fray for their own reasons. Finally, the LDP had to referee the dispute and impose a political settlement.[62]

From one angle of vision this is a classic example of a political negotiation undertaken by the members of iron triangles. But from a broader perspective, this issue would never have reached the formal political arena if millions of small savers had not created a new field of political action through their aggregated efforts to exploit a legal opportunity to minimize taxes. Their behavior in many ways shaped the parameters within which the formally negotiated political settlement occurred, and—as Frances Rosenbluth suggests—the final solution did redound to their benefit.

In this case escaping taxes many times over on a small scale fomented what became a difficult political issue. In another way concerns about taxes helped to bring two central issues to the political agenda of the 1980s, the size of the state and its expenditures. Charles Horioka has gathered figures to illustrate how taxes and social security payments began to

60. Eisuke Sakakibara, "The Japanese Politico-economic System and the Public Sector," in Kernell, *Parallel Politics*, 65.

61. Ibid.

62. Frances Rosenbluth, *Financial Politics in Contemporary Japan* (Ithaca: Cornell University Press, 1989), 167–208.

eat into the disposable incomes of Japanese families after 1976.[63] As taxes rose from 10 percent of nonconsumption expenditures to more than 16 percent in 1986, disposable income fell (in the aggregate) from 90 percent of gross income to 84 percent. Families continued to save about the same percentage of their incomes, so they found themselves with a shrinking percentage of income to spend. Realization of these tendencies on the part of many households undoubtedly contributed to the supportive atmosphere underlying the administrative reform movement. And if families did not appreciate their dilemma from this perspective, an outpouring of reports stressing the dangers of rising government expenditures surely drove the point home. The "English disease"—national decline owing to big government—became anathema.

In many of the succeeding chapters we address aspects of the administrative reform movement of the 1980s, but it is necessary here to describe its general characteristics. The movement began in 1981 with the creation of the Second Provisional Commission on Administrative Reform (Rinchō), which had a two-year charge. (The first council operated between 1962 and 1964.) This commission consisted of nine members representing different segments of Japanese society and a large number of subordinate, consultative bodies. The commission recommended several changes aimed essentially at reducing the role of the state and the public sector. As a consequence of its recommendations, the national railway and the public telephone monopoly were privatized, bureaucratic regulations were simplified, national budgets were reduced, and managerial reforms (such as a stronger prime minister's office) were made. A special Administrative Reform Promotion Council was created in 1983. It operated for three years to assure the implementation of the commission's recommendations.

One man chaired both Rinchō and the promotion council, Dokō Toshio. He was a prominent businessman who had just completed a six-year term as chairman of Keidanren. Born at the turn of the century to a farming family of modest means, Dokō was a classic example of a rags-to-riches story.[64] He was a graduate of a nonimperial university. He spent his early business career working in predecessors to the current Ishikawajima Harima Heavy Industries (IHI). He first demonstrated his managerial prowess to the Japanese business community when he presided over the merger that created this firm and the difficult reorganization that ensued. Shortly after, he assumed the leadership of one of Japan's oldest electrical

63. Charles Horioka, "Consumption and Saving in Postwar Japan" (Typescript, 1988, Department of Economics, Osaka University).
64. Tōkyō shoten henshūbu, ed., *Ningen Dokō Toshio* [The human Dokō Toshio] (Tokyo: Tōkyō shoten, 1983); and Dokō Toshio, *Watakushi no rirekisho* [my vitae] (Tokyo: Nihon keizai shinbunsha, 1983).

firms, Tōshiba, and rescued it from managerial collapse. Dokō had a public reputation as a diligent, earnest, and plainspoken individual known for his personal integrity and parsimony. One tale, possibly apocryphal but widely known, holds that he did his own laundry on international trips to save money. He was an ideal figure to articulate and promote a political movement that advocated economy in government and imposition of business values on public life.

It is important to distinguish Dokō and the administrative reform movement from Prime Minister Nakasone Yasuhiro and his reform efforts. Nakasone initiated administrative reform in the early 1980s when he held the cabinet post of Administrative Management Agency director. He also appointed Dokō to chair the reform commission. And he was energetic in his support of the reform movement throughout. When he rose to become prime minister in 1982, however, Nakasone began to appropriate the vehicle employed by the administrative reform movement—the advisory council of experts and societal representatives—and used it to promote a much wider political agenda. This agenda was a product of his distinctive personal vision for Japan and its future. Educational issues, international policy, and land use were just three of the broader matters that his later advisory councils addressed.

It was a presidential style that made Nakasone's reform efforts distinctive.[65] He employed policy-promoting advisory councils of a strongly personal hue to appeal directly to the people and to circumvent such vested interests as the bureaucracy and the party. In this way he effectively created a new field of political action that linked his administration with the populace. He tried—consciously it appears—to exploit urban middle-class anxieties over taxes, welfare, and materialism for the long-term benefit of the LDP, but his efforts produced mixed results. They are assessed in the chapters by Michio Muramatsu, Frank Schwartz, and Hideo Otake.

The social fragmentation analyzed in the first half of this chapter underpinned LDP hegemony after 1970. Party segmentation led to the emergence of a tacit covenant honored by the electorate, which awarded the LDP a durable but precarious mandate to rule. Voters accepted the covenant with varying degrees of enthusiasm because it appealed to their pragmatic tendencies during an age of affluence. Women also acquiesced to the covenant, but they formed a social body whose internal divisions weakened their influence as a collective force in Japanese politics. A tense standoff between voters and the LDP, coupled with factional problems and Tanaka's quizzical influence, constrained the short-term prime ministers of the 1970s from acting decisively on very many issues. In the

---

65. See Muramatsu, "In Search of National Identity."

1980s, however, the LDP managed to link its policy agenda with the implicit concerns of an increasingly more affluent populace. A reform movement that challenged entrenched bureaucratic authority gave expression to the unarticulated aspirations of a society enjoying broader economic citizenship, not to mention stronger feelings of nationalism. Nakasone forcefully articulated the latter values and the forthright Dokō, the former. Together they were a potent duo communicating a newfound confidence in national strength and material well-being. It remains to be seen, briefly, how in other ways big business, small enterprises, interest groups, and the labor movement fit into this political picture.

The Pursuit of Interests and the Negotiated Polity

Dokō Toshio in his role as leader of the administrative reform councils personified the authority of a more autonomous, self-confident business community.[66] It is no coincidence that he was the first Keidanren chairman to hail from a purely business background. He did not possess the sense of noblesse oblige that his bureaucratic predecessor, Uemura Kōgorō, communicated as a samurai descendant born to rule. Instead, Dokō's commoner origins, his lack of a Tōdai pedigree and bureaucratic career, and his consistent success as the leader of major corporations actually imparted a democratic aura to his service. He was especially well suited to articulate in plain, blunt language the morality of a resurgent business community intent on putting its stamp on the nation's political life.

The actual power of Japan's big business community in the postwar era has often been exaggerated. The ruling triad model contributed to this dilemma by offering a static portrait of a structure of power that seldom conformed closely with the vicissitudes of historical change. Analysts have also attributed more homogeneity to the big business world than it has often displayed in practice.[67] Finally, observers have not always acknowledged how restraining have been MITI's controls over foreign exchange and technology imports and MOF's direct and indirect controls over corporate finance.

The astonishing expansion of Japanese firms after the 1960s has done a great deal to diminish these restraints, however. In the process business has won a higher measure of autonomy.[68] Domestic pressures and foreign

66. See Allinson, "Japan's Keidanren," 395–407.
67. On internal divisions within Japan's business community see Chapter 10 by Hideo Otake.
68. Greg Noble, "The Japanese Industrial Policy Debate," in Stephen Haggard and Chung-in Moon, eds., *Pacific Dynamics* (Boulder, Colo.: Westview Press, 1989), 53–96.

demands alike helped to eliminate MITI's controls over foreign exchange and technology imports by the end of the seventies. Japanese firms engaged in international markets won ready access to foreign sources of capital. They also built up massive reserves that enabled them to draw down their corporate debts.[69] As a consequence, big firms found themselves with increasingly more freedom from bureaucratic regulations, which gave them a stronger position when they engaged in contests of power with individual ministries.[70] It may also have emboldened big business to pursue in the 1980s what was an unprecedented course of action. Its support of Dokō and the administrative reform movement denoted a frontal challenge to the political standing of the bureaucracy in Japanese political life and was a fitting commentary on the rich and audacious Japanese business community.

Small business firms, as discussed earlier, had, perhaps paradoxically, grown to be a more important feature of the Japanese economy after 1970. Purely economic tendencies contributed to their enhanced importance, but so did political support won through long efforts at organizing and negotiating. Small business groups existed in Japan well before the war ended in 1945. On various occasions during the prewar era they were able to demonstrate their influence, even in the face of military and bureaucratic opposition.[71] After the war small enterprises organized more extensively and by the early 1950s had become a major force in domestic politics.[72] Throughout the fifties, sixties, and seventies, organized pressure from small business groups produced major returns to the small enterprise sector. These returns took the form of subsidies, noncollateralized loans issued through local Chambers of Commerce, government assistance in developing human resources, preferential tax rates, the legal regulation of predatory behavior by large firms, generous depreciation allowances, government procurement programs, and lax enforcement of laws that facilitated tax evasion and labor abuses.[73] By the 1980s small business organizations were intimately linked with the support networks of LDP politicians, and, through them, the party itself.[74] They had become an indispensable element in the party's electoral and financial equation, and represented a classic example of the way in which "compensatory" policies fostered mutually beneficial exchange relationships in the Japanese polity.

69. Lincoln, *Japan*, 130–210.
70. See Haley, "Government by Negotiation."
71. See the chapter by Sheldon Garon and Mike Mochizuki, "Negotiating Social Contracts in Postwar Japan," in Gordon, *Postwar Japan as History*.
72. Ibid; Calder, *Crisis and Compensation*, 312–348.
73. Yokokura, "Small and Medium Enterprises."
74. Muramatsu, Itō, and Tsujinaka, *SNAD*, 248.

In his chapter Frank Upham offers a fascinating example of one way in which small businesses pursued their interests in a very wide field of political action. MITI vacillated over its implementation procedures for the Large-Scale Retail Stores Law for two reasons. The ministry worried about the direct political costs it might suffer if it intervened too intimately in such a controversial policy area. It also faced practical restraints. MITI simply did not have enough personnel with enough time and resources at their disposal to deal directly with all the cases that were likely to arise. The obvious solution was to delegate authority to disputants, and that is just what MITI did. This approach legitimated negotiation on, or even beyond, the periphery of the bureaucratic arena. By diffusing and delegating the task of negotiation MITI produced long, painful delays. Domestic interests eventually grew accustomed to them, but cloying foreign pressure finally brought the arrangements to an end. The solution announced in late 1990 lent MITI the appearance of power, responded on the surface to American pressures, and offered prospective benefits to urban consumers. The decision may also contribute to the further decline of small retail stores; it was a signal that government protection of all small businesses would not persist indefinitely.

Small business associations are just one type of interest group that has become highly influential in recent decades. Many others represent a congeries of interests that span the social spectrum. The 1980 survey of interest groups cited confirms persuasively that they have become deeply vested interests fully integrated into the nation's political life. Interest groups recruit former bureaucrats and Diet members to serve as officers and leaders. They strive to put their own representatives on shingikai. They work assiduously to keep in contact with the party and the bureaucracy alike. The bureaucracy, however, is a favored target, and many groups maintain contacts at all levels from section chief to cabinet minister. They strive energetically to advance their interests in every corner of the formal polity. Most groups are also quick to acknowledge the success of their endeavors whether through the positive promotion of policies or the defeat of harmful initiatives.[75]

When powerful interest groups enjoy too much success, however, it can sometimes boomerang against them. For many years after the war, one of Japan's most influential interest groups was the Japan Medical Association (JMA).[76] Its influence derived from the stature of its long-time chairman, Takemi Tarō, from the contacts that he sedulously cultivated in the LDP, and, perhaps, from the high status physicians enjoyed. In pursuit of

75. Ibid., 215–272.
76. William E. Steslicke, *Doctors in Politics: The Political Life of the Japan Medical Association* (New York: Praeger, 1973).

its interests, the JMA faced a weak bureaucratic representative in the Ministry of Health and Welfare (MHW). MHW was a new ministry that attracted limited resources during the years of rapid economic growth. It was during this period that Takemi often rode haughtily over the ministry to preserve and expand the benefits of the JMA.

These conditions gradually changed and led in the 1980s to new relationships between the JMA and MHW.[77] Health and welfare issues became more salient owing to the environmental crisis and to concerns about an aging populace. Welfare benefits were expanded in the 1970s and quickly became one of the most rapidly growing government outlays. They were, thus, a cause for concern when the national financial crisis worsened in the early 1980s. At just this point, significant personnel shifts took place in the association and the ministry. Takemi Tarō resigned in 1982 as head of the JMA. He was replaced by a man with more moderate views because the JMA itself was rent by divisions. Wealthy, private physicians who operated their own clinics and younger, salaried doctors working in public agencies held opposing views about health care delivery. Meanwhile, at MHW men, who as low-level officials had long chafed at Takemi's haughty behavior, began to rise to key positions as bureau chiefs.

Emboldened by the ideological climate of the administrative reform movement and forced to act by the financial crisis, these ministry officials launched a counteroffensive against the association in alliance with LDP members interested in health matters. They succeeded in carrying out key changes that altered fundamental premises held dear by the JMA. In this instance the negotiated polity witnessed an assertion of power by a once-weak ministry carried out against a strong interest group that may have overplayed its hand for too long. Popular anxieties about the costs of health care and a growing public disdain for physicians were essential adjuncts to this effort.

Welfare policy-making in the early 1980s was important in its own right, but this case is important for another reason as well. It echoes findings from several of the following studies. Masaru Mabuchi, for example, finds that the MOF employed legal devices in the late 1980s that helped to arrest a decline in its control over financial issues. Hideo Otake illustrates

77. Two illuminating sources on these events are Takahashi Hideyuki, "Atsuryoku dantai: Nihon ishikai" [Pressure group: The Japan Medical Association], in Nakano Minoru, ed., *Nihon-gata seisaku kettei no hen'yō* [Transformation of the Japanese style of policy-making] (Tokyo: Tōyō keizai shinpōsha, 1986), 237–266; and Katō Junko, "Seisaku kettei katei kenkyū no riron to jisshō [Fact and theory in research on the policy-making process]," *Revaiasan*, no. 8(1991): 165–184. Another excellent study appeared too late for me to incorporate it into this account. See especially chapter 9 of John Creighton Campbell, *How Policies Change: The Japanese Government and the Aging Society* (Princeton: Princeton University Press, 1992).

how officials in the Ministry of Construction (MOC) were able to thwart the deregulatory designs of the Nakasone government and to achieve land policies that accorded with ministerial preferences. And Frank Upham demonstrates how MITI, after a long period of rather helplessly ceding authority to its clientele, acted with dispatch in 1990 to retrieve authority and impose its own will on the distribution sector. All of these cases confirm the perduring influence of bureaucracy in Japan's political life. They suggest how the bureaucracy can use its expertise, its strategic participation, and even its exploitation of foreign pressure to retrieve and preserve its power. A stronger and more capable ruling party, resource-rich interest groups, and an affluent citizenry have encroached on bureaucratic power in many ways, but the bureaucracy remains an implacable force fully capable both of slogging on and fighting back.

One organized interest that never before the 1980s managed to integrate itself with established powers was the labor movement. Its importance as the principal support for the JSP and the DSP is one reason why its role deserves attention. Its dramatic retreat from power during the course of the 1980s is another. Although we examine labor's alteration in some detail in the chapters in Part 3, a brief overview is warranted in the context of matters under consideration here. In Part 1 of this chapter I described how economic fragmentation in the small enterprise sector produced a structural transformation to which labor could not adapt. This failure to adapt led to a sharp drop in the share of the labor force that belonged to unions and was one crucial cause of labor's declining influence.

A second phenomenon undermining organized labor was moderation among workers. One can trace the beginning of this attitude to the 1950s and 1960s.[78] But as the economy grew, real wages rose, and workers became more affluent, the signs of moderation multiplied. For example, after peaking in 1975 at around 3,400 disputes per year, the number of strikes and lockouts of more than half-day duration dropped to only 10 percent of that level by the late 1980s. The number of workers involved in such disputes dropped even more sharply from nearly 3 million in 1975 to less than 100,000 in 1989. Days lost to work also plummeted from 8 million to 220,000.[79] This is evidence of a more docile labor force. Moderation also manifested itself in other forms. Younger workers, animated by materialist values and averse to the Marxian ideologies of the JCP and JSP, stopped affiliating with unions altogether. This trend was especially disastrous in some formerly strong public sector unions such as Nikkyōso, the national union of public school teachers. Ikuo Kume, in Chapter 6,

78. Gary D. Allinson, "The Moderation of Organized Labor in Postwar Japan," *Journal of Japanese Studies* 1(Spring 1975): 409–436.
    79. *Ntn* (1990), 116.

describes how the tendency toward moderation also shaped behavior in two important private-sector unions.

The third and final force promoting labor weakness was political divisiveness. There had always been divisions within a union movement whose members supported political parties across the full political spectrum from the LDP to the JCP. Such divisions had spawned and sustained the DSP, the JSP, and the JCP. Events of the eighties, however, magnified these divisions further. First, the LDP tried to co-opt the moderate, private sector wing of organized labor by granting unprecedented access to top officials.[80] Later, the party-business coalition promoting administrative reform launched an assault on the public sector unions affiliated with the JSP. Privatization of the Japan National Railway and the telecommunications monopoly produced deep and possibly lasting effects on the most important unions in the public sector. Mike Mochizuki assesses these changes in Chapter 7. The effort to co-opt moderates facilitated the rise of Rengō, whose role Yutaka Tsujinaka analyzes in Chapter 8.

Structural transformation, moderation, and political divisiveness have, thus, all contributed to labor's difficulties. They have reduced the size of the labor movement, rendered unions more docile, undermined commitment to oppositionary politics, and weakened support for the JSP. It is too early to determine with assurance what the future holds, but events of the recent past have dramatically altered the role of organized labor as a collective force in national political life.

Metaphorically, renegotiation has become an inherent practice in Japan's dynamic polity since 1970. The LDP is obliged at nearly every election to renegotiate its tacit covenant with the electorate. By exploiting a firmer citizenship and by holding the LDP in check for pragmatic reasons, families and individuals have employed the formal electoral arena to renegotiate a stronger collective presence for themselves in Japan's political life. The big business community during the 1980s renegotiated a more central role in national affairs, following a lengthy eclipse in the wake of the environmental crisis. The small-business sector has continually renegotiated a "social contract" that enhances its economic importance and confers penetrating political influence.[81] And labor is in the process of renegotiating its very existence within the political order. All of these tendencies confirm the effects of continuous structural transformation and the more competitive, strenuously negotiated character of recent Japanese politics.

80. Tsujinaka Yutaka, "Rōdōkai no saihen to 86-nen taisei no imi" [Labor's reorganization and the meaning of the 1986 system], *Revaiasan*, no. 1(Fall 1987): 47–72.
81. This is the term used by Garon and Mochizuki, "Negotiating Social Contracts."

In a more realistic sense, however, negotiation has become the hallmark of Japanese politics during an age of expanded economic citizenship and social fragmentation. Political bargains can be, and are, struck by a wider range of participants engaged on a much broader field of action than ever before. In this chapter I have sought to describe the socioeconomic context in which these recent modes of political practice have appeared. In the chapters that follow we will explore in greater detail just how political practice itself has evolved in Japan's negotiated polity.

CHAPTER TWO

PATTERNED PLURALISM UNDER CHALLENGE:

THE POLICIES OF THE 1980S

Michio Muramatsu

ONCE THE ORTHODOX INTERPRETATION OF JAPANESE POLITICS, THE bureaucracy-dominant model was challenged in the 1980s by the alternative of a pluralist polity. The concept of "patterned pluralism" that I advocate originated as an attempt to criticize the bureaucracy-dominant model.[1] However, various political developments that called pluralism itself into question occurred in the 1980s. In this chapter I detail my use of "patterned pluralism," suggest how patterned pluralism relates to my concept of the weak state and how postwar patterned pluralism arose, and argue that the political events of the 1980s transformed Japanese politics but sustained patterned pluralism.

Patterned Pluralism and Other Models

Pluralism is a form of politics in which the interests of various groups are accommodated through negotiation among them or through representative organs such as political parties. Such pluralism is based on the formation of diverse social groups and on the participation of individuals in a variety of such groups. This process occurs in response to environmental changes.[2]

1. The concept of patterned pluralism was first developed in Michio Muramatsu and Ellis Krauss, "The Conservative Policy Line and the Development of Patterned Pluralism," in Kozo Yamamura and Yasukichi Yasuba, eds., *The Political Economy of Japan*, vol. 1: *The Domestic Transformation* (Stanford: Stanford University Press, 1987), 516–554.

2. Arthur Bentley, *The Process of Government* (Cambridge: Harvard University Press, 1967); and David Truman, *The Governmental Process* (New York: Knopf, 1951). For a

I add the modifier "patterned" to pluralism because in the Japanese context one can observe two institutional characteristics that are not emphasized in ordinary pluralism. One concerns public administration. In most policy matters, bureaucratic decisions are almost final. Bureaucrats are engaged in the complex, difficult work of accommodating various interests. Their work also becomes highly political because important activities carried out in their own jurisdictions will increase their budgets and personnel and enhance the posts they will assume in the private sector after retirement. Jurisdictional competition among ministries is, therefore, extremely severe. Otake Hideo contrasts the United States with Japan, pointing out that the former does not specify which powers belong to which department, agency, or committee because Congress and its members can directly decide or intervene in many policies without letting administrative agencies participate in the decision-making process. In contrast, Japan clearly specifies the location of authority or power, so agencies in the executive branch decide policies without intervention by politicians.[3] Otake's findings suggest that jurisdiction can become subject to rivalry in Japanese politics.

Jurisdiction, as Richard Samuels points out, is separate from control or influence.[4] Ministries with specified authority do not automatically decide matters within their jurisdictions. Although the ministry with relevant jurisdiction is the basic decision-making unit, other interests can and do influence its decisions, leading to the emergence of "subgovernments" in each ministry. Politicians inject their views into the deliberations of subgovernments. Provisional decisions by such subgovernments often take the form of draft bills submitted to the Diet. Unless influential Liberal Democratic party (LDP) politicians interfere with such bills later, probably under special circumstances, they are usually confirmed as laws. Most decisions are made by many actors but within the procedures and jurisdictions of ministry arenas. Pluralism in Japan thereby becomes highly patterned.

During the long postwar period in which the LDP has controlled the majority in the Diet, bills in draft form approved by the dominant party have almost always been passed into law.[5] It must be noted, however, that a procedure has existed to honor the opinion of minority parties (the

more recent discussion, see Theodore Lowi, *The End of Liberalism* (New York: Norton, 1981).

3. Otake Hideo, *Gendai Nihon no seiji kenryoku keizai kenryoku* [Political and economic power in contemporary Japan] (Tokyo: San'ichi shobō, 1979), 197.

4. Richard Samuels, *The Business of the Japanese State* (Ithaca: Cornell University Press, 1987).

5. T. J. Pempel, ed., *Uncommon Democracies: The One-Party Dominant Regimes* (Ithaca: Cornell University Press, 1990).

Japan Socialist party (JSP), in particular) even under single-party dominance. Thus, the second element of patterned pluralism is that opinions of
the opposition (most of whom oppose LDP proposals) are taken into account and built into the party system.

The very process by which opposition party opinions are honored is
patterned because the relationship between policies likely to pass the Diet
and ones likely to be blocked is patterned. Bills that pass the Diet are those
supported by the majority coalition. Under democratic rule, the LDP
could pass almost any bill it wished throughout nearly the entire postwar
period. But opposition parties, especially the JSP, have been particularly
concerned about such issues as constitutional reform and national security. When opposition dissent in these issues is strong, the LDP withdraws
its proposals from Diet deliberations, thereby respecting the political position of the JSP. The stronger the dissent is, the larger the blocking force
becomes. It is weakest when just the JSP opposes the bill. It strengthens
when the JSP and one or more other opposition parties join in dissent,
becomes even stronger when all of the opposition parties dissent, and is
strongest when newspapers join the opposition parties to bring the power
of the masses to bear. Under these circumstances even opposition elements
within the LDP can become extremely vocal as in the controversy over introducing a consumption tax during the Nakasone administration.[6] The
patterned pluralism that I advocate is often confused with the "compartmentalized competition" model of Murakami, the "canalized pluralism"
of Satō and Matsuzaki, and the "bureaucracy-led, mass-inclusionary pluralism" of Inoguchi.[7] Murakami's model tries to explain the rules that define the relationship between government and business but fails to relate it
to the pluralistic political system that emerged in the 1960s and 1970s.
Satō and Matsuzaki, while acknowledging the increased influence of the
LDP, stress the bureaucracy's "guidance" to political parties. Inoguchi's
model is a variation of the bureaucracy-dominant model; it is not a pluralist democratic model. Instead, Inoguchi points out the close relationship between the bureaucracy and social groups. No political party
dominance emerges from his model. My concept of patterned pluralism is
a more sharply conceptualized model which I use to explain why Japanese
politics in the 1960s and 1970s were pluralistic.

6. Sone Yasunori and Iwai Tomoaki's model is useful for understanding the political process of policy-making in Japan. See their "Seisaku kettei ni okeru rippōbu no yakuwari" [The
role of the legislature in the policy process], in Nihon seiji gakkai, ed., *Seiji katei ni okeru
rippō kinō* [Legislative functions in the political process] (Tokyo: Iwanami shoten, 1989).

7. Murakami Yasusuke, *Shin chūkan taishū no jidai* [The age of the new middle mass]
(Tokyo: Chūō kōron sha, 1983); Satō Seizaburō and Matsuzaki Tetsuhisa, *Jimintō seiken*
[LDP power] (Tokyo: Chūō kōron sha, 1985); and Inoguchi Takashi, *Gendai Nihon no seiji
keizai* [Modern political economy in Japan] (Tokyo: Tōyō keizai shinpōsha, 1982).

Japan has had a long tradition of effective bureaucracy. Postwar Japanese politics, however, saw the evolutionary development of the Diet-centered dominant party system even while the polity continued to allocate important roles to the bureaucracy. The majority in the Diet appoints the prime minister and determines the ruling party. Under the dominant party system, the policy preferences of the ruling party need to be identical with or similar to the preferences of its supporters. Thus, groups having connections with the LDP have realized their demands through what I call a "pre-Diet procedure" in the internal policy-making process within the LDP. In addition, groups not aligned with the LDP also have acquired far more influence than normally alleged through activities of the opposition, both inside and outside the Diet.

I believe that patterned pluralism arose during and after the 1960s. In the 1980s, however, two factors emerged that challenged pluralism: the national deficit and the pressure for change from the United States. How patterned pluralism developed after the 1960s and what the impact of these two factors has been is best understood by reflecting briefly on problems accompanying the weak state in modernizing Japan and how political leaders tried to overcome them.

The Weak State and Its Problems

The decentralization of authority that one detects in the postwar Japanese polity is a legacy of the weak state of the prewar era. To implement a strong policy Japanese governments had to overcome decentralized authority by making special efforts.

Late to modernize, the Meiji government carried out policies to foster economic growth and enhance industrial productivity by relying heavily on the bureaucracy and modernization strategies. As is well known, financial resources were not sufficient, nor were high-quality human resources, such as engineers. Thus, in many areas the nation had to take the initiative, and the efficient use of limited resources became commonplace. Under these circumstances the Meiji government was characterized by its extensive but weak presence.

The task of overcoming limited resources in diverse ways for many purposes was pursued in four ways. First, people at the top of the government delegated their authority to power groups at the next level, forcing them to share the burden. For example, the highest political leaders delegated authority to the ministries of the central government. Delegation fostered a pattern of decentralized authority exemplified by the *genro,* leaders of the

Meiji Restoration who after 1890 were elevated to the high-status positions of imperial advisers. The Meiji constitution intentionally avoided a strong premiership so that powers were actually dispersed among numerous clan oligarchs and the genro and was pluralistic in some degree. But the pluralism in the period was shared among the various elites who lacked bases of popular support. Yamaguchi calls this *plutocracy*.[8]

Second, the government circumvented the problem of scarce economic resources by mobilizing nonpolitical resources. A good example can be found in the relationship between the central and local governments after the city/town/village ordinance was issued in 1889. The central government was compelled to minimize its investments in time and funds to resolve local issues so that it could fully devote itself to vital national issues, such as revision of the unequal treaties.[9] To meet its needs the central government tried to use the social authority and resources of local influential figures. For this reason, it granted more autonomy to local communities than would be expected of a relatively new state. Similarly, the central government inspired the nation with the ideology of the emperor (*tennō*) system to reinforce government authority with minimal expenditure. Historians argue that the Meiji government actually created an excess of imperial ideology that made it difficult in time to curb the ambitions of the Japanese military.

Third, the informal procedure of prior negotiation that laid the groundwork (*nemawashi*) helped to make up for the lack of resources and the dispersed authority of decision makers.[10] Many social scientists have failed to understand that extensive authority can be inherently weak just because it is extensive. Even if the central government issued an order, it was difficult to implement it thoroughly if forces resisted it. On this point, John Haley makes two interesting observations:[11] tax collectors in Japan resisted compulsory enforcement of tax collection because the system of support was weak, and land rarely was expropriated by the government because resistance from land owners was strong. The government historically avoided politically sensitive issues owing to defects of the "weak state." Officials tended to postpone decisions on vital issues as, for example, in the decision-making process that led to Japan's participation in World War II. After the war, despite fundamental constitutional reform

8. Yamaguchi Yasushi expressed this view in a symposium with Professor Theodore Lowi at the Kyoto American Center in September 1984.

9. Nagahama Masatoshi, *Chihō jichi* [Local government] (Tokyo: Iwanami shoten, 1952); and Mitani Taichirō, *Nihon seitō sei no keisei* [The formation of party politics in Japan] (Tokyo: Tōkyō daigaku shuppankai, 1968).

10. Too often the social system in Japan is interpreted in cultural terms. I argue that most cases of cultural explanation can be reinterpreted with rational theory. *Nemawashi* is one case in point.

11. John Haley, "The Myth of the Reluctant Litigant," *Journal of Japanese Studies* 4(Summer 1978): 359–390.

that shifted sovereignty from the emperor to the people, the government still tended to postpone major decisions as a clever strategy against opponents. Only when the particular controversy cooled did Japanese leaders adopt the policies that they deemed necessary. They had to do so because the resources available to them were limited.

Fourth, the Meiji leaders invented the method by which they determined a target and used resources intensively on it. For example, in 1872 the Meiji government constructed a government-controlled silk mill in Tomioka. When the factory achieved sufficient productivity, they transferred it to private ownership and moved on to another task. The priority production system (*Keisha seisan hoshiki*) of the postwar era was just one application of the well-established prewar target system to the postwar economy.

Delegation of authority, mobilization of nonpolitical resources, informality, and targeting were first devised by a weak state during the Meiji era and continued to be used by Japanese governments after 1945. The Japanese polity in the postwar period, therefore, has had problems similar to those of Meiji governments in a weak state and has needed similar devices to overcome them.

What was the role of an active bureaucracy in postwar policies of the Japanese government? In the context of a weak state an active bureaucracy was the outcome of efforts to overcome the state's weakness. Between 1945 and the early 1950s, when Japan was mostly under the control of the occupation forces, the Japanese government temporarily enjoyed the fruits of a strong state. The government had the power to allocate foreign exchange to the industries it chose and, also, the power under law to restrict foreign investments. But this was an exceptional period. Japan later had to open the market and abolish the law concerning foreign exchange control. Facing a loss of power, the Ministry of International Trade and Industry (MITI) tried to introduce a new law that would permit it to exercise legal measures to guide businesses. But the Diet failed to pass the law, and MITI resorted to extensive use of administrative guidance. When the Police Agency failed to win passage of a law concerning implementation of police duties, it, too, invented new measures to supplement its weak power.[12]

The Postwar System and Patterned Pluralism

The political elements of Japan's patterned pluralism became apparent in the 1960s. But it was during the 1970s that they acquired concrete form.

12. Peter Katzenstein and Yutaka Tsujinaka, "Japan's Internal Security Policy: Political Responses to Terrorism and Vioient Social Protest in the 1970s and 1980s" (Typescript, Department of Government, Cornell University, 1991).

During that decade, political parties succeeded in penetrating the bureaucracy-centered policy-making process, and the so-called *zoku* politicians, who specialize in particular policy areas, were born. For example, politicians with special interests in road construction were called *dōro-zoku*, and those supporting the interests of hotels, inns, and restaurants were called *kankyōeisei-zoku*. During the seventies, also, the principle of a balanced budget, which the Ministry of Finance (MOF) tried hard to maintain, began to fall by the wayside. In the end an increase in financial rigidity marked the beginning of pluralistic pressure politics. MOF adopted a campaign to resist increasing political pressure. The campaign, however, ended in failure not because pressure politics disappeared but because financial resources increased with the recovery of the Japanese economy. As for political parties, the LDP and the Japan Socialist party (JSP) both lost influence in the late 1960s, while the Democratic Socialist party (DSP), Komeito (Clean Government party [CGP]) and the Japan Communist party (JCP) gained power significantly by representing interests that had not been heard until then. As a result, so-called multiparty politics emerged.

In the 1970s the government expanded its welfare programs. The new welfare policies, such as free medical care for the aged, originated from local politics, as did new environmental policies. These developments around 1970 marked the second stage of patterned pluralism.

The trend toward pluralism is well marked by expanding national expenditures. Between 1965 and 1980 general expenditures in the national budget increased by a total of 60.5 percent. In table 2.1 one can trace the periodic rate of increase in each category from 1965 to 1980. In general, spending on welfare and spending on some categories of nonpublic goods rose. More specifically, overseas development assistance and energy expenditures increased. Among welfare outlays, the increases in social insurance and social services were pronounced. The rate of expenditure declined in judiciary, police, and fire, defense, education, and reservation and development of land, which are, on the whole, outlays related to the basic functions of a state that are often called public goods. In contrast, expenditures increased for categories such as nonpublic goods in which politics came into play. Thus, one can detect a tendency toward the politicization of the budget. Why?

Pressure politics increased, so budgetary expenditures grew in policy areas in which pressure groups became active. Welfare organizations and citizen groups belatedly took the stage in Japanese politics in the 1970s, and it became necessary for the Japanese government to respond to such groups (see table 2.2).

The expansion of political party influence brought about an increase in the scale of the budget. For most of the postwar era the MOF succeeded in imposing its balanced-budget policy. In 1966, however, the country first

Table 2.1. Trends in the composition of national expenditures: FYs 1965, 1970, 1975, and 1980 (percentage of national budget)

National budget categories	1965	1970	1975	1980
General administration	8.0	6.6	6.5	5.1
Judiciary, police, fire	3.4	2.7	2.4	1.9
Foreign affairs	0.6	0.6	0.7	0.8
Others	4.0	3.3	3.4	2.4
Local government transfers	19.2	21.6	20.9	17.5
Defense	8.2	7.2	6.3	5.3
Reservation and development of land	18.7	16.2	12.2	13.5
Industry and economy	8.5	11.8	11.3	8.8
Education and culture	12.8	11.4	12.0	10.7
Social welfare	17.0	15.8	20.6	21.7
Social insurance	7.1	7.7	11.2	12.4
Social security	2.9	2.7	2.5	2.2
Social services	1.7	1.7	3.1	3.4
Housing	1.0	1.2	1.4	1.8
Others	4.2	2.4	2.4	1.9
Pensions	4.2	3.6	3.6	3.9
Civilians	0.5	0.4	0.3	0.3
Veterans	3.6	2.9	2.9	3.2
Others	0.1	0.3	0.3	0.4
National debt	0.3	3.5	4.9	12.5
Others	2.9	2.1	1.7	1.0
TOTAL	99.8	99.8	100.0	100.0

Sources: Ōkura shō, ed., *Kuni no yosan* [National budgets] (Tokyo, 1968, 1973, 1978, and 1983).

experienced some financial rigidity. The problems of that period were solved, but in the late 1970s the MOF had to resort to issuing government bonds to finance growing deficits. Some foreign pressure was behind these developments, but more important was a desire on the part of the LDP to secure its domestic political base. The functions of *zoku giin,* who had first appeared in the mid-1960s as interest mediators, and the importance of the LDP Political Affairs Research Committee (PARC) both increased markedly in the late 1970s as they became established vehicles for politicizing the budget. As LDP party influence grew, the MOF was obliged to expand budgetary outlays.

As interparty competition heightened, the 1970s witnessed a new diversity of interests and values. Some of these were reflected in opposition party pressures on the LDP that made it more responsive to the public. Many other features of the 1970s were destabilizing, including the move to a floating exchange system in international currency markets, the restoration of diplomatic relations with the People's Republic of China, and the oil crisis. All of these events elevated competition between the LDP and its opponents.

Table 2.2. Founding periods of pressure groups by type of organization (percentage)

Type of organization	1868–1924	1925–1945	1946–1955	1956–1965	Post–1966	Number of organizations
Agricultural	4.3	4.3	73.9	13.0	4.3	23
Welfare	0	3.3	40.0	33.3	23.3	30
Economic (business and financial)	3.4	4.5	44.3	34.1	13.6	88
Labor	0	3.8	51.9	28.8	15.4	52
Administrative	33.4	6.7	40.0	13.3	6.7	15
Educational	0	8.3	83.3	8.3	0	12
Professional	22.2	0	55.6	22.2	0	9
Citizen/Political	0	5.3	26.3	36.8	31.6	19
Other	0	25.0	50.0	25.0	0	4
TOTAL (all types)	4.4	4.8	48.8	28.2	13.9	252

Source: Based on a 1978 survey by Michio Muramatsu of 252 of the most influential interest groups. See Muramatsu Michio, Itō Mitsutoshi, and Tsujinaka Yutaka, eds., *Sengo Nihon no atsuryoku dantai* [Postwar Japan's pressure groups] (Tokyo: Tōyō keizai shinpōsha, 1987).

Table 2.3. Frequency of contacts between bureaucrats and LDP and opposition parties (percentage of total bureaucrats interviewed)

	No response	Daily	Weekly	Monthly	More than once monthly	Scarcely
LDP	0.4	18.7	23.1	15.5	37.5	4.8
Opposition	0	3.2	26.7	31.1	21.1	17.9

Source: Based on interviews with 251 bureaucrats conducted in the late 1970s and reported fully in Muramatsu Michio, *Sengo Nihon no kanryōsei* [Postwar Japan's bureaucratic system] (Tokyo: Tōyō keizai shinpōsha, 1981).

Amid these crises, the LDP tried to surmount its problems by relying on spending policy. By fulfilling welfare provisions and expanding outlays for nonpublic goods, the LDP sought to mollify the opposition and to strengthen its rural base. Some international appeals, of course, were behind these increases. Prime Minister Fukuda returned from the summit conference in 1976 to announce, "I don't know the numbers, but we're moving ahead at 7 percent," the result of his promise at the summit to expand Japan's budget. He pushed forward with this promise despite opposition from the MOF and other government agencies. However important these international considerations were, the LDP's emphasis on spending policy derived even more from its efforts to overcome a domestic political crisis.

The extent to which bureaucrats of each ministry valued individual actors during this period is obvious in table 2.3. It was not sufficient for bureaucrats to obtain approval from only the LDP and other ministries when they wished to push forward policies. As long as the Diet was the supreme decision-making organ, bills could not be enacted unless some tacit approval was also obtained from the opposition. Bureaucrats laid considerable groundwork to deal with opposition parties (see table 2.3). Thus, Japanese politics from the 1960s through the 1970s was characterized by three elements.

Political resources (education, income, leisure time, and so forth) increased and were distributed relatively widely throughout the entire society. Many industrial groups were organized. Later, welfare groups were organized to influence government policy-making. Active political competition rose perceptibly.

The bureaucracy played a more important role in Japanese politics than that in the United States. The Japanese bureaucracy represented various interests in the policy-making process. A symbiotic relationship emerged between specific bureaucratic agencies and specific interest groups, and demands from groups were efficiently translated into policies. Bureaucracy, therefore, grappled positively to transform the interests of its own organization and its clients into policies, but within the LDP's policy framework. It was the important duty of bureaucrats to coordinate inter-ests with other ministries or government agencies, with the LDP Political Affairs Research Council, and with zoku politicians representing partic-ular policy areas.[13] Under these pressures from society, bureaucracy was motivated positively to initiate projects, and competition among bureau-cratic agencies over jurisdiction was extremely severe.

The LDP made the final decision on political competition between groups and the bureaucracy or between agency-group coalitions. Pat-terned pluralism promotes competition among ministry bureaucracies to push forward new projects that appeal to their constituents. Ministerial bureaucracies propose, and the LDP decides. Opposition parties play an important role in changing governmental policies by opposing and criti-cizing governmental proposals in the various stages of Diet procedure, particularly in the policy areas "belonging" to them. Welfare, environ-ment, salaries of public employees, defense, and so forth, are the areas in which they claim to share power. Because the LDP has been the final ar-biter in this process, however, it has reaped the fruits of this competition.

Challenges to Patterned Pluralism

Two factors seem to have driven changes in Japanese politics in the 1980s: decreasing resources and economic friction with the United States. Has bureaucratic initiative decreased as a consequence of American pressure and decreased financial and other resources? Has the people's voting be-havior changed despite LDP dominance? Have policies adapted to envi-ronmental changes? Have the opposition parties changed in terms of policies or political strength?

The issue of financial resources rose to the surface when the Japanese government sharply increased deficit-covering bonds in 1976. Prime Min-ister Ohira, when elected in 1978, tried to introduce a large-scale con-sumption tax to rectify the national finance problem. When he failed, "overload" and "governability" became politically controversial issues

13. One can observe the emergence of the zoku phenomenon in the 1960s or even before, much earlier than Inoguchi Takashi and Iwai Tomoaki point out in their "*Zoku giin*" *no kenkyū* [Research on "tribal parliamentarians"] (Tokyo: Nihon keizai shinbunsha, 1987). See also Mikuriya Takashi, "Mizushigen kaihatsu to sengo seisaku kettei katei" [Develop-ment of water resources and the postwar policy decision-making process], in Kindai Nihon seijishi kenkyūkai, ed., *Kanryōsei no seisei to tenkai* [The formation and development of the Japanese bureaucracy] (Tokyo: Yamakawa shuppankai, 1986).

well beyond academic circles.[14] In the 1979 general election when voters strongly objected to the large-scale consumption tax, the LDP lost forty seats in the Diet. Conflicts heightened within the LDP. When big business also opposed the introduction of the new tax, the LDP under the Suzuki administration decided to curtail expenditures as the first step toward eliminating deficits and reconstructing the government's financial framework. For these purposes the Second Provisional Commission on Administrative Reform (SPCAR) was organized in 1981.

In contrast to the politics of financial expansion of the preceding years, the Suzuki (1980–1982) and Nakasone (1982–1987) administrations were characterized by the politics of austerity. Austerity coupled with pressure from the United States made the 1980s a stormy decade. The government, instead of responding favorably to demands of various groups, as it had during periods of high growth, persuaded them to accept budget cuts and deregulation. Fortunately, the times were politically favorable to the LDP. Support for conservatives grew after the late 1970s probably because of the public trust earned as they overcame such problems as the oil crisis of the mid-1970s.[15] The LDP government, therefore, managed to carry out drastic measures, including cuts in welfare and the reduction of farm subsidies, to the great disadvantages of the interest groups and people concerned. Administrative reforms, such as the so-called zero ceiling and minus ceiling budget principles, were set and maintained for three years to reduce national deficits. Salary increases for public servants were stopped. Three public corporations (Japan National Railway, Japan Telephone and Telegraph, and Japan Tobacco and Salt Corporation) were privatized, and the telecommunications, transportation, and banking industries were deregulated. In 1988 a consumption tax was introduced after nine years of devoted efforts by four successive cabinets.[16]

The 1980s was the decade of privatization and deregulation, undertaken to address the various political issues (such as libertarianism, size of government, technology developments, etc.) perceived as critical by conservative leaders. These changes, however, were also carried out in response to foreign pressures. Economic friction between the United States and Japan intensified in the 1980s and assumed a form different from that

14. For the concepts of governability and overload, see Samuel Huntington, Michael Crozier, and Joji Watanuki, *The Governability of Democracies* (New York: Trilateral Commission, 1975); and Anthony King, "Overload: Problems of Governing in the 1970s," *Political Studies* 23 (1987), 227–248.

15. Miyake Ichirō et al., eds., *Nihon seiji no zahyō* [The locus of Japanese politics] (Tokyo: Yūhikaku, 1984), 282–300.

16. Michio Muramatsu and Masaru Mabuchi, "Introducing a New Tax in Japan," in Samuel Kernell, ed., *Parallel Politics: Economic Policymaking in Japan and the United States* (Washington, D.C.: Brookings Institution, 1991), 184–207.

in the 1970s. In particular, the Japan-United States Structural Impediments Initiative (SII) talks and American demands to export more agricultural products into Japan began to exert an influence on policy-making that had a more systematic, and less piecemeal, effect than ever before.

The Elections of 1986, 1989, and 1990

Support of political parties became quite unstable in the 1980s. After the landslide victory of the LDP in 1986, the JSP and other opposition parties defeated the LDP for the first time since the war in the 1989 election for the House of Councillors. In 1990, however, the LDP reaffirmed its strength in the election for the Lower House.

The LDP won 304 seats in the Diet in the 1986 election largely because Nakasone's presidential style and opinion-oriented politics attracted wide popular support. Particularly influential was his assertion of Japan's international position on the diplomatic front and his politics toward urban dwellers. By appealing to urbanities Nakasone was trying to realign LDP electoral support. Some observers believe that he was almost successful. It must be remembered, however, that support from urban dwellers has been volatile. Furthermore, farm support for the LDP, regarded as "constant" for a long time, swayed in the 1989 election.[17] I believe the LDP's defeat in the 1989 election for the House of Councillors resulted from its decision to reduce agricultural subsidies. It is, of course, difficult to determine which factors produced the heaviest damage to the party. Many factors degraded its image: the introduction of a consumption tax, the Recruit scandal, and Prime Minister Uno's sex scandal, to name just a few. Among the many aspects of the damage to the LDP, the LDP losses in the thirty local electoral districts in the election for the House of Councillors is noteworthy. The defeat in these electoral districts came as many agricultural cooperatives, longtime retainers of the LDP, supported candidates allied with the JSP and/or the newly organized Rengō. In the 1990 election for the House of Representatives, however, most voters in these constituencies again supported the LDP. The interpretation of the results of these three national elections is, thus, complicated. Whatever the interpretation, it is true that once rural voters become volatile, the LDP's conventional support base is no longer fixed.

In the relationships between the LDP and the opposition parties on the Diet level, a cleavage persists. The JSP has not completely abandoned the ideologies of traditional socialism and idealistic pacifism, but it is impor-

17. For the results of the 1989 elections for the House of Councillors, see Kobayashi Yoshiaki, *Nihon no senkyo* [Japanese elections] (Tokyo: Tōkyō daigaku shuppankai, 1991).

tant that the party has begun taking a more flexible stance than ever before on many issues. It is possible that the LDP's adoption of a "realignment strategy" to shift its support base to urban areas and the JSP's adoption of realistic policies will both bear some fruit. Revisions of election laws and laws that regulate political contributions could bring further, far-reaching changes to party and electoral politics if they are passed by the Diet.

The weak position of the LDP in the House of Councillors will continue at least until the election in 1992. The 1989 election results made it difficult for the LDP to steer the government as it did when it had a majority in the upper house. This became clear in 1990 when the government had to grapple with the issues raised by the Gulf War. Conversely, the 1989 election results helped the JSP. It had been losing influence, owing to its long-standing position as the party out of power. Gains in the upper house, however, have enabled it to retain some influence over policy-making and to sustain the system of patterned pluralism. However, the party's long-term popular support, and, therefore, its very future, depends on many factors, not least the strength of Rengō (the new peak association for labor discussed by Yutaka Tsujinaka in Chapter 8).

Changes in Public Administration and
Policies in Government Ministries

The political changes of the 1980s affected the bureaucracy in two ways. They altered the relationship between the bureaucracy and the prime minister and they made the bureaucracy itself far more defensive.

Resource constraints and trade frictions between Japan and the United States promoted a more presidential style among Japanese prime ministers. During the G7 economic summit of 1976 Prime Minister Fukuda was persuaded that Japan should become the "locomotive" for international economic recovery. After returning to Japan he formulated financial policies based on an annual economic growth rate of 7 percent. It is well known that he cut taxes on one hand and expanded public projects on the other, worsening the already poor financial condition of the country. When the economic frictions between Japan and the United States intensified, American requests became demands to economic agencies to modify macroscopic policies (such as total spending for public works) and rules to encompass individual microscopic issues (such as consumer behavior). U.S. demands were gradually made even on the implementation level. Prime Minister Nakasone, in the Maekawa Report, promised to stimulate domestic demand and transform the Japanese economic structure so as to encourage imports. He also called on the general public in a television address to buy imported products.

A more recent example of presidential behavior by a prime minister is the response to very specific American demands in the SII talks between the United States and the Kaifu government. After discussions concerning the Large-Scale Retail Stores Law (discussed at greater length by Frank Upham in Chapter 11), Prime Minister Kaifu responded favorably to American demands, allowing construction of new supermarkets and issuance of shop-opening permits within a much shorter period than before. Kaifu had to persuade relevant government agencies and industries to understand and approve revisions to the retail stores law. Kaifu's foundation within the LDP was weak, and a weak Kaifu cabinet could not have survived the SII without special considerations from the U.S. government. When Kaifu found it difficult to persuade relevant government agencies and interest groups within Japan, the United States either weakened or strengthened its demands in ways helpful to his negotiations. Although one might not regard American influence over governmental decisions through a prime minister as part of the political process of patterned pluralism, according to Otake, who observed the politics of textile disputes between the United States and Japan twenty years ago, the growing role of the prime minister has been one of the most important factors that has broken the monolithic rule of ministerial bureaucracies and brought about pluralistic politics in Japan.[18] Some new elements in prime-ministerial politics, developed in conjunction with negotiations with the United States in the 1980s, have thus enhanced patterned pluralism.

Government ministries have become more defensive. Ministerial bureaucracies have changed their behavior and strategies in response to the impact of administrative reform and American pressures. Curiously, new political cleavages have become more salient than before, whereas old cleavages based on Right and Left seem to be retreating. A new cleavage is seen in the policy conflicts between those who support a large government framework and those who advocate a small government framework. Most businesses, labor unions in large companies, salaried persons in the large cities, and the leadership groups of the LDP and the DSP support small government, whereas farmers, welfare recipients, some business leaders such as those in construction, and many other groups advocate large government. Government ministries have also divided along the lines of large versus small government, with economic ministries on the side of small government and spending ministries on the side of

---

18. Otake Hideo finds the conspicuous emergence of prime-ministerial politics in the textile negotiations between the United States and Japan around 1970. See Otake, *Gendai Nihon*, 140–150.

large government. Ministeries on both sides change their strategies to defend their interests.[19]

After the postwar abolition of the Home Affairs Ministry, MOF became the most influential ministry. Until the fall of 1965, when the MOF issued deficit-covering bonds for the first time in the postwar period, it had managed to maintain a "balanced budget" policy, rejecting all excessive requests and demands. That year, however, marked the beginning of MOF's concessions to political pressures. In 1966 national finances became very restricted owing to an economic recession. The financial rigidity that ensued weakened MOF's influence on other ministries because resources allocated to those ministries decreased. Throughout the 1970s MOF had to issue deficit-covering national bonds to cope with internal and external pressures. Japan's national deficits grew each year and reached ¥ 200 trillion in 1980. To resolve this situation, Prime Ministers Suzuki and Nakasone endeavored to curtail expenditures for several years, using the influence of the Second Provisional Commission on Administrative Reform. The MOF served as the prime minister's right hand both in cutting expenditures during the eighties and in introducing the consumption tax in 1988.

External pressures also worked to reduce MOF autonomy. The liberalization of interest rates in 1983 by the MOF originated in U.S. pressures. To respond to the U.S. demand for abolition of Japan's nontariff trade barriers, the MOF adopted various deregulation measures, among them monetary relaxation (liberalization of interest rates). Liberalization further developed into measures that permitted banks to advance into new arenas, such as dealing in government securities. Banks also demanded access to business areas where securities companies had operated profitably and monopolistically. The MOF was unable to resist these pressures as Frances Rosenbluth explains in Chapter 4. Securities firms demanded more freedom, too. By that time, neither the MOF Banking Bureau nor its Securities Bureau was any longer able to favor the industries it controlled because the MOF's control over both banks and securities companies had weakened so much.

Masaru Mabuchi, in Chapter 5, further supports my claim that MOF was on the defensive by the 1980s. He illustrates how both resource constraints and external pressure forced the solidification and clarification of MOF authority. In his view and mine, these trends also confirmed some decline in MOF power.

19. The following comments are based on the results of collaborative research on a project that I led for the Center for Management Studies in Tokyo in which Professors Kitahara Tetsuya, Mabuchi Masaru, Kume Ikuo, and Kitayama Toshiya participated. See *Shakai keizai no henka to gyōsei sutairu no henyō* [Changes in style of Japanese public administration in changing environments], Research Report of the Agency for Management and Coordination of Japanese Government (Tokyo, 1990).

In the 1960s the United States began demanding that Japan relax its control of trade and capital. Liberalization caused MITI to lose its right to allocate foreign exchange and, among others, the right to issue various business licenses. The loss of these policy tools did not entirely reduce MITI's influence because it continued to issue extensive administrative guidance under the premise of cooperation between the government and the people. After the eras of control and administrative guidance, MITI entered a third era, which is characterized in the 1990s by the use of extremely soft administrative techniques, such as forming networks and supplying information. It is true that MITI has sought to gain regulatory influence over foreign investments in Japan and over Japanese firms when they try to move abroad. On the whole, however, MITI's strong influence over enterprises and groups is gone. Nevertheless, MITI has become increasingly assertive in defining its own territory against other ministries, for example, in its "Telecom War" with the Ministry of Posts and Telecommunications. Like the MOF, MITI has watched its declining authority force it to assume a more defensive posture.

The Ministry of Labor (MOL), established by the Katayama cabinet, has also become defensive but it is one of the few ministries that has gained some measure of initiative. Under the Labor Standards Law, the MOL at first extended its protection, which had been limited to female workers and workers under age twenty, to workers in general. To ensure that the law was strictly observed, the MOL often intervened in specific companies. After 1960, however, as part of the labor reconciliation policy begun by the Ikeda cabinet, the labor standards issue was left to labor and management. The measure permitted overtime work, which, in turn, enhanced the country's economic growth. After 1980, however, Japanese workers and foreign nations demanded international standardization of working hours that made the MOL adopt new, positive administrative measures. Shortened working hours were realized smoothly in contrast to the slow pace of international standardization in other fields, mainly as a result of the great political influence exerted by Labor Minister Yamaguchi, who was versed in international development. Although exacting administrative policy for shortened working hours was implemented through legislation, MOL's implementation of the policy allowed considerable flexibility among job types.

In this policy area internationalization benefited MOL, but the impact of resource constraints and internationalization in other policy areas proved MOL no exception to larger trends toward defensive ministries. Retraining programs in declining industries were abolished in 1986 and deregulation has been under consideration in several policy areas. MOL has jurisdiction over companies engaged in employment information circulation. The Recruit Company contracted with almost all the major companies to deliver information on those companies to recent graduates. When deregulation of this business was under consideration, the president of Recruit bribed many influential politicians. The scandal resulted in the resignation of the prime minister and the arrest of several high officials, which subsequently drove MOL on the defensive.

Keeping pace with Japan's economic growth, resources for the two main bureaus within the Ministry of Construction (MOC) increased steadily. The River Bureau's budget in absolute terms has been kept at a high level since the end of the war as has that of the Road Bureau. This generosity is explained by the similar interests that MOC shares with farming areas. The LDP's *kensetsu-zoku* (which represents the interests of the construction industry) draws heavily on Diet members elected from constituencies in farming areas strongly supported by the MOC. The MOC's strong ties both to farm districts and construction firms ensured its abundant resources. Locally elected LDP Diet members have frequently intervened in the ministry's decisions on budget distribution (e.g., budgets for roads) in their locales. This is an opportunity for Diet members to show their constituents how useful they are to them.

The MOC is engaged in two other types of activities, according to the analysis of T. Kitahara:[20] "plan activities" and "market-activity promotion." City planning is a typical example of the former, and invigoration of the private sector is an example of the latter. Some say that the MOC is shifting its activities away from public construction toward activities of the second type; it no longer feels safe after the "zero ceiling" was set in 1980 although the ministry has been assured adequate funds. To cope with this situation the MOC reinforced its regulatory authority in the age of deregulation to make up for a decrease in resources. In SII talks in 1989 the MOC negotiated hard with the United States over the *dangō* (preliminary consultation) issue. Further observation is needed to know to what extent outside pressures will affect the MOC.

Despite the change in policy emphasis from resource-consuming river administration to plan activities, the MOC has made every effort to increase or maintain its existing level of expenditures. The MOC advocates large government as do, for example, the Ministry of Transportation and the Ministry of Health and Welfare (MHW). In contrast, economic ministries such as the MOF and MITI have accepted the economic theories of small government. As social and economic groups have divided into those advocating large government (benefits recipient groups) and those in favor of small government, so too have the governmental ministries divided into political ministries advocating large government and economic ministries in favor of small government.

20. Kitahara's comments appear in the research report cited in n. 19.

The development of postwar regulatory administration can be divided into three periods: control, whose origin can be traced back to the prewar years (1945–1960); control abandonment and a shift in commitment to the society and economy by means of administrative guidance and resource distribution (1960–1970); and deregulation (1981–). Project administration can be divided by trends in expenditures into implementation of the national policy to establish sufficient infrastructure (1945–1965); project expansion (1966–1980); and project cessation (1981–). These observations suggest that Japan once attempted to create a large government, but in the 1980s it began to move toward a "smaller government" through deregulation and curtailment of expenditures. Because of the changes forced by SPCAR and pressures from the United States, the Japanese bureaucracy is becoming generally defensive for fear it will lose authority.

In the years before 1960 institutional conditions for patterned pluralism were prepared. A parliament-centered constitutional system emerged in which one-party dominance was the norm. Ministerial initiative and ministerial rivalries also developed, such as those between MITI and MOF over economic policies. In the 1960s and 1970s patterned pluralism blossomed. A combination of new forces, especially the LDP and its interest groups, appeared in the 1960s and brought about a truly pluralistic political process. In a third stage, during the 1980s, patterned pluralism was challenged because of limited resources and increased foreign influence.

Assessing policies adopted in the 1980s, I believe that the producer-centered policy-making system is being eroded. The abolition of subsidies and deregulation by the SPCAR were obviously measures to weaken vested interests. What the United States stressed through the reduction of agricultural protection in 1988 and the SII talks were changes that would benefit Japanese consumers. One researcher attributed these pressures to "the U.S.-consumer coalition." Liberalization of agricultural production, minimized requirements for establishing supermarkets, and prohibition of dangō all enhance the interests of Japanese consumers, in general, and urban dwellers, in particular. Since the 1986 election, the LDP has intentionally adopted a realignment strategy to shift its support base to urban areas although the party still takes steps forward and backward.

Have political changes in the 1980s undermined the concept and reality of patterned pluralism? Despite the various changes and fluidity shown in bureaucratic and voting behavior in the 1980s, patterned pluralism still offers a valid explanation of Japanese politics.

The 1980s did witness diverse tendencies in the bureaucracy. It was an age of deregulation and austerity. All ministries were involved in the politics of defending jurisdictions and influence. The MOF, for example, tried to guarantee a minimum influence, not by the conventional method of administrative guidance but by codification of laws (as Masaru Mabuchi explains in Chapter 5). Such measures were adopted to reconfirm the jurisdiction of the MOF. The same defensive behavior was observed in the Ministry of Transportation and in other ministries. Such efforts to secure minimum influence imply weakened control over affiliated groups. The MOL's active policy for shortening working hours was exceptional. Deregulation and scarce resources, however, were major problems in organizational developments at MOL, too. It was there, after all, that the Recruit scandal (bearing, in part, on the deregulation of employment information) drove the ministry onto the defensive in a wholly unexpected way.

Prime-ministerial politics are still emerging. Therefore, a new style of "presidential politics" has not wholly displaced patterned pluralism. The fact that Prime Minister Kaifu was able to overcome difficulties during the SII talks in spite of his weak administration implies a change in the location of policy-making initiative. The general public felt that the strong leadership of Prime Minister Nakasone was somewhat related to the personal charisma of Nakasone himself. If the same sense of strong leadership can apply to a weak Kaifu, then the Japanese political system is becoming a system of prime-ministerial politics. Other prime ministers modified policies in important ways from time to time. After 1960, Ikeda's inclusive strategy, Satō's Okinawa reversion and environmental policies, Tanaka's welfare policy, and Miki's amendment of the Antimonopoly Act were all the results of prime ministers' decisions. They made drastic policy modifications through the administrative means of a weak state while they avoided confrontation with competing and varying interests. It would be a mistake to say that only in the 1980s did prime ministers engage in prime-ministerial politics. If, however, the change from producer-centered policy-making to consumer-centered policy-making was triggered by pressures from the United States, then something different from conventional prime-ministerial politics must be occurring.

In the 1989 election for the House of Councillors, agricultural cooperatives in many farming areas did not vote for LDP candidates. The JSP appealed to the interests of the farming population by opposing the LDP's proposed agricultural policies, thus attracted farmers' votes, and achieved an unprecedented victory. Faced with outside pressures, the LDP was compelled to adopt policies that ran counter to the interests of the distribution industry, the construction industry, and farmers, all of whom had been traditional LDP supporters. Patterns will not change overnight, and it seems likely that past political dividing lines will become more fluid than ever. In the 1990 election for the House of Representatives, the LDP won again. Bases for political support are not fixed anymore. In the wake of the 1990 election and the Gulf War, specialists on Japanese politics see no chance for the JSP to assume power. Although many new things happened in Japanese politics in the 1980s, no single factor will remove the LDP from power.

The LDP has been involved in a realignment strategy since the Nakasone administration that has blurred party lines among voters. In the midst of growing political turmoil during the 1980s, Nakasone decided to link the urban middle class's preferences for "small government" and "greater internationalism" to his own policies of administrative reform and diplomacy. In doing so, he created a means to rebuild public support for the LDP. Behind the effort to cut income taxes and compensate for them with an indirect tax was one explicit goal—to shift away from the LDP's traditional base of support in the coalition of farmers and small business in order to accommodate better the interests of an urban, middle-class constituency with a radical income tax reduction policy.[21]

This aim was easily defeated when Nakasone's proposal for a flat-rate sales tax to be paid by manufacturers ran into opposition. He won the 1986 election only when he promised not to introduce the tax he was considering. The LDP could not afford to depend solely on an urban constituency, however, because urban voters have proved to be highly volatile. To convert its failures of 1986 and 1987 into the successfully implemented reforms of 1988 and 1989 the party realized that it had to make major concessions to groups with vested interests. Even if the LDP recognized the desires of urban dwellers, it would not be able to win a majority of seats in the Diet on their votes alone. It was, thus, politically dangerous for the LDP to adopt policies that shifted entirely toward an accommodation for the urbanites.

Pressures have been more strongly felt among the opposition parties to change their basic policies, especially toward defense. It is apparent that Japan's international responsibilities should be enlarged. The opposition's problem is, thus, a large one. Opposition supporters are still against any changes in defense policy (they would not allow the Self-defense Agency to send troops even for mine-sweeping duty in the wake of the Gulf War) although some opposition party leaders seem to have accepted the need for change. In the near future the LDP will be reorganizing its electoral strategies and the JSP will be concerned with an antiquated conservative-leftist rivalry. For some years to come, the two largest parties will be struggling to create a new alignment strategy within the framework of patterned pluralism.

Patterned pluralism offers a viable means of interpreting Japanese politics through the 1980s. Interest-group negotiation and the role of representative parties remained strong and were accentuated by events of the

21. Michio Muramatsu, "Bringing Politics Back In," *Daedalus* 119 (Summer 1990): 141–154.

period. The two essential patterns associated with this type of pluralism concern the bureaucracy and the opposition. Although bureaucratic resources declined and bureaucrats became more defensive, they struggled mightily to maintain their jurisdictional boundaries and their policy-making authority. In addition, opposition opinions were taken more seriously. For all of these reasons, patterned pluralism persisted in Japan during the 1980s despite the many challenges to it from a rapidly changing society.

CHAPTER THREE

STATE STRENGTH AND

THE PUBLIC INTEREST

Margaret A. McKean

A QUESTION THAT CONTINUES TO FASCINATE OBSERVERS OF JAPAN IS HOW
that country produces what appear to be its most admirable accomplishments against what ought to be great odds. These accomplishments con-
sist not only of recovering "miraculously" after utter destruction in war,
of producing exportable merchandise that competes in price, quality, and
technological superiority but also of emphasizing long-term over short-
term interests, avoiding the British-American stagflation disease and recovering well from national and world recessions, and responding to
environmental tragedy with effective environmental policies, to energy crises with effective energy policies, and to government fiscal disaster with
effective administrative reform that alone among the advanced industrial
democracies produces balanced budgets as intended. These recent crises
have pitched most of the other advanced industrial democracies into internal political squabbling that puts aggregate social income at risk,[1] but
Japan somehow prevents this kind of internal conflict from reaching ru-
inous totals and addresses the fundamental problem, time after time.

Thus far, comparativists either note but do not explain the Japanese
anomaly or explain Japan's accomplishments through reference to a
strong state, strong enough not to be done in by sectoral interests that

I am indebted to Hayden Lesbirel, T. J. Pempel, Mark Ramseyer, Richard Samuels, and
Mark Tilton for insightful suggestions and criticisms.
1. Mancur Olson attributes the decline of many advanced industrial economies to the
proliferation of nonencompassing special interest groups, which are willing to put total social product at risk to claim more for themselves. See Mancur Olson, *The Rise and Decline
of Nations: Economic Growth, Stagflation, and Social Rigidities* (New Haven: Yale University Press, 1982).

manage to penetrate the centers of power elsewhere.[2] T. J. Pempel located the strength and wisdom of the state in the central bureaucracy and described Japan as "state-led capitalism."[3] Chalmers Johnson narrowed the search further to the central economic bureaucracy, particularly in the Ministry of International Trade and Industry (MITI), and he described Japan as an example of "soft authoritarianism" rather than democracy.[4] Their views have greatly influenced such comparativists as John Zysman, Robert Wade, and Peter Katzenstein, who along with Johnson have spread the message of the strong state, especially the strong bureaucracy, far and wide.[5]

From within the study of Japanese politics, however, now comes a veritable chorus of voices, many included in this volume, stating that Japan does *not* have a strong state or a dominant bureaucracy, that sectoral squabbling in Japanese politics frequently penetrates and overpowers the bureaucracy and the dominant Liberal Democratic party (LDP), that the LDP's perpetual electoral victories are based on a strategy of perpetual concessions to interest groups old and new. In addition to the chapters in this volume—particularly those by Muramatsu, Mabuchi, Rosenbluth,

2. Some of the best recent work is international enough to incorporate Japan in basic data collection so that Japan appears on graphs and charts with other nations (or apart from them, in a corner for deviants), even if more detailed case studies are reserved for European countries. See Fritz W. Scharpf, *Crisis and Choice in European Social Democracy* (Ithaca: Cornell University Press, 1991), and John Freeman, *Democracy and Markets: The Politics of Mixed Economies* (Ithaca: Cornell University Press, 1989), particularly 137–148. Scholars using aggregate data are increasingly likely to include Japan in their analysis and explanations. See Peter Lange and Geoffrey Garrett, "The Politics of Growth: Strategic Interaction and Economic Performance in the Advanced Industrial Democracies, 1974–1980," *Journal of Politics* 47 (August 1985): 792–827; and David R. Cameron, "Social Democracy, Corporatism, Labor Quiesence, and the Representation of Economic Interest in Advanced Capitalist Society," in John Goldthorpe, ed., *Order and Conflict in Contemporary Capitalism* (New York: Oxford University Press, 1984), 142–178.

3. T. J. Pempel, "The Bureaucratization of Policymaking in Postwar Japan," *American Journal of Political Science* 18 (November 1974): 647–664; Pempel, *Policy and Politics in Japan: Creative Conservatism* (Philadelphia: Temple University Press, 1982); and Pempel, "Organizing for Efficiency: The Higher Civil Service in Japan," in Ezra N. Suleiman, ed., *Bureaucrats and Policy-Making* (New York: Holmes and Meier, 1984), 72–106.

4. Chalmers Johnson, *MITI and the Japanese Miracle: The Growth of Industrial Policy, 1925–1975* (Stanford: Stanford University Press, 1982).

5. John Zysman, *Governments, Markets, and Growth: Financial Systems and the Politics of Industrial Change* (Ithaca: Cornell University Press, 1983); Robert Wade, *Governing the Market: Economic Theory and the Role of Government in East Asian Industrialization* (Princeton: Princeton University Press, 1990); and Peter Katzenstein, "Conclusion," in Katzenstein, ed., *Between Power and Plenty: Foreign Economic Policies of Advanced Industrial States* (Madison: University of Wisconsin Press, 1977), especially 313–316, as well as Katzenstein, *Small States in World Markets: Industrial Policy in Europe* (Ithaca: Cornell University Press, 1985). Although Katzenstein characterizes Japanese political economy as statist (because of high centralization of both state and society and very little differentiation between the two in Japan), he is not at all sure that the state is smart. See *Small States,* 19–20.

Upham, Mochizuki, Kume, and Tsujinaka in which they explicitly raise the question of state strength—in reams of new empirical research on Japan scholars argue that Japan has pluralism or social corporatism or a weak or soft state rather than a strong state or state corporatism. In this new literature they maintain that the center of gravity in Japanese politics has moved out of the bureaucracy and into the LDP and its support groups, that the centralized power of the unitary state is a fiction concealing considerable local initiative and bargaining strength, that labor may have played a larger part in determining its own fate than the statists ever dreamed possible, and that the bureaucracy's original proposals do not prevail but are converted into policies designed to suit powerful private interests, leaving the state with little need for a will or imagination of its own.

If the Japanese state is not really strong, then the strong state explanation of Japanese successes is invalid, contaminated from the start by inaccurate assumptions. Obviously one will have to explore this debate over the "true nature" of politics, the relative strengths of different political actors, and the way interests are met or ignored in policy-making before one can hope to explain Japan's ability to produce socially desirable results. In this chapter I first disassemble the empirical evidence in this dispute against the background of statist theory and then pick up the pieces, assembling an explanation of how Japanese political processes do seem, when it really counts, to produce outcomes that serve the public interest rather than a few private interests. My aim is to explain how those processes can sometimes mediate and even convert private conflict into public-regarding results.

The Strong State Thesis

Part of the problem in explaining Japan's accomplishments with the strong state thesis may be the strong state thesis itself. To get anywhere in assessing the validity of statist and antistatist explanations of politics in Japan, one must define "the state" and develop a reasonable measure of state strength or weakness.

Some scholars who write about the state use the term as a substitute for "nation" or "country," as a substitute for "government," and, sometimes, as a substitute for "bureaucracy" (and their arguments would suffer little, perhaps even become clearer, if the words were changed all the way through). But many statist theorists insist that the state is more than the sum of career central bureaucracy plus elected ruling coalition; they sometimes want to throw in historical memory, independent goals, institutional will, and other ghostly abstractions.[6] A definition of "state," however, that prevents a differentiation between the state's components just dumps everything into a huge, black box that the extreme statists would then forbid anyone to open or risk dismissal as a mere pluralist who sees only trees, never forests.[7] I am willing to acknowledge the possible existence of the forest, even to give it a name, but not to give it collective intelligence without overwhelming evidence, just as one should hesitate to give the attributes of a central nervous system to entities that do not have one, whether forests or human institutions.[8] So in this chapter, I sweep aside the ghosts and goblins and use "state" as shorthand for just the bureaucrats plus the ruling party, without assuming that these people always share monolithic interests and goals.[9]

Many statists also assume, rather than define and test, state strength. Whenever they see state activity or state involvement, they infer strength, quite incorrectly, without doing any policy tracing, or "political archaeology,"[10] a detailed analysis of the origins of a particular political outcome. But statists admit upon challenge that the definition of state strength (or autonomy or capacity) has to be based on who pushes whom

6. This is most often the case among theorists in the Weberian tradition. See Albert Stepan, *The State and Society: Peru in Comparative Perspective* (Princeton: Princeton University Press, 1978); and Theda Skocpol, *States and Social Revolutions: A Comparative Analysis of France, Russia, and China* (Cambridge: Cambridge University Press, 1979). For an analysis of the transcendental mythology of the state and state-society boundaries, see Timothy Mitchell, "The Limits of the State: Beyond Statist Approaches and their Critics," *American Political Science Review* 85 (March 1991): 77–96.

7. Theda Skocpol argues for the reexamination of states and state capacity as an antidote to pluralism and structural-functionalism in her "Bringing the State Back In: Strategies of Analysis in Current Research," in Peter B. Evans, Dietrich Reuschemeyer, and Theda Skocpol, eds., *Bringing the State Back In* (Cambridge: Cambridge University Press, 1985), 3–43.

8. Several of the chapters in James A. Caporaso, ed., *The Elusive State: International and Comparative Perspectives* (Newbury Park, Calif.: Sage Publications, 1989), are very helpful treatments of problems of definition and methodology in this field. See particularly Caporaso, "Introduction: The State in Comparative and International Perspective," 7–16; James N. Rosenau, "The State in an Era of Cascading Politics: Wavering Concept, Widening Competence, Withering Colossus, or Weathering Change?" 17–48; and Bert A. Rockman, "Minding the State—or a State of Mind? Issues in the Comparative Conceptualization of the State," 173–203.

9. Eric Nordlinger, usually considered a statist, insists, as I would, upon defining the state as some collection of individual persons in order to avoid anthropomorphisms, reification, and Hegelian implications about the preferences of the state. See Nordlinger, *On the Autonomy of the Democratic State* (Cambridge: Harvard University Press, 1981); Nordlinger, "Taking the State Seriously," in Myron Weiner and Samuel Huntington, eds., *Understanding Political Development* (Boston: Little, Brown, 1987); and Gabriel A. Almond, "The Return to the State," *American Political Science Review* 82 (September 1988): 853–874, as well as the commentaries by Nordlinger, Lowi, and Fabbrini that follow on 875–901.

10. This is Kent Calder's apt term for researching the origins of a policy in order to find out who won. See "Linking Welfare and the Developmental State: Postal Savings in Japan," *Journal of Japanese Studies* 16(Winter 1990): 31–59.

around: strength or power is quite definitely the ability to make others do what they would not otherwise do. Thus, state strength or capacity can never be assumed because the only way to diagnose it is to go through a case-by-case comparison of initial positions with final results, an examination of who actually wins prelegislative battles over policy design and who actually wins the postlegislative battles over implementation.[11] Mere knowledge of which parties are involved cannot reveal the actual distribution of power among them and how much of whose initial demands survived the negotiations to affect the outcome. John Zysman, who readily assumes that it is not even controversial to call Japan a strong state, devises a typology of policy-making in the advanced industrial countries with these three alternatives: state-led policy, company-led policy (in which the state is not involved at all) and tripartite (corporatist) bargaining among labor, capital, and government. Zysman, thus, forces himself to declare the state the leading partner if it is involved and labor is not and, thereby, overlooks the possibility that the state might be involved without being the leader, either as referee or as loser.[12]

It is difficult to diagnose the paths of influence for any political struggle that is already completed because one must absorb the story in retrospect, always contaminated by knowledge about the appearance of the final outcome and without the benefit of following the struggle in daily detail over a long period. In Japan, it is especially easy to confuse the arena with the winner of a political battle. Because many laws are drafted in the bureaucracy, their contents fought out within the halls of Kasumigaseki, and their implementation mediated by bureaucrats, it often seems that the bureaucrats have controlled the entire process from start to finish.[13] But one must remain open to the possibility of confusing place with power, literally mistaking the stadium itself, or, perhaps, the referees in the black and white stripes, for the winning team (and its owners). One would laugh if a visitor to a baseball game thought that the bleachers, or the referees, or providers of hot dogs (or green tea and sake?) were the true winners of the game. But this is precisely the kind of mistake made when one does not recognize all the roles actors may play in political battles and that visibility may not go with victory. As Rosenbluth points out in Chapter 4, the active

11. Unhappily, this fact creates the possibility that a given state may turn out to be strong in some conditions and weak in others at the same time rather than displaying a certain strength across all sectors and look like different things to different analysts, depending on the policy area they examine. This is particularly so in Japan, hence, a good portion of the confusion and disagreement over the strength of the Japanese state.

12. Zysman, *Governments, Markets, and Growth.*

13. David Friedman comes to this conclusion in his study of bureaucratic politics and policies aimed at the machine tool industry in postwar Japan. See Friedman, *The Misunderstood Miracle: Industrial Development and Political Change in Japan* (Ithaca: Cornell University Press, 1988).

state is often the conductor but not the composer and may not be determining an outcome but brokering the outcome. Of course, all those involved, including bureaucrats and other state actors, have more impact than if they were entirely absent, and sometimes they make enough difference to make enemies (as do referees—hence, the slogan, "Kill the umpire!"), but serious mistakes arise when appearance is confused with reality—all the more so if appearances are artfully crafted compromises to save face for the losers or are actually designed to conceal a sordid or embarrassing reality. The only protection against making these kinds of errors is to examine decision making from its beginnings and take note of all the actors who participated, not just those who announced the final compromise.

There are two reasons for the increasing doubts about the view that Japan has a strong-and-perhaps-smart state. One reason, which readers in this field can arrive at only after considerable slogging through the literature, is nothing more than an artifact of semantic sloppiness in the use of the term "state." Slippery boundaries around the definition of the "state" make it possible for two observers to look at exactly the same thing and disagree over whether they see a strong or a weak "state." Some state theorists, although they would admit when questioned that private interests technically belong to society rather than to the state, include the favored client groups of the ruling party along with the bureaucracy and the ruling party as part of the state. (Others sometimes go to the other extreme and use "state" as if it means the bureaucracy alone, unwittingly omitting even the elected party regime.) Imagine a policy-making conflict in which the bureaucracy was overpowered by private business interests in the determination of final policy; this contest allows one to describe the bureaucracy as weak and the client groups as strong. The observer who quite improperly includes these private societal interests that interact with bureaucrats within the state then claims to see a strong state. But including a private societal interest, however powerful, in one's operational definition of the state is a grievous error. If the societal actors dominate the policy outcome, then what one has is a strong societal actor, and the state itself is not strong but captured. Thus definitions and boundaries are crucial, and sloppiness can invert one's conclusions.[14]

The second reason for doubting that Japan has a strong-and-perhaps-smart state is the accumulating empirical evidence of something that cannot be called a strong state.

14. Marxists argue deductively that the capitalist class will capture the state. Although I am not a Marxist, I have to admit that I reach the same conclusion, that this happens more often than not in Japan, although I do so inductively on the basis of accumulated empirical examples.

The Empirical Evidence

Some of those who challenge the strong state thesis have noted the pluralization of participation and influence from active private interest groups. Other challengers have noticed how frequently Japanese interest groups expand or federate into encompassing groups that essentially represent all of their latent members, and they have talked about the inclusive, essentially corporatist quality of interest group representation in Japan. Lest one frets that pluralism and corporatism are not supposed to coexist, one can remember helpful comments by Yutaka Tsujinaka: participation and influence are undergoing pluralization (new actors are gaining entry and influence), but the mode of interest group representation is highly corporatist whether through formal structures or through informal "osmotic" networks.

Pluralization of Participation

One major assault on the strong state or dominant bureaucracy view of Japan comes from the accumulating evidence that bureaucrats are losing power to politicians. Muramatsu Michio, Ellis Krauss, Sone Yasunori, Satō Seizaburō and Matsuzaki Tetsuhisa, Inoguchi Takashi, and, recently, Kabashima Ikuo and Jeffrey Broadbent all argue on the contrary that Japan is pluralist.[15] They find the LDP and even the Diet becoming much

15. On *patterned pluralism*, see Muramatsu Michio, *Sengo Nihon no kanryōsei* [Postwar Japan's bureaucratic system] (Tokyo: Tōyō keizai shimpōsha, 1981); and Muramatsu Michio, Itō Mitsutoshi, and Tsujinaka Yutaka, eds., *Sengo Nihon no atsuryoku dantai* [Postwar Japan's pressure groups] (Tokyo: Tōyō keizai shimpōsha, 1986) (hereafter cited as *SNAD*); Michio Muramatsu and Ellis S. Krauss, "Bureaucrats and Politicians in Policymaking: The Case of Japan," *American Political Science Review* 78 (March 1984): 126–146; and Muramatsu and Krauss, "The Conservative Party Line and the Development of Patterned Pluralism," in Kozo Yamamura and Yasukichi Yasuba, eds., *The Political Economy of Japan*, vol. 1: *The Domestic Transformation* (Stanford: Stanford University Press, 1987), 516–554. On *predominant party pluralism*, see Sone Yasunori, "Nihon no seisaku keiseiron no henka" [Changes in the theory of Japanese policy formation], in Nakano Minoru, ed., *Nihon-gata seisaku kettei no hen'yō* [Transformation of the Japanese style of policy-making] (Tokyo: Tōyō keizai shimpōsha, 1986), 301–319; and Sone Yasunori, "Tagen Minshushugi ron to gendai kokka" [The debate over pluralist democracy and the modern state], *Nempō seijigaku* (1982): 117–149. On *mixed party–bureaucracy-led compartmentalized pluralism*, see Satō Seizaburō and Matsuzaki Tetsuhisa, *Jimintō seiken* [LDP Power] (Tokyo: Chūōronsha, 1986). On *bureaucratic mass–inclusionary pluralism*, see Inoguchi Takashi, *Gendai Nihon seiji keizai no kōzu: Seifu to shijō* [The composition of the modern Japanese political economy: government and market] (Tokyo: Tōyō keizai shimpōsha, 1983). Finally, *on referent pluralism*, see Kabashima Ikuo and Jeffrey Broadbent, "Referent Pluralism: Mass Media and Politics in Japan," *Journal of Japanese Studies* 12 (Summer 1986): 329–361. For a review of the debate over these pluralisms, see Gary D. Allinson, "Politics in Contemporary Japan: Pluralist Scholarship in the Conservative Era—A Review Article," *Journal of Asian Studies* 48 (May 1989): 324–332.

more important than before both as arenas of policy-making and as prevailing voices in the shaping of policy.[16] Nakano Minoru has edited several empirical case studies of policy-making that indicate that pluralist interest group politics is replacing bureaucratic dominance.[17] T. J. Pempel now describes both Japanese politics and the ability to perceive it as coming unbundled as the bureaucracy loses its earlier power and as analysts begin to see the parts (which can now include alliances with foreign actors) and not just the whole with greater clarity.[18]

Satō and Matsuzaki, as well as Gerald Curtis, argue that the changing career profiles of LDP politicians suggest that the "center" in Japanese politics is moving out of the bureaucracy and into the LDP. Whereas the LDP in the 1950s and 1960s was heavily infiltrated by retired senior bureaucrats, today the LDP is composed largely of career politicians, and bureaucrats who enter political life do so now by abandoning the bureaucracy early before they have developed many useful connections there.[19] The implication is that power is to be acquired not through a bureaucratic career but by entering the LDP early and that the LDP no longer needs senior bureaucrats as sources of expertise and connections because it has its own expertise in policy *zoku* (tribes or clans), a phenomenon studied by Inoguchi Takashi, Iwai Tomoaki, and Lee Farnsworth.[20]

Muramatsu, Nakano, and Reed find considerable evidence that local governments are not entirely constrained by their dependence on the central government for budgetary transfers. On the contrary, they can use local demands for services as a bargaining chip to extract central funds and even to use those funds in ways disapproved by the center; they are not punished for these "misdeeds" in future budgetary allocations; and they can be policy innovators ahead of the central government.[21]

16. On the Diet's rising influence, see Ellis S. Krauss, "Conflict in the Diet: Toward Conflict Management in Parliamentary Politics," in Krauss, Thomas P. Rohlen, and Patricia G. Steinhoff, eds., *Conflict in Japan* (Honolulu: University of Hawaii Press, 1984), 243–293; and Mike Mochizuki, "Managing and Influencing the Japanese Legislative Process: The Role of Parties and the National Diet" (Ph.D. diss., Harvard University, 1982).

17. Nakano, *Nihon-gata seisaku kettei no hen'yō.*

18. For T. J. Pempel's new views, see Pempel, "The Unbundling of 'Japan, Inc.': The Changing Dynamics of Japanese Policy Formation," *Journal of Japanese Studies* 13 (Summer 1987): 271–306, later printed in Kenneth B. Pyle, ed., *The Trade Crisis: How Will Japan Respond?* (Seattle: University of Washington Society for Japanese Studies, 1987), 117–152.

19. Satō and Matsuzaki, *Jimintō seiken;* Gerald L. Curtis, *The Japanese Way of Politics* (New York: Columbia University Press, 1988), especially 80–116.

20. On the emergence of LDP policy expertise (*zoku*), see Inoguchi Takashi and Iwai Tomoaki, *"Zoku giin" no kenkyū* [Research on "tribal parliamentarians"] (Tokyo: Nihon keizai shimbunsha, 1987), and Lee W. Farnsworth, "'Clan Politics' and Japan's Changing Policy-making Structure," *The World Economy* 12 (June 1989): 163–174.

21. Michio Muramatsu, "The Impact of Economic Growth Policies on Local Politics in Japan," *Asian Survey* 15 (September 1975): 799–816; Muramatsu, "Center-Local Political Relations in Japan: A Lateral Competition Model," *Journal of Japanese Studies* 12 (Summer 1986): 303–327; Steven R. Reed, "Is Japanese Government Really Centralized?" *Journal of*

Ramseyer and Rosenbluth have turned the strong-bureaucracy argument on its head and reanalyzed Japanese politics as a test of the hypothesis that the bureaucrats are, in fact, obedient agents of the LDP, so well trained, even docile, that the top LDP leadership can usually trust the bureaucrats to draft legislation "correctly" without elaborate instructions from the LDP in every instance. Similarly, they also argue that the highest-ranking judges in the land win their positions through similar displays of learning and obedience to the wishes of senior LDP politicians. Thus, the judiciary displays the courage to challenge the status quo in its verdicts only in the lower ranks, after which high courts and the Supreme Court routinely reverse such rulings in favor of the established order. Not only is this analysis persuasive but the crucial evidence is particularly compelling: maverick bureaucrats and judges who try to innovate or go beyond the strictures laid out for them are punished with slow promotion rates, poor job assignments, and unattractive postretirement positions.[22]

The mounting evidence that the arena for decision making is shifting from the bureaucracy to the Diet, that policy experts in the LDP are telling the bureaucracy what has to go into draft legislation rather than the other way around, could be considered merely a sideways shift *within* a still-strong state from a weakening bureaucracy to an invigorated LDP. This shift would not be evidence of declining power of the state as a whole. After all, as a dominant party, the LDP is in an excellent position to alter rules and institutions to enhance its dominance over other parties apart from the external support it receives from voters and organized groups. But this kind of manipulation has limits: reapportionment of urban and rural seats in the Diet, ordered by the Supreme Court, has worked against the LDP by replacing safe LDP Diet seats with seats the LDP must struggle to win; the era of partisan balance (*hakuchū*) may be over but the LDP's electoral successes seem to alternate with near disasters. And in almost every instance when the LDP must actively intervene in drafting legislation or implementing policy, the party does so as conveyor of private interests who have appealed to the LDP for representation or balance. It is crucial to appreciate the fact that the LDP's own strength and power is highly derivative and based on the interests of societal actors. Therefore, the LDP's strength vis-à-vis the bureaucracy is also, in part, a measure of the power

---

Japanese Studies 8 (Winter 1982): 133–164; Reed, *Japanese Prefectures and Policymaking* (Pittsburgh: University of Pittsburgh Press, 1986); and Nakano Minoru, "Chihō rieki no hyōshutsu, baikai to kōkyōteki ishi kettei" [Public interest decision making and the revelation and mediation of local interests], in Nakano, *Nihon-gata seisaku kettei no hen'yō*, 111–155.

22. J. Mark Ramseyer and Frances McCall Rosenbluth, *Voters, Politicians, Bureaucrats, and Judges: Principals and Agents in Japan* (Cambridge: Harvard University Press, 1993), especially chaps. 7–9.

of private interests to penetrate the bureaucracy directly when they can or to seek a champion of their cause in a nervous LDP anxious to please.

This is not to say that a weakening state is automatically a more democratic one than in the past. When the successful private interest groups are long associates of the LDP, representation and political power do not broaden compared to the past. The state is simply weaker and penetrated more successfully by the old regulars. Only when, as occasionally happens, new groups without long track records of political lobbying manage to operate successfully through the LDP can one say that state strength has declined and the range of private interests heard has broadened.

Thus, the discovery that the Japanese labor movement is becoming increasingly involved in policy-making seriously challenges the strong state view, which encompasses the widely accepted picture of the Japanese labor movement as hopelessly fragmented and essentially missing from political decisions, offering no significant resistance to big business or to state policy.[23] The chapters by Kume, Mochizuki, and Tsujinaka in Part 3 of this volume challenge this tidy image.[24] Some portion of the labor movement, either the moderate unions or secretly moderate leaders of radical unions, increasingly have been consulted in wage negotiations and other economic issues during the postwar period, especially since the 1960s. Fragmentation and ideological disputes were real and assuredly weakened the labor movement compared to what it might have been, but consultation was taking place and cumulating into a routine. Even before formal federation of most unions into Rengō in 1989, Japan essentially had corporatist wage negotiations and an incomes policy, conducting negotiations through the press, by megaphone, and by personal networks, and setting wage increases with pacesetter firms in model sectors.[25]

State Leadership or State Followership

So many observers now think that state power in general and bureaucratic autonomy in particular are declining because scholars are finally

23. T. J. Pempel and Keiichi Tsunekawa, "Corporatism without Labor? The Japanese Anomaly," in Philippe C. Schmitter and Gerhard Lehmbruch, eds., *Trends toward Corporatist Intermediation* (Beverly Hills, Calif.: Sage Publications, 1979), 213–230.

24. Sheldon Garon and Mike Mochizuki, "Negotiating Social Contracts in Postwar Japan," in Andrew Gordon, ed., *Postwar Japan as History* (Berkeley: University of California Press, forthcoming); Tsujinaka Yutaka, "Rōdōkai no saihen to 86-nen taisei no imi" [Labor's reorganization and the meaning of the 1986 system], *Revaiasan*, no. 1(Fall 1987): 47–72; and Ikuo Kume, "Changing Relations among the Government, Labor, and Business in Japan after the Oil Crisis," *International Organization* 42 (Autumn 1988): 658–687.

25. Ronald Dore describes the spring offensive negotiations as a mechanism for implementing an income policy in Japan in *Taking Japan Seriously: A Confucian Perspective on Leading Economic Issues* (Stanford: Stanford University Press, 1987), 69–84.

accumulating case studies of policy-making so that they can begin to probe beyond outcomes and appearances and find out who actually fought a battle and who among the parties were winners, losers, and referees. When people did not have the empirical evidence that challenged the appearance of a strong-state-or-bureaucracy, they accepted that appearance. The intimacy of the government-business relationship in Japan is well known, and it is often assumed to signify a strong state. Because Japanese firms and business organizations do not speak angrily about state interference the way self-respecting independent capitalists should, and because both government and business repeat often the importance of doing the socially desirable thing, it is usually assumed that this situation signifies government power over docile business interests. Why so few outside of Japan think this could just as easily signify business power over a docile government—an equally plausible situation in which business would have no need to make impolite or resentful remarks—I have never understood.[26]

In many case studies of policy-making for specific economic sectors, however, the bureaucracy and the LDP often give way to demands from well-organized trade associations, ranging from agriculture to small business to major industries. In many instances, then, government follows and business leads in these relationships; in industrial policy and regulatory policy, in Japan as in many other places, the targeted and the regulated rather than the targeters and the regulators are calling the shots.[27] A strong state leads, but a state that follows is by definition penetrated by private interests and, therefore, weak. Thus, this distinction between government (or bureaucratic) leadership and followership is a make-or-break matter for the strong state thesis.[28] In the following review of this evidence to discern the roles and relative power of the bureaucracy, the LDP, and

26. Similarly, it is often thought that *amakudari*, the descent from "heaven" of retired bureaucrats into highly paid jobs in business, was a device by which the bureaucracy maintained its hold on business. Kent Calder has, at last, reversed this standard interpretation. His evidence on which firms hire former bureaucrats suggests instead that firms hire bureaucrats to increase their influence in the bureaucracy. See Kent E. Calder, "Elites in an Equalizing Role: Ex-Bureaucrats as Coordinators and Intermediaries in the Japanese Government-Business Relationship," *Comparative Politics* 21 (July 1989): 379–403.

27. George Stigler developed the theory of regulation and within it the prediction that the regulated will usually capture their regulators, in "The Theory of Regulation," *Bell Journal of Economics and Management Science* 2 (1971): 3–21.

28. Robert Wade has articulated this distinction with greater clarity than I have seen elsewhere: if the state leads, it is persuading others to do what they would not otherwise do through reallocation of resources that can be large or small. If the state follows, it is reallocating resources by following the suggestions and demands of those who receive the resources. Unfortunately, Wade is not interested in figuring out when it is big followership and when it is big leadership; he takes as an article of faith that in Japan big leadership (materially substantial intervention by a strong state) is the rule. See *Governing the Market: Economic Theory and the Role of Government in East Asian Industrialization* (Princeton: Princeton University Press, 1990).

private interests in political disputes, I attempt to discern patterns that might explain when the configuration of power can serve broad or even public interests, and when the configuration of power serves only a few.

Dominant party though it is, the LDP is often vulnerable (or at least it thinks it is) and in its frequent moments of anxiety it is easily persuaded by interest groups to design compensatory distributive policies to suit these groups—side payments, often massive, for the noisy and boisterous. Kent Calder has documented this response in six nontraded or nonexport sectors of the economy and notes that the aggregate result for Japanese society is reduced efficiency.[29] Calder's findings reveal an easily penetrated state and further imply poor economic performance in the nontraded sectors where the state practices big followership and simultaneously agrees to protect these sectors from competition.

MITI wins much praise from statists for administering socially gentle euthanasia to industries facing permanent decline, for easing industries in a temporary slump through recessions, for masterminding the growth of basic heavy industries, and for targeting promising sectors (the neglected winners) for future expansion.[30] But case studies of how such policies evolve suggest that MITI's own ideas are often rejected and that more often it follows the lead of the industry concerned. In his study of the history of regulation in the energy sector Richard Samuels shows that the policies promulgated by the energy bureaucracy in MITI have, in fact, been utterly transmogrified by the energy industry and that every government attempt to go into the energy business has been thwarted and converted instead into public subsidies of private energy research and development.[31] David Friedman believes it was Japan's good fortune that the rapidly changing

29. These sectors are agriculture, regional policy (packages of benefits for areas outside of the Tōkaidō complex), small business, welfare, land use, and defense. See Kent E. Calder, *Crisis and Compensation: Public Policy and Political Stability in Japan* (Princeton: Princeton University Press, 1988). Calder believes that the distinguishing feature of these politically powerful sectors is that they are nontraded. All six sectors are somewhat insulated from international competition and opportunities for growth either for natural reasons or because they were already organized enough to maintain protectionism and, therefore, were motivated and capable of applying pressure to keep things that way. Daniel Okimoto suggests another explanation: certain sectors are notoriously able to lobby for protection because they come under the narrower jurisdiction of ministries other than MITI, whereas MITI's large jurisdiction gives it responsibility for the health of the entire economy and makes it less vulnerable to parochial appeals. See Daniel I. Okimoto, *Between MITI and the Market: Japanese Industrial Policy for High Technology* (Stanford: Stanford University Press, 1989). However, plenty of protection and coddling takes place within MITI's knowledge and jurisdiction.

30. This is the theme in most of the essays in Chalmers Johnson, Laura D'Andrea Tyson, and John Zysman, eds., *Politics and Productivity: The Real Story of Why Japan Works* (New York: Ballinger Publishing, 1989), and it is explicit laid out in "Preface: The Argument Outlined," xiii–xxi, by Tyson and Zysman.

31. Richard J. Samuels, *The Business of the Japanese State: Energy Markets in Comparative and Historical Perspective* (Ithaca: Cornell University Press, 1987).

and highly competitive machine tool industry was able to reject routinely the bureaucracy's schemes for consolidation and cartelization.[32] In Gregory Noble's studies of two very different sectors, steel minimills in decline and video equipment under development, MITI found itself unable to orchestrate either a capacity reduction cartel or standardization of videotape, videodisc, and camcorder formats.[33] In a similar way, Marie Anchordoguy finds that MITI began with ambitious plans for the state to enter computer production and relegate existing electronics firms to producing parts, but the firms themselves insisted instead that the Japan Electronic Computer Company leave production to them, guarantee them computer sales at propped-up prices, up-front cash flow, and an administratively guided rental market and sponsor collaborative research and development with cheap loans. MITI was not without wisdom in this episode and should be credited with insisting upon competition among firms and weeding out poor performers from research projects.[34] But as in energy, machine tools, steel minimills, and consumer electronics, so in computers, MITI's original schemes were rejected. Similarly, Rosenbluth finds in Chapter 4 that the highly respected Ministry of Finance (MOF) does not lead but defers to its clients, the banking industry, and, lately, the securities industry as well, even if their demands yield social *in*efficiency (protection of small banks, abandonment of MOF plans for bank mergers, etc.).

MITI's much-admired industrial policy for declining industries actually operates through outright delegation of decision making to industrial associations. Mark Tilton found from his studies of cement, aluminum, steel, and petrochemicals during periods of sectoral decline that MITI delegates both policy-making and implementation to industrial associations, frequently allowing or encouraging them to collude and form cartels, legal and otherwise, to manipulate prices, current production levels, and long-term production capacity. In the few cases where MITI "wins" and persuades an industry to do something it did not originally want to, MITI must make concessions of other kinds to "buy" this deference, so these "victories" are hollow, not signs of a strong state either.[35]

32. David Friedman, *The Misunderstood Miracle: Industrial Development and Political Change in Japan* (Ithaca: Cornell University Press, 1988).

33. Gregory W. Noble, "The Japanese Industrial Policy Debate," in Stephan Haggard and Chung-in Moon, eds., *Pacific Dynamics: The International Politics of Industrial Change* (Inchon: Inha University Center for International Studies; Boulder, Colo.: Westview Press, 1989), 53–95.

34. Marie Anchordoguy, *Computers, Inc.: Japan's Challenge to IBM* (Cambridge: Harvard University Press, 1990), especially 59–92.

35. For example, MITI successfully cajoled the aluminum rollers into a merger they did not want with the aluminum refiners' association but only in return for a six-month production and price cartel. Mark Campbell Tilton, "Trade Associations in Japan's Declining

Big followership can also occur in growing industries whether the industries are concentrated, or fragmented and highly competitive. Growth industries are perfectly capable of lobbying for assistance and often welcome tax breaks, subsidies, and low-cost loans, as well as government-endorsed protection of particular markets or products. They will also indulge in building what might later turn out to be excess capacity if they can persuade the government to offer guarantees to free them from the risk of overdoing as aluminum, steel, and shipbuilding all did in their heyday. Thus, some of the measures that growth industries ask for produce social *in*efficiency in exchange for protected markets and high prices that guarantee a certain profit margin subsidized by their customers. But growing industries are also known to reject MITI advice that threatens to cut them off from profit-making opportunities. During their periods of rapid expansion, both the automobile and the steel industries, each with just a few firms, rejected MITI attempts to intervene and promote mergers. MITI has even less luck in high technology, where there are hundreds of firms in electronics, hardware, and software, none willing to self-destruct or forego possibilities for profit during boom years. One might say that MITI had the "market-conforming wisdom" to leave well enough alone here, but it is clear from MITI attempts to exert influence at the outset that these episodes are defeats for MITI.[36]

State Retreat and Deregulation

Several observers noted during the 1980s a pattern of government retreat from policy areas that are increasingly difficult to regulate. Big followership is, obviously, easy for the LDP and the bureaucracy when pressure on a particular issue comes mainly from a unified and powerful source, but it becomes as difficult as leadership for issues in which there are countervailing pressures. Increasing demand and economic competition at home creates political competition among interest groups with opposing claims so that designing a satisfactory policy is quite difficult.

Industries: Informal Policy-making and State Strategic Goals" (Ph.D. diss., University of California at Berkeley, 1990).

36. The automobile case is documented in Ira Magaziner and Thomas Hout, *Japanese Industrial Policy*, Policy Papers in International Affairs no. 15 (Institute for International Studies, University of California at Berkeley, 1981); and William Duncan, *U.S.-Japan Automobile Diplomacy: A Study in Economic Confrontation* (Cambridge, Mass.: Ballinger, 1973). On electronics and high technology, see Daniel I. Okimoto, *Between MITI and the Market*, 129; and Okimoto, "Political Context," 78–113, in Daniel I. Okimoto, Takuo Sugano, and Franklin B. Weinstein, eds., *Competitive Edge: The Semiconductor Industry in the U.S. and Japan* (Stanford: Stanford University Press, 1984).

Increasing competition from abroad removes many variables from the realm of control in Japan, making policy implementation through government-business agreement or any other means quite impossible.

One bureaucratic response to increasing difficulty is to delegate decisions and, therefore, discretion and actual power to others, even while retaining the right to exercise bureaucratic discretion on paper as MITI did through 1990 in regulating retail distribution and sales. Upham (in Chapter 11) finds that MITI faced conflicting pressures from department stores, existing superstores and discount chains, convenience stores, successful small retail outlets with the ambition to become large, and truly small family retail shops threatened by all of the others. MITI attempted to "regulate" retail sales through the Large-Scale Retail Stores Law by delegating the nastiest bits of the job to those regulated, leaving local chambers of commerce and entrepreneurs to fight it out and, thereby, abdicating responsibility for the outcome. This is another convincing case in which we see MITI bureaucrats caving in (sometimes to baseball bats and worse things wielded by small store owners), certainly a sign of weakness. Only pressure from Keidanren and others, accentuated by loud foreign protest against this arrangement as a giant nontariff barrier, empowered MITI to undertake reluctant reform of the regulations in 1990.

Another response to countervailing pressures is to proceed deliberately toward deregulation. In the struggle over coking coal, the government was caught between pressure from the coal miners' unions and LDP politicians based in Kyushu and conveniently positioned on the Policy Affairs Research Council's special coal policy committee to slow the decline of coal and pressure from coking coal buyers (the steel industry) to let market restructuring take its course and allow them to buy inexpensive coal abroad. The resulting agreement displayed political expediency by protecting coal mines in politically sensitive districts in Kyushu, but it honored market efficiency by allowing plants located in Hokkaido and those producing largely coking coal to close first and by preventing an import tax on coking coal.[37] In my study of energy pricing and energy conservation policy MITI was willing to retreat from the headache of regulating the prices of petroleum products in the late seventies and early eighties once it became clear that this task simply put MITI into the line of fire between producers and consumers of petroleum products, creating work but no glory.[38] Similarly, both Rosenbluth and Mabuchi (in Part 2 and elsewhere)[39] found

37. See S. Hayden Lesbirel, "Structural Adjustment in Japan: Terminating 'Old King Coal,'" *Asian Survey* 31 (November 1991): 1,079–1,094.

38. Margaret A. McKean, "Energy Conservation Policy through the Oil Shocks of the 1970s" (Typescript, January 1987, Department of Political Science, Duke University).

39. See also Frances McCall Rosenbluth, *Financial Politics in Contemporary Japan* (Ithaca: Cornell University Press, 1989).

that the Ministry of Finance would rather give up than retain portions of regulatory jurisdictions that are fraught with conflict (between big banks and little banks, between banking and securities, and between banking and securities on the one hand and the postal savings system on the other). Having to regulate from such a hazardous political battlefield is not only burdensome but risks propagating the impression of ministerial incompetence or unfairness—hence, the shift to deregulation that permits banks and securities firms to compete with each other for depositors and borrowers, and to compete with the postal savings system for depositors. Mabuchi's description of MOF's retreat, clarification, and legalization of jurisdiction brings the analogy of pruning trees to mind: a tree cannot survive if its top is larger than its root base, so pruning after transplant or in drought is essential to maintain the vitality of the tree. Bureaucrats and the LDP both have sufficient survival instincts to know when they need to reduce their responsibilities in order to avoid trouble.

Most of the evidence of state slippage and increasing penetration by private interest groups comes from studies of politics in the 1960s and since, but some evidence goes back to the 1950s and even into the prewar period to confirm that the strong state may have been a fiction all along. Campbell argues that rule by subgovernments in which private (nonstate) interests speak loudly has been customary since the 1950s and 1960s—it was the dominant mode of budgetary politics—and it is only researchers' discovery of this penetration of decision making by private interests that is new, not the fact itself.[40] Indeed, Samuels's historical research in the energy sector found this pattern before and during the war, not simply after the crises of the 1970s when it began to receive notice, so he shares Campbell's view that state-society bargaining rather than state autonomy has been the rule much longer than realized. Muramatsu argues in Chapter 2 that the modern Japanese state has been weak all along since the Meiji period. In these analyses, the change of the last few decades is not one from a strong state to a weak one but a change from well-veiled state weakness to more transparency, so that one can no longer fail to see what they believe has always been true.

Most observers agree that a ruling coalition of the state (the bureaucracy and LDP combined) and regular LDP clients used to be fairly strong. Within this arrangement, the bureaucracy inherited considerable discretion and power from wartime and occupation controls. The new evidence concerning the relationships among the parts of this coalition, however, suggests that the state institutions are weak insofar as they are often penetrated by very powerful client groups who transmit their wishes through

40. John Creighton Campbell, "Fragmentation and Power: Politicians and Bureaucrats in the Japanese Decision-Making System" (Paper presented to the Midwest Seminar on Japanese Studies, Ann Arbor, October 24, 1987).

the LDP. This new evidence thus suggests that both the coalition as a whole (the state plus its regular clients) and the bureaucracy in particular have been weakening further as a result of increasing invasions by interest groups, including many new ones that are not part of the regular LDP clientele. Moreover, the LDP has increasingly found its regular clients in conflict with each other and has had to make hard choices at times—especially in the post-1973 era of somewhat slower growth—between agricultural and industrial groups and, within the latter, between subgroups of big and small business, between healthy and troubled sectors, and so on. Most observers agree on the timing as well; bureaucratic control started to slip in the early 1960s. But one also finds evidence that this conflict within the LDP's "regular" client groups is not new, has been going on since the 1950s, but has increasingly come out into the open.

Picking up the Pieces: Coordination for the Public Interest

The evidence described indicates that rather than the state leadership posited by the strong state argument, one finds plenty of state followership. It appears in nontraded sectors as well as in export-oriented industries and domestic industries subject to considerable foreign competition. Similarly, one finds followership both in sectors that can collude and engineer protection for themselves and in others that are willing and even eager to engage in healthy competition. One finds followership when industries want more regulation and state involvement (read "aid") *and* when they want less. And one finds followership associated with socially beneficial results and with socially detrimental results. Thus, the evidence has two implications. First, the strong-and-perhaps-smart-state/bureaucracy thesis dissolves upon scrutiny and is no longer available as a handy explanation for Japan's admirable accomplishments. More often than not when one actually looks at what happens to initial government proposals as they go through the pummeling of pressure group politics, one finds a government fairly easily penetrated by well-organized private interests.

Second, one cannot simply substitute followership as a handy explanation because followership is *too* prevalent to explain what is admired in Japan; it also goes with what is not admired. One cannot overlook the fact that Japan actually does have nasty political corruption accompanying elections, electoral politics based on bribery and illicit service to particular rather than general constituency needs, notorious diversions from the public purse to coddle a considerable variety of underproductive economic sectors (from agriculture to basic industries to distribution to small and medium business in general, all of which has to be a serious drag on economic growth), and wasteful pork barrel contracts for public works boondoggles.[41] The challenge is to explain the coexistence of these all-too-familiar crimes against the public interest and Japan's undeniably impressive aggregate economic performance—a rare combination of economic growth and distributive equality—which still leaps to the eye out of OECD (Organization for Economic Cooperation and Development) statistical tables.[42] Why does pork barrel disease not spread into every area of politics? Or, conversely, if the Japanese government seems able to put collective above particular interests in some issues why is it not possible to do this in other areas? Worded differently, when do a few sectoral private interests dominate the outcome, and when are many competing private interests amalgamated into a balanced and fairly complete whole, essentially the public interest?

The distinctions worth further thought are those between simple (e.g., abject) followership of a single, powerful private interest and coordination of multiple conflicting private interests, and those between followership to protect and followership to deregulate. Faced with a single unified interest and no countervailing pressure, a bureaucratic agency is highly likely to follow or be ordered to do so by the LDP as representative of that client. Neither the bureaucracy nor the LDP can overpower a single unified interest without the support (permission, endorsement) of some other single unified interest in conflict with the first one. But the emergence of conflicts of interest instantly eliminates for the bureaucracy and LDP the possibility of simple-minded followership and creates other opportunities.

When one does not find simple followership, one tends to find not leadership (the ability to make others do what they would rather not) but *coordination* among conflicting interests. Coordination can be supplied by a single sector-specific bureau within a ministry when there is disunity among firms in a single industry, by a single ministry or agency when all the parties to the conflict come within its jurisdiction, and by the LDP when the parties to the conflict spill beyond a single bureaucratic jurisdiction and create parallel conflicts among ministries. If politics is public conflict, and the function of government is to process conflict, then what the Japanese state (bureaucracy and LDP combined) is particularly good at is taking care of conflict: marginalizing it when that works, delegating the resolution of conflict to groups that have powerful internal incentives to fix it, and, when the state has to jump into the fray itself,

---

41. Eisuke Sakakibara, "The Japanese-Politico-Economic System and the Public Sector," in Samuel Kernell, ed., *Parallel Politics: Economic Policymaking in the United States and Japan* (Tokyo and Washington, D.C.: Japan Center for International Exchange and the Brookings Institution, 1991), 50–79, argues that most Japanese policy-making is the wasteful pork barrel variety in the public works sector.
42. See, for instance, Freeman, *Democracy and Markets,* 137–148.

attempting to resolve it in a way that will win the cooperation and compliance of the parties that have the power to disrupt. This is not strength per se, but skill.

Many observers have noted the importance of coordination—collaboration, bargaining, negotiation, networking, reciprocity, and so on—in the relationships between government and interest groups in Japan, even arguing that this is the quintessential feature of state-society relations that one must understand.[43] I agree. Moreover, I think one can understand how these consultative practices and structures can sometimes serve larger collective interests and even the public interest in Japan, if one examines them in the light of collective action theory built on elements of rational choice and game theory.[44]

Theories of Collective Action and Cooperation

Game theory views interest mediation as an iterative game among rational players all trying to enhance their benefits, reduce their costs (possibly by finding someone else to bear them), and improve their position vis-à-vis competitors and opponents. It also alerts those who study it to the conditions that foster and inhibit cooperation and collusion among players. Whenever a group of actors can maximize their collective benefit by cooperating, but single actors can improve their positions even more by defecting while the rest continue to cooperate (thereby riding free on the efforts of the other players), and where an actor's worst option is to cooperate while others defect (ending up a dupe), one has the classic Prisoner's Dilemma. All simultaneously want and fear cooperation, and in one-shot play mutual defection (as insurance against being deceived) is the likeliest outcome or dominant solution. The tragic message here is that when incentives are structured this way, individuals cannot pursue both their individual interests and their interests as members of a group without the help of other group members. Without that help, they will have to abandon their interests as group members and seek only their interests as

43. In addition to Allinson's Chapter 1 in this volume and his "Structure and Transformation of Conservative Rule," book-length works arguing this case are those already cited: Calder, *Crisis and Compensation;* Okimoto, *MITI and the Market;* Samuels, *Energy and the Business of the Japanese State;* Tilton, *Trade Associations;* Muramatsu, Itō, and Tsujinaka, *SNAD;* and Tsujinaka Yutaka, *Rieki shūdan* [Interest groups] (Tokyo: Tokyo daigaku shuppankai, 1988).

44. Collective action theory, sometimes described also as the Prisoner's Dilemma or the free-rider problem and used to explain political and economic problems, can be found in Mancur Olson, *The Logic of Collective Action: Public Goods and the Theory of Groups* (Cambridge: Harvard University Press, 1965, 1971); Olson, *Rise and Decline of Nations;* and Russell Hardin, *Collective Action* (Baltimore: Johns Hopkins University Press and Resources for the Future, 1982).

risk-averse individuals. Thus, all players end up worse off than if they had somehow orchestrated mutual cooperation.

In politics, the first challenge to collective action is mobilization itself, in which interested individuals must decide whether to make personal investments in an effort that will succeed only if large numbers join and will then yield benefits to all interested individuals, active or not. Many people are tempted, of course, to let others organize and to wait for any benefits from the organizers' efforts to flow. Many also try to avoid the reverse risk of investing without succeeding in extracting any benefits at all. Thus, a small number of players, each with large per-person stakes in the outcome, is much more likely to overcome the collective action problem than a large group containing many individuals with small per-person stakes in the outcome.

The immediate implication is obvious and depressingly antidemocratic: concentrated industries have organizational advantages over fragmented competitive ones as do business over labor, producers over consumers, corporate taxpayers over citizen taxpayers, big savers over small savers, polluters over pollution victims, and so on. Collective action problems alone can mean that large diffuse groups of interested individuals do not mobilize to protect their interests or to withhold their consent as savers, taxpayers, consumers, or workers when, in fact, they would like to. Silence can signify organizational helplessness, not complacence. To be sure, "larger issues" may be involved that mean the "losers" are paying to prevent even worse disasters and are, thus, in some sense "winners" in the long run, but those who "lose" in the short run in such situations may not be aware of their roles (as all-purpose, handy-dandy subsidizers) and may not have given their consent to the outcomes. Thus, this approach can make one sensitive to the existence of *un*mobilized, *un*voiced interests.

Politics is essentially a collection of Prisoner's Dilemma and bargaining games, simultaneous, sequential, and nested, fought over goods that cannot be procured through individual action (as in the marketplace). The analysis presented thus far might seem to imply that the collective interest of large groups (which are even more seriously afflicted with free-rider temptations than small groups whose members have higher per-person stakes) would never be served, that political mobilization would never be democratically spread across all latent interest groups, and that the public interest of society would never emerge out of competition among private groups. Fortunately, this is not always so, and collective action theory offers some hope, not just despair.[45]

45. Game theory can take the reality of cooperation among human beings in stride. All life is not a Prisoner's Dilemma game; unstable games like Chicken and other bargaining games can result in collectively desirable outcomes some of the time, and sometimes life is an Assurance game, in which the dominant (stable) outcome is mutual cooperation even in

First, over time crises appear to give large diffuse groups sufficient per-person stakes to mobilize, so societies with long periods of stable democracy (with freedom of speech and assembly and the like) gradually undergo more balanced mobilization.[46] Once a group has overcome the start-up costs of mobilization, the maintenance costs appear to be less problematic. Moreover, in iterated play, players can "signal" to each other either directly or by their plays and move toward patterns of mutual cooperation.[47] In fact, in iterated play players can make pacts and rules to identify and punish free-riders, enforce cooperation, and maximize the long-run benefit of all. These pacts can emerge on their own, but the presence of a neutral coordinator (whose goal may simply be to find a solution, any solution, to a conflict) can accelerate the process. And the presence of a trusted, or at least neutral, enforcer can enhance compliance and the longevity of the pact. Herein lies a powerful explanation for the Japanese bureaucracy's occasional successes at coordination.

Second, even though a small group may unite easily to pursue its collective, but still narrow and very private, interest, when the group of collectively successful actors is "encompassing"—incorporates an interest that pervades the entire society—then suddenly, the group has to become concerned about broader and longer-term issues. Not only is the number of actors served larger, but the group itself is more likely to suffer from long-term ill effects of its own short-term actions and is, therefore, more likely to concern itself with long-term costs and benefits.[48] In economists' language, one gets more socially efficient outcomes when imposers of

---

one-shot play. Sometimes for a subset of players the value of a cooperative outcome is so great that they will undertake the full cost of provision. Best of all, even in Prisoner's Dilemma, iterated play brings good news and mutual cooperation. See Michael Taylor, *The Possibility of Cooperation* (Cambridge: Cambridge University Press, 1987); and Russell Hardin, *Collective Action.*

46. Olson, *Rise and Decline of Nations,* views the passage of time as a prerequisite for mobilization, but if too much time passes and interest-group formation is only by sector and never encompassing, time becomes the enemy. Thus, societies like Britain and the United States are ravaged by the clashing of strong, mature sectoral interests, with no groups interested in overall collective outcomes, compared to Japan and Germany, which "started over" in 1945.

47. This is the cheerful conclusion of Robert Axelrod, *The Evolution of Cooperation* (New York: Basic Books, 1984), who got mutual cooperation in repeated computer simulations on the basis of a simple tit-for-tat strategy (you cooperate, I cooperate; you defect, I defect), and his players were just computer fabrications and could not even smile or eat dinner together.

48. Thus, a labor union of auto workers alone may choose to demand egregiously high wage increases, figuring correctly that any damage to the economy as a whole from their own and other unions' wage push would be spread throughout society, whereas their own wage increase would be sufficient to make the trade-off acceptable to them. But a peak association of all workers would be worried about the average wage increase across all trades and the macroeconomic effect of this on future wage increases and would be more moderate in its demands.

costs suffer them (so become reluctant to generate those costs) and when producers of benefits can capture them (so become happy to produce those benefits)—that is, when externalities are internalized.[49] Oddly enough, the more encompassing an organization gets, the more moderate and compromising it gets. Mancur Olson and the scholars of social corporatism argue that tripartite interest mediation among government, encompassing business groups, and encompassing labor federations is the mechanism by which corporatist societies seem to push out their time horizons and arrive at wage settlements and other economic policies that both business and labor will agree to and that can prevent long-term decline.[50]

A final contribution of collective action theory is that it can help construct a meaningful definition of "the public interest," a term that otherwise evades definition and suffers from rhetorical abuse. The value of a particular course of action to a *group* of players in any game is the sum of the payoffs to the individual players in the cell representing that course of action. It is in the collective interest of the players to choose the course of action with the highest net payoffs to the group as a whole. Games can vary in the way payoffs are arrayed. In Assurance, maximizing individual payoffs coincides with the collective interest, so mutual cooperation is absolutely risk free and is guaranteed to occur. Assurance is the happy and all-too-rare situation that requires no coordination, no external intervention, and essentially requires neither government nor contracts between players. But in other games some contradiction can be involved between the course of action that maximizes individual payoffs and the one that maximizes collective payoff. In Prisoner's Dilemma, mutual cooperation is the course of action with the highest net payoff to the group as a whole, but the tragic dynamics of free-riderism (the fear of terrible individual payoffs to dupes) cause the players to choose mutual defection, in which they are much worse off as a group *and* as individuals than if they had arrived

49. If polluters have to breathe their own emissions and use their waste water as an input, they will produce clean emissions and clean waste water, and society achieves economic efficiency and justice both. If somebody can make money by preserving endangered species, they will undertake to preserve them (this is the argument for assigning ivory and rhino horn rights to particular groups of people who then have powerful incentives to keep herds alive and punish poachers while they themselves crop the herds at a sustainable level).

50. Some of the very important works in neocorporatism include Philippe C. Schmitter, "Modes of Interest Intermediation and Models of Societal Change in Western Europe," *Comparative Political Studies* 10 (1977): 7–38; Philippe C. Schmitter and Gerhard Lehmbruch, *Trends towards Corporatist Intermediation;* Gerhard Lehmbruch and Philippe C. Schmitter, eds., *Patterns of Corporatist Policy-making* (London: Sage Publications, 1982); Alan Cawson, ed., *Organized Interests and the State: Studies in Meso-Corporatism* (London: Sage Publications, 1985); and Wyn Grant, ed., *The Political Economy of Corporatism* (New York: St. Martin's Press, 1985). On the macroeconomic consequences of corporatist and consensual wage regulation, see Lange and Garrett, "Politics of Growth," and Cameron, "Social Democracy." Mancur Olson makes the same case, without using the term *corporatism* to label policy-making by encompassing organizations, in *Rise and Decline of Nations*.

at mutual cooperation. One can use the idea of collective interest among players of a game or members of a group to construct a notion of public interest. As the number of players grows to include more and more citizens and as the games groups play become nested in larger ones involving other groups, the collective interest of all of the players becomes increasingly "public."

How does collective action theory help determine when the public interest does and does not get served in Japan?

Corporatism: Encompassing Organizations and Longer Time Horizons

First, collective action theory states that encompassing or peak organizations encourage the pursuit of long-term goals. Japan has more of these than meet the eye, both formal ones and informal ones maintained through personal networks. Producers are very well organized, not only into industrial sector groups but, more importantly, into peak associations that represent all big business (Keidanren), all small business (Japan Chamber of Commerce and Industry), and all employers (Japan Federation of Employers' Associations), regardless of sector. These peak associations mute the sector-first demands of the industry and trade associations and sometimes give the bureaucracy and the LDP the leverage and the leeway to promote broader "public" interests (as in administrative reform and recession treatment) over egregious sector-only demands (bailouts to coddle the unproductive). It is the encompassing nature of so many organizations in Japan and the resulting corporatism underlying decision making in an increasing number of arenas that deserve credit for Japan's "successes," not a strong state.

Pempel and Tsunekawa were the first to recognize the corporatist phenomenon in Japan, though they now seem to have been incorrect in thinking that labor was not included.[51] Since 1989 labor has been formally organized into a growing peak association, Rengō, that represents labor, period, regardless of sector. Debate continues about Rengō, of course, with some skeptics feeling that in its moderation Rengō constitutes a sellout of labor, but it is hard to believe that a peak association for labor will hurt labor. The evidence that Yutaka Tsujinaka presents in Chapter 8 plausibly suggests that for the past two decades or more, networks of consultation substituted for a formal peak organization. These networks clearly played a role in muting short-term wage demands after the oil shocks in the interest of long-term recovery, making Japan the first industrial country to emerge from the resulting recession.

51. Pempel and Tsunekawa, "Corporatism without Labor?"

Another peak association, I will argue, is the LDP itself because it pursues a catchall strategy and continues to hold a legislative majority. Unlike a political party with a narrow electoral base, which has to give priority to its primary constituency before trying to appeal to others, the LDP also tries to "catch all" constituencies. If the LDP could maintain its dominance with a narrow constituency and without worrying about the departure of centrist floating voters, its dominance would not have these socially redeeming effects, but since the era of hakuchū the LDP seems convinced that it must appeal to all in order not to lose a crucial group of voters. Ramseyer and Rosenbluth point out that the macroeconomic successes often credited to a strong-and-smart bureaucracy are also policies that an encompassing or catchall LDP would initiate and endorse anyway: "Many observers forget . . . that what is good for the country is often good for the LDP."[52]

It is not much of a stretch to argue that the same paradoxically mellowing effect that monopolistic representation has on peak associations in corporatism works for the LDP, too. The LDP will suffer the effects of its own errors, and it will benefit in the form of continued power from its successes. It has little to fear except its own errors, and in this sense has "control" over its fate. Having this much control can encourage responsible behavior. The LDP's very dominance as a political party makes it accountable and, in that sense, gives it long time horizons.[53] It must think beyond the next election, which it will surely win anyway, to the distant day when it may be blamed for problems it does not address now and might lose an election as a result. Compare this to the United States, where alternation in power is fairly frequent and where executive and legislative bodies are often held by different parties; failures can be blamed on the other party, particularly if they take a long time to materialize, and this reduces both need and ability to worry about failures in the distant future, shortening time horizons to the next election.[54]

Encompassing organizations are a very important reason for Japan's successes, but the conflicts between sector-specific organizations also work sometimes to the benefit of some larger public interest chiefly because they come to the bureaucracy or the LDP for mediation. Farmers

52. Ramseyer and Rosenbluth, *Voters, Politicians, Bureaucrats, and Judges,* chap. 7, 25.

53. Several of the contributors to T. J. Pempel, ed., *Uncommon Democracies: The One-Party Dominant Regimes* (Ithaca: Cornell University Press, 1990), argue on the basis of empirical evidence, rather than as a proposition extracted deductively from collective action theory, that dominance goes with accountability and long-term vision.

54. For an introduction to the literature on divided government as the explanation for the American disease, see Roger G. Noll and Haruo Shimada, "Comparative Structural Policies," in Samuel Kernell, ed., *Parallel Politics: Economic Policymaking in the United States and Japan* (Tokyo: Japan Center for International Exchange; Washington D.C.: Brookings Institution, 1991), 211–229, as well as other essays in the same volume.

and small business have been politically successful against all Olsonian odds for entrepreneurs so tiny and numerous.[55] Their influence, insofar as they have secured benefits for farming and small business alone, has not resulted in economic efficiency for Japan as a whole—agriculture and small business are probably the most coddled and least productive parts of the Japanese economy—but other social benefits have accrued from their participation. Postwar Japan has undergone incredibly rapid structural change without anything like the social disruption one might have expected. Perhaps the interventions on behalf of farmers and small business have been worth some portion of their economic price in social tranquility and in providing some variety and breadth to the LDP's political base.[56]

Benefits to the Underorganized

In spite of the producer bias that is clear where the strongest organizations represent producers, the general health of the economy that highly organized producers seek produces diffuse benefits for others, even some of the *un*organized, that one would never see if producers and workers were only organized into sector-specific groupings. The healthy growing economy that producers' peak associations have fought for has included full or high employment, and this has produced more favorable labor market conditions for temporary nonunion labor than would exist if Japan spent long periods in deep recession with high rates of unemployment. The same goes for consumers who pay high prices for commodities but continue to get richer because economic growth continues so that high prices today are not as high as they were yesterday. And the same is true for taxpayers, particularly future taxpayers, who may count themselves one day as beneficiaries of the administrative reform campaign.[57]

Japanese consumers, taxpayers, environmentalists, and other components of the mass public are relatively less organized than their counter-

---

55. It is a sweet irony that the wartime government incurred the start-up costs for mobilizing many groups in the population and in doing so contributed to democratizing the array of organized groups that entered the postwar period. Oligopolistic producers would have organized anyway, but farmers, small business, labor, women, and, perhaps, neighborhoods received a crucial head start from wartime mobilization and after the war could convert this infrastructure to serving member needs rather than transmitting wartime directives.

56. For an elaboration of this point, see Margaret A. McKean, "Equality," in Takeshi Ishida and Ellis S. Krauss, eds., *Democracy in Japan* (Pittsburgh: University of Pittsburgh Press, 1989), 201–224.

57. Japanese citizens benefit from fairly low tax rates, a relatively egalitarian income distribution that protects everyone against dire poverty, an impressive rate of pollution cleanup, high employment levels, and the restoration of some fiscal solvency into government spending that protects them against egregious tax increases and inflation in the future. Although clearly good for producers, Japan's aggregate economic performance has also brought many benefits to Japan's citizens that people in other countries justifiably envy.

parts in other countries—not because of any cultural predispositions but because of the collective action dilemma and the tremendous challenge of penetrating a system already heavily infiltrated by their likely opponents. They do organize, and they are learning to penetrate the bureaucracy.[58] But these groups get more consideration in policy-making than they themselves demand, beyond just the accidental spillover effects of a healthy economy, because of the long time horizons exercised by the peak associations, particularly the LDP. A few crises showing the LDP that these groups can get mad enough to mobilize and to hurt the LDP at the polls has taught the LDP to think about these groups' reactions in advance. From the government's point of view, it is almost certainly better, easier, and cheaper to invent a policy that can prevent *un*mobilized groups from getting involved in the policy-making process than to ignore them so long that they mobilize, get involved, and complicate the process immensely. Not only can the government win credit for anticipating popular needs rather than blame for ignoring them but the actual process of design is much less likely to spin out of control. The challenge is knowing when mobilization of the voiceless is imminent because it is obviously not worthwhile for the government to worry about the voiceless if they plan to remain that way. Bureaucrats involved in drafting legislation have often spoken to me of their own or the LDP's anxiety about potential citizen reactions. Whether the LDP and the bureaucrats preemptively modify their proposals out of sympathy or fear is unimportant: the resulting policy is slightly democratized anyway.

Moreover, collective action theory reminds one of the value of voluntary cooperation in arriving at social pacts. This fact also confers some power on the otherwise *under*represented when their cooperation (perhaps, just in the form of continued passivity!) is needed for a policy to work. These groups, thus, have latent or passive power that they might not in a political system where the winning party panders only to certain sectors or groups or is willing to commit the additional resources needed for coercive policy-making. The underrepresented are clearly not as well off as they would be if they did organize, but they are not as completely ignored as they would be in a noncorporatist polity whose politicians have shorter time horizons and a narrow political base.

The Japanese electoral system plays a part in this. Japan's multimember single-nontransferable vote system regularly returns the LDP to office, but it pushes LDP candidates into competition with each other and not just with the opposition candidates and, therefore, throws most individual LDP politicians into total panic about whether they or their rivals within

58. See Michio Muramatsu and Ellis S. Krauss, "The Dominant Party and Social Coalitions in Japan," 282–305, in Pempel, *Uncommon Democracies*.

the party will be going back to Tokyo.[59] Top LDP politicians and faction leaders have more secure support networks in their districts although they have to spend plenty of time and effort maintaining their networks to avert defeat (idle incumbency is no guarantee of future success in the Japanese electoral system). But to the extent that top LDP politicians and faction leaders are confident that they will continue as leading members of the party that will rule Japan, they should have very long time horizons and, essentially, embody the interests of the party as an institutional abstraction. This long-term view is yet another reason one might expect top LDP politicians to make some effort to consider the underorganized before they become a threat to the regime's longevity. Junior LDP politicians would have much narrower, shorter-term interests in getting reelected, but the erratic qualities of the electoral system push most of them toward the middle of the political spectrum to hang onto floating voters whose support may turn out to be crucial in lifting them above the line between winners and losers. If my speculations about the differential time horizons of LDP politicians are correct, then this system produces top LDP leaders worried about the defeat of the party someday and junior LDP politicians worried about imminent personal defeat and gives both a reason to worry about the LDP voters most likely to leave the fold—the unorganized with grievances.

Some supporting evidence for the notion that the LDP leadership has longer time horizons than the rank and file of the party comes from Sakakibara Eisuke, who argues from his insider experience that the real debates in policy-making are between the top leaders of the LDP and the Ministry of Finance, on the one hand, and the LDP's policy divisions and the individual spending ministries, on the other hand. The former tend to advocate the long-term "public interest," whereas the latter are the voice of sector-first interests and wasteful pork barrel projects.[60] And it was a victory of the former, under Nakasone, that postponed expensive and inefficient district-specific pork barrel projects in the interest of accomplishing economywide administrative reform and streamlining the national budget during the 1980s. Muramatsu and Mabuchi point out the same split between LDP national leadership pursuing national goals and a party

59. On the mechanics of the electoral system, see Hans H. Baerwald, *Party Politics in Japan* (Boston: Allen and Unwin, 1986); Gerald L. Curtis, *The Japanese Way of Politics* (New York: Columbia University Press, 1987); and Ronald J. Hrebenar, *The Japanese Party System: From One Party Rule to Coalition Government* (Boulder, Colo.: Westview Press, 1986), especially the first three chapters. On the policy-making consequences of the multimember single–nontransferable-vote (SNTV) system, see Mathew D. McCubbins and Frances M. Rosenbluth, "SNTV and the Organization of Policymaking in the LDP" (Typescript, 1991). On the risks incumbents face and their coping strategies, see Steven R. Reed, "The Incumbency Advantage in Japan" (Typescript, 1991, Department of Political Science, University of Alabama).

60. Sakakibara, "Japanese Politico-Economic System," especially 73–76.

rank and file concerned mostly with smaller matters and note that the LDP leadership must select the issues with highest priority in order to arrive at compromises with the rank and file over which few truly public-regarding policies a given legislative session will enact.[61]

Government as Enforcer of Cooperative Pacts and Producer of Public Goods

Collective action theory would suggest that the notorious Japanese preference for consensual decision making, time consuming for new decisions but swift in more familiar territory, is, above all, economical. One often encounters the statement that the Japanese government does not dare use the formal or coercive powers it does have because that would jeopardize future cooperation on which it is dependent for future "success." Collective action theory would support this argument because cooperative outcomes depend essentially upon voluntary decisions by each player to cooperate. Having the skill to construct agreements that elicit voluntary cooperation, especially from parties (like large business conglomerates or even labor unions) that have the resources to challenge the state if they want to, is clearly less wasteful of everyone's time, energy, and GNP than an endless series of public showdowns between the state and private interests would be. When I queried a senior Japanese energy bureaucrat about how MITI persuaded reluctant firms and industries to go along with MITI policy, he and his colleagues in the room replied that they never asked for what they could not get, and thanks to perpetual consultation and networking with industry (*nemawashi*) they always knew in advance what they could get.

One must acknowledge that the ability to coordinate brings risk: the hazards of collusion rather than competition in the marketplace.[62] When the bureaucracy is encouraging cooperative problem solving within a particular industrial sector that is beset by conflict, the bureaucracy turns easily into an advocate for the industry's collective interests rather than for society's interests; collusion rather than competition in an industry will result; and, worse, any pact will probably favor the most powerful firms in a relatively lopsided industry. This was certainly the case in the Sumitomo Metals incident of 1965, in which MITI served as the steel association's

61. Michio Muramatsu and Masaru Mabuchi, "Introducing a New Tax in Japan," in Kernell, ed., *Parallel Politics*, 184–207.
62. Mark Tilton has pointed out to me that consumers and social efficiency do not have to suffer as much as one might think even under price collusion because a price-fixing pact will not eliminate competition between cartel members on product quality, after-service, add-ons, and the like.

police in punishing Sumitomo, the maverick upstart.[63] Most probably disapprove of both the social inefficiency likely to result and of the producer bias (or "big capital bias") implicit in these political arrangements.

But collective action theory also alerts observers to the circumstances in which collusion and cooperation can sometimes be better for society than competition (or mutual defection), namely, wherever one is concerned about public goods, those that are chronically underprovided by market and by contracting among individual economic actors. Here the bureaucracy's services as coordinator permits policy options not available to polities where this kind of coordination is either illegal or unlikely to emerge for structural reasons. In sector-specific industrial policy such options include managed shrinkage for declining industries where impact on aggregate employment and regional economies is a serious problem and cooperative research and development for new industries that require very high initial investments. Perhaps more significantly, in macroeconomic policy the state's role as coordinator and enforcer of cooperative agreements can occasionally turn "fiscal responsibility in government" from mere slogan into actuality. These policies—structural change with minimal unemployment, cutting-edge research that is too expensive for individual firms to contemplate, and belt tightening in government—can be considered public goods (goods from which all benefit whether they contribute or not). It is not strength (the capacity to push others around) but the Japanese government's availability as a skilled coordinator, able to design cooperative solutions where lack of trust would normally prevent cooperation, that gives Japanese the ability to produce more of these public goods than other nations can.[64]

The Japanese government's practice is to orchestrate decline by delegating policy design and policy implementation to interest groups and industrial associations, what Mark Tilton calls "decentralized corporatism."[65] Thus, in concentrated sectors where collective action theory would predict easy cartelization (and where the theory of regulation would further predict that free market solutions are politically unlikely in any polity), the Japanese government does manage to use production and capacity cartels to apportion sacrifice, spread risk, and smooth the ugly process of decline, all without the even greater expense on government's (taxpayers') part that would ensue from bailouts involving no sacrifice, adjustment, or actual shrinkage.

63. Frank Upham, *Law and Social Change in Postwar Japan* (Cambridge: Harvard University Press, 1987), 176–185.
64. The particular public good that the Japanese polity seems relatively *dis*inclined to produce (in comparison to that in the United States) is vigilant antitrust policy. It appears unlikely that a nation would produce both antitrust enforcement and coordinated industrial policy in the quantities that citizen preferences would actually demand. This unhappy paradox is left to public choice theorists and ethicists to consider.
65. Tilton, *Trade Associations*.

But even the Japanese government cannot always overcome problems of mutual trust in its attempts to orchestrate shrinkage for declining industries. It is much easier for the firms in question to form and maintain a cartel to restrain production or eliminate excess capacity in a concentrated industry than in a fragmented one. The resulting cartels can achieve proportionately larger quantitative reductions, and reductions that are more evenly shared among firms, in the concentrated industries. In relatively fragmented industries, orchestrating cooperation is much more difficult, free-rider defections from reduction pacts are endemic, and in the end, reduction appears to be driven by the market, with the least-efficient firms leaving the industry first.[66] Thus, government-guided shrinkage in shipbuilding remains the clearest example of MITI-refereed success, whereas MITI has been much less successful in having any impact at all on orchestrating reductions for steel minimills or aluminum.[67] In addition to debate over whether MITI makes a difference, there is plenty of debate over whether managed decline or decline-by-market is more socially efficient. Neoclassicists argue correctly that unguided shrinkage through the brutal process of bankruptcy is more efficient in driving out the least efficient firms first, but large dislocations in the labor force and regionally concentrated unemployment are, clearly, socially inefficient too.

Coordination of industries with a rosy future is even more difficult than for declining industries because the prospects for individual firms that try to defect from a pact are quite promising. As a result, the Japanese government's attempts to encourage cooperation in research for high technology have often encountered problems of mistrust among firms, which send their second-rate researchers to the consortium while keeping their top people in-house, and which fuss understandably about red tape, ownership, and earnings from any discoveries of the consortium. Cooperation among firms is extremely difficult to achieve, with or without MITI, the closer the product is to competitive commercial sales.

But MITI coordination of research and development projects is more likely to win the cooperation of industry where there are high risks, heavy capital needs, long gestation periods, steep learning curves, a need for *pre*-commercial prototypes, the promise of advancements in other areas as a result, and potential commercial utility across several industries.[68] The mainframe computer industry is such a case, and the cooperation achieved over a decade made Japan the only industrial democracy with a computer

66. Merton J. Peck, Richard C. Levin, and Akira Goto, "Picking Losers: Public Policy toward Declining Industries in Japan," *Journal of Japanese Studies* 13 (Winter 1987): 79–123.

67. Noble, "The Japanese Industrial Policy Debate"; Richard J. Samuels, "The Industrial Destructuring of the Japanese Aluminum Industry," *Pacific Affairs* 56 (Fall 1983): 495–509.

68. Okimoto, *Between MITI and the Market*, 66–83; Jonah D. Levy and Richard J. Samuels, "Institutions and Innovation: Research Collaboration as Technology Strategy in Japan," MIT Japan Program Working Paper MITJSTP 89–02, 1989.

industry not dominated by IBM.[69] These are precisely the areas in which collective action theory would predict that private parties would avoid investment on their own because they could not capture all of the returns on their investment but where there is benefit to them as a group and to society as a whole in cooperating if the difficulties with mutual trust can be overcome.

Finally, in competition between rival sectoral interests that try to use political salve for their wounds instead of fighting it out in the marketplace, the government functions as stripe-wearing referee. As mediator, the government has the opportunity to introduce some balance between rival sectors whether all of the rivals are among its regular clients or not. This fact increases the likelihood that various sectors will be able to pursue their private sectoral interests but also the likelihood that no particular private interest will be able to ride utterly roughshod over other organized private interests. In engineering deals between rival sectors, between growing and declining sectors, between upstream and downstream producers, the arithmetic of political competition is likely to produce "balance," which may inadvertently protect some sort of "public interest." Coordination and compromise is much better and, probably, cheaper to those who bear any social costs involved than are stalemate or uncoordinated (escalating) payoffs to rivals.

The opportunity and necessity to coordinate rather than simply follow is increasing, and it results in bureaucrats and the LDP mediating when they have to and deregulating when the market can do the job. Corporatist interest representation in Japan, driven by the existence of encompassing organizations (including the LDP itself) and becoming more democratic over time through the increasing incorporation of labor and other interests, gives the major actors an interest in having government referee societywide pacts. Because encompassing organizations can have longer time horizons and by definition more "public" interests than sector-based organizations, they worry about social efficiency and social product. Such organizations can become vocal opponents of too much coddling, too many boondoggles, too much public waste, and too sluggish a transition in industrial structure. Thus, an organization like Keidanren can overcome the private sectoral interests of its components and speak instead for many of the same things that consumer groups advocate: administrative reform, streamlining Japan's distribution system, lowering agricultural protectionism, responsiveness to American complaints on trade issues, and even deregulating altogether when countervailing pressures risk the generation of escalating government payoffs to each side in turn. Corporatism, encom-

69. Anchordoguy, *Computers, Inc.*

passing organizations, and long time horizons are no guarantee of public-regarding policies or of producing public goods in precisely the right amounts and types dictated by aggregate taxpayer preferences. But these institutional patterns provide a channel by which collective interests do get voiced, in addition to all of the private, sectoral, and individual interests already voiced. They, thus, provide not the guarantee but the possibility of coordinated outcomes to produce public goods in the collective interest alongside the uncoordinated production of private goods by the market. Corporatism, encompassing organizations, and long time horizons increase the likelihood that the Japanese government will use regulatory interventions where these are needed to produce public goods and will avoid them when the market does well on its own.

Japan's superior performance is not based on a strong-and-smart market-conforming state (if there is one, it might be Singapore, though I am instinctively skeptical). It is not based on a strong-but-lucky state (most observers are fairly convinced that strong-without-smart is unlucky indeed). It is not based on unfettered market competition plus a minimal state (the Japanese government really does intervene quite heavily in markets and rarely to promote competition and resist collusion, even if it does so on a comparatively lean budget). Rather, this review of the evidence suggests that Japan's significant traits appear to be a market economy characterized by considerable competition and collusion, a gradual formalization of corporatist institutions and practices that began with a strong producer bias, and a dominant political party made anxious and, therefore, responsive to new groups and interests by the precariousness of its hold on power. This finding implies that it is the corporatism in economic organization and the ruling party itself that makes Japan better than the United States at producing public goods like high employment, low inflation, and fiscal responsibility in government and that it is the relatively small size of the government's share of the economy that makes Japan moderately better than many European social democracies in producing growth. I hope that more careful specification of Japan's institutions and political processes will provide the basis for a new round of comparative analysis of aggregate economic data to test hypotheses like these.

Japan does not have a strong state. Rather, the state follows when it can, coordinates when it must, and deregulates when it cannot coordinate. The pluralization of participation so evident over the last two decades is enhancing Japanese democracy. Increasingly visible and challenging conflicts between interests are causing the state to shy away from impossible tasks and to formalize its responsibilities for the tasks that remain. Finally, the mode of interest mediation that is being adopted during this process of retreat and redefinition, one which results from the organizational topology of Japanese politics more than from any holistic or public-minded ethic, is increasingly corporatist. Not only business and labor are now represented by peak associations but the LDP itself serves as an encompassing organization. Each of these needs for its own selfish reasons to consider, occasionally, the interests of society at large and the needs of the otherwise *un*represented. These simultaneous trends—the mobilization of new interests and new publics, the state's skill at diagnosing when conflicts among competing interests can be solved by coaxing and coordinating the parties in disagreement toward cooperative solutions, and the encompassing nature of economic and political representation—contribute greatly to policy outcomes that, perhaps surprisingly, sometimes serve collective or public interests.

PART TWO

NEGOTIATING
FINANCIAL REFORM

JAPAN'S MINISTRY OF FINANCE (MOF) HAS LONG BEEN REGARDED AS ONE of the most important ministries of the central government. The talented graduates of the law department of the University of Tokyo who have staffed the upper echelons of the ministry were both a cause of its influence and an emblem of its prestige. Their intangible influence was greatly enhanced by the possession of a range of legal and quasi-legal authority as well. These forms of authority made it possible for the ministry to exercise close supervision over the nation's banking and securities industries, to prepare the national budget, to determine interest rates, to control foreign exchange transactions, and to regulate the presence of foreign parties in Japanese finance. Firm, adroit application of these powers made it possible for the MOF to act as one of the key agents of Japan's economic expansion in the postwar period.

Beginning as early as the mid-1960s, however, a variety of forces conjoined to transform the general environment in which the MOF had once worked. LDP encroachment on the ministry's budgetary prerogatives was one of the first changes to which the MOF had to adapt. Other changes followed in quick succession. Japan's increasing participation in the international economy enhanced the financial leverage of private corporations and forced the domestic banking industry to take notice. An expanding national debt after 1975 imposed constraints on governmental actions in general and MOF actions in particular. Slower economic growth at home in the face of steadily increasing depository balances created problems in the financial industry and threatened its profitability. More Japanese yen circulating in the international economy weakened the MOF's ability to control domestic finances as it once had. And in the face of all these problems, the ministry also came to suffer more outspoken demands from foreign governments to alter its ways.

Frances Rosenbluth and Masaru Mabuchi offer two perspectives on these changes and their political significance. Rosenbluth employs a theory of regulation set forth by George Stigler to assert that organized pressure brought to bear by producer groups was the fundamental stimulant to financial deregulation. Her argument contends that benefits to consumers arose largely as unintentional by-products of political negotiations in which they did not participate. Although her analysis focuses on the domestic contours of financial deregulation, she makes clear that wider participation by Japanese corporations in international markets was an indispensable adjunct to change. In her view, direct political pressures from foreign governments were not a major force for change until, perhaps, the late 1980s and then only when they coincided with pressures for change sought by domestic groups.

Mabuchi explains not only deregulation but also an ensuing process of reregulation. His findings, thus, differ somewhat from those of Rosenbluth. As she does, he recognizes the consequences of Japan's financial internationalization after the early 1970s, but he attributes importance both to access to foreign markets and to direct foreign political pressure. He also emphasizes how purely domestic forces contributed to financial deregulation and reregulation. But rather than point to pressure group activity, he highlights the political dilemmas caused by Japan's increased deficit financing after 1975. His penetrating analysis of the complex crosscurrents set in motion by domestic and international pressures and their effects on de jure and de facto bases of authority offers a unique perspective on Japan's financial politics.

As different as their emphases might be, both Rosenbluth and Mabuchi leave an image of the Ministry of Finance that is fundamentally similar. They both see it as an administrative agency strongly buffeted by domestic and international forces to a large extent beyond its full control. Yet they both acknowledge that the ministry has struggled with ingenuity, persistence, and determination to retain as much influence as possible. From Mabuchi's point of view, MOF may have pulled in its horns by retreating to the solidification and clarification of its authority, but it still remains a hard character that "means business." Rosenbluth employs a much softer metaphor but conveys a similar impression. In her felicitous phrase, the MOF strives to "orchestrate" domestic interests, but it has to do so by "following a political score it did not compose." Beleaguered as it may be, the MOF—like other ministries noted in Chapter 1—slogs on and fights back.

CHAPTER FOUR

FINANCIAL DEREGULATION AND

INTEREST INTERMEDIATION

Frances McCall Rosenbluth

THE SPECTACULAR SUCCESS OF JAPANESE FINANCIAL INSTITUTIONS IN GLO-
bal financial markets is well known. In the late 1980s the world's ten largest banks, measured by assets, were all Japanese. Even when measured by
shareholders' equity, five of the top ten banks in the world were Japanese.[1]
The "Big Four" Japanese securities firms were also among the largest in
the world. In the early 1990s Japanese financial institutions dominated
bond underwriting in the Euromarket and partly or fully owned twelve of
the forty-two primary dealers in the U.S. government securities market.[2]

In Japan, financial markets seem to be moving toward the freer market
practices of the Euromarket. Interest rates are becoming more flexible; the
Ministry of Finance is studying ways to lower further the barrier between
banking and securities activities; and it has become easier for corporations to issue bonds and commercial paper in Japan. Why has Japan been
deregulating its financial markets? And what, if any, is the relationship
between Japanese financial institutions' performance abroad and domestic liberalization?

Recognizing that international market forces must filter through the
domestic political economy, one might suggest three possible explanations
for financial deregulation. First, Japan may be a strong state in the sense
that it has an administrative apparatus capable of mobilizing and direct-
ing the resources of society toward the attainment of national goals.[3] In

---

1. "The Euromoney 500 Ranked by Shareholders' Equity," *Euromoney* (June 1989):
83–85.

2. Federal Reserve Bank of New York, *News Bulletin*, August 21, 1989.

3. For this widely used definition of a "strong state," see John Zysman, *Governments,
Markets, and Growth* (Ithaca: Cornell University Press, 1983).

this view it is the Japanese bureaucracy, having coddled the Japanese private sector, that is deregulating financial markets because it now deems Japanese corporations and financial institutions competitive enough internationally to fare well in a liberalized environment.

A second possibility is that Japan is a populist state. Granted, this is a rarely voiced view but one, perhaps, not unthinkable in the wake of the sharp Liberal Democratic party (LDP) setback in the Upper House election of July 1989 and the strong showing of the Japan Socialist party (JSP) in the Lower House election of February 1990. This view attributes to taxpayers and consumers of financial services a victory in rolling back bank protection and winning more competitive rates on deposits and loans.

A third explanation draws from the theory of regulation and assumes a general collective action advantage in the policy-making process for producer groups—in this case, producers of financial services—over the unorganized public. Deregulation, in this view, is proceeding because changes in the international environment have rendered the original protective regulation no longer advantageous to the banks that benefited from the rules in the first place. This explanation would lead one to expect the retention of protective regulations wherever such protection does not place domestic banks at a competitive disadvantage in retaining clients.

I employ Japan's financial deregulation as a vehicle to address two broader sets of issues: to examine the theory of regulation and lay out the circumstances under which the producer-dominance version of the theory of regulation will most likely hold and to use these theoretical tools to analyze the process of interest mediation in Japan. I want to know, in Lasswell's succinct terms, who gets "what, when, and how."

I argue that the Japanese financial sector comprises several well-organized interest groups that have successfully employed their political resources to influence financial policy. In conformity with the producer-dominance hypothesis, deregulation is indeed occurring most rapidly at the wholesale end of the financial industry where customers are corporations with access to foreign markets.[4]

Deregulation has lagged behind at the retail end of the market where customers are individuals who have neither comparable access nor the political resources to change the rules of the game. A "second image reversed" phenomenon is at work here: the impact of the international system is greatest where the involvement of Japanese corporations in foreign markets introduces leakage into the domestic system.[5] Even in retail

4. This conclusion is in many ways close to Richard Samuels's characterization of Japanese government-business interaction, which he terms "reciprocal consent," in *The Business of the Japanese State* (Ithaca: Cornell University Press, 1986). See especially the conclusion.

5. Peter Gourevitch, "The Second Image Reversed: The International Sources of Domestic Politics," *International Organization* 32 (Autumn 1978): 911.

finance, however, consumers of financial services are beginning to enjoy higher yields on their savings deposits—not because of a successful consumer revolt but because of a crack in the bureaucratic edifice.

It is not difficult to see how the strong-state theorists derive their conclusions: the Ministry of Finance is the primary government actor involved in financial regulation, and it takes considerable pains to obviate the direct interference of politicians or other outsiders. To thereby conclude that the MOF is calling all the shots, however, is mistaken. Although the institutional structure of the MOF allows it to orchestrate private sector interests effectively, thus modifying the trend toward greater involvement of politicians, the MOF is following a political score it did not compose.

What Is Being Deregulated?

Before World War II, Japan's financial system resembled the universal banking system still prevalent in continental Europe today. As in relatively late-developing Germany, Japan's financial system emerged during a period of capital-intensive industrialization in the 1870s and 1880s. Banks and manufacturing concerns developed in close connection, with banks owning corporate shares and handling a wide range of financial transactions from lending and deposit taking to bond and equity underwriting. Securities firms existed but were left in a rather small niche to sell bonds and stocks to the public.[6]

It was the U.S. Occupation (1945–1952) that conferred upon Japan a Glass-Steagall-equivalent, Section 65 of Japan's Securities Exchange Act of 1948, separating the banking and securities businesses.[7] This action by a foreign power thus vested in the securities industry greater stature in the Japanese economy and political world. Predictably, the banking sector

6. Takahashi Kamekichi, ed., *Nihon no koshasai shijō* [The Japanese bond market] (Tokyo: Diamond, 1963), 128; and Senda Jun'ichi, ed., *Henkakuki no ginkō to shōken* [Banks and securities firms in a period of transition] (Tokyo: Yūhikaku, 1986), 164–168. For the classic explanation of the late-developer thesis and implications for bank-firm relations, see Alexander Gerschenkron, *Economic Backwardness in Historical Perspective* (Cambridge: Harvard University Press, 1962).

7. Congress passed the U.S. Banking Act of 1933, popularly known as the Glass-Steagall Act, in the wake of the market crash of 1929. Although the prevailing view is that Congress wrote the bill to protect the public, evidence also suggests that an important impetus for the new bill was the eagerness of Chase and other commercial banks to break up the Morgan financial giant into a commercial bank and an investment bank, thus reducing competition in commercial banking. For this revisionist view see Thomas Ferguson, "From Normalcy to New Deal: Industrial Structure, Party Competition, and American Public Policy in the Great Depression," *International Organization* 38 (Winter 1984): 41–94.

lobbied for the elimination of Section 65 upon the conclusion of the U.S. Occupation, but the securities firms reputedly made their survival worthwhile to the politicians who had control of their fate by plying them with stocks on the rise.[8]

Despite the emergence of the securities firms as an important new group on the financial landscape, commercial banks remained central to the postwar economy. The prewar industrial combines (zaibatsu) were broken up by the Occupation officials, but in their place emerged keiretsu, bank-centered firm groupings that maintained varying degrees of intragroup cross share holdings and business relationships.[9] Most large corporations maintained close ties with a "main" bank, typically the keiretsu bank, in addition to holding credit lines with several other banks. Japan's postwar economic growth was characterized by bank-dependent investment and high debt-equity ratios.[10]

In an exemption from the Antimonopoly Act, the Temporary Interest Rate Control Act of 1948 allowed banks to collect deposits at low interest rates, thereby guaranteeing to banks a low cost of funds. The purported goal of this law was to induce banks to provide low-interest loans to corporations. But Japan's so-called low interest rate policy has been overstated in much of the writing on Japan's industrial policy. In war-depleted Japan, banks had money, and corporations, which needed it for their ambitious investment plans, did not; this placed the bargaining power with the banks. Banks demanded compensating balances, commonly as high as 20 percent of the total loan, thereby sharply raising the effective rates of

8. Tatsuzawa Takuji, *Watakushi no ginkō Shōwashi* [My Shōwa history of banks] (Tokyo: Tōyō keizai shinpōsha, 1985), 108–109. The practice among the large securities firms of tipping off politicians about certain stocks and then ramping up the prices by urging less-favored clients to buy is widely believed to have been quite common in postwar Japan. The Recruit scandal was one such example. The reason Recruit was exposed, and others not, probably is attributable to Recruit's position as an outsider corporation trying to break into the charmed inner circle of the business world with more massive and widespread payoffs than is usually the case. It was thus less able to cover its tracks, and others were also less inclined to support it.

9. Paul Sheard, "Corporate Organization and Structural Adjustment in Japan" (Ph. D. diss., Australian National University, 1986).

10. Iwao Nakatani described the bank-firm relationship within an association of affiliated firms (*keiretsu*) as an implicit insurance scheme, in which firms would pay a premium for loans in good times with the understanding that the bank would come to their rescue in bad times. Iwao Nakatani, "The Economic Role of Financial Corporate Grouping," in Masahiko Aoki, ed., *The Economic Analysis of the Japanese Firm* (Amsterdam: Elsevier Science Publishers B. V., 1984), 227–258. More recently, scholars have challenged the benevolent depiction of banks. Mark Ramseyer points out that banks bail out firms for the hefty price of management control if at all. See Ramseyer, "Bankers, Borrowers, and Bandits: Cooperating in the Shadow of Cheats in Japan" (Typescript, June 1989, UCLA Law School), and Shin'ichi Fukuda, "What Role has the 'Main Bank' Played in Japan?" *Journal of Japanese and International Economics* 2 (June 1988): 159–180.

interest paid on corporate loans.[11] If, for example, a corporation borrowed ¥ 100 million at 5 percent, ¥ 20 million was typically placed in an account bearing almost no interest. The firm was actually paying ¥ 5 million in interest for the use of ¥ 80 million, making the effective interest rate 6.25 percent. Banks were able, with this device, to protect their profits when faced with the low interest rate policy.[12]

A second important institutional feature benefited banks. In spite of Section 65's separation of banking and securities's activities, banks succeeded in obstructing the development of the corporate bond market through their cartel-like Kisaikai, or Bond Arrangement Committee. Formed in 1933, the Kisaikai continued in the postwar period to set strict terms for domestically issued corporate bonds, thereby enhancing banks' loan business.[13]

It is reasonable to ask why, if deposit rates were so low, did depositors not switch to market-based financial instruments for a better return. The answer is that there were no such instruments because the MOF restrained competition by other institutions for bank deposits. The corporate bond market was small and sluggish owing to the Kisaikai's control. Sometimes bank competitors did offer consumer investment alternatives. For example, in 1965 securities firms offered a corporate bond savings account, an instrument that would pass on to small savers the interest corporations paid for bond issues minus the commission that went to the securities firms. This instrument proved to be popular because it was marketed in small denominations but bore a higher yield than bank deposits. Its success was halted by the MOF, however, to keep the securities and banking businesses in balance.[14]

Several changes in Japan's economic environment in recent decades have eroded bank preeminence in the Japanese economy. First, slower economic growth ushered in by the oil price hike of 1973 left its mark on every aspect of Japan's political economy; finance was no exception. In contrast with the heady years of rapid growth when corporations had an insatiable appetite for bank loans to plow back into expansion plans and new projects, corporations were no longer willing to pay banks a high premium for a line of credit.

11. Akiyoshi Horiuchi, "Economic Growth and Financial Allocation in Postwar Japan" (Discussion paper, Research Institute for the Japanese Economy University of Tokyo, August 1984).

12. Morimoto Tadao, *Ginkō daisensō: Hakaisuru Nihon no kin'yū kōzō* [The great banking wars: Japan's crumbling financial structure] (Tokyo: Diamond, 1979), 165–167.

13. Nagatomi Yūichirō, *Antei seichō jidai no koshasai shijō* [Japan's bond market in a period of stable economic growth] (Tokyo: Ōkura zaimu kyōkai, 1978), 20–22.

14. Abe Yasuji, *Ginkō shōken kakine ronsō oboegaki* [Memorandum on the disputed regulatory barrier between banks and securities firms] (Tokyo: Nihon keizai shinbunsha, 1980), 43.

Second, despite Japan's slower growth, many firms had become international giants with excellent credit ratings in global financial markets. An increasing number of firms found they had access to more flexible and often cheaper funds from the Eurobond market. More cautious and eager to shave expenses in an era of slower growth, Japanese corporations began issuing bonds in the Euromarket with growing enthusiasm in the mid-1970s. In the early 1970s the Euromarket accounted for a total of 1.7 percent of Japanese corporate financing. During the second half of the 1970s that figure rose to 19.6 percent, and by 1984 it was 36.2 percent. As a portion of all Japanese corporate bonds issued, the Euromarket accounted for 51.9 percent in 1984.[15]

Japanese banks have fought to keep their best customers by cutting their spreads and phasing down compensating balances. Banks have also agreed to ease the conditions for domestic corporate bond issuance; the minimum capitalization requirements for issuing firms are gradually lowering, and a growing number of firms are permitted to issue debt without collateral. In exchange, banks have gained greater freedom to operate in the private placement market.[16]

Even as banks were having to make terms more attractive for borrowers, they faced depositors with stronger bargaining power. Large depositors, primarily corporations with cash and often excellent credit ratings, no longer blithely placed funds in low-yield accounts because they discovered the opportunities of financial management *(zaitekku)* in global markets. When firms felt freer to take their money elsewhere, banks raised the yields on large deposits at the expense of their own profitability. To do otherwise would have courted extinction. Banks countered the burgeoning securities repo *(gensaki)* market, for example, with large denomination certificates of deposit (CDs) in 1979 that offered far better yields than regular bank accounts.[17]

Small deposit deregulation has been much slower in coming because there have not been viable substitutes for savings accounts. Lacking alternative opportunities in the marketplace, small savers can theoretically demand that their political representatives change the rules of the market by, for example, abolishing the "Temporary" Interest Rate Control Act still

15. Ichikawa Nobuyuki, "Kigyō kin'yū no kōzō henka wa doko made susunde iru no ka" [How far have the structural changes in corporate finance proceeded?] *Kin'yū zaisei jijō* (December 8, 1986): 34–39.

16. For more on Japanese bond market deregulation, see Takeo Hoshi, Anil Kashyap, and David Sharfstein, "Bank Monitoring and Investment: Evidence from the Changing Structure of Japanese Corporate Banking Relationships" (Typescript, June 1989, Department of Economics, MIT).

17. See Robert Feldman, *Japanese Financial Markets: Deficits, Dilemmas, and Deregulation* (Cambridge: MIT Press, 1986); and James Horne, *Japanese Financial Markets* (London: Allen and Unwin, 1985).

in place after more than four decades. But collective action theory explains why small savers do not have recourse to the political arena. This is a classic case in which the potential benefits of higher deposit yields are diffused across a wide swath of the electorate, giving no one a high per capita incentive to change the existing system even though the costs of such a change would be borne by the highly organized commercial banks.[18]

The two changes in Japan's economy just noted were the growing bargaining leverage of bank borrowers and the growing leverage of, at least, large depositors. A third change that also disadvantaged banks was the sudden increased issuance of government bonds that began in 1975 to battle the recession caused by wild price increases in 1973–1974. Since 1965, when the Japanese government first issued deficit bonds, banks had absorbed about 60 percent of the bonds issued. This posed no particular burden because the Bank of Japan repurchased the bonds from the banks as part of their supply of money in the system. After 1975, however, the quantities were too large for the Bank of Japan to reabsorb without fueling massive inflation; banks were incensed because they had to hold the bonds to maturity.[19]

The MOF made several attempts to placate the banks, usually by adjusting accounting practices. Unappeased by such minor measures, the banks boycotted the government-bond placement syndicate and forced the MOF to relent. In the Banking Act of 1982, the MOF allowed banks to do what heretofore only securities firms had been permitted to do under the Securities Exchange Act: sell government bonds to the public, trade government bonds for customers, and deal for their own account in government bonds to profit on price fluctuations. For the first time since the early postwar reforms, the MOF redrew the lines dividing the banking and securities businesses.[20]

The MOF made a subsequent adjustment of this sort when it established a commercial paper market in November 1987. Commercial papers are, in the United States, unsecured, negotiable notes with a fixed but typically short maturity (30 days to 270 days) agreed upon by issuer and investor.[21] Banks had long resisted the establishment of a commercial

18. Mancur Olson, *Logic of Collective Action* (Cambridge: Harvard University Press, 1982).

19. Yukio Noguchi, "Public Finance," in Kozo Yamamura and Yasukichi Yasuba, eds., *The Political Economy of Japan*, vol. 1: *The Domestic Transformation* (Stanford: Stanford University Press, 1987), 186–222.

20. See Frances McCall Rosenbluth, *Financial Politics in Contemporary Japan* (Ithaca: Cornell University Press, 1989), especially chap. 4.

21. Ulrike Schaede, "The Introduction of Commercial Paper: A Case Study in the Liberalization of the Japanese Financial Markets" (Typescript, March 1988, Center on Japanese Economy and Business, Columbia University).

paper market in Japan, despite increasing corporate demand, because it would compete directly with their short-term loan business. Because commercial paper was treated as a security in the United States and the Euromarket, the securities industry could profit at the banks' expense by underwriting the instrument outside Japan. Once corporations found a way around the banks by issuing commercial paper in foreign markets, however, the banks were ready for a compromise. The MOF struck a bargain between the banks and securities firms by defining commercial paper as a promissory note, thus avoiding the legal issue of whether or not banks could underwrite corporate securities. This decision enabled both banks and securities firms to underwrite commercial paper in Japan.[22]

The Theory of Regulation

The economist George Stigler is known for his formulation of the classic supply and demand model of regulation. Stigler argued that private-sector groups obtain regulation from politicians to enhance their profitability.[23] Regulation, in this view, is essentially a transfer of wealth from the consumers to the regulated groups because consumers are less well organized than producers.[24] According to collective action theory, interests in society facing the lowest barriers to getting organized are most likely to be successful in capturing their regulators. Groups bearing concentrated costs or benefits are generally more successful in obtaining regulation favorable to themselves. Conversely, widely dispersed interests have difficulty protecting themselves through regulation. Members of the general public face high transaction costs in gathering information about interests and in getting and staying organized, all in the face of small per capita gains. Typically, then, regulation produces a small number of winners and a large number of losers.

How well does this simple model help one understand Japan's financial deregulation? What motivates the players in Japanese financial politics? How do they interact? Stigler's model posits only one political actor supplying regulation, the politician/bureaucrat. This conflation of what in reality are two separate actors may yield accurate results if the bureaucracy

22. For a careful and detailed comparison of how commercial paper is treated in Japan and the United States, see David Litt, "Introduction of Commercial Paper in Japan: A Case Study of Financial Services Decision Making" (Typescript, April 1989, UCLA Law School).

23. George Stigler, "The Theory of Regulation," *Bell Journal of Economics and Management Science* 2 (1971): 3–21.

24. Sam Peltzman, "Toward a More General Theory of Regulation," *Journal of Law and Economics* 19 (1976): 211–240; and Gary Becker, "A Theory of Competition among Pressure Groups for Political Influence," *Quarterly Journal of Economics* 98 (1983): 377.

is a reliable agent of political representatives. Is this the case in Japan? The strong-state hypothesis suggests that the bureaucracy is capable of operating quite independently of the politicians despite the primacy of the Diet under the Japanese constitution.

The Bureaucrats

Bureaucrats, maximizing their personal success, will behave in a variety of ways depending on who is assessing their performances.[25] In Japan, what constitutes a bureaucrat's success is determined largely by the bureaucracy itself. In the MOF in particular, bureaucrats stay with their agencies for their entire careers to move up the ladder before parachuting into comfortable private-sector jobs upon retirement.[26] Only the minister and one vice-minister are political appointees, and their jobs largely are to coordinate policies with the rest of the cabinet when necessary.

Given this immediate chain of command, a MOF official's job proceeds most smoothly and, hence, chances of success are best when politicians stay out, allowing the MOF to preside over the delicate balancing of interests, and when the financial institutions believe the MOF can enforce the compromises over which it presides. Unlike William Niskanen, I argue that a bureaucracy tries to maximize its jurisdiction only when its more important goal, ease of regulation, is also attained.[27] In fact, the MOF will voluntarily cut back its territory in some cases to avoid politicization or unenforceability.[28]

Because the MOF is a single institution, it is able to forge decisions that take into account its various parts. The highest court of appeal, as it were, is within the MOF itself. Consider, by contrast, the United States, which has a Federal Reserve Board, twelve regional Federal Reserve Banks, the

25. I am adopting the rational actor hypothesis in the absence of a more consistently precise assumption. On bureaucratic behavior, see J. Q. Wilson, "The Politics of Regulation," in Wilson, ed., *The Politics of Regulation* (New York: Basic Books, 1980), 375–376; and R. G. Noll, "Government Regulatory Behavior: A Multidisciplinary Survey and Synthesis," in Noll, ed., *Regulatory Policy and the Social Sciences* (Berkeley: University of California Press, 1985), 44.

26. On the topic of bureaucrats who "descend from heaven" (or experience *amakudari*) in Japan, see Kent Calder, "Elites in an Equalizing Role: Ex-Bureaucrats as Coordinators and Intermediaries in the Japanese Government-Business Relationship," *Comparative Politics* 21 (July 1989): 379–404; and Tuvia Blumenthal, "The Practice of *amakudari* within the Japanese Employment System," *Asian Survey* 25 (March 1985): 310–321.

27. For an explication of the budget-maximizing thesis, see William A. Niskanen, *Bureaucracy and Representative Government* (Chicago: Aldine, 1971).

28. One such case was the MOF's reluctance for many decades to dirty its hands with the regulation of the loan shark business. It was only after the Liberal Democratic party, by dint of pressure from the opposition parties, passed an interest-ceiling bill in 1983 that the MOF was forced to regulate the loan shark business.

Securities Exchange Commission, the Department of the Treasury and its Comptroller of the Currency, the Federal Deposit Insurance Corporation, and, until 1990, the Federal Savings and Loan Insurance Corporation, not to mention the state agencies that regulate state-chartered banks. Lacking interbureau coordinating mechanisms, differences among these many, diverse institutions are settled by politicians, the courts, or, by default, the marketplace.[29] Japan's Ministry of Finance is the equivalent of all these American administrative bodies rolled into one entity.

To borrow Stigler's metaphor, the "price" the MOF bureaucrat charges for regulation varies according to what other interests the MOF must weigh. The price can range from almost nothing, if the group bearing the cost of regulation is a dormant public, to a costly compromise with another tightly organized interest group. That MOF is one entity with an encompassing jurisdiction enables it to preside over a wider range of compromises than is possible in a fragmented regulatory system such as that of the United States. But even the MOF, with its wide authority, is accountable to the politicians and must set its "price" in accordance with the will of the political representatives, lest it subject itself to unwanted political intrusion. What do the politicians want?

The Politicians

Politicians may strive for a variety of goals, such as gaining status within the party or even achieving a particular policy objective. But because they must first get elected each time their seats are up, they must maximize their chances for reelection subject to these other interests. And because reelection forces them to be concerned with their net support, they will not champion a cause, for whatever sum of campaign money or number of votes, if they would lose more potential support from a disgruntled party than they could gain from the beneficiaries of their efforts. If, on the other hand, the interest group's only opponent is an unaware, unorganized public, politicians will likely attempt to increase their support by using regulation to give favors.

The Liberal Democratic party influences the MOF with its potential to intervene on behalf of aggrieved groups in the financial sector. The principal-agent relationship works, as Stigler's model requires. But the LDP would rather delegate to the MOF the delicate balancing operations

29. For an interesting account of financial regulators in the United States competing over regulatory jurisdiction, see Sam Peltzman, "Entry into Commercial Banking," *Journal of Law and Economics* 8 (1965): 11–50.

between Japanese banks and their rivals, the securities houses, because the LDP would forfeit money and/or votes, on balance, if it favored one more than the other.[30] Phrased differently, banks and securities firms would prefer that the MOF preside over compromises between them because the alternative is an expensive, upwardly spiraling competition for preferential treatment from the LDP.

The Courts

Another at least potential actor in financial politics is the judicial system. Readers familiar with the financial regulatory process in the United States know that the courts are probably the central actors in U.S. banking regulation. In Japan, the role of the courts is remarkable principally for its absence.

In the United States, as in Japan and, for that matter, in any representative democracy, political representatives prefer to delegate problem solving that vexes one or another important constituency. Given America's fragmented bureaucracy, however, even if Congress passes burdens to it, the responsibility does not stop there in the vast number of cases that concern two or more regulatory bodies. Many issues are, therefore, settled in the marketplace or, if either of the competing groups is dissatisfied with that arena, before the courts.

In U.S. banking regulation, for example, each time the Federal Reserve permits commercial banks to advance slightly into the securities business, the Securities Industry Association challenges the regulation in the courts.[31] Neither the Republican nor the Democratic party has been willing to legislate against either commercial or investment banks in the ongoing competition between the two groups of financial institutions. Therefore, the courts rather than the bureaucrats or politicians have set the pace for the erosion of the Glass-Steagall Act.[32] This will likely continue to be the case until or unless commercial banking profits lag behind investment banking profits to such an extent that politicians feel

30. For more on the general propensity of legislators to delegate to administrative bodies, see Morris Fiorina, "Group Concentration and the Delegation of Legislative Authority," in Noll, *Regulatory Policy and the Social Sciences,* 175–197, especially p. 180.

31. See Frederick Karr, "Is the Cash Management Account Innovative Brokerage or Unlawful Competition for Smaller Banks?" *Banking Law Journal* 96 (1979): 307–312; and John Adams, "Money Market Mutual Funds: Has Glass-Steagall Been Cracked?" *Banking Law Journal* 99 (1982): 4–54.

32. For an interesting analysis of the Glass-Steagall issue and of international coordination of financial regulation, see Wolfgang Reinecke, "Commercial Banks and the Internationalization of Finance: The Politics of Regulatory Reform and Global Cooperation" (Typescript, June 1989, Department of Political Science, Yale University).

politically justified in picking favorites. They could hide behind plenty of rhetoric about shoring up an important industry in the face of the global competitive challenge.[33]

Japanese courts figure scarcely at all in the financial regulatory process primarily because the MOF's jurisdiction encompasses both the banking and securities industries as well as most other kinds of financial institutions. Few disputes cannot be handled by the MOF itself. Even if financial institutions were inclined to challenge the MOF through the courts, the administrative courts in Japan are reluctant to hear cases that concern the relationship between a ministry and an industry under the ministry's jurisdiction.[34] The courts have taken themselves out of the running as a major actor in Japanese financial regulation.

The Regulated Groups

The Japanese financial system comprises several different kinds of banks, ranging from twelve city banks, seven trust banks, and three large long-term credit banks to more than one hundred regional banks and even more credit associations, credit unions, and agricultural cooperatives, and more than two hundred securities firms.[35] The groups I am primarily concerned with here are the large, competitive banks represented by their peak organizations, the City Bank Roundtable (Toshi Ginkō Konwakai), the National Federation of Bankers' Associations (Zenkoku Ginkō Kyōkai), and the large, competitive securities firms led by the "Big Four" securities houses, Nomura, Daiwa, Nikkō, and Yamaichi.

From unequal points of origin just after World War II, the banking and securities industries have become interest groups of roughly equal political strength. Banks individually and as a group contribute more reported political campaign funds to the LDP than do the securities firms. They are consistently among the top three corporate contributors. But untold sums

33. The U.S. Savings and Loan industry got into trouble because it "purchased" unduly lenient regulation through the political process. Typical of what Fiorina calls "legislative sins of omission," concentrated interests were rewarded at the expense of the diffuse interests of the general public—at least until this rich mess fermented and bubbled into public view.

34. John Haley, "Toward a Reappraisal of the Occupation Legal Reforms: Administrative Accountability" (Typescript, November 1986, School of Law, University of Washington). See also Shokitsu Tanakadate, "A Summary of the Limitations on Administrative Adjudication under the Japanese Constitution," *Law in Japan* 18 (1985): 108–117.

35. The structure of the Japanese financial system is described in a host of books. See, for example, Horne, *Japanese Financial Markets;* Thomas Cargill and Shoichi Royama, *The Transition of Japanese Finance and Monetary Policy in Comparative Perspective with the United States* (Stanford: Hoover Institution Press, 1987); and Suzuki Yoshio, *Kin'yū jiyūka to kin'yū seisaku* [Financial liberalization and financial policy] (Tokyo: Tōyō keizai shinpōsha, 1985).

make their way into politicians' pockets from the securities firms through the practice of stock price ramping.[36]

Examples of Financial Policy-making

Bureaucratic Preemptive Balancing: Bank Entry into Securities Activities

As noted earlier, the MOF has resolved, without LDP intervention, disputes over the extent to which banks would be allowed to participate in securities activities. Although the Banking Bureau and Securities Bureau each leaned toward the position of the sector it regulates, they finally reached a compromise solution. Failure to do so would have incited either the banks or the securities firms or both to invite politicians to overrule the MOF in their favor. The LDP, in any case, would not intervene uninvited and uncompensated because it would bring no net gain in campaign contributions.

Once the MOF provided a solution, the banks and securities firms were unwilling to pay huge sums to the LDP because the MOF's equilibrating service had a lower price tag. If the Banking Bureau and Securities Bureau were institutionally discrete and, thus, lacking incentive to settle the issue "in house," the banks and securities firms would surely have taken their cases to the politicians for resolution.

Disclosure: The Case of Unwanted Regulation

The MOF's desire has always been to have a strong, highly concentrated financial sector. It would be easier to regulate and less likely to produce panics and scandals that invite political intrusion. But political reality has dictated otherwise. Bank profits have been strained with the trend in recent decades away from corporate dependence on bank loans, and numerous small banks have fallen into serious trouble. Instead of allowing weak financial institutions to go bankrupt, the MOF has often had to shore up politically influential small banks with loans and to arrange bank mergers when possible.[37] In 1981, as part of the new Banking Act

36. See, for example, Lawrence Repeta, "Declining Public Ownership of Japanese Industry," *Law in Japan* 17 (1984): 153–184; and Hirota Katsuhiro, *Seibi jiken: Kōhan dokyumento* [The Seibi incident: Public documents] (Tokyo: Koju jisha, 1984).
37. Nakajima Toshihiro, *Aru ginkō gappei no zasetsu* [The collapse of a bank merger] (Tokyo: Tōyō keizai shinpōsha, 1979), 143–212; and Hirata Takujirō, *Dare no tame no ginkō* [Banks for whom?] (Tokyo: Ōtsuki shoten, 1981), 226.

mentioned earlier, the MOF attempted to tighten up bank disclosure rules in hopes of using market forces to consolidate small financial institutions. The MOF felt that more stringent disclosure requirements and greater public exposure of bad loans would force weak banks to acquiesce to the MOF's merger plans.

The banks fought back. They launched a political campaign with the LDP to roll back the tightened disclosure requirements, and they succeeded. The two LDP Policy Affairs Research Council committees that deal with finance, the Finance Committee (Zaisei Bukai) and Financial Affairs Research Committee (Kinyū Mondai Chōsakai) met jointly and deleted in toto the MOF's chosen disclosure provision before submitting the Banking Act bill to the Diet for approval.[38] In an interesting twist on the capture theory, the MOF tried to get out of its cage but could not.

Retail Banking: Fragmentation of Regulatory Jurisdiction

The cases examined so far all corroborate the expectations of Stigler's model rather well. Although Stigler does not delve into the intricacies of the policy-making process itself, he predicts that regulation should benefit industry and that regulations will be changed if that benefit dissipates. The MOF has reinterpreted the Section 65 division between the banking and securities industries in accord with changing economic factors in order to maintain an equilibrium between the two industries that reflects their relative political clout. Stigler would also predict, by way of his strict principal-agent assumption, that politicians would force bureaucrats to retreat from proposed regulation that proved unpopular with important constituencies. Indeed, the principal-agent relationship between the LDP and the MOF appears to be consistent with Stigler's views as shown in the MOF's vain attempt to tighten bank disclosure rules.

In retail banking, however, one now confronts what at least appears to be an exception to the policy outcomes predicted by the capture theory. The simple capture version of the theory of regulation would predict no compromises with the interests of banks in the area of retail banking because small borrowers and depositors do not have easy access to competitive foreign financial services. Domestic financial institutions should, therefore, have no incentive to compete for the patronage of small customers.

38. *Nihon keizai shinbun*, February 17, 18, 21, 24, 1981, and March 3, 5, 24, 25, 1981, and April 8, 14, 1981. See also "Shin ginkō hōan ōhaba shūsei" [Broad amendments to the new banking law proposals], *Kin'yū zaisei jijō* (April 27, 1981): 14–16; and Rosenbluth, *Financial Politics in Contemporary Japan*, 112–131.

But, in fact, they do. In Japan, the Ministry of Posts and Telecommunications (MPT), not the MOF, operates the largest bank in Japan, indeed, in the world. More than ¥ 100 trillion in deposits makes the postal savings system larger in terms of assets than the five largest city banks combined.

Perhaps even more important is the postal system's political power. Nearly twenty thousand local notables, located in villages and communities all over Japan, are MPT-appointed postmasters, many having inherited the title from fathers and grandfathers. These postmasters are paid on commission to market the postal savings instruments and insurance plans. They also are reputed to wield considerable vote-gathering power for sympathetic LDP politicians at election time. Although this sort of political machine is less potent in Japan today than it was a decade or so ago and is even less effective in urban than in rural districts, risk-averse politicians prefer not to cross the commissioned postmasters if at all possible.[39]

The MPT keeps LDP politicians favorably disposed toward its operations through the electoral support of the commissioned post officers and through the political campaign contributions from telecommunications companies under MPT jurisdiction. The ongoing struggle between the Ministry of International Trade and Industry (MITI) and the Ministry of Posts and Telecommunications for jurisdiction over the telecommunications industry has been told well elsewhere.[40] The MPT has also battled with the MOF for authority to set interest rates.

Since the postal ministry (then the Ekitei Ryo) was established in 1873 with independent authority over postal savings interest rates, the MOF has attempted to integrate the postal interest rates into the rest of the financial system, but the postal ministry has persistently defended its turf. Known in Japan as the Hundred Years' War, this jurisdictional squabble has now outlived one century and is still raging.

Free from the Temporary Interest Rate Control Act that limits competition for deposits among banks, the postal savings system offers an instrument with slightly higher yields. This bête noire of the private banks, the *teigaku chōkin,* is a ten-year, fixed-amount savings deposit with biannual compounded interest and free withdrawal without penalty after six months. Banks cry foul, claiming that no institution concerned with its bottom line could offer such a generous savings instrument and that the MPT subsidizes the postal savings system from its profitable

39. Osada, a former MPT bureaucrat, for example, overwhelmingly won an Upper House seat reputedly because of the commissioned postmasters' electoral machine. See Chalmers Johnson, "MITI, MPT, and the Telecom Wars: How Japan Makes Policy for High Technology," in Chalmers Johnson, Laura D'Andrea Tyson, and John Zysman, eds., *Politics and Productivity: How Japan's Development Strategy Works* (New York: Ballinger, 1989).
40. Ibid.

postal services as a way of paying off the commissioned postmasters.[41] The available evidence is inconclusive concerning the basis for these accusations, but it is certainly true that many small banks would go under if they had to openly compete with the postal savings system.

Unlike the competition between the banking and securities industries that pits the MOF's Banking Bureau against the Securities Bureau, the struggle between the MPT / postal savings system, on the one hand, and the MOF and private banks, on the other, lacks an administrative mechanism to resolve the problem short of politicization. Politicians necessarily become involved because there is no other overarching institution to which they can delegate this sort of dispute.

After years of pulling and hauling and political maneuvering on both sides, the MOF and MPT finally agreed in the 1980s to a compromise solution: the MPT would still control the interest rates of the postal savings system, but banks and the postal savings system both would offer an identical higher-yield savings account beginning in June 1989. This money market certificate (MMC) would require a ¥ 3 million (roughly $23,000 at ¥ 130 to the dollar) minimum deposit and its interest rate would be set at a fixed spread from banks' certificates of deposits and government bonds.[42]

Banks were by no means overjoyed by this resolution of the interest rate dispute. Higher-yield, small-denomination accounts would raise their cost of funds. They wanted the MOF to enforce a lower interest rate ceiling on the postal savings system. But they got the best they could hope for, given the political clout of the MPT and the commissioned postmasters, because the outcome did avert unbridled price competition for deposits. The MPT, in exchange for its side of the compromise, was granted a slightly larger percentage of the postal savings funds, from 2 to 4 percent, which it could invest on its own without handing the proceeds over to the MOF's Fiscal Investment and Loan Program.[43]

41. "Ginkō to yūbin chōkin no keihi" [The expenses of banks and postal savings], Kin'yu (April 23, 1977): 47–48; and "Yūbin chōkin ni kansuru kihonteki kangaekata" [A basic view of postal savings], Kin'yū (November 1980): 9.

42. "Ninki no sūpa MMC: Isoide kau no wa son desu" [The popular MMC: Buying quickly invites loss], Shūkan asahi (June 16, 1989): 29–31.

43. The Fiscal Investment and Loan Program, four-fifths of which is financed by postal savings deposits, is a government investing and lending program supervised by the MOF's Finance Bureau. It makes loans to public and quasi-public corporations or to the private sector through various government financial institutions, such as the Japan Development Bank for big business projects or the Peoples' Finance Corporation for small business financing. See Chalmers Johnson, Japan's Public Policy Companies (Washington, D.C.: American Enterprise Institute, 1978), 84; and Kent Calder, Crisis and Compensation: Public Policy and Political Stability in Japan, 1949–1986 (Princeton: Princeton University Press, 1988), 179–182.

That small savers have gained higher yields on their deposits was clearly not the result of consumer awareness and activism but a by-product of a territorial squabble between two ministries unable fully to protect their clients. The key factor producing a different outcome from that expected in Japanese finance is, therefore, jurisdictional fragmentation, not some sort of grassroots campaign.

In addition to Japan's own small savers, a second group has also benefited from the higher yields on small savings deposits—foreign banks. Some foreign banking operations in Japan predate World War II, but all seventy-four foreign banks still have a combined share of less than 3 percent of the Japanese loan market, a level that has persisted for decades.[44] The thorniest problem for foreign banks has been the Temporary Interest Rate Control Act, which provides established domestic banks with a wealth of low-cost funds with which to make low-cost loans (if necessary), whereas foreign banks, lacking the name recognition to attract a large number of small deposits, must rely on the more expensive interbank market for funds. The more Japanese banks must pay for their deposits, the greater is the competitive advantage for foreign banks.

Japanese Politics

These cases from financial politics in Japan provide illuminating material for challenging the strong-state thesis. Finance is a highly regulated sector in most countries because of its close connection with the health of the entire economy, and in Japan it is regarded as one of the government's most willing agents.

As the primary administrative agency overseeing the activities of the financial sector, the MOF is certainly involved in policy formulation and implementation. But as noted, the Ministry of Finance does not dictate its wishes to the financial sector. One must not mistake an active state for a strong one.

Bureaucratic performance, the MOF's highest goal, depends in large measure on bank compliance because politicians are always available as a last resort for the regulated parties. Hence, it is the political cost that sets the bureaucratic price for dispute settlement.

As long as small banks are powerful in local districts and as long as the postal network continues to operate as a powerful local vote gathering

---

44. Louis Pauly, *Opening Financial Markets: Banking Politics on the Pacific Rim* (Ithaca: Cornell University Press, 1988).

machine, streamlining the Japanese financial system remains a distant goal for the MOF. An example of unfulfilled aspirations in another administrative agency is the Ministry of International Trade and Industry and its relationship to small business. Although MITI would prefer to preside over globally competitive industries, the LDP compels it to enforce legislation protecting small businesses from the encroachment of large conglomerates.[45]

Finance also presents a strong case against the thesis that Japan is a populist state. As noted, higher yields on small denomination deposits were not the result of political pressure from the public. Consumers of financial services remain as unorganized as ever. Politicians brokered an interministerial battle between the MOF and MPT to prevent an all-out skirmish for deposits that would have crippled the banks. Establishing higher but capped interest rates was the second-best solution for the banks and an inadvertent windfall for savers and foreign banks.

The MOF continues to protect banks in a number of ways in the name of guaranteeing the integrity of the banking system. Granted, depositors in Japan have never lost their bank savings in the postwar era as a result of bank failure. But the still relatively low yields on savings accounts are a high, forced premium depositors pay for safety. The small depositor could be protected by other means, such as strict balance sheet requirements or better deposit insurance. The rhetoric of "depositor protection" continues to disguise bank protection.

Despite the formidable lobbying power of interest groups, overtly protective regulation is at least hypothetically vulnerable to censure from political entrepreneurs who are not allied to the special interests that seek regulation for their own purposes.[46] Why do not ambitious politicians in the Liberal Democratic party or in the opposition parties attempt to incite the silent voters to depose long-standing vested interests? After all, if strong leadership helped consumers of financial services to overcome their free rider problem, vast numbers would reward the reformers at the polls.

The short answer is that the LDP, which since 1955 has been the only party with the Diet majority necessary to formulate national policy, imposes strict voting discipline on its Diet members to prevent would-be mavericks from capitalizing on potential voter dissatisfaction with established policies. As in all parliamentary democracies, the LDP rank and file accepts strict voting discipline because the party leadership controls the

45. Calder recounts this story in *Crisis and Compensation.*
46. R. G. Noll and B. M. Owen, eds., *The Political Economy of Deregulation* (Washington, D.C.: American Enterprise Institute, 1983), 158–159; Wilson, "Politics of Regulation"; Martha Derthick and Paul Quirk, *The Politics of Deregulation* (Washington, D.C.: Brookings Institution, 1985); and Sam Peltzman, "Current Developments in the Economics of Regulation," in Gary Fromm, ed., *Studies in Public Regulation* (Cambridge: MIT Press, 1981).

allocation of party and cabinet posts and because a vote of no confidence against the leadership would mean that they would all have to recontest their seats in another election.

The more complete answer requires a look at Japan's rather unique electoral system to understand why the opposition parties have not formulated electoral strategies and won elections on the basis of proconsumer, protaxpayer platforms. Members of Japan's Lower House are elected from a multimember district system in which each voter has a single nontransferrable vote (SNTV). Because the LDP must run several candidates against each other in most districts to retain a Lower House majority, LDP candidates must campaign on personal attributes and constituency services rather than on broad-based issues.[47] This electoral system and the LDP's factional adaptation to it produce, in other words, patronage-based rather than issue-based political campaign strategies. The LDP will retain its majority in the Lower House as long as its candidates are able to satisfy—or promise to satisfy, in the case of new candidates— their constituencies with favors that distract attention from broader-based consumer and taxpayer issues.[48]

This electoral system only minimizes, but does not obliterate entirely, the political salience of broad-based issues. The opposition parties can and do score well electorally when they succeed in raising enough public concern about LDP policies to overshadow the LDP's constituency services. One example of genuine entrepreneurship by the opposition was over the loan shark problem that had begun to receive splashy news coverage in 1981. Taking advantage of public anger over reports of suicides because of inability to repay loans and of hired gangsters harrassing overdue borrowers, the Japan Socialist party and the Democratic Socialist party launched a widely publicized campaign to lower the legal ceiling on the interest rate for consumer loans from the existing level of 109.5 percent. Despite heavy lobbying of the LDP by the consumer loan industry, the LDP had to give in to the opposition, lest it lose support of the aroused public. The Diet passed a law lowering the interest rate ceiling to 40 percent, scarcely a bonanza for small borrowers but enough to remove the spotlight of public concern.[49]

47. For what is still the best in-depth examination of an LDP candidate's electoral strategy, see Gerald Curtis, *Election Campaigning, Japanese Style* (New York: Columbia University Press, 1971).

48. To be reported more fully in a forthcoming work by Mathew McCubbins and Frances McCall Rosenbluth.

49. See, for example, "Ginkō no sarakin yūshi" [The salaryman loans of banks], *Kin'yū zaisei jijō* (October 30, 1978): 6. Mark Ramseyer has noted that the Japanese loan shark industry is a classic example of Akerlof's "market for lemons." Because of the difficulty of checking the credit-worthiness of individuals under the existing credit information system in Japan, bad borrowers have taken advantage of the market, thus forcing up the interest rates

Under the charismatic leadership of Doi Takako and with the help of the Recruit scandal, sexual improprieties of prominent LDP politicians, and the unpopular sales tax, the Japan Socialist party fared significantly better in the Upper House election in July 1989 and the Lower House election in February 1990 than it had for decades. The LDP's loss of a majority in the Upper House temporarily crimped its ability to formulate and implement policy with only token concessions to the Opposition. But the electoral system for the Lower House will continue to assist the LDP in retaining its majority there. Broadly based public concerns still fare poorly in Japan's political system.

When Do Producers Dominate?

Under which circumstances are regulators most likely to do the bidding of the regulated industries? When does capture theory best apply?

One criterion is the existence of a unified state authority. The propensity of legislatures to delegate delicate issues has been documented generally and in Japanese financial politics in particular. If an administrative agency has an encompassing jurisdiction over an issue area, it has both the motivation and capability to contain any conflict that erupts among competing groups under its jurisdiction. If it fails to broker a compromise, the sparring groups take the issue to another arena, such as the political one, for resolution. Because this would be undesirable both for the administrative agency trying to maintain its discretion and for the regulated groups trying to maximize profits, this move is unlikely to occur. The preferred outcome for all groups concerned is a bureaucratically administered solution. This result allows the bureaucracy to retain its procedural integrity, the competing groups to obtain a resolution at less cost than would be required in all-out political lobbying, and the politicians to retain the usual, uninterrupted flow of campaign contributions from both sides in the dispute.

Where the MOF functions as a single regulator, such as in the regulatory process between banks and securities firms, the capture pattern holds. The MOF maintains the balance between these two industries while managing to retain its own procedural integrity by preempting any adjustment that would result from political intervention. It is important to recognize,

---

with their high default rate and making the market unattractive to borrowers who would like the money for nonspeculative purposes. See George Akerlof, "The Market for 'Lemons': Quality Uncertainty and the Market Mechanism," *Quarterly Journal of Economics* 84 (August 1970): 424–449.

however, that the MOF retains its procedural autonomy at the expense of substantive autonomy. For the MOF to fight for policy outcomes independently of the interests of important LDP constituents would invite quick and sure political redress.

The regulatory process between ministerial boundaries, such as between the MOF and the MPT, more closely resembles what typically occurs in the United States: much public debate, much competing rhetoric about public interest, and open involvement by political representatives. A key difference, however, is the absence of an important role for the courts in Japan. As a result, outcomes in Japan parallel the underlying political clout of the competing groups.

Consumers "prevailed" in the United States in 1978 when courts ruled that securities firms could, indeed, issue money market certificates at attractive yields even though these MMCs would draw money away from bank accounts. Defeated, the banks had to give up their Regulation Q that placed a ceiling on bank account interest rates and, hence, limited competition. Limiting competition among banks no longer made sense if more attractive substitutes for bank deposits were permitted. As in the battle between the MPT and the MOF, the consumer victory was not achieved through consumer consciousness and action. In this case, the absence of an overarching regulatory body and the active role of the U.S. courts mandated recourse to the marketplace.

A second condition that fosters producer dominance is the ability of the regulated groups to organize effectively for political action. Geographic concentration and small numbers typically are advantages because members of groups with such attributes have less difficulty consulting among themselves and presenting the government with a unified request than do scattered groups with large numbers.

In Japan both banking and the securities industry are organized more or less hierarchically; they enjoy strict barriers to entry, and they have coordinating bodies centrally located in Tokyo even though members are scattered across the country. The MOF, with its encompassing jurisdiction, helps the financial industries reach agreements and keep them, further buttressing their existing collective action advantages.

Third, regulatory capture is most likely to occur in a political system characterized by weak issue-based competition for votes. LDP politicians do not win their seats on the basis of an "LDP platform" because that would provide no means for dividing the vote among the several LDP candidates who must run against each other from the same district. Rather, the LDP's continued success at the polls since 1955 is largely the result of the effectiveness of its incumbents' and new candidates' personal support groups. Issue politics have been crowded out by personalistic politics and constituency service.

This is not to say that Japanese politics have been entirely devoid of electoral competition. Although strong party discipline has mitigated political entrepreneurship by individual LDP politicians and the electoral system has weakened the effectiveness of the opposition's rhetorical challenges, the LDP has demonstrated a healthy taste for survival by incorporating key electoral blocs whenever its margin at the polls has become too thin. The LDP's inclusion of farmers in the early 1950s, of small business people and shopkeepers in the 1960s, and of much of the urban vote in the 1970s was in direct response to electoral challenges by the opposition.[50]

Nonetheless, the opposition has been no match for the LDP in the battle for the votes of consumers and taxpayers even though it is these dispersed interests that bear the costs of producer-dominated policies. Because the LDP wins votes on constituency services and personal loyalty, voters are not mobilized in their capacities as consumers and taxpayers except on issues in which they have sizable per capita stakes. The consumption tax introduced in 1989 seemed to be such an issue; indeed, the Socialists used it to their electoral advantage in the Upper House election in July 1989 and the Lower House election in February 1990. Nonetheless, the LDP still held onto its majority in the Lower House. The political environment, in other words, remained conducive to producer dominance.

Financial deregulation in Japan reflects the interests of the same financial institutions that sought regulation in the first place. The changing economic environment in which the financial institutions operate has forced them to relinquish some protection to compete with institutions in markets beyond the MOF's reach. This is as true in the retail market vis-à-vis the MPT/postal savings system as it is in the United States and the Euromarket.

Jurisdictions with fragmented regulatory structures, such as the United States and the Euromarket, started the deregulatory process in motion, at least at the wholesale end of the market. Economic interdependence is the transmission belt whereby countries with encompassing bureaucracies—Japan and Germany, for example—must also deregulate lest they lose business.

Some Japan observers have expected to see greater involvement of politicians as Japan's economy becomes more interlocked with the world economy. Politicians have intervened when internationally salient issues fell across the jurisdictions of two or more ministries, as in the telecommunications tug-of-war between the MPT and MITI.[51] But financial deregulation has not been wholly politicized in Japan because the MOF

---

50. Calder, *Crisis and Compensation;* and Gerald Curtis, *The Japanese Way of Politics* (New York: Columbia University Press, 1988), 24–25.
51. Johnson, "MITI, MPT, and the Telecom Wars."

balances competing interests under its jurisdiction in anticipation of political interference. The salient factor for the likelihood of politicization is the scope of bureaucratic jurisdiction, not internationalization. In the ongoing competition between the banks and the securities firms, the regulatory/deregulatory process gives them back at least part of what they lose in the marketplace. The MOF, following political cues, is redrawing the boundaries between these two industries to allow banks gradual entry into the more lucrative securities business. The MOF will continue this anticipatory balancing for the foreseeable future because not only the MOF but the financial institutions and the politicians as well find it in their interests to do so.

That the policy-making process is little affected by increasing internationalization does not mean, however, that Japan's financial institutions can rest assured entirely. The instances of deregulation recounted here demonstrate that internationalization of Japan's corporate sector does weaken the MOF's ability to shield financial institutions from the winds of global competition. As long as Japanese nonfinancial corporations have access to less strictly regulated financial services in the Euromarket and the United States, Japanese financial institutions will have to agree to parallel deregulation to retain their clients. Japan's financial deregulation has been the result of banks' grudging recognition that they must relinquish certain kinds of protection to compete, even with slimmer profits. The most the MOF can do is moderate the rate of change, adjust the interests of groups treated differently by market forces, and maintain protective regulation in areas that do not impinge on competitiveness abroad—as long as foreign governments will tolerate it.

CHAPTER FIVE

DEREGULATION AND LEGALIZATION

OF FINANCIAL POLICY

Masaru Mabuchi

IN THIS CHAPTER, I EXAMINE CHANGES IN THE FINANCIAL POLICIES OF THE Ministry of Finance (MOF), identify the reasons for those changes, and interpret their meaning in a context of state strength.

One such change is financial deregulation. Since the 1980s the regulated financial system has slowly been breaking up, as evidenced by deregulation of interest rates, easing of regulations on financial institutions, creation of new financial instruments, and increased use of the yen in international markets.

Legalization of regulations represents another change. Although the Ministry of Finance has been relinquishing some of its regulatory authority, it has simultaneously been giving a legal basis to what remains. Movement has been toward legally regulating the new markets that have emerged as a result of deregulation. In addition, the MOF has recently been using legal regulations to clarify the basis and standards of its regulatory activities for the benefit of foreign countries. These changes can be viewed as part of a movement away from financial policy operated chiefly on administrative "guidelines" to a policy run more according to laws. Thus, recent developments in financial policy encompass both deregulation and the legalization of financial policy, or reregulation.

At first glance, deregulation and reregulation may seem contradictory. Deregulation appears to be a retreat by the government, whereas reregulation apparently is an advance. But both of these movements are progressing side by side. My purpose here is to prove that these two seemingly contradictory movements are, in fact, two sides of the same coin and that the objective of both is to respond to similar changes in the financial environment.

The background of the recent movements toward financial market deregulation has been explained chiefly by economists who generally focus on changes in market forces. Few explanations have been made from a political standpoint.[1] Based upon fragmentary observations and general explanations of Japanese politics, however, the recent trend toward deregulation can be explained by international pressures, MOF inducements, and pressure from the Liberal Democratic party (LDP).

The first explanation focuses on external or international pressure. This position takes the view that the United States and Europe forced Japan to open restrictive financial markets and that this further led to the deregulation of domestic financial practices. According to this position, the United States sought to lay the blame for its enormous trade deficit on Japan, whom it accused of deliberately letting the exchange rate of the yen rest at unreasonably low levels. It further states that the value of the yen is so low because the Japanese financial system is so tightly regulated. It then asserts that the United States, in an effort to improve the situation, demanded that Japan open up its financial markets and that Japan responded to this pressure.

The second explanation attributes the movement toward deregulation to inducements by the MOF. According to this approach, the MOF decided that Japanese industries and private financial institutions had reached a point where they were capable of competing in international markets and needed no further protection through regulation. Having determined that it would be far better if they could enjoy the merits of free competition, the MOF decided on a policy of deregulation. Although very few, if any, openly take this stance, such an explanation would not be unnatural at all if one adopted the traditional position of bureaucracy dominance.

The third explanation states that pressure from the Liberal Democratic party caused the deregulatory movement. Whether they had the interests of consumers (savers) or producers (private financial institutions) in mind, the ruling Liberal Democratic party, out to grab either more votes, more political donations, or both, decided to pursue financial deregulation. As with the second explanation, few if any adopt this stance openly. But if a major change in policy occurs in a system under party dominance, then this explanation is possible, at least theoretically.

Although internal forces certainly had much to do with the movement toward deregulation, the acceleration of this trend from a certain point

1. Important exceptions are James Horne, *Japanese Financial Markets* (London: Allen and Unwin, 1985); Frances Rosenbluth, *Financial Politics in Contemporary Japan* (Ithaca: Cornell University Press, 1989); and Louis W. Pauly, *Opening Financial Markets: Banking Politics on the Pacific Rim* (Ithaca: Cornell University Press, 1988), chap. 4.

has to be attributed to a great extent to external pressure.[2] LDP politicians, who attach great importance to continued good relations with the United States, played a significant role in converting external pressure into deregulatory policies. In particular, the decision to deregulate the financial system taken by the prime minister is of great importance.[3] It cannot be denied that the Ministry of Finance attempted to anticipate expected foreign demands for deregulation. Thus, domestic political actors responding to foreign pressure drove deregulation policies.

These three explanations, however, share one common defect. None of them explains the current movement toward reregulation, or legalization. It is certainly true that Japanese financial policy is being deregulated. The highly regulated financial system is slowly but steadily being loosened and is currently undergoing what some even call a "financial revolution." But viewing only one aspect of current changes ignores the legalization of regulations.

If the central feature of financial policy is viewed as regulation or intervention by the state, then the liberalization of financial regulations indicates a major revision in administration style. If, however, the central feature is viewed as governmental guidelines, or governmental notifications, legalization of financial regulations would also mean an important change in administrative style on a par with the movement toward deregulation. In this chapter I characterize the changes in administrative style that have occurred in Japan under the simultaneous policies of deregulation and reregulation, or legalization.

Theoretical Hypotheses

Hypothesis

Simultaneous movements toward deregulation and reregulation have altered the administrative style of financial policy-making. The explanatory variables I stress are a reduction in administrative resources and an increase in external pressure. For a diagram of the hypotheses that must be considered, see figure 5.1.

As shown in the center of the diagram, the force within Japan that is pushing the trend toward liberalization is a reduction in administrative re-

2. See Pauly, *Opening Financial Markets*, 66. For the general relation between domestic politics and international politics, see Robert D. Putnam, "Diplomacy and Domestic Politics: The Logic of Two-level Games," *International Organization* 42 (Summer 1988): 427–460.
3. Funahashi Yoichi, *Tsūka retsu retsu* [Managing the dollar] (Tokyo: Asahi shinbun sha, 1988), chap. 4.

Figure 5.1 Causal relationships underlying legalization and deregulation

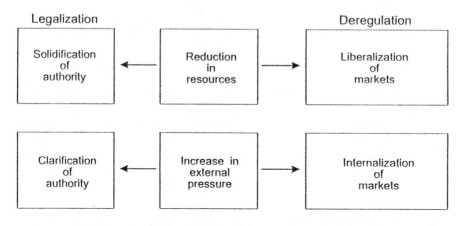

sources. The force outside Japan that is pushing the trend toward internationalization is the increase in foreign pressure.

If the reduction in administrative resources is synonymous with the government's decreased ability to secure revenues, as symbolized by the large-scale issuance of national bonds, then the two *kokusaika* (in Japanese, the terms for internationalization and for a heavy dependence on national bonds are both pronounced *kokusaika,* although the characters are different) can be said to be driving forces behind the deregulation movement. Although I define reduction in administrative resources widely and do not limit it to the government's ability to secure revenues, my hypothesis concerning causes of deregulation does not differ greatly from the one that economists use.

The same forces that promote deregulation act simultaneously as the driving forces behind the movement toward the solidification and clarification of authority, that is, the legalization of financial regulations. To explain the legalization of regulations, which has received little attention, the domestic factors of change must be understood in a wider sense than as an increased reliance on bonds, namely, as a reduction in administrative resources. If this hypothesis concerns *structure,* the next concerns *process.*

Administrative styles can be divided into three periods: period 1, from the 1960s through the 1970s, during which regulations responded to the needs of the period of high growth; period 2, from around 1980 to 1985, when regulations were liberalized and solidified to respond to a reduction in administrative resources; and period 3, from 1985 to the 1990s, when internationalization and clarification were called for to respond to foreign pressure. It is difficult to separate periods 2 and 3. The logic prevalent in period 2 did not disappear completely in period 3 but persisted and supported it instead. Because solidification / liberalization and clarification / internationalization were responses to different changes in the environment, however, the two periods will be treated separately here, partly to clarify the differences in the structure of change during these periods.

Many economists would probably support a three-part chronological division. Shoichi Royama, for example, points out that "the issuance of national bonds on a large scale began in 1975. After that, the changes in Japan's financial system assumed a certain directional bearing. Thus, one can say that 1975 was an epoch-making year. Following numerous preliminary indications in 1984, 1985 became yet another epoch-making year. If 1975 was the first year of the Period of Bonds, then 1985 can be called the first year of the Period of Internationalization."[4]

Terms and Definitions

Of the two facets of deregulation, liberalization and internationalization, *liberalization* means in this chapter the actions taken by the government to ease or eliminate the various regulations applied to domestic financial institutions. In general, financial activities tend to be more widely regulated by the government than other economic sectors. The need for this sort of regulation has been recognized by most economists (e.g., Milton Friedman):[5] unless a complete gold standard is followed, some sort of intervention by the government is necessary to stabilize the value of currency, which is the point around which all economic activity revolves.

Many aspects of the postwar Japanese financial systems have been so regulated by the government that its efforts were often referred to by the public as the "convoy system." Just as transport ships are grouped when crossing the high seas in wartime to enable fast escorts to protect slower transports and cargo vessels, the Japanese financial system has been characterized as one in which large, efficient financial institutions observe the slower pace set for small, inefficient institutions.

Internationalization is used, first, to refer to an increase in the movement of capital to and from foreign countries, that is, an increase in business conducted by Japanese firms or individuals with foreign parties or an increase in such business conducted in foreign currency. Second, it means an increase in the roles played by Japanese financial institutions in international financial transactions. Third, it includes the development of Ja-

---

4. Royama Shōichi, *Kin'yū jiyūka* [Financial liberalization] (Tokyo: Tokyo daigaku shuppan kai, 1986), 21.
5. Milton Friedman, *Capitalism and Freedom* (Chicago: University of Chicago Press, 1962).

pan's financial and capital markets as places where the international distribution of capital takes place. Fourth, it entails an increase in the role of the yen overseas. In all instances, internationalization is viewed as an economic phenomenon.

I use internationalization here to mean the governmental actions to ease or eliminate regulations pertaining to overseas transactions or business involving foreign parties, for example, actions to facilitate the international transfer of capital or to increase the international use of the yen.

A typical example is the easing and removal of the laws regulating foreign currency exchange. Such laws were basically intended to restrict financial transactions between residents and nonresidents. In fact, the Foreign Exchange Law was originally set up to regulate transactions by prohibiting them as a rule and permitting them only as an exception. As a result of amendments to the law in 1980, financial transactions basically became free through liberalization of the inflow and outflow of capital and of overseas activities. Movements in overseas financial markets and overseas interest rates began directly to affect Japanese markets and rates. Internationalization in this sense, that is, the opening up of Japanese markets, was brought about by demands made by foreign countries.

The legalization of regulations gave a legal basis to regulatory activities that were previously conducted by means of administrative guidelines or notifications. Such legalization had two objectives: to *solidify* governmental authority and to *clarify* the existence and basis of such authority. Authority was solidified to cope with the reduction in governmental resources and clarified in response to foreign pressure.

The government must mobilize many legal and nonlegal resources when it wishes to regulate the private sector. The first is legal authority. Government agencies can, based upon their legal authority, demand obligations of the citizenry and, when such obligations are not met, carry out governmental policies. If failure to meet obligations becomes a breach of law, then the government can inflict penalties on the person responsible.

First among nonlegal resources[6] is a general respect for government departments and agencies and their legitimacy. The tradition within Japan that ranks bureaucrats higher than others within the social hierarchy functions as a strong resource. Second, public support of a particular governmental activity is likely to deter opposition to it. Anybody who opposes the government will, therefore, be left with little choice but to accept, however grudgingly, its authority. Third, the government can take punitive actions against those who do not obey it: on-the-spot inspections, reporting requirements, revoking operating or business permits, withholding or rejecting applications, denying use of public facilities, and reducing the

6. Yamauchi Kazuo, *Gyōsei shidō* [Administrative guidance] (Tokyo: Kōbundō, 1977), chap. 4.

foreign currency distributed to import raw materials. The legal basis for such punitive actions is often rather informal and should, therefore, be distinguished from direct legal sanctions. Finally, resources take the form of benefits: financial aid, low-interest loans, assistance in obtaining loans, special consideration in the granting of permits, government purchasing orders, and information.

Solidification of authority, then, is defined as the replacement of non-legal resources, which supported government activities in the past, with legal resources. This shift occurs when the utility of nonlegal resources begins to decline; legal resources are expected to produce the same results as nonlegal resources. Bureaucrats try to use the law as cement to repair a wall that is crumbling.

Not all nonlegal resources can be replaced by legal resources. If public support for a certain activity by the government declines, any attempt by the government to force such support through legal means would probably result only in more public resentment. Replacement of the other three nonlegal resources, however, is possible.

Solidification in Japanese financial policy occurred in one instance: in the period of high economic growth between 1955 and 1973, private companies borrowed heavily from private banks to meet their high investment needs. When private banks did not have sufficient funds to meet these needs, they had to depend upon the central bank for the money. The Bank of Japan (BOJ) used several special techniques to distribute its valuable resources as it wished. Although the relationship between the Ministry of Finance and the Bank of Japan was not simply that between ruler and subject, in many respects the Bank of Japan was under the influence of the MOF. The influence exercised by the BOJ on the private banks was, therefore, also a resource to the MOF when the ministry wished to influence the private financial sector. The MOF and the BOJ "proffered benefits" to influence the financial world in many areas.[7] In this case, legal authority was only secondary as the MOF and BOJ controlled the actions of private banks without recourse to legal resources.

When the money shortage ended and banks no longer had to borrow from the government, then the government's ability to lend money lost its importance as a resource and the effectiveness of de facto regulations imposed by the government on the banks was diminished. To rectify this situation the government solidified its authority by replacing de facto regulations with de jure regulations.

Government agencies need clarification of standards when conducting regulatory activities. Although some standards are clearly defined, others

7. Yoshio Suzuki, *Money and Banking in Contemporary Japan* (New Haven: Yale University Press, 1980), 215. See also John Zysman, *Governments, Markets, and Growth* (Ithaca: Cornell University Press, 1983), 234–251.

are not revealed to the public. The basis or standards in the latter case are vital information to private corporations.

Kent Calder notes that, in Japan, "the percentage of such standards which have been made publicly available and are accessible at any time are, in comparison to the U.S. and western European countries, severely limited."[8] For example, although the MOF has revealed its general policies regarding the opening of new branch offices by financial institutions, it has not revealed the standards it follows when granting or refusing permits to open such new offices.

The relative secrecy concerning the reasons for regulatory decisions effectively widens the government's range of discretion. Although the secrecy has a number of disadvantages for those regulated, they benefit because it prevents the entry of new parties into the market. When foreign parties increasingly desire to enter an ever more attractive Japanese market, only to realize that they have been shut out by invisible rules and decisions made by the Japanese government, the lack of accessibility to such information comes under criticism. An effective countermeasure would be to clarify the standards of governmental activities by legalizing them and making this information public.

Japan's Regulated System of Finance

Japan's postwar financial system before the late 1970s had three basic features, the regulation of business activities, interest rates, and foreign participation.

Regulation of Business Activities

The first characteristic of Japan's postwar financial system was its rigid segmentation by regulation. The business each type of financial institution was permitted to engage in was limited by laws, orders, and administrative guidance. The financial industry was divided into a number of sectors. Under the Securities and Exchange Law of 1947, banks were prohibited from engaging in securities transactions other than those involving national bonds, which created a division between banks and securities firms. A second division distinguished between long-term credit and short-term

8. Kent Calder, "Elites in an Equalizing Role: Ex-bureaucrats as Coordinators and Intermediaries in the Japanese Business Relationship," *Comparative Politics* 21 (July 1989): 379–403.

credit. City banks relied upon deposits made by their customers as a source of lending money and, by discounting bills, among other methods, offered short-term credit. Long-term credit banks, on the other hand, offered long-term credit for new investment by private corporations. They raised their capital by issuing financial debentures. A third division permitted only the trust banks to deal in trust and custodial services; other institutions had to secure funds through deposits and other means. A fourth and final distinction rested on differing loan practices. City banks and other large banks made loans to major corporations, whereas regional banks, mutual banks, credit associations, and credit cooperatives lent to small businesses. These boundaries protected the smaller banks, which lacked competitiveness, by preventing competition among different types of banks.

The Ministry of Finance played two roles in this regimented system. First, the ministry was responsible for enforcing the boundaries through laws, executive orders, and organizational method.[9] In other words, within the MOF, the Bureau of Banks was solely responsible for overseeing the activities of banks, whereas the Bureau of Securities was solely responsible for administering the activities of securities firms. Each of these bureaus was further subdivided. For example, the Bureau of Banks was divided into three sections, each responsible for a different banking sector.

The second role of the ministry was to maintain order within each area of finance as defined by the boundaries. The Bureau of Banks controlled bank expansion (the opening of new branches) and the types of financial instruments the institutions could offer. The Bureau of Securities likewise exercised strong control over the opening of new branches by securities firms, new entry into the bond market, characteristics of the bond market, and returns on securities.

Regulation of Interest Rates

A second characteristic of Japan's postwar financial system was regulated interest rates. The Temporary Interest Adjustment Law passed in 1947 gave the Policy Committee of the Bank of Japan the authority to set the upper limits on interest rates in many different areas. Interest rates not covered by the 1947 law, such as long-term prime rates, were, for all practical purposes, set by the government. The result was a highly regulated system in which all interest rates were tied to the official discount rate.

9. T. J. Pempel, "Japanese Foreign Economic Policy," in Peter Katzenstein, ed., *Between Power and Plenty: Foreign Economic Policies of Advanced Industrial States* (Madison: University of Wisconsin Press, 1978), 24.

The role of the MOF in this system was to coordinate all other interest rates with the discount rate.

Regulation of Foreign Participants

The third characteristic of Japan's financial system was its control over foreign parties. Financial officials tightly controlled the flow of foreign and domestic capital to and from Japan by using the old Foreign Exchange Law to maintain Japan's international balance of payments at a given level. It was necessary to shut out any foreign influence in order for the domestic regulations to function effectively. If the inflow and outflow of capital were unregulated, the domestic system of regulated interest rates could easily be circumvented, thereby undermining the system. As T. J. Pempel points out, the Japanese government stood between Japan and the foreign countries and acted as a "doorman" during the period of high economic growth. It was able to determine what entered and left Japan and under what conditions.[10] In its role as doorman the Ministry of Finance was extremely selective and stubborn.

Deregulation

Liberalization

Liberalization took place in many areas: the deregulation of interest rates, an increase in the variety of financial instruments offered by banks and other institutions, a diversification in the business activities of financial institutions, and so on. I discuss two key measures, certificates of deposit and national bonds, and the causes that brought them about.

Banks issued certificates of deposit (CDs), large-sum, transferable time-deposit certificates issued at market interest rates, and increased their availability to more depositors in 1979. At first, banks required a minimum deposit of ￥ 500 million for a period of maturity from three to six months.

The banks indicated their desire to introduce CDs in the mid-1970s as private companies began saving their excess money in short-term money markets (the *gensaki* market) thereby reducing their deposits in banks. As a countermeasure, the banks requested approval by the Ministry of Finance to introduce CDs. The MOF ignored their request.

10. James Horne, "Politics and the Japanese Financial System," in J. A. A. Stockwin et al., eds., *Dynamic and Immobilist Politics in Japan* (London: Macmillan Press, 1988), 173.

The situation changed, however, in the late 1970s. By then the government increasingly depended upon procuring funds by issuing national bonds. Until fiscal year (FY) 1974 borrowing was only a marginal source of revenue. The average bond dependency ratio was around 10 percent from FY 1965 to FY 1974. A significant change, however, occurred in the supplementary budget of FY 1975. Tax revenue dropped sharply because of the recession caused by the first oil shock. Consequently, it became necessary to increase the bond dependency ratio from an initial budget level of 9.4 to 25.3 percent. In the initial budgets of FY 1976 and FY 1977, the dependency ratio was still less than 30 percent, at 29.9 percent and 29.6 percent, respectively. But in FY 1978, the dependency ratio broke the 30-percent barrier, reaching 32 percent. In FY 1979, the year in which CDs were introduced, the dependency ratio reached 39.6 percent.[11]

In the same year, the Ohira government admitted that the government had serious fiscal problems, hinted at the introduction of a general consumption tax (a kind of value-added tax), and lost the general election. As a result, the government had to continue to procure revenues by issuing national bonds.[12] Banks had been buying a large portion of such bonds, but on this occasion they rebelled at the demand to continue. Therefore, the Ministry of Finance had little choice but to yield to bank demands to introduce CDs.

The conditions attached to CDs, deposit minimums and periods of maturity, were unchanged for five years after their introduction. During this period, the banks asked the MOF to approve the easing of the conditions under which CDs could be issued, but the ministry refused. It was not until 1984 that the required minimum amount of deposit was lowered to ¥ 300 million from ¥ 500 million, and the banks were permitted to issue CDs up to 75 percent of their equity. After this, the lowering of the minimum sum of deposit and an increase in the percentage of the bank's equity held by CDs continued periodically as the periods of maturity available for CDs diversified.

National bonds also played a role in the decision of 1984. If the 1979 decision to permit banks to issue CDs was caused by the shock of the large-scale issuance of bonds, the 1984 decision was caused by the shock of bonds maturing. The ten-year-maturity national bonds issued in large numbers after 1975 began maturing in 1985, and financial authorities predicted that these bonds would begin appearing in the secondary market in large numbers shortly before that time, as near-maturity bonds. They also

11. Yukio Noguchi, "Public Finance," in Kozo Yamamura and Yasukichi Yasuba, eds., *The Political Economy of Japan:* vol. 1: *The Domestic Transformation* (Stanford: Stanford University Press, 1987), 186–222.

12. Michio Muramatsu and Masaru Mabuchi, "Introducing a New Tax in Japan," in Samuel Kernell, ed., *Parallel Politics: Economic Policymaking in Japan and the United States* (Washington, D.C.: Brookings Institution, 1991), 187–189.

predicted that these would be used by private firms in the same way as fixed-time deposits. Because the interest on these near-maturity bonds exceeded the interest on fixed-time deposits, the money that would have been invested in the time deposits would be invested in the near-maturity bonds instead. To prevent such an occurrence, the banks pressed ever more loudly for an increase in their ability to issue CDs.

During this period the MOF was also studying the possible effects of the maturing bonds on financial markets. According to a Finance Ministry official, "Around 1983, many heated discussions were held about whether near-maturity bonds would be circulated. The majority voiced the opinion that they would not be circulated, but on the other hand, some persons said that 'If they will be circulated, and if they will capture a large share of deposits, we must speed up the deregulation of interest rates.' "[13] In 1983 an optimistic mood still prevailed in the MOF, but the atmosphere within the ministry would change in less than one year.

The MOF could no longer ignore bank demands to ease the conditions for the issuance of CDs because the banks sensed danger in the massive government bond issues. The national bonds were being bought by the syndicate of national bond underwriters, whose major members were the banks. On the one hand, the government was extremely dependent upon the banks for its revenues, whereas, on the other hand, the government was laying the groundwork for the deterioration of the banks' management environment. Under such conditions, the MOF had no choice but to give in to bank demands. In 1984 the conditions for CD issues were eased for the first time in five years.

In 1984 the Yen-Dollar Committee produced its report. The MOF, in response to that report, published its own report entitled "Current Perspectives for the Liberalization and Internationalization of the Financial and Capital Markets"[14] in which it stated that although steady progress has been made in recent years regarding the liberalization of the interest rates on bank deposits, "further liberalization measures will be taken in the future." It is, therefore, possible to recognize foreign pressure behind the easing of regulations on interest rates. Domestic pressures were the primary causes of interest rate liberalization, however, because the massive national bond issues and their maturing occurred independently of any foreign influence.

Another liberalization measure was the easing of regulations concerning the activities in which financial institutions could engage. Here, too,

13. Ebato Tetsuo, *Kasumigaseki no kōbō* [The rise and decline of administrative agencies in Japan] (Tokyo: Chikuma shobō, 1987), 65.

14. For the process and background of the Yen-Dollar Committee, see Tadokoro Masayuki, "Aru gaiatsu no kenkyū" [A case of U.S.-Japanese financial friction], *Himeji hōgaku* 1 (1988): 209–255.

the role played by national bonds was large. The division of activities between banks and securities firms was defined by ARTICLE 65 of the Securities Exchange Law. ART. 65, however, also states that banks may handle transactions of public bonds. This article caught the banks' attention, and the banks promptly applied its provisions to near-maturity bonds so that they could handle them and survive in a financial system characterized by large-scale government bond issues.

The gap between securities firms permitted to handle national bonds and the banks prohibited from doing so would have widened unless the banks resorted to such methods. In January 1980 the securities firms introduced "mid-term national bond funds," which heightened the banks' sense of danger as the high-interest-rate funds immediately became popular. They increased the securities firms' share of the market as they competed with the regular and time deposits of the banks. The banks had been assigned a major share of national bonds, but the all-important handling of the bonds was a monopoly of the securities firms.

If, in addition, the securities firms began offering high-interest instruments that made full use of national bonds, the disparity would become unbearable. To counter this situation, the banks introduced new financial instruments, such as specified-date time deposits with which depositors could, on dates specified by them in advance, withdraw a portion of the amounts deposited without penalty. They were introduced in June 1981. Banks also strengthened their demands to the Ministry of Finance for permission to handle national bonds. This demand by the banks naturally met furious opposition from the securities firms. But, when a new Banking Law was passed in 1981, the banks finally succeeded in working in clauses that permitted them to handle transactions of national bonds. Events moved forward, and from April 1983 banks began handling over-the-counter transactions of long-term national bonds and, after approval in June 1984 to sell midterm national bonds, also began to deal in bonds already circulating in the market.

Reduction of the MOF's Resources

If I were to give the reason for the deregulation of finance in one phrase, it would be "the end of high economic growth." Owing to the high economic growth sustained for nearly twenty years before 1974, most Japanese had become wealthier and diversified the ways excess money was used or invested. But uniform, low-interest rates on banks deposits no longer provided satisfaction.

As the period of high growth came to an end, the government found that it could no longer count on tax revenues to grow automatically, and

Figure 5.2 The percentage of national bonds in the general account budget

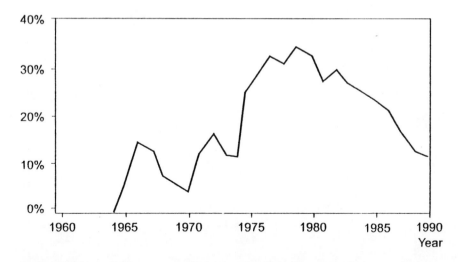

it had to issue bonds in ever-increasing numbers to maintain its existing policies and programs. To persuade more people to invest more in its bonds, the government had to make them more attractive. To decrease its procurement costs, however, the MOF (in particular, the Budget Bureau) tried to hold interest rates on national bonds to a low level. Unfortunately, if it succeeded, the ministry would not be able to reach its procurement goals because few, if any, would invest in such low-interest bonds. This dilemma knocked a hole in the policy of artificially maintaining low interest rates, which had been the linchpin of Japan's financial policy.

Changes in the financial markets would have resulted in the gradual removal of the regulations that blanketed Japan's financial system. When faced with the demands of the market and decreased resources, the MOF, while ignoring many requests from financial institutions, was forced to give ground and supervised the slow easing of regulations.

It is clearly evident in figure 5.2 that after 1975 MOF dependency on bonds increased suddenly. Large volumes of national bonds were purchased by the syndicate of national bond underwriters. As a consequence, the government's finances came to depend heavily on the cooperation of the banks.

The difference between the gross and net budgets in figure 5.3 is the equivalent of the debt-servicing costs. The gross budget and the cost of national bonds increased rapidly after 1975 because the redemption of bonds issued in 1965 began in 1975. This trend continued until the late 1980s when debt-servicing costs increased to 25 percent of the general account budget. Because banks were holding the bulk of this debt, when

Figure 5.3 The Ministry of Finance budget as a percentage of the general account budget

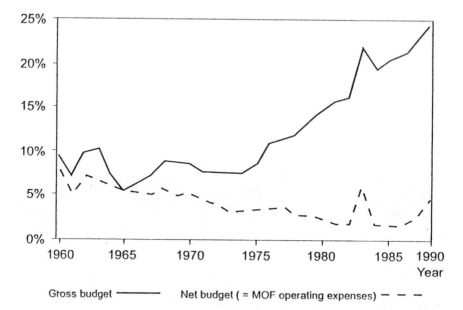

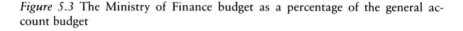

Gross budget ————   Net budget (= MOF operating expenses) — — —

they pressured the MOF for other concessions (especially the right to sell other financial instruments), the ministry was nearly forced to oblige. It had few if any alternatives; revenue demands weakened the ministry's bargaining power.

The MOF's net budget steadily decreased from the 1960s to the mid-1980s. The funds that the Ministry of Finance could use to carry out its own policies amounted to only 2 percent or so of the general account budget during the mid-1980s. Especially after the growth of the general account budget itself came to a halt as a result of the Second Provisional Administrative Reform Commission of the early 1980s, the absolute budget funds of the MOF were more or less frozen at a very low level.

Ironically, although much research has focused on the MOF as the controller of the budget,[15] little if any research has analyzed the budget and the budget making of the MOF itself. What stance does the MOF take when it submits a budget to itself for approval? Is the relationship in that situation the same as the relationship with other ministries when they submit budgets to the MOF? How is the MOF's budget actually used? No one knows. In information available to the public, only such uses of the

15. John C. Campbell, *Contemporary Japanese Budget Politics* (Berkeley: University of California Press, 1977).

budget as "Housing Expenses for Civil Servants" or "Transfer to Special Account for Industrial Investment" can be found. Allocations for the implementation of the MOF's policies seem to be lumped together under the single item "Central Office of Finance Ministry," and the details are unknown. (The single exception is "Foreign Assistance," which is listed separately.) It, therefore, does not seem possible to show, by using actual data, how the reduction of the MOF's budget influenced the ministry's financial policies.

But, because the MOF needs a certain amount of money to carry out its functions, such as inspections of bank activities, budgetary limitations are certain to affect its operations. In some cases already the MOF has not exercised its right to conduct inspections and audits authorized under laws and orders owing to budgetary limitations.[16] One of the reasons why financial institutions obey MOF guidelines is because they fear the ministry's periodic random inspections. Even such punitive actions by the ministry, however, are effective only when it is able to bear the financial cost of implementing them. Although much more information on this point is needed, it is certain that, just like the Ministry of Construction or the Ministry of International Trade and Industry, the Ministry of Finance, when exercising its authority, is forced to work under budget restraints. On the basis of the evidence available, I believe that the MOF's low budget in the 1980s reduced its potential for regulatory control.

During the period of high growth, savings consisted primarily of deposits made by individuals, whereas massive investments made by private corporations used up these savings. During this period the public sector pursued a policy of balanced budgets, and its importance as a net borrower was small.

After the first oil crisis in 1973, however, the flow of money within Japan changed greatly. Private corporations freed themselves from chronic money shortages, and the public sector, through the massive issuance of national bonds, found itself in the midst of severe money shortages. In addition, money left over after the public sector finished borrowing began to flow overseas.

During the period of high economic growth, private corporations made up for their money shortage by borrowing from the banks for capital investments. This practice led to high rates of investment as a proportion of GNP, but it also led to the phenomenon of "overborrowing." Prohibitions against borrowing abroad also fostered overborrowing at home. Overborrowing, in turn, prompted "overloans" by banks, which loaned more money than was prudent because they knew that the Bank of Japan would guarantee such loans.

16. Interview with an official of the Ministry of Finance. Tokyo, June 17, 1990.

The twin phenomena of overborrowing and overloans, together with the policy of artificially low interest rates, formed the basis for the influence exercised by the "MOF-BOJ dynasty"[17] over private banks and corporations. In the case of overloans, not all of the banks that attempted to procure money through market transactions and at interest rates set by the Bank of Japan succeeded in doing so because the financial authorities, not the market, determined who gained resources.

The escape by the private firms from money shortages meant not only a change in the structure of the money flow but a change in the relationship between the financial authorities and the banks. Although the ability of the financial authorities to offer credit had not been reduced absolutely, they had suffered a relative loss of influence. Richer corporations able to borrow abroad, therefore, also contributed to a decline in MOF power.

The change from a bureaucracy-dominated system to a political party-dominated system has been pointed out since the early 1980s.[18] Muramatsu contends that initiative for the formulation of the budget passed from the Budget Bureau to the Policy Affairs Research Council of the Liberal Democratic party. The loss of influence of the MOF in budget formation is a trend that, according to many observers, has been in progress since the mid-1960s.[19] The MOF's reduced role in the budget process also diminished the ministry's general prestige in financial matters.

Foreign Pressure Issues in the MOF

The trade friction between the United States and Japan was, for a long time, something that was happening to somebody else, as far as the MOF was concerned. Trade friction had begun with labor-intensive industries, such as textiles and footwear,[20] and then moved into capital-intensive industries, such as automobiles, steel, and color televisions[21] before focusing on intelligence-intensive industries, such as computers, in the 1980s,[22] industrial areas all under the jurisdiction of the Ministry of International Trade and Industry (MITI). The focus of the trade friction spread beyond

17. Sakakibara Eisuke and Noguchi Yukio, "Ōkurashō-Nichigin ōchō no shūen" [The end of the Ministry of Finance-Bank of Japan dynasty], *Chūō kōron* (August 1977): 96–150.

18. Muramatsu Michio, *Sengo Nihon no kanryōsei* [Postwar Japan's bureaucratic system] (Tokyo: Tōyō keizai shinpōsha, 1981).

19. Mabuchi Masaru, "Zaisei kōchokuka dakai undō no kenkyū" [A study of the movement to break fiscal rigidification], *Handai hōgaku* no. 136 (September 1985): 1–27.

20. I. M. Destler, Haruhiro Fukui, and Hideo Sato, *The Textile Wrangle* (Ithaca: Cornell University Press, 1979).

21. I. M. Destler and Hideo Sato, eds., *Coping with U.S.-Japan Economic Conflicts* (Lexington, Mass.: Lexington Books, 1982).

22. Daniel Okimoto, *Competitive Edge: The Semiconductor Industry in the U.S. and Japan* (Stanford: Stanford University Press, 1985).

the MITI sphere as issues involving biotechnology and public works arose after the late 1970s.[23] Because such issues did not involve the MOF directly, it continued to act as if it were a purely staff-agency with no authority over the business world.

But, from about the time of the Yen-Dollar Committee in 1984, the focus of the trade friction shifted toward macroeconomic policies and away from individual products or sectors. In the latter half of the 1980s the target of foreign pressure switched from the MITI to the MOF. The change in targets also signaled a change in the content of the attacks by foreign countries. Heretofore, disputes had centered on the policies of the Japanese government that aimed to increase the growth of certain industries. Naturally, the relationship between the Japanese government and Japanese industries provoked foreign criticism. However, criticism aimed at the structure of Japanese industry was essentially theoretical. During this period no foreign government demanded actual structural changes. To resolve the finance problem, however, foreign governments, and especially the United States, demanded reforms in Japan's financial system itself. In this sense, the friction between the United States and Japan over Japan's financial system was the first problem involving "structural impediments."

The logic of the U.S. government was simple. The United States had a huge trade deficit with Japan because the yen was undervalued against the dollar. This imbalance was caused by the distorted structure of Japan's financial system, which killed all demand for the yen. If restrictions on transactions using the yen were removed and if the financial markets involving the yen were completely internationalized, the value of the yen would increase until it accurately reflected the fundamentals of the Japanese economy. As countermeasures to such a situation, the United States demanded that the Japanese government remove all restrictions on interest rates involving the yen, abolish all restrictions on transactions in yen bonds by foreign investors, and establish a yen-TB (treasury bill) that would be open to foreigners.

Negotiations between the United States and Japan resulted in the publication of two reports: one in May 1984 by the Yen-Dollar Committee, "Report of the Activities of the Special Meeting to Discuss the Yen-Dollar Rate and Financial-Capital Market Problems," and the other by the MOF, "Current Status and Prospects for Financial Liberalization and Internationalization of Yen." Based on the results in these reports, the MOF agreed to provide foreign banks with trust banking licenses, to eliminate swap limits altogether, to expand the scope of foreign bank dealing in government bonds, and to promote greater flexibility in interbank, foreign exchange, and Euroyen markets. The liberalization of the Euroyen was one

23. Hugh Patrick, ed., *Japan's High Technology Industries* (Tokyo: Tokyo University Press, 1986).

of the most visible results. The Japan Offshore Market was established in 1986 through a partial revision of the Foreign Exchange Law. If private corporations were able to raise money freely by issuing private bonds in the European market, to which the authority of the Japanese government did not extend, the regulated domestic market could be bypassed. The United States believed that Japan would deregulate its domestic market to prevent such a situation from occurring. Because only dealings between foreign parties are approved in the Japan Offshore Market, its influence on the domestic market is indirect. Nevertheless, its establishment had a certain undeniable effect.

How did Japan's financial world respond to such pressure from the United States? In a survey the International Financial Information Center asked, How do you feel about the report of the Yen-Dollar Committee and the response by the Finance Ministry? Most of the respondents felt that the demands of the United States, even if they had been somewhat hastily made, were inevitable, given the changes in the financial environment. Little difference could be seen between the responses by different banking sectors. Notably, most of the regional banks and mutual banks, which according to general belief had little chance of surviving liberalization and internationalization because of their relative lack of competitiveness, responded, "It cannot be helped." One imagines that the regional and mutual banks believed that they would enjoy the merits of deregulation in retail banking. Apparently, they selected a survival strategy, intending to fill in the gaps that would appear as a result of deregulation.

Legalization

A reduction in administrative resources and an increase in foreign pressure stimulated financial deregulation. How did these two forces bring about the legalization of regulations? I suggest that the reduction of resources led to the solidification of authority while foreign pressure led to the clarification of authority thereby promoting the legalization of regulations.

Revisions in Financial Laws

The movement toward legalization can be revealed through a quantitative examination of laws, executive orders, ministry orders, and notifications related to finance.

The convenient way to display the movement toward legalization is to count the number of such actions on a year-to-year basis. But because the

Figure 5.4 Changes in numbers of laws and orders and of notifications

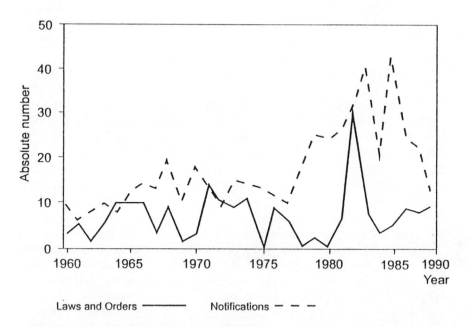

Laws and Orders ———— Notifications — — —

absolute number of laws and executive orders in this case is fairly small, a clear trend cannot be derived. By adding the numbers of laws, executive orders, and ministry orders and computing three-year averages the trend becomes clear (see fig. 5.4).

The number of laws and orders was relatively stable until 1980. After 1980, however, a change is evident. In 1982, approximately twenty laws and orders were handed down, the highest number since the 1960s. Most were ministry orders related to the previous year's revisions in the Banking Law, the first such revision in fifty-five years. The number of laws and orders then decreased for a few years but gradually began to increase again. Although it is not possible to predict future trends, an upward trajectory is indicated.

Notifications, on the other hand, remained steady until the mid-1970s, after which they suddenly increased and peaked in the first half of the 1980s before dropping suddenly again. The sudden increase in the first half of the 1980s can be attributed to the revising of the Banking Law and the effect of the friction over financial issues. It is important to note that after peaking in that period, the number of notifications greatly diminished while, almost as if in contrast, the number of laws and orders began to increase. This fluctuation suggests that the ministry first responded to foreign pressure with more notifications, but, after it determined that the opening of Japan's financial markets was inevitable, it applied the brakes to its traditional methods of administration by notification and switched to governing by more visible legal means.

Revisions in the Banking Law

The old Banking Law was established in 1927. During the next half-century, a few technical revisions in the Company Law and other related laws were made, but no changes were made in the Banking Law until a full-scale revision in 1981. The MOF cited the following changes in the economy and society as the underlying reasons for the major revision: change in the structure of the economy brought about the transition from a high-growth to a slow, steady-growth economy; diversification and increased accessibility of banking activities; large-scale national bond issues; and internationalization problems.

Regarding internationalization, the MOF said, "As the economy internationalizes, progress in the financial system towards internationalization is also great. Japanese banks are expanding overseas, while foreign banks are entering Japan. It is necessary to review the existing guideline-oriented administrative methods and to prepare a more open legal system."[24] Certainly, the MOF responded to the expected demand for internationalization by revising the Banking Law. But given the fact that pressure for internationalization was not critical at the time, it would probably be more correct to interpret the ministry's actions as a reaction to the reduction in its resources.

The solidification of authority becomes apparent when one examines differences in the old and new Banking Laws. The old Banking Law is short; it has only thirty-seven articles. Simplicity is a major reason why the Banking Law was able to survive in the totally different economic environments of the prewar, wartime, and postwar periods. During the prewar and wartime periods, the law functioned with the support of the related National Mobilization Law, the Special Law for Military Finances, and others. In the postwar period, because the Banking Law was simple and left much to interpretation, it was able to survive alongside such laws as the Antimonopoly Law.

This characteristic of the Banking Law also meshed perfectly with the heavy use of notifications and other administrative guidelines used by the MOF to implement its financial policies. The Banking Law functioned only as a broad framework, and the actual administrative actions were carried out through the use of guidelines.

24. Interview with an official of the Ministry of Finance. Tokyo, June 17, 1990.

In comparison, the number of articles in the new Banking Law increased to sixty-six because the administrative regulation is more explicit in the new law and each article is more detailed than those in the old law.[25] Furthermore, the number of articles within the systematic Execution Order was increased from ten to thirty-seven. The objective of the MOF was to solidify its authority by putting it in writing and by codifying it.

One of the issues raised during the revision of the Banking Law was the extent to which the banks should be permitted to handle securities. The initial proposal of the MOF worked to the advantage of the securities firms. The banks opposed this, however, and ultimately a compromise proposal was made. The banks also opposed the MOF's proposal because the new law seemed to give the MOF much more control than the old law. In other words, the banks criticized the proposals regarding the MOF's authority to advise as well as the proposed articles concerning disclosure and the regulations for offering large-scale credit.

In response to the banks' criticism, the MOF offered the following explanation: "The authority to advise was inserted to respond to inquiries from foreign banks regarding the basis of administrative guidance, and for no other purpose. Regarding disclosures, it is fine for disclosures to be made voluntarily, but codifying the requirements is a natural action taken in order to respond to the people's wishes. The article concerning large-scale credit was also merely the codifying of something which had previously been done through administrative guidance. The true intention of the Banking Bureau is to put into writing, as much as possible, that which was performed through administrative guidance in the past, and thereby to reduce the work which is done through administrative guidelines."[26] In the end, the banking industry succeeded in eliminating the articles in question, ARTS. 36 and 37 in the draft, and in inserting a clause in ART. 1, regarding the objective of this law, which paid respect to "the independence of the banks" alongside "the necessity of banking activities to serve the public."

As the power of the MOF weakened, the ministry was forced to give in to the demands of the banking industry. What is more interesting is the

25. See Leon Hollerman, *Japan, Disincorporated: The Economic Liberalization Process* (Stanford: Hoover Institution Press, 1988), chap. 3. Administrative activities formerly conducted through administrative guidance were inserted in the new law as follows: regulations concerning large-scale credit (regulated previously by executive and ministerial orders), regulations relating to foreign banks, regulations regarding branch offices (previously regulated by ministerial orders), and regulations regarding the activities that may be performed by representatives (previously regulated by ministerial orders). The administrative activities codified in greater detail in the new law were standards for examining business licenses, standards for examining mergers and business transfers, standards for granting approval for business closures and liquidations, and the range of business activities permitted.

26. Ōkura Mondo, *Ōkurashō ginkō kyoku* [The Banking Bureau of the Ministry of Finance] (Tokyo: Paru shuppan, 1985), 72.

MOF's explanation that the law was revised to convert what had previously been de facto authority into de jure authority. If such de facto authority had functioned properly in the past, then it was because it was supported by administrative resources of one kind or another. The need to put such de facto authority into writing was caused by none other than the reduction in such resources. The MOF's strategy—to compensate for a loss in its resources by improving the law upon which its authority rests— is an underlying cause of the revisions in the Banking Law.

The Establishment of a Financial Futures Law

The establishment of a Financial Futures Law is one more example of the legalization of regulations. A futures market is a hedge against the risks that will be caused by finance deregulation. In Japan a futures market first emerged in 1985 in connection with transactions involving long-term national bonds. The two laws related to futures were established in 1988 to place such transactions within a legal framework.

It appears that the MOF is attempting to gain control of new financial instruments by setting up a legal system to control the financial futures market. In this case, financial futures are a new corner of the economic world. They offer new business opportunities while simultaneously presenting the MOF with a chance to expand its legal jurisdiction.

The laws relating to financial futures, however, cannot be used as an example of reregulation in the true sense of the word. Trading in futures is a new economic phenomenon and is, therefore, not something that came under the MOF's jurisdiction in the past. It would be more correct to say that regulations concerning futures are "new regulations." Nonetheless, this movement to regulate, through new laws, new markets that emerged as a result of liberalization is the clearest example of the seemingly conflicting trends that have been examined in this chapter.

Deregulation and legalization trends are graphed in figure 5.5. The $O–X$ axis is de facto regulatory activity, and the $O–Y$ axis is de jure regulatory activity. Any given points along the arbitrary circle with O as its center (A and C) are points where the number of regulations is the same. However, point C, which is close to the Y axis, represents a point where the role of the law as a basis for regulations is greater than at point A, which is close to the X axis. According to this diagram, the movement toward deregulation is a shift from A to B. Likewise, the movement toward legalization is a shift from A to C. Deregulation and legalization are, therefore, vectors that are independent from one another. If recent changes in financial pol-

Figure 5.5 Legalization and deregulation

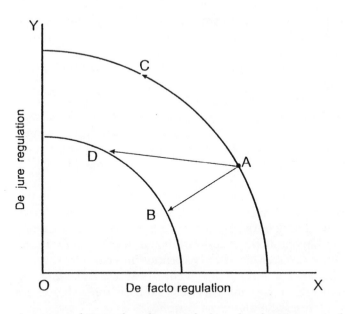

icy are understood as discussed, then the changes as a whole are shown by vector **AD**, which is the sum of vectors **AB** and **AC**.

How universal are the conclusions I have drawn concerning financial policy? More specifically, how reliable is the strategy of maintaining influence over the private sector by legalizing regulations? What implications does the progress of deregulation and legalization of financial policy have for the Japanese state?

Many researchers are debating whether Japan is a strong state or a weak state. According to Samuels, "Jurisdiction is the territory within which authority can be exercised, and control is the exercise of that authority."[27] His argument is that the two yardsticks of jurisdiction and control must be kept foremost when determining whether a state is strong or weak. In a strong state the government's jurisdiction is wide and its control is tight, whereas in a weak state the government's jurisdiction is narrow and its control is loose.

To classify states with two different yardsticks, however, there must be at least four different types of states. Two types of states remain: a state with wide jurisdiction and loose control ("soft state") and a state with narrow jurisdiction and tight control ("hard state"). In a soft state, the

27. Richard Samuels, *The Business of the Japanese State* (Ithaca: Cornell University Press, 1987).

government is present everywhere but is not really serious, and its actions do not have much effect. The government can, therefore, be compared to a diluted solution. The amount of the solution may be large, but the dissolved solute has little effect. In a hard state, on the other hand, the government does not act very often, but when it does, it means business. Like a concentrated solution, the amount of solution may be small, but when applied, the effect of the dissolved substance is great.

When the types of states are categorized by control and jurisdiction, then in most recent research Japan is classified as a soft state. Samuels's "reciprocal consent" and Okimoto's "network state"[28] are typical examples. Rosenbluth's analysis of decision making in this volume regarding financial policy also appears to support the hypothesis that Japan is a soft state.[29]

In the 1990s Japan is in a transitional period from a soft state to a hard state if the observations of Samuels, Okimoto, and Rosenbluth are correct and if a reduction in administrative resources and an increase in external pressure are pushing Japan toward liberalization and internationalization. While the scope of the government's involvement in the economy is gradually narrowing, the powers of the government to enforce its actions regarding the economy are strengthening as the legal basis for such actions increases through solidification and clarification.

28. Daniel Okimoto, *Between MITI and the Market* (Stanford: Stanford University Press, 1989).
29. Rosenbluth, *Financial Politics in Contemporary Japan,* 8–9.

PART THREE

NEGOTIATING
LABOR'S ROLE

ORGANIZED LABOR HAS HAD A CHECKERED HISTORY AS A POLITICAL FORCE in Japan. Before 1945 government policies, police repression, the structure of industry, and the composition of the labor force itself all militated against a strong union movement. Legalization of unions immediately after the war created a radically new environment for labor, which responded with a burst of organizing activity. By the late 1940s nearly half of all eligible workers had joined a union. Their support was indispensable for the opposition parties on the political left. By the early 1950s, however, domestic economic problems, the policies of Allied occupiers, and the cold war all conjoined to reduce the strength of organized labor and the parties that labor supported. Thereafter, strong unions remained in large, private manufacturing concerns and in the public sector, but unions never secured a foothold in small firms or the tertiary sector. Workers in private firms, who usually affiliated with the Democratic Socialist party (DSP), came to adopt a rather accommodating approach to labor relations. Their counterparts in the public sector, most of whom affiliated with the Japan Socialist party (JSP), pursued a far more adversarial approach through public political action.

In Chapter 6 Ikuo Kume advances a highly original explanation for the accommodationist approach of workers in large private-sector firms. He chooses two important industries to make his case. Coal and steel had a long history of government involvement as strategic industries essential to the nation's economic development. When government structured markets to limit competition, labor won its demands by cooperating with managers. Under such conditions managers found it easy to transfer costs to others, either in the form of subsidies or higher prices. When an industry confronted a less regulated and more competitive environment, however, management was often forced to adopt rationalization programs. Workers who challenged management and refused to cooperate under these circumstances often saw wages drop and jobs decline. This was the fate of coalminers. Perhaps learning from their plight, steel workers eventually chose to cooperate with management. In return for enhanced participation and commitment to managerial goals, steel workers eschewed labor activism, joined a crusade for productivity, retained jobs, and won a stable livelihood. Kume argues that such workers consciously chose to cooperate out of self-interest that was rewarded by the play of the market. Private-sector labor accommodation thus emerged in the 1960s and 1970s as workers consciously abandoned their struggle against the system and worked instead to negotiate a place for themselves within the system.

To summarize the crucial implications of Kume's argument, labor's role is the shifting outcome of a continuous process of negotiation in which the state, management, and labor all participate with some measure of equality. For workers, cooperation serves better than confrontation. Labor knows this and pursues its goals accordingly. These claims are particularly striking because they find strong echoes in Chapters 7 and 8, in which Mike Mochizuki and Yutaka Tsujinaka examine public-sector unions and Japan's new peak association for labor, respectively.

Kume's explanation for accommodation in the private sector bears a strong similarity to Mochizuki's analysis of labor in the former public sector. As Mochizuki makes clear, conservative displeasure with labor activism in public enterprises was one motive behind administrative reform and privatization. Converting public monopolies to private firms would force workers to join the private-sector labor movement and breaking up state monopolies would reduce the size and disperse the influence of once-large public unions. Both objectives promised to weaken support for opposition parties. Railway and telecommunications workers responded in ways reminiscent of coalminers and steel workers and with comparable results. Unions that adopted a defiant posture of opposition suffered numerous losses. In contrast, unions that chose to cooperate did so out of the same desire to preserve jobs and enhance wages that drove the steel workers Kume discusses. Cooperation seems to have achieved the economic objectives that charismatic union leaders sought for their members. However, Mochizuki strongly implies that economic gains have been purchased at the expense of a clear commitment to political objectives sought in alliance with the opposition parties.

Yutaka Tsujinaka's assessment in Chapter 8 of Rengō's early influence confirms the trends toward political moderation and economic accommodation that Kume and Mochizuki find in Japan's labor movement. Although the emergence of a single peak association for organized labor is unprecedented in Japan's history, it remains to be seen whether this organization will become a strong political force. Tsujinaka argues vigorously that it already shows many signs of influence. He attributes Rengō's strength to its role as an information node that connects osmotic networks to which labor unions are linked. This capacity to build wide contacts and to create shared visions enhances the influence of Rengō. It also distinguishes Rengō from its predecessors on the Left, especially Sohyo. In Tsujinaka's view, Sohyo's militant socialist line kept it aloof from Japanese society and ensured its exclusion from the corridors of power. Rengō, in contrast, is building deep and broad relationships with many establishment organs in the public and private sector. Such relationships are an analogue on the national level to the kind of joint management councils that Kume identifies in the steel industry and that Mochizuki has uncovered among the newly accommodationist unions in the former public sector.

Throughout the postwar period organized labor has provided essential support for Japan's opposition parties, in the form of votes, organizational resources, finances, and personnel. The fate of the union movement, thus, has a direct bearing on the destiny of a viable political opposition in Japan. The chapters in Part 3 illustrate just how volatile labor's situation is on the brink of the 1990s, and they highlight effectively the critical issues that labor and the opposition face. Can unions and their members loyally cooperate with management to achieve their economic ends and still constitute the base for a viable political opposition? Or will they, by negotiating a secure niche within the system, so compromise their oppositionary principles that they will be wholly co-opted? If organized labor is co-opted, can the Japanese polity sustain a real alternative to the Liberal Democrats' one-party dominance?

CHAPTER SIX

A TALE OF TWIN INDUSTRIES:

LABOR ACCOMMODATION

IN THE PRIVATE SECTOR

Ikuo Kume

THIS IS A TALE OF TWINS IN JAPANESE INDUSTRY: DYING COAL AND prospering steel. Both industries have played an important role in Japanese industrial development. The Japanese government, from time to time since the Meiji Restoration, has tried to support the development of these two industries. In the reconstruction period after 1945, the two industries were major targets of the Priority Production (Keisha Seisan) program and received generous support from the government. They both followed similar paths through the industrial development of Japan until the 1950s.

There the similarity stopped. The coal industry faced a final decision to detach its life-support equipment, whereas the steel industry maintained its competitiveness with those in the United States, Europe, and the newly industrializing states. The labor movement in the Japanese coal industry is often remembered as very radical, sometimes revolutionary, whereas that in steel is regarded as cooperative, sometimes co-opted. These contradictory features reflect a division in the entire Japanese labor movement; despite recent perceptions of Japanese labor as docile, it was very radical in the 1940s and 1950s. To analyze what causes this duality in the Japanese labor movement I examine differences between the alignment of labor, business, and government in coal and steel.

The introduction of mass production technology requires management to incorporate labor in the production system, and this situation gives labor some opportunity for political exchange with management. If the industry in which such labor-management relations emerge is supported by the government, labor and management tend to form a coalition and pursue more benefits from the government. In this situation, labor tends to be militant in its demands and pursues a politics of unproductivity. If the industry becomes privatized, management and labor tend to cooperate in rationalizing their production, and labor tends to keep its demands in line with growth in the industry by pursuing the politics of productivity.[1]

The Politics of Unproductivity: The Japanese Coal Industry

In many countries, labor unions in the coal industry are among the most radical, attributable, perhaps, to their unique work conditions. Clark Kerr and Abraham Siegel argue that coalminers are prone to strike because they "form isolated masses, almost a 'race apart,' . . . [and] all of the members . . . have the same grievances."[2] For some analysts, the Miike strike of 1960 was the most important labor dispute after World War II. Some even see the coalminers' movement as a heroic political struggle. If analyzed in terms of economic activities, however, union movements were based upon rational economic calculations or, sometimes, miscalculations.

Unions act to maximize their economic benefits. Sometimes they demand higher wages from management, and sometimes they cooperate with management to demand support from the government. I argue that, basically, labor and management in the coal industry implicitly formed a kind of coalition against the government and / or its user industries. In this sense, the alignment of labor, management, and the government in this industry is a prototype of that in other industries whose unions and management formed coalitions in the 1960s.

The Japanese coal industry has a long tradition. It has been a leading industry since the Meiji era (1868–1912) and was essential to the industrialization of Japan. Perhaps for this very reason, it was destined for an early death. Coal was a volatile industry, and it changed significantly on two occasions: in the middle of the 1930s and at the end of the 1950s. A new mining technology, longwall face mining, in which a group of miners cooperates as a team, replaced older techniques that used two-man teams in the 1930s. Industrial relations in the industry changed significantly. This new technology eventually destroyed the *naya* (bunkhouse) system, in which owners of the naya managed, as well as exploited, the miners at the workplace for the company. Instead, companies began to regulate miners directly. Labor shortages and increasing demand for coal during the war and postwar reconstruction period, as well as technological change,

1. See Charles S. Maier, *In Search of Stability: Explorations in Historical Political Economy* (Cambridge: Cambridge University Press, 1987), 121–152.
2. Clark Kerr and Abraham Siegel, "The Interindustry Propensity to Strike," in Arnold Kornhauser et al., eds., *Industrial Conflict* (New York: McGraw-Hill, 1954), 189–213.

resulted in yet another alignment among labor, management, and the government. In a word, an implicit, but deformed, coalition of labor, management, and government emerged. However, this coalition began to dissolve at the end of 1950s although labor and management tried to maintain it by demanding political remedies from the government.

The Japanese Coal Industry Takes Off

The Meiji Restoration marked the beginning of modern state building in Japan. "To foster a prosperous nation and strong military" became a principal goal. The Meiji government first planned to establish a strong economy by creating and owning some fundamental industries, such as textiles, steel, and coal. The Mining Industry Law (Nippon Kōhō) of 1873 enabled state ownership and control of coal mines. Nationalization was a defensive action against foreign capital as well as an effort to eliminate competing feudal local powers. However, the Meiji government did not philosophically commit itself to nationalization per se and, relatively soon, it sold most nationalized industries. The coal industry was totally privatized by 1888.

The Japan-China War of 1894 and subsequent economic development propped up demand for coal, and it became a leading industry. In this booming industry, however, labor suffered from terrible working conditions, and miners occasionally rioted. Poor working conditions were a result of the naya system. Under this system, owners of the bunkhouse recruited and organized miners, allocated jobs, and forced them to live in the bunkhouses; in a sense, they regulated miners for the mining companies. They were not just foremen external to the companies. They received wages in place of miners, picked money out of the wages allocated to miners, sold living goods at high prices, and made excessive profits. All in all, the naya system was a perfect system to exploit miners and a useful institution for the mining companies because it lowered the cost of labor management.

Miners' riots and public opinion sympathetic to the miners, however, forced the government to make some effort to alleviate working conditions in mines. The Mining Law of 1892 was a minor, but first, step by the government to protect miners. It set up the regulating agencies of the Mining Police (Kōgyō Keisatsu) and the Office of Supervising Mines (Kōzan Kantokusho). But the owners of the mines were not eager to cooperate with the government at first. It is true that a few mining capitalists were planning to reform the naya system because they wanted to rationalize work by regulating miners directly. The indirect regulation of the naya system had shortcomings. Sometimes bosses were powerful enough to demand a lion's share of the profits from the company. Sometimes the bosses controlled the pace of work to maximize their own profit regardless of the company's plan. These problems posed threats to the mine owners and, thus, led them to try to abolish the naya system.

Hokutan, Hokkaidō Mines and Steamship Company, in 1893 introduced the direct management system as did Yasukawa Keiichirō, an owner of Tagawa Coal Mining Company, in 1899. Their efforts failed[3] because mining was labor intensive and miners were difficult to control. At that time mining was not mechanized. It was usually based upon the cooperation of two miners, one skilled worker and one apprentice. Mining technology was very craftlike, and miners had so much discretion over their work that they were unlikely to follow the company's direct, standardized supervision. Company managers allegedly faced severe problems in controlling miners because the miners had a totally different subculture.[4] In addition, miners tended to move around the country and did not stay at one mine for long. It was, thus, advantageous for the company to delegate recruitment to the naya owners. They remained firmly entrenched throughout the industry until the 1920s.

Incorporation of Labor in the Company System

Stagnation in the coal industry after World War I forced the mining companies to rationalize their production, and mechanization became dominant in most mines by the middle of the 1920s. Mechanization changed the entire mining system and removed the technological bottleneck to the company's direct control of workers. Longwall mining, which used powerful equipment such as the coalpick, was important in that it enabled as well as necessitated direct regulation of labor by the company. Longwall mining demanded the cooperation of a large number of miners rather than a team of two or three. Miners were organized as a group and directed by the management at the worksite. The new technology made mining easier and enabled unskilled miners to work in the mines. Mechanization also reduced the need for craftlike skills, thereby undercutting worker discretion. Mining procedures became standardized, and direct regulation of work became easier. The new technology depended upon certainty of labor input rather than labor flexibility. Thus, the company had every reason to control labor by introducing a direct management system.

To achieve a direct management system, coal mining companies bought up the bunkhouses or closed them by compensating bunkhouse owners. In

---

3. Arisawa Hiromi, ed., *Nihon sangyō 100-nen shi* [One hundred years of Japanese industry] (Tokyo: Nihon keizai shinbunsha, 1965), 185.

4. Yano Makio et al., eds., *Sekitan no kataru Nihon no kindai* [Modern Japan related through the coal industry] (Tokyo: Soshiete, 1978), 150.

their place companies set up new company-run dormitories and housing facilities. Companies employed more married miners, who were expected to be less mobile than unmarried miners, to stabilize the labor supply. Management often tried to build company towns and company-supervised communities by appointing caretakers among the miners to supervise community life and keep social order. By the 1910s at the Mitsui mines and in 1922 at the Hokutan mines the bunkhouse management system was abolished, and a new company-oriented labor force grew up.

During rationalization, many miners were fired, but this was not an attack against labor as a whole. Companies pursued a well-planned elimination of part of the labor force while they incorporated remaining labor into the company system. After World War I many companies introduced some form of management-labor cooperation. Its predecessor, the miners' fraternity, Tomoko Dōmei, was a kind of guild, set up in the Edo period (1600–1868), based upon skills needed in the mines. But as mining technology became more mechanized, this fraternal organization began to lose its power. Coalminers' strikes occurred, and several labor unions were organized in the coal industry, but employers soon started their own efforts to preempt labor movements in the 1920s. They set up labor organizations in their companies to provide miners with some benefits, such as injury compensation. But the major purpose behind these organizations was to make miners cooperate with their companies and to foster good labor-management relationships. In other words, mining companies began to incorporate miners into company systems while they excluded unproductive labor.

The world economic downturn after World War I continued, however, and the Japanese coal industry fell into a deep recession. Stagnation promoted not just rationalization but also cartelization efforts by the coal companies. The companies and the Japanese government wanted to stabilize coal prices by regulating domestic coal production and by limiting imports from Manchuria. In 1931 after a long but ineffective self-regulation effort by the coal companies, the Showa Coal Company was set up to control coal production and imports.[5] In 1940 the Japan Coal Company was established to control coal prices, and the government won the power to allocate productive materials, labor, and money within the coal industry.

This process can be viewed as the beginning of a new alignment of state, capital, and labor in the coal industry. Coal capital succeeded in setting up a stable coalition in which labor was definitely an inferior partner. The inferior status of labor changed as the Japan-China War started, not because of labor efforts but because of the increasing importance of coal

5. Richard J. Samuels, *The Business of the Japanese State: Energy Markets in Comparative and Historical Perspective* (Ithaca: Cornell University Press, 1987), chap. 3.

for wartime production. A coal industry boom amid labor scarcity improved labor's situation although corvée miners were introduced and forced to work under terrible conditions. After 1937, Japanese coalminers began to receive relatively higher wages than workers in most manufacturing industries. Subsequent wartime mobilization further increased the importance of the coal industry and helped maintain this alignment of state, capital, and labor.

Postwar Reconstruction: Labor as a Full Actor

Japan's defeat in the Pacific War resulted in the Allied Occupation. The Supreme Commander for the Allied Powers (SCAP) quickly realized that shortages of coal and steel were the main causes of a downward spiral of production shortfalls. Therefore, SCAP ordered maximum coal production as early as September 1945, and the cabinet also adopted new emergency measures for coal production.[6] In November 1945 the government decided to increase state-controlled coal prices in order to increase coalminers' wages in an effort to solve labor shortages. In June 1946 the government decided to give priority to food distribution and housing construction for miners and subsequently began priority production (keisha seisan) to increase coal and steel output. It established the Reconstruction Finance Bank in 1947 to better finance these industries and set up the Coal Distribution Public Corporation (Haitan Kōdan) in 1947 to purchase, sell, and distribute coal under the direction of the Economic Stabilization Board.

In 1948 state control of coal mines was officially introduced by the first Socialist cabinet under Katayama, although state control was weakened by many compromises in the legislating process. The small and medium-sized companies did not want to have any state control for fear that their inefficient mines would be scrapped to set up rationally planned coal production. In due course they succeeded in transforming the law into a state support system for the coal industry from a system of state ownership.[7] The relationship between the coal industry and the state seems to be very similar to that of the wartime period (1937–1945), but labor's role in it had changed drastically. In the wartime coal production system, Japanese coalminers won relatively better wages, but miners were never full partners in this industry because their autonomous organization was banned in the prewar authoritarian political system. The U.S. occupation and its democratization of society changed their situation, however, and the miners began to organize labor unions.

6. Ibid., 91.
7. Ibid., 102.

In 1946 after a number of union movements at the local level, two national federations of coalminers' unions were set up. Zentan consisted of
workers in large mines with a leftist orientation. Nichikō consisted mainly
of small and medium-sized unions with a reformist orientation. Originally,
both were industrial unions rather than groups of company unions. But in
1947 these two national organizations and the other independent coalminers' unions established a single national center, Tankyo, in order to
achieve equal pay for equal work across the coal industry.[8] This move was
also supported by the coal companies and the government because coal
prices were controlled nationally and it was easy for management to negotiate wages with labor at the national level. Militant union movements,
especially wage strikes, enabled coalminers to earn wages that were consistently 20 percent above those of other workers in manufacturing. The
relationship between labor and management in the coal industry, however,
was not as antagonistic as is often believed. In the 1940s labor and management were on good terms.

During reconstruction coal sold itself because of widespread shortages.
The only concern of management was how to produce as much coal as
possible. Companies preferred stable production to low-cost or low-wage
production, which might result in production disturbances by strikes.
Companies solved a high labor-cost problem by selling coal at a higher
price and transferring their labor costs to the coal users. Coal users, in
turn, received government grants, price differential subsidies, to buy coal.
Thus, government grants subsidized high labor costs. In addition, the coal
industry acquired special government funds (fukkin yūshi). In general,
these were the bases of the labor-management coalition in the early postwar coal industry.[9] Even though the revolutionary demands to control
production advocated by radical union members caused a lot of severe
conflicts, such demands were rather easily met by the system.[10]

This cooperative system was institutionalized in several organizational
forms. Each company set up a Management Council, later a Production
Council, consisting of representatives from union and management. In addition, parallel organizations arose at the national level. In February 1947
labor and management set up a voluntary cooperative organization to increase coal production, the National Council for Reconstructing Coal
Production, issued various demands concerning the well-being of miners.[11]

8. Okazaki Saburo, *Nihon no sangyōbetsu kumiai* [Japan's industrial unions] (Tokyo:
Sōgō rōdō kenkyūjo, 1971).

9. Mitsui kōzan, *Shiryō Miike sōgi* [Documents on the Miike conflicts] (Tokyo: Mitsui
kōzan kabushiki kaisha, 1961), 30.

10. Ibid., 8.

11. Nihon tankō rōdō kumiai, *Tanrō 10-nen shi* [A ten-year history of Tanrō] (Tokyo:
Rōdō junpōsha, 1963), 118.

During this period, management and labor in the coal industry enjoyed enormous economic benefits, thanks to government support. Thus, the alignment of labor, management, and government that appeared in the wartime economy was not destroyed with Japan's defeat. During the post-war reconstruction period, the alignment was actually strengthened, and labor became a more equal partner.

The Declining Coal Industry: The Politics of Unproductivity

The situation changed in 1949 when SCAP forced the Japanese government to adopt a series of strong anti-inflationary policies called the Dodge line. Reconstruction assistance was totally abolished and state control of the coal industry was eliminated in an effort to bring the market mechanism into the coal industry. The ensuing liberalization of the coal industry undermined the cooperative alignment of labor, management, and the government by reducing state support and by stirring conflict between labor and management.

Without government grants, the coal user industries, such as steel, had to pay higher costs by themselves, which made them complain about coal prices. The coal companies responded by rationalizing their production. Conflict arose between the small and medium-sized companies and the large ones because severe competition soon concentrated coal production in the hands of the larger companies. Within only one year of liberalization, the market share of the smaller companies decreased from 29 percent to 26 percent.[12] In March 1951 coal mining associations formed: the Nihon Sekitan Kōgyō Rengōkai for smaller companies and the Nihon Sekitan Kyōkai for the larger ones. Large companies were eager to rationalize their production in a capital-intensive way (for instance, by introducing Kappe mining technology), whereas the small labor-intensive mines were not able to and, instead, tried to decrease labor costs by workforce reductions and wage cutbacks. As a result, in 1949 the unions in the small mining companies started organizing strong strikes against massive dismissal. The main goal for Tankyo's successor, Tanrō, in 1949–1950, however, was not to organize antidismissal strikes but to demand wage increases. Evidently, Tanrō's major concern reflected the interests of miners in large coal companies.

This split exemplified the division in the coal industry. The coal union movement after liberalization changed substantially. During the reconstruction era, coalminers' unions tried to introduce the principle of equal

12. Ōhara shakai mondai kenkyūjo, ed., *Nihon rōdō nenkan* [Yearbook of Japanese labor] (Tokyo: Ōhara shakai mondai kenkyūjo, 1951), 238.

pay for equal work in a movement mainly led by the national center of coal unions. But thereafter, unions began to pursue their individual interests within the company system rather than on an industrywide basis. The labor movement became decentralized, and company unions became the main actors in labor disputes. In other words, unions in the large companies, which were the mainstream of Tanrō, gave up the concept of equal pay for equal work and sought high wages from their own companies. Conflict grew between the large and small company unions, and in 1949 Nichikō, consisting mainly of unions in small companies, left Tanrō. After this departure, the coalminers' movement was mainly led by the unions at large companies.

In the 1950 spring wage negotiation, the first after liberalization, Tanrō demanded an increase of ¥ 730 per day per miner in the standard wage without increasing standard job obligations. Owing to the economic downturn, however, management offered only ¥ 363 coupled with new standard job obligations. Management's offer would actually have reduced the pay per output ratio. After a series of strikes, the unions failed to realize their demands; in several companies, they won no increase in the standard wage. Management had committed itself to a rationalizing effort to deal with the economic downturn and a more competitive market. This might seem to imply that the basically cooperative alignment among labor, management, and the government was dissolving in a new environment. But this negotiation did not yet set a new pattern because the economic boom caused by the Korean War brought enormous benefits to the coal industry. In the fall wage negotiation of 1951, the unions in eight large coal companies, after two forty-eight-hour strikes, gained a wage increase of 20 percent.

Labor unions also succeeded in achieving a substantial wage increase after "the sixty-three-day" strike (called Densan-Tanrō Sōgi) in 1952. The government finally had to mediate the dispute. It authoritatively directed that management should increase wages by 7 percent without increasing standard job obligations and pay a special bonus. This strike is often characterized as a defeat for the union. It is true that union demands were not fully met, and the struggle was stopped by the government order. But it is also true that the unions achieved a substantial wage increase. Therefore, I believe that the alignment among labor, management, and the government still continued.

During this time, large companies began to rationalize production, and in due course they planned to reduce the workforce in order to improve production efficiency. In August 1953 Mitsui Mining Company dismissed 3,464 workers as part of a rationalization plan. Unions at Mitsui immediately organized in strong opposition and mobilized miners' wives and families to keep their solidarity. Eventually, after 113 days of labor disputes, the union succeeded in forcing management to cancel the dismissal of 1,815 workers.

It is crucial to note that large coal companies did not pursue a vigorous program of job reduction and rationalization. This is in contrast with other firms, such as Nissan Motors, where company management strongly committed itself to rationalize its production and drastically strengthened its managerial power following a strike in 1953.[13] This difference is attributable to the strength of the coalminers' union and also to the spoiled "capitalist spirit" of coal company management. As long as costs could be transferred to someone else, coal management did not mind compromising with labor and destroying their own rationalization plans. This tendency can also be found in the relationship between coal firms and government. In 1955 in response to the recession in the coal industry after the Korean War, the Coal Mining Rationalization Special Measures Law was passed. The Coal Mining Rationalizing Public Corporation was set up to purchase a number of inefficient mines and to restrict the opening of new ones. The second postwar boom and the Suez crisis of 1956, however, stimulated domestic coal demand. Coal firms, faced with this opportunity, chose not to use profits to streamline production. Instead, they expanded production to take advantage of government subsidies and to reap handsome short-term profits.[14] They definitely lacked a long-term strategy, probably because market competition among coal companies was not high. Thus, the basic alignment among labor, management, and government persisted into the mid-1950s.

Coal itself, however, began to lose its competitive edge against oil in the late 1950s. In 1957 many people began to realize that the decline of the coal industry was inevitable. But labor unions still tried to achieve high wage increases while opposing management's rationalization efforts. Coal companies still tried to pass labor costs to their customers and the government. They also succeeded in having the government maintain import restrictions on foreign fuel and in winning reductions on interest payments for government loans.

In the famous Miike strike (1959–1960) management finally committed itself to rationalization. In 1959 Mitsui Mining Company announced the layoff of 5,000 workers, but the union immediately refused to cooperate in choosing volunteers for early retirement. Management dismissed 1,277 workers, including 300 union activists, and a ten-month, fierce struggle began. Nikkeiren mobilized business nationwide while Sohyo mobilized labor support. Financially exhausted and politically defeated, in

13. Ōkochi Kazuo and Matsuo Hiroshi, *Nihon rōdō kumiai monogatari: Sengo hen* [The story of Japanese labor unions: The postwar segment] (Tokyo: Chikuma shobō, 1973), 136–139.

14. Samuels, *Business of the Japanese State,* 111.

the end the union accepted the original layoff plan.[15] The coalminers' unions lost their biggest struggle against management after World War II. In the wake of this loss and faced with oil import liberalization coming in 1963 Tanrō drastically changed its strategy and began to lobby for the LDP government to introduce an industrial policy for the coal industry in a tactic called the Policy Transformation Movement. At this point unions realized it was necessary to restore their cooperation with management in order to lobby the government. Union leaders did not mind naming this new strategy "avec struggle," or a struggle with management. They demanded policies to protect the domestic coal industry against foreign competitors, such as a heavy tariff on oil imports, price supports, and public finance to rationalize industry. The unions actively lobbied the government and the LDP, in cooperation with management, by sending many miners to Tokyo to put pressure on the government. Although some policy demands were met by the government, the unions' main demand, to secure employment within the coal industry, was not achieved.

The coal industry was dying, and no one could stop it. Several policies, however, were introduced to alleviate unemployment. The most important was the active labor market policy, which contributed to Japan's low unemployment rates. The government set up a new system to facilitate labor mobility and to decrease unemployment with retraining programs, an active job placement service, and subsidies for employers of some categories of unemployed workers (miners), and so forth. The coal industry almost died, but the union's final efforts cushioned the worst consequences for their members and left an active labor market policy as a legacy.[16]

The Politics of Productivity: The Japanese Steel Industry

The steel industry has been indispensable to industrial development in every country. In Japan, steel has been called "rice for industries." After the postwar reconstruction period, labor was very active in getting as many economic benefits as possible from companies while management was on the defensive. Management, however, gradually began to recognize the need to reorganize its production system and did so. Labor unions opposed this move and resorted to strikes. In return for the introduction of some participatory mechanisms, such as company production committees,

15. Peter Katzenstein, "Japan, Switzerland of the Far East?" in Takashi Inoguchi and Daniel I. Okimoto, eds., *The Political Economy of Japan*, vol. 2: *The Changing International Context* (Stanford: Stanford University Press, 1988), 290.

16. Ōta Kaoru, *Shuntō no shūen* [The end of *shuntō*] (Tokyo: Chūō keizaisha, 1975), 122–123.

the unions finally acquiesced. This deal, coupled with a boom in the steel industry, led to the emergence of productivity politics whereby the union cooperated with management in rationalizing production in return for growth dividends.

Prewar Development

Iron making in Japan has a long tradition, but it was in the Meiji period that the Japanese iron and steel industry started using modern technology. The Japanese state played an important role in establishing the iron and steel industry by creating national steel mills. At the turn of the century, the Japanese government built the Yahata Mill, Japan's first large, modern, integrated steel facility. Until World War I began, the Yahata Mill's share of domestic iron and steel production was 70 percent and 80 percent, respectively. Increasing demand caused by the war, as well as the Steel Industry Encouragement Law of 1916, initiated many private steel firms. In 1917 more than two hundred private steel companies existed. However, the recession after the war forced twenty-two of these companies to close by 1922. Indian steel then began to compete with Japanese, which forced steel company management and the government to adopt efforts to rationalize and stabilize the steel industry.

First, management made every effort to rationalize and modernize production facilities. In due course, they fired workers and reduced labor costs while introducing new technology. The result was the biggest steel workers' strike before World War II in the Yahata Mill in 1919; fifteen thousand workers participated. After the strike, supervisors organized to represent workers and to incorporate them into the firm.

Second, the import of iron from India caused complex changes within the industry. The integrated steelmakers, which produced iron as well as steel, demanded a higher tariff on Indian iron, whereas the steel companies, which only had open hearth furnaces, welcomed cheap Indian pig iron. The integrated steelmakers and ironmakers organized a Cooperative of Ironmakers and demanded that the government set a higher tariff on iron and steel imports. The tariff on steel, which was welcomed by both iron- and steelmakers, was elevated from time to time, but no tariff on iron was introduced until 1932.

Third, the government tried to create one national champion for the steel company by merging most steelmakers in a move advocated by the Research Council on Steel set up by the Ministry of Agriculture and Commerce in 1924. But the private companies, especially steelmakers of the zaibatsu, opposed this plan and stopped it. In 1930 when the depression struck the Japanese economy, the government again advocated a merger between private and national steel firms, but it failed. As the depression posed more severe problems for these companies, the Japan Steel Corporation (Nittetsu) was formed by merging Yahata with the six largest private steel companies in 1933. The government held a 70 percent share in the new firm. Even then, however, several large private firms, such as Nippon kōkan, did not join the merger because the market activated again by the Manchurian War gave them enough opportunity to earn a profit outside. The subsequent Japan-China War further increased demand for steel, and the steel companies, both national and private, built new facilities and expanded production.

Growth peaked in 1938 when the Japanese steel industry was faced with a shortage of raw materials, especially scrap iron. The United States totally banned the export of scrap to Japan in 1940 in response to the Japanese invasion of China. The Japanese government responded by undertaking more and more intervention with the Act of Steel Business in 1937, the establishment of the Steel Control Council, and the Decree of Steel Rationing in 1938. In 1941 just before the Pacific War, the government assumed full operational control over the industry for the duration of the war.

Postwar Reconstruction and the Incorporation of Labor

World War II was devastating for the steel industry. In 1943, 35 blast furnaces and 208 open hearth furnaces were working. By 1946, only 3 blast furnaces and 22 open hearth furnaces were in operation. In addition, the general headquarters of the Allied Occupation (GHQ) originally planned to seize three-fourths of Japanese steel facilities for war reparations. Thus, prospects for the Japanese steel industry just after the war were extremely dim.

The start of the cold war helped the Japanese steel industry by changing American policy from destroying the Japanese economy to reconstructing it. In 1948 the reparation plan was finally abandoned by the GHQ. Meanwhile, in 1946, the government started priority production (keisha seisan), in which steel as well as coal was given special priority to use capital and raw materials. The steel industry also received low-interest credit from the Reconstruction Finance Corporation (Hukkō Kin'yū Kōko), which helped steelmakers to restart their businesses smoothly. Steel, like coal, was in absolute demand, so it sold itself. As the government introduced price subsidies (kakakusa hōkyūkin), management increased wages at labor's demand. Under this system, steelworkers won relatively better wages than workers in other industries. Their wage increases were never automatic; they were achieved through aggressive negotiations and strikes. This basic relationship was institutionalized in the National Council for Reconstructing the Steel Industry (Tekkō fukkō kaigi) in 1948, and iron production increased from 648,000 metric tons in 1946 to 2,093,000 metric tons in 1948.

This system collapsed in 1949, however, as the Dodge line's anti-inflationary policy was introduced. The government still maintained some financial assistance for the steel industry, but abolished the price subsidy for steel. Consequently, steel prices for users went up, and steelmakers were pressured to lower steel prices.[17] In addition, GHQ, in 1950, ordered the Japan Steel Corporation (Nittetsu) divided into four separate firms: Yahata Steel, Fuji Steel, Nittetsu Steamship, and Harima Firebrick, all fully private. These changes drastically increased market competition in the steel industry and required firms to rationalize.

The main rationalizing effort was the introduction of new technology and plant modernization based on it. In the 1950s steel firms used the most advanced basic oxygen furnace (BOF), an Austrian invention that reduced unit costs 20–40 percent in older open-hearth furnaces.[18] This rationalizing effort was supported by the government with government loans, import protection, and a tax exemption policy. The Japanese government implemented two rationalizing programs: the first, in 1951–1955, emphasized capital investment for plant modernization and the second, in 1955–1960, investment for new plant construction. As a result, the Japanese steel industry became highly competitive in the world market by the 1960s. In 1957, the unit production cost of ordinary steel in Japan was 121 percent of that in the United States; by 1960 it was only 71 percent. Japanese steel firms reaped substantial benefits from the government policies of the 1950s.[19]

Workers in the steel industry were deeply affected by these changes. Just after World War II labor unions were actively organized in many plants. In 1946 a national organization of steel workers, Zentetsurō, was organized. But the steelworkers' unions were faced with severe conflict between the Right and Left wings of the labor movement, and in due course Zentetsurō dissolved. In 1951 after the Communist wing lost its power to the Red Purge, the Federation of Japan Steel Industry Unions (Tekkō rōren) was established.

In the postwar reconstruction period unions demanded higher wages and sometimes tried to control production itself by eroding managerial prerogatives. During priority production unions achieved wage increases

17. For example, machine makers criticized steel makers for high steel prices. See Shin Nihon Seitetsu, comp., *Honō to tomo ni: Yahata seitetsu kabushiki kaisha* [In the cauldron: Yahata Steel Company] (Tokyo: Shin Nihon seitetsu kabushiki kaisha, 1981), 14.

18. Thomas Howell et al., eds., *Steel and the State: Government Intervention and Steel's Structural Crisis* (Boulder, Colo.: Westview Press, 1988), 198.

19. Yamakawa Hideki, "Tekkōgyō" [The steel industry], in Komiya Ryūtarō et al., eds., *Nihon no sangyō seisaku* [Japanese industrial policy] (Tokyo: Tōkyō daigaku shuppankai, 1984), 255–276.

with relative ease because management could transfer labor costs to the government. But after the Dodge line was implemented, unions went on the defensive, fighting against management labor cost cuts and rationalization. Management's exit from the National Council for Reconstructing the Steel Industry can be seen as the symbolic move denoting labor and management divisions.

New labor-management relations were also established after the war at the company level. At Yahata the union was active in demanding wage increases after World War II but also faced a management offensive after the Dodge line. In 1949 management tried to introduce a new wage system of efficiency pay. The union opposed it by arguing that average wages would be cut and struck in 1950. The strike resulted in a 40-percent production cut in iron and a 10-percent cut in rolled steel production. In addition, because it occurred just before the establishment of the new Yahata Steel Company, management was more vulnerable to the strike than it otherwise would have been. Management, thus, made some concessions to the union in a pattern similar to that in the coal industry in the 1950s.

In the steel industry, however, management was more determined to take the lead in labor-management relations. In 1952 after the Tekkō rōren national strategy, the Yahata union demanded wage increases based upon a living stipend increase and undertook a series of strikes. But this time management replied with a lockout and made no concessions. The union eventually gave up its original demands and returned to work after achieving some increase in bonus payments.

In 1957 Tekkō rōren demanded another wage increase and organized an industrywide struggle. Workers struck for thirteen days in eleven incidents. Again, management offered no increase in wages because of an economic downturn and fear of industrywide centralized negotiation. The Yahata union thus changed its goal from a regular wage increase to an ad hoc bonus increase and made a deal with management. These strikes caused serious economic damage to the steel industry, but management held to its line and rejected the unions' demands. This position contrasted with that of management in the coal industry in the 1950s because steel management was very determined. Management did not deny every benefit to workers but offered a bonus increase, which permitted the company flexibility in labor-cost management while it prevented the union from being regarded as a complete loser. After these events, labor-management relations gradually became more cooperative. In addition, the union achieved improved arrangements at the firm level. In 1947 as a result of postwar democratization, the traditional differentiation of status within a firm was abolished, and a new egalitarian personnel system was introduced. Under this new system, however, management found it very difficult to motivate workers because the new system had few promotion mechanisms. Consequently, management tried to set up a new rational job classification in 1953. In this system, shopfloor workers, who had been employed on a daily basis, were given regular employee status. In 1962 supervisors, who had started as shopfloor workers, became nonunionized and began to assume managerial responsibilities. Shopfloor workers could now expect to climb career ladders as high as the plant manager rank. In the same year a partial job-oriented wage was introduced amid the generally seniority-oriented wage system. These changes homogenized steelworkers.[20] The changes were necessary because the introduction of a new production technology rendered obsolete the abilities of former skilled workers and required totally new skills in all workers.[21]

During these changes the union raised some opposition, especially against the nonunionization of supervisors. Faced with the union's opposition, management agreed to some demands and, for example, abolished traditional job classifications and incorporated shopfloor workers into regularized worker positions with monthly salaries. The most important concession was the establishment of a labor-management consultation system. In 1951 a Production Council was set up at the company level. It enabled labor and management to discuss issues such as production plans, rationalization programs, and working conditions. In 1962, in return for the nonunionization of supervisors, management agreed to set up the Shopfloor Production Council.

During the latter half of the reconstruction period the union could not achieve all that it wanted because of management's hard-line policy. But the union did receive economic benefits in the form of a bonus increase and reasonable wage increases, and it achieved some participation in management decisions. In a sense, the union succeeded in transforming the company system into a more employee-oriented one[22] as a result of a "political exchange" between management and the union.[23] This fact has often been ignored and, consequently, many observers have claimed that steel managers co-opted steelworkers. The role of labor should not be overlooked in this incorporation process. Within the steelworkers' movement two factions, one radical and one economic, competed with each

20. David Gordon, Richard Edwards, and Michael Reich, *Segmented Work, Divided Workers: The Historical Transformation of Labor in the United States* (Cambridge: Cambridge University Press, 1982).

21. Mainichi shinbunsha, ed., *Shōgen: Kōdō seichōki no Nihon* [Witness to Japan during the period of rapid growth], 2 vols. (Tokyo: Mainichi shinbunsha, 1984), 2:221.

22. See Masahiko Aoki, *Information, Incentives, and Bargaining in the Japanese Economy* (Cambridge: Cambridge University Press, 1988); Aoki, *The Cooperative Game Theory of the Firm* (Oxford: Clarendon Press, 1984); and Itami Noriyuki, *Jinponshugi kigyō* [Personnel-oriented enterprises] (Tokyo: Chikuma shobō, 1987).

23. Hiroshi Komatsu, who was in charge of labor-management relations at Yahata Steel during the 1950s, has said that without labor's cooperation it would have been impossible to introduce the new personnel management system. See Mainichi shinbunsha, *Shōgen*, 2:221.

other in the 1940s and 1950s.[24] During the political exchange with management, the economic faction cooperated with management and attacked the radicals. Leaders of "economic unionism" and management both had their own reasons for attacking the radical faction, to wit, securing union leadership for the former and achieving domestication of labor for the latter. This was the political basis for the accommodation of labor and management, on one hand, and for the exclusion of the radical faction, on the other.[25]

The Politics of Productivity and Its Transformation

After the incorporation of labor, industrial relations in the steel industry became apolitical. The severe labor dispute in 1957 gave both management and labor incentives to settle wage negotiations without strikes. The ensuing wage-negotiation pattern is proudly called *ippatsu kaitō* (one-shot response). In it management offers as high a wage increase as possible, and the union takes it at once.[26] Labor and management share a wage increase calculus based upon "rational" evaluation, rather than bargaining with bluff and tactical maneuvering. This does not mean that labor and management do not negotiate; instead, both regard wage negotiation as a process to distribute economic benefits among the agencies of the firm.[27]

This perception is found in the union's declaration. In 1968 Tekkō rōren adopted the principle of trade unionism. The union advocated the need to focus on increasing economic benefits within the existing capitalist system, and it criticized the union movement as a class struggle. Furthermore, the union admitted the need for the continuous rationalization of production, which had been a hot issue between management and labor until the 1960s. Thus, the union's own goal became enhancing economic benefits through rationalized production.

The continuous growth of the Japanese steel industry made the union movement in this industry possible because a positive-sum game arose. From 1960 to 1975 Japanese gross crude steel capacity grew from 28 million metric tons to 140 million metric tons. Many people argue that government intervention in the 1960s, as well as in the 1950s, played an important role in steel industry growth in Japan. But the fact that government predictions of steel output have been systematically lower than

24. For example, in union elections at the Yahata mill in the 1950s radical and economic factions won in turn. See *Honō to tomo ni*.

25. Takanashi Akira, *Shōgen: Sengo rōdō undō shi* [Witness to postwar labor history] (Tokyo: Tōyō keizai shinpōsha, 1985), 298.

26. Mainichi shinbunsha, *Shōgen*, vol. 2.

27. Aoki, *Information, Incentives, and Bargaining*.

what was really produced casts some doubt upon the thesis of government omnipotence. Recently, in an excellent economic study of the industrial policy of steel Yamakawa has persuasively shown that government intervention in the 1960s under the Third Rationalization program did not have the intended effect.[28] In this program the Ministry of International Trade and Industry (MITI) tried to control production investment and price fluctuation. MITI feared that excessive production capacity would result in excessive competition and damage the steel industry as a whole.

First, MITI introduced a system to control production investment, relying on a self-regulation mechanism. A company that planned to enlarge its production facility under this system reported its plan to MITI, and the Deliberation Committee on Industrial Rationalization checked it to prevent excessive competition. When the committee found the plan inadequately competitive, it advised the company to change it. MITI, however, did not have any sanctioning power; it could only ask for self-regulation. As shown in the study, despite this system, steel companies could invest as much as they wanted.

Second, MITI also tried to stabilize steel prices. In 1950 governmental steel price controls were abolished. They were replaced with a private price stabilization effort. The two leading companies, Yahata and Fuji, tried to set steel prices following some formula of correct production cost plus a fair profit. Late-starters, such as Kawasaki, Sumitomo, and Kobe, however, did not follow their lead and competed against the leading companies with lower prices. In the recession of 1958, MITI introduced the Public Sale system (Kōkai Hanbaisei). It required companies to set prices without discounting and it was based upon the famous administrative guidance (*gyōsei shidō*). From 1958 to 1961 the system worked relatively well. But, again, severe competition among steel companies, which resulted in discounting during the recession, broke down the system.

The steel industry in the 1960s was not only growing it was becoming more privatized and market oriented than in the 1940s and the 1950s.[29] Companies were more competitive among themselves. Late-starters such as Kawasaki and Sumitomo were notoriously aggressive in the market, and from time to time they defied MITI's intentions. Competition among companies definitely influenced union strategy in the 1960s. If a union in one company used aggressive tactics and disturbed its own company production too much, the union itself paid the price in decreasing company profits. In addition, the fact that the union in Kawasaki Steel was not affiliated with Tekkō rōren increased the vulnerability, or sensitivity, of the unions to market competition among companies.

28. Yamakawa, "Tekkōgyō," 255–276.
29. In a personal communication Kitayama Toshiya has noted that government intervention in Japan is the result of harsh competition in industry. Despite government attempts to control competition, it has vigorously persisted.

Following this line of strategy, the steelworkers' federation formally set up the Industrial Policy Committee in 1970. In 1971 it established a labor-management consultation meeting of five major steelmakers to express union demands and interests at the industry level. In 1972 the steelworkers' federation formulated the "Demands for a Long-term Vision of the Steel Industry." After consulting with management, it handed this proposal to the government. "Demands" is based upon a view of the steel industry that is similar to that of the steelmakers. It can be seen as an outcome at the industry level of the kinds of proposals developed by production committees at the company level. After the oil crisis of 1973, when faced with a severe recession in the industry, the steelworkers became more active in demanding policies such as increasing public spending, permitting cartels, and so forth, to alleviate the problems in steel. The steelworkers' federation, cooperating with other private-sector unions, succeeded in making the government establish some policies for structurally depressed industries.[30] At the company level, too, the union actively negotiated with management to adjust the production system to the new situation.

Cooperative labor-management accommodation, built up during the 1960s and the early 1970s, faced new challenges thereafter. It has not broken down, but strengthened. Labor and management in the steel industry cooperated with each other in further rationalizing production. Together they began to demand public policies to help the steel industry from a government faced with an economic downturn. They also struggled against international competition, especially from the developing countries.[31] After the mid-1970s, labor put priority upon employment, rather than maximization of short-term economic gain, and cooperated with management. For instance, in the thirty-fifth semi-institutionalized meeting between management and labor of the five large integrated steel companies held in 1988, the topic was how to keep employment high and maintain the international competitiveness of Japanese steel.[32] In 1981 management and labor in electric furnace companies organized a negotiating forum with the government.[33] In 1984 labor and management in the steel industry demanded an increase in subsidies from the Ministry of Labor to maintain employment.[34] Labor-management accommodation continued into the 1980s. In contrast with the coal industry, workers and managers in steel cooperated to sustain the industry itself and employment within it.

30. Ikuo Kume, "Changing Relations among the Government, Labor, and Business in Japan after the Oil Crises," *International Organization* 42 (1988): 659–689.
31. Chiba Toshio, "Tekkō sangyō no kōzō kaizen to kongo no kadai" [Structural reform in the steel industry and future problems], *Tekkō shinbun*, September 20, 1989.
32. *Tekkō shinbun*, August 4, 1988.
33. *Nikkei sangyō shinbun*, May 27, 1981.
34. *Nikkei sangyō shinbun*, March 13, 1984.

A Comparison: Coal and Steel

The coal and steel industries share some similarities and differences. In both industries as technological change progressed, labor was incorporated in one way or another. The introduction of longwall coal mining required management to incorporate labor into the production system to stabilize labor inputs. The result was a management-labor coalition although labor originally was an inferior partner. As modern steel technology, such as BOF, was introduced after World War II, management incorporated labor into the production system by establishing a new personnel system, which homogenized labor. When the personnel system changed, a "political exchange" with management secured some institutionalized mechanisms for labor that influenced the production process. In a word, technological development produced one condition for a cooperative relationship between management and labor.

The importance of these two industries to the national economy gave them the leverage to acquire substantial support from the government. A general lack of resources forced both industries to rely on state support, and the many government benefits they received from the beginning were maintained after World War II to reconstruct the economy. The impact upon labor-management relations was substantial. Management accepted labor's demands in order to stabilize labor input because costs could be transferred to the government or to the user industries under this system. Labor was relatively free from restraints and demanded higher wages and better working conditions. This relationship was nurtured by postwar democratization, which strengthened labor's position and made it a full actor in the political economy. What had been an implicit coalition became, with labor's increasing power, an explicit coalition.

Contrary to the general perception, coalminers' unions mostly adopted a material-oriented approach (economism) rather than a revolutionary class-struggle strategy.[35] The result was somewhat similar to that of the "First Industrial Divide,"[36] in which American labor and business formed a coalition based upon the politics of productivity. But the unions in the Japanese system did not conform to market competition discipline. They aggressively pursued as many economic benefits as possible, challenged managerial prerogatives, and strongly opposed rationalizing efforts. Steelworkers' unions in the 1940s and the 1950s struck aggressively to achieve higher wages and also challenged management efforts to rationalize, although to a lesser degree than did the coalminers. State support and a lack

35. Union leaders at the national level often complained about the economism at the company level. See, for example, Nihon tankō rōdō kumiai, *Tanrō 10-nen shi.*
36. Charles Sabel and Michael Piorre, *Second Industrial Divide: Possibilities for Prosperity* (New York: Basic Books, 1984).

of market competition in these industries were the conditions necessary for labor to pursue economic benefits aggressively, and for management to accept labor's demands relatively easily—the politics of unproductivity.

In the late 1950s both industries became privatized and vulnerable to market competition. From this point onward, the twins followed different paths. In the 1950s the liberalization of the coal industry from state control and subsequent market competition required coal companies to adjust industrially. They began efforts to rationalize production by introducing more mechanization and by demanding assistance from the government. But both management and labor were relatively slow to change. Labor sought to maximize short-term economic gains and aggressively opposed rationalizing efforts. Management did not take rationalization seriously and also sought short-term economic benefits by demanding government support and by exploiting market fluctuations. Thus, the basic relation between labor and management in the coal industry continued. The Korean War boom and the Jinmu boom at first glance seemed to prove the effectiveness of their strategy. The on-going decline of the coal industry after 1957, however, forced management to commit fully to rationalization. Labor failed to recognize that it could not continue to embrace economism until its dramatic defeat in the strike of 1960.

In the steel industry management began to rationalize efforts earlier and with more seriousness than in the coal industry. The unions at first opposed rationalizing efforts, but unlike coal management, steel executives strongly committed to rationalization. The degree of competition in the steel industry was higher and state intervention lower than in the coal industry. Kawasaki Steel's decision to build a new integrated steel mill in Chiba while defying the government in 1950 indicates how cutthroat the competition was.[37] In the 1960s as competition increased and the value of state support decreased more privatization occurred. As management found it more difficult to transfer labor costs to the government or to users, it deepened its commitment to rationalization. Labor was quick to adopt a new strategy, cooperate with management rationalization efforts, and demand its fair share of benefits. At the company level, unions at Yahata and Kawasaki adopted this strategy in the late 1950s.[38] At the national level, Tekkō rōren explicitly admitted the necessity of rationalization and adopted this approach in 1966.[39] A higher degree of competition in the steel industry and increasing productivity enabled labor and management to choose the "politics of productivity." The difference between the twins in adopting a rationalization strategy seems to be attributable to

37. Arisawa, *Nihon sangyō 100-nen shi*, 384.
38. *Honō to tomo ni*, 76–80.
39. Tekkō sangyō rōdō kumiai rengōkai, *Tekkō rōren undō shi* [A movement history of the steelworkers' federation] (Tokyo: Tekkō sangyō rōdō kumiai rengōkai, 1981), 177.

a different level of market competition, which was much higher in the steel than in the coal industry despite their similar industrial structures.

What happened in these two industries when they encountered hard times in the 1960s and 1970s? In the coal industry, after the defeat of Miike, labor changed its strategy and cooperated with management to demand government support. The crisis caused by unproductivity in the coal industry finally cemented an explicit coalition between labor and management. Both actively participated in the policy-making process to protect the industry as a whole. As coal lost its strategic importance in the national economy, however, the government lost its incentives to support the industry. To maintain social harmony the government responded to labor's demands by introducing some political remedies for unemployment in accordance with an active labor market policy.

In the steel industry, the depression struck in the 1970s after the first oil crisis. The unions and management cooperated actively to demand help from the government. The government, recognizing the importance of steel, responded with several policies, such as Measures for Structurally Depressed Industries. But, probably because of pressures to open the Japanese economy imposed by the U.S. and European countries, the state limited protection of the steel industry, and competition persisted, especially from the developing countries. Competition continued to drive cooperative management and labor rationalization efforts well into the 1980s.

Technological change contributes to the formation of labor-management coalitions. Japan's role as a late-starter gave the coal and steel industries incentives to seek government support, and the importance of the industries to the national economy forced the government to respond. Under this system of state-aided production without severe intercompany competition, management could easily compromise with labor and maintain a basically cooperative relationship because labor costs could be transferred to the government or to users. Labor could achieve relatively higher wages and boycott many rationalizing programs. Consequently, a semi-cooperative alignment among labor, management, and government arose, and labor achieved its benefits by using a very active and militant strategy. Increasing intercompany competition, however, changed the alignment. Usually, challengers do not like government support because it tends to maintain the status quo and to protect the leading companies. Therefore, challengers promote privatization of industries and force management and labor to recognize the implications of severe competition. At this point, management commits itself to rationalization, and labor, carefully calculating its benefits, often cooperates.

The dual image of Japanese labor as both docile and militant is related to the development of this alignment among labor, management, and government. In the 1940s and 1950s the "politics of unproductivity" was prevalent. It leaves the impression of an aggressive labor movement. The "politics of productivity" caused by the increasing privatization of Japanese industries fosters an image of a docile labor movement in Japan. But as I have argued, the docile labor movement resulted from a political exchange between labor and management that grew out of the "politics of unproductivity." Japanese labor in the private sector is not co-opted by capital. Rather, private-sector labor has succeeded in forming a coalition with management based upon the "politics of productivity." Labor joined that coalition willingly with the intention of achieving its own interests.

CHAPTER SEVEN

PUBLIC SECTOR LABOR AND THE PRIVATIZATION CHALLENGE: THE RAILWAY AND TELECOMMUNICATIONS UNIONS

Mike Mochizuki

THE JAPANESE LABOR MOVEMENT IN THE POSTWAR ERA PRESENTS A SHARP contrast between private and public sectors. After the tumultuous late 1940s and early 1950s, private-sector unions evolved toward economic unionism, and labor-management relations became basically cooperative. The public-sector unions, however, continued to espouse political unionism, and industrial relations remained highly conflictual. The reasons for this divergence are not difficult to find. Public-sector workers did not enjoy organizational rights comparable to those in the private sector. They expended much of their energy trying to regain the right to strike that was denied in 1948. They pressed their case in the Diet, in the courts, in various government commissions, and in the International Labour Organisation (ILO) without much success. Frustrated by the lack of progress, workers in this sector resorted to militant tactics that resulted in a vicious cycle of illegal strikes and dismissals. Moreover, the limited autonomy that public-sector management had in setting wages contributed to the politicization of labor relations. Because wage settlements were contingent upon government and Diet approval, collective bargaining was more a political conflict than economic negotiations.

The public-private asymmetry in the labor movement had important political consequences for the Left. This division in the labor movement provided the social basis for the split between the Democratic Socialist (DSP) and the Japan Socialist parties (JSP). It was no accident that private-sector unions formed the core of the pro-DSP Dōmei labor federation and that the public-sector workers tended to affiliate with the pro-JSP Sohyo federation. The conflictual issues in the public sector caused sharp divisions among public workers themselves. In many public enterprises and in the civil service "second unions" formed that espoused a more moderate line and cooperation with management authorities. Moreover, a number of the more militant "first unions" were plagued by internal factionalism. In short, the politicization of labor relations in the public sector not only obstructed the organizational unity of the labor movement but also exacerbated the fragmentation of the opposition political camp.

The inability of public workers to restore their right to strike should not imply that unions failed completely in pressing their interests in organizational rights. The government ratified the ILO Convention no. 87 in 1964 and repealed the restrictions on union membership eligibility for public workers that clearly violated the freedom of association principle. Public-sector unions also negotiated joint consultation agreements with management authorities regarding the introduction of new technology and rationalization efforts that occurred after the late 1950s.

There were also gains on the wage front. During the early 1950s the government refused to implement the wage recommendations of the Public Corporation and National Enterprise Labor Relations (PCNELR) Commission. But in 1957 the government began to respect the commission's arbitration awards. In 1964 Prime Minister Ikeda Hayato confirmed the government's commitment to pay comparability between the public and private sectors during his meeting with Ohta Kaoru, then secretary-general of Sohyo. After 1971, the payroll budget system was gradually relaxed so that authorities would have greater flexibility in negotiating wages. During the 1970s, also, "hidden arrangements" were developed to give public enterprise workers supplemental benefits such as falsified travel expenses (*karashutchō*) and overtime (*karachōkin*). Managers in the public enterprises illegally manipulated financial loopholes to get union cooperation for various rationalization programs.[1]

This uneasy accommodation between unions and management within a framework of intense political conflict provided one of the critical contexts for the administrative reform campaign of the 1980s. The reform movement was spearheaded by the Second Provisional Commission on Administrative Reform (Rinchō), which was chaired by the austere but highly respected business leader Dokō Toshio. Indeed, one of the implicit objectives of the neoconservative reformers was to end the public-private asymmetry by transforming the public-sector labor movement to resemble the "cooperative" big business unions. While the administrative reform campaign was getting underway, the electoral resurgence of the Liberal Democratic party (LDP) and the alarming decline in trade union membership posed a crisis for the Left. Labor leaders responded with a re-

1. Kazutoshi Koshiro, "Labor Relations in Public Enterprises," in Taishiro Shirai, ed., *Contemporary Industrial Relations in Japan* (Madison: University of Wisconsin Press, 1983), 289.

newed push for labor unity and groped for a more realistic strategy. And so administrative reform, which was primarily motivated by a desire to resolve the fiscal crisis without a tax increase, became inextricably intertwined with the labor movement's quest for unity and a new strategy.

In November 1987 Japanese labor took a major step toward unification by forming Rengō (Zen Nihon Minkan Rōdō Kumiai Rengōkai, the Japanese Private Sector Trade Union Confederation). Consisting of 62 industrial and other unions, Rengō boasted a membership of about 5.55 million workers and comprised about 45 percent of the unionized work force. The privatization of Nippon Telephone and Telegraph (NTT) and the Japan National Railway (JNR) contributed immensely to this development. Zendentsu (Japan Telecommunication Workers Union), which represents almost all NTT workers, and Tetsudōrōren (Japan Confederation of Railway Workers Unions), which organizes a majority of workers in the new Japan Railway (JR) firms, were important components of the Rengō movement. Two years later, Sohyo disbanded, and its major public-sector unions joined the private-sector unions in Rengō to form the New Rengō (Shin Rengō). New Rengō encompasses about 65 percent of unionized workers; it is the largest labor federation in Japanese history.

I examine change in the labor movement and industrial relations in two public corporations: the Japan National Railway and the Nippon Telephone and Telegraph. Both JNR and NTT experienced major changes in enterprise structure, management policies, and labor relations because of administrative reform (including privatization and deregulation) as well as shifts in market conditions. And unions in both sectors generally became less militant and labor-management relations more cooperative. Despite these similarities, the two public enterprises differed regarding the role that unions played in shaping the reform process, the attitudes and policies of unions toward reform, and the reform outcomes in both the configuration of labor organization and the character of labor-management relations.

Zendentsu at an early stage participated actively in informal discussions about NTT privatization in order to protect and promote the interests of its members. By pursuing a cooperative strategy, the union succeeded in establishing a joint Management Council based on labor-management equality to shape NTT policies on new technology, the development of new services, and other future business plans. The union also won shorter working hours and higher wages for NTT workers while preventing any dismissals of redundant employees. During the privatization process Zendentsu avoided organizational splits and adroitly managed its internal differences. About 99.6 percent of NTT workers belong to the union.

The experience of JNR reform could not be more different. Union involvement in the deliberative stage of reform was minimal and perfunctory. Except for the promanagement Tetsurō, the railway workers' unions resisted radical reform that would break up and privatize JNR. When reform became imminent, Dōrō, the militant union of locomotive engineers, completely reversed its position and decided to cooperate with privatization. The largest union, Kokurō, became mired in internal conflict and finally split. Although those who cooperated with the reforms managed to find employment in comparable positions in privatized JR firms, the unionists who resisted faced discrimination. The work force was reduced dramatically, and labor-management relations in the 1990s still have not normalized.

I analyze the privatization process for JNR and NTT to delineate the general transformation of public-sector labor organization in the context of administrative reform and to explain differences in both process and outcomes across these two enterprises. I use the following variables and hypotheses to explain the cross-enterprise variation: the economic status of the public enterprise, the organizational characteristics of labor unions in the sectors, and political factors such as state policies and linkages with political parties.

Japan National Railway

The Context of JNR Reform

The story of JNR reform with respect to labor begins in 1971 with the launching of the productivity movement known as Marusei Undō. Faced with a rapidly increasing deficit, management and the "second union," Tetsurō, promoted this rationalization campaign. Overzealous JNR managers and Tetsurō activists used the movement to expand the moderate union's membership. They offered promotions and wage increases to entice them away from the militant Kokurō. Needless to say, relations among employees became tense. As its membership declined by more than 18 percent in eighteen months, Kokurō appealed to the PCNELR Commission, charging the railway authorities with unfair labor practices. Of the more than thirty complaints filed, the PCNELR Commission ruled completely in Kokurō's favor in two cases. Even the mass media came out against Marusei Undō. The JNR president was forced to apologize in public, and many of the JNR managers who implemented the campaign at the worksite level were removed and/or transferred.

In the wake of this victory, Kokurō and the radical Dōrō gained the upper hand and began to exert their influence at the shopfloor level through a system of worksite conferences (*genba kyōgi*). According to one of the key architects of this strategy, the idea of the conferences was to promote meaningful labor participation in management from below.[2] Management consultation with labor, however, was not new. In 1958 JNR had established prior consultation mechanisms with unions for labor programs, transfer and retraining, and the abolition and/or retrenchment of worksites. In 1962 further agreements had been reached regarding employment stabilization and rationalization.[3] But after the JNR's embarrassing defeat, Kokurō and Dōrō unionists in many instances used the worksite conferences to harass supervisory personnel with political questions and to paralyze staff organization. Although the conferences were in principle to be held once a month for two hours, in some locations, as many as fifty conferences were held per year with some lasting five to seven hours. Some supervisors even committed suicide because of the pressure. Labor discipline began to decline, and the practice of falsified allowances, unauthorized time offs, and idle work became prevalent. But to prevent an explosion of labor conflict at the shopfloor level, JNR management bent over backward to please Kokurō.[4]

Kokurō leaders also used intraunion factionalism to get lenient policies from JNR authorities. Kokurō divided into three groups in the 1950s: the Mindō faction, the pro-Communist party Kakudō faction, and the Shakaishugi Kyōkai (the Socialism Association) faction affiliated with the left wing of the JSP. Because the union leadership tended to be dominated by the *relatively* moderate Mindō faction, Kokurō officers induced JNR managers to be accommodative to prevent the rise of the more radical Kakudō group.

Confident about their power and misled by a member of the Miki cabinet who claimed that the government was likely to grant public workers the right to strike on a conditional basis, Kokurō and Dōrō along with other public sector and transportation unions launched a ten-day strike for the "right to strike" in 1975. Not only did the strike fail to apply the necessary pressure to change government policy regarding strikes but the mass media and the public became less sympathetic toward the unions. The misguided strike, however, did not move JNR management away from its accommodative labor policy. As the JNR fiscal situation worsened, the authorities needed union consent for their 1980 Management Improvement Plan, which included a personnel cut of seventy-four

2. Interviews with Hosoi Shoichi, April 13 and May 17, 1988, in Tokyo.
3. Koshiro, "Labor Relations," 274.
4. Ōno Mitsumoto, *Kokutetsu o utta kanryōtachi* [The bureaucrats who sold JNR] (Tokyo: Yoshimoto sha, 1986); and Sankei shinbun kokutetsu shuzaihan, *Kokutetsu no ichiban nagai hi* [JNR's longest day] (Tokyo: PHP kenkyūjo, 1987), 132–138. The JNR ideology of industrial familialism (*kokutetsu ikka*, or "one railroad family") helped to legitimize this system of labor-management relations. See Paul H. Noguchi, *Delayed Departures, Overdue Arrivals: Industrial Familialism and the Japanese National Railways* (Honolulu: University of Hawaii Press, 1990).

thousand. It is widely suspected that JNR secretly offered to retract the ¥ 20.2 billion damage suit against the unions for the illegal strike in exchange for labor cooperation on rationalization.

Labor Participation in the Reform Process

The driving force behind the policy to break up and privatize JNR was a coalition of Rinchō members (especially those from academics, business, and journalism) and three JNR officials who were critical of the half-hearted reform efforts of the past. As early as July 1981 when the Rinchō deliberations were just beginning, the mid-level JNR executives (known as the "gang of three") decided to cooperate with the Rinchō process in defiance of their superiors. Although they were not yet willing to embrace the drastic solution of breakup and privatization, they firmly believed that JNR reconstruction demanded the restoration of labor discipline. For them, the JNR crisis was more than a financial problem; it was a labor problem.

Rinchō and the gang of three worked closely with the JNR Reform Subcommittee of the LDP chaired by Mitsuzuka Hiroshi to overcome party resistance. The proreformers in JNR provided Rinchō and the Mitsuzuka Subcommittee with internal documents revealing the deterioration of worker discipline. They helped to arrange unannounced site visits and surveys of supervisory personnel for members of the LDP subcommittee. Meanwhile, journalist Yayama Tarō, a member of the Rinchō division dealing with public corporations, published a series of influential articles revealing the labor relations problem in JNR. Steadily, the mass media turned against Kokurō.

In July 1982 Rinchō released its third report in which it explicitly recommended JNR breakup and privatization, a policy far more sweeping than the 1980 Management Improvement Plan. In June 1983 a JNR Reconstruction Supervisory Committee (JNR-RSC) was established as a deliberative council to develop a concrete reform program. Fourteen months later, the JNR-RSC formally backed the breakup/privatization plan. By this time, the Mitsuzuka Subcommittee in the LDP was also coming around to this position. As a government consensus for radical reform was forming, the JNR top officials made a feeble attempt to resist it by calling for privatization without a clear commitment for a breakup of JNR. After both Prime Minister Nakasone and the chairman of the JNR-RSC expressed their displeasure, the JNR president and seven other top officers resigned their posts. They were replaced by officers clearly committed to the Rinchō line. In October 1985 the Nakasone cabinet formally approved the outline for JNR reform, and the implementing legislation passed the Diet in November 1986.

As Kusano Atsushi argues in his excellent book on JNR reform, although labor was definitely a target of the reformers, the unions were peripheral in shaping the final policy.[5] Initially, Kokurō and Dōrō were relatively complacent that radical reform would be blocked by the top JNR officials and the LDP transportation policy specialists (*zoku*) who brokered JNR contracts to constituents. To the extent that they supported reform, the unions indicated their willingness to cooperate with the 1980 JNR Management Reform Plan, which spelled out personnel cuts of seventy-four thousand by 1985. But they opposed a fundamental change in JNR organization, resisted a reassessment of the worksite conferences, and defended the free railway passes for employees. By contrast, Tetsurō actively called for an improvement of worker discipline, and Dōmei representatives in Rinchō supported the reform cause. Even so, the promanagement labor organizations played primarily a cheerleading role. The five-member JNR-RSC did not have anyone from labor.

Union Responses to JNR Reform

One of the most dramatic moves in the reform process was the turnaround of the "demon Dōrō" (*oni no Dōrō*) led by the New Left radical Matsuzaki Akira. As sweeping JNR reform appeared inevitable, Matsuzaki in one brilliant stroke led his union in January 1986 to join Tetsurō and the small Zenshirō in concluding a Labor-Management Joint Declaration. According to the declaration, the unions agreed to cooperate with management to encourage transfers and voluntary retirements, to forego illegal strikes, and to secure employment. In August 1986 they signed another declaration supporting the JNR breakup and privatization, promising restraint about strikes even after privatization, and announcing their willingness to drop all lawsuits against JNR. Matsuzaki's explanation for this switch is that he wanted to preserve jobs for his union members. After the debacle of the 1975 strike, demand for freight train transport declined dramatically. Given the change in the transportation industry, Matsuzaki believed that the only viable course to save JNR was to cooperate with the reforms.[6] What is amazing is that the policy reversal of Dōrō took place with only a minor split. A pro-Communist group broke off to form Zendōrō, but in the 1990s it has less than fourteen hundred members. It appears that Matsuzaki's tight grip over the rank-and-file based on both charisma and shrewdness made the turnaround possible.

The response of Kokurō was more problematical. After the LDP's stunning electoral victory and the JSP's shocking defeat in July 1986, Sohyo

5. Kusano Atsushi, *Kokutetsu kaikaku* [JNR reform] (Tokyo: Chūō kōron sha, 1989).
6. Interview with Matsuzaki Akira, April 15, 1988, in Tokyo.

began to pressure Kokurō to moderate its opposition to the JNR breakup and privatization and to concentrate on securing employment. By the fall, Kokurō president, Yamazaki Shunichi, tried to lay the groundwork for a shift to a cooperative line. Union activists at the shopfloor level, however, resisted this move and forced a formal vote in an emergency convention. Yamazaki's proposal to conclude a joint labor-management declaration was soundly defeated by a 183–101 vote. Yamazaki's Mindō faction leadership was then replaced by a coalition of the Kakudō and Shakai-shugi Kyōkai factions.

Explanations for Kokurō's response differ. Those who interpret the reform process as a union-busting scheme argue that the JNR authorities responded hostilely when Kokurō began to show flexibility. They deliberately proposed conditions for the conclusion of a joint declaration that the Kokurō activists could not possibly accept, such as withdrawing the complaints of unfair labor practices before the various labor commissions. If Kokurō refused to sign the agreement, then the authorities could justify discriminating against Kokurō members for reemployment in the privatized JR firms.[7] Others claim that Rinchō recognized from the beginning that successful reform was not possible with the support of only Tetsurō. Consequently, commission members approached *both* Dōro and Kokurō behind the scenes to get their cooperation. Although Matsuzaki of Dōro was responsive, Kokurō leaders showed no interest.[8] The explanation for Kokurō's recalcitrance, therefore, lies not with the authorities' hostility toward the union but with the attitudes and structure of the union itself.

The failure of Kokurō to reach an accommodation with JNR had dire consequences for the organization. Its membership dropped sharply from about 187,000 in June 1985 to about 110,000 in November 1986. In February 1987 those supporting the defeated Yamazaki line seceded from Kokurō and formed Tetsusanrō (Japan Railway Industry Workers Union). The new union then concluded a joint declaration with management and decided to cooperate with the reforms. By the time JNR was privatized in April 1987, Kokurō was down to only 44,000 members.

Outcome of the Reform Process

The 1990s union configuration comprises three major unions representing workers in the JR companies. Tetsurō, Dōro, and a couple of small

7. Tateyama Manabu, *JR no hikari to kage* [The light and shadows of JR] (Tokyo: Iwanami shoten, 1989), 120–122; and Onomichi Hiroshi, *Kore ga Rengō da!* [This is Rengō!] (Tokyo: Yoshimoto sha, 1987), 180–181.
8. Interview with Katō Hiroshi, chairman of the Fourth Division of Rinchō, which dealt with public corporations, May 2, 1988, in Tokyo.

Table 7.1. Railway union memberships, April 1988

Labor Union	Number of Members	Percentage of Total
Tetsudōrōren	132,265	67.4
Kokurō	33,575	17.1
Tetsusanrō	24,822	12.7
Other unions	2,404	1.2
Unaffiliated	3,089	1.6
TOTAL	196,155	100.0

unions coalesced in July 1986 to form Tetsudōrōren. Tetsusanrō still refuses Tetsudōrōren's overtures for unification although both belong to Rengō and both pursue a policy of labor-management cooperation. Kokurō survives as the second largest union. As of April 1988, the membership figures and percentages of the JR unions were as they appear in table 7.1. The JNR-RSC had drawn up a plan that projected the status of JNR employees in April 1987. The expected disposition of former JNR employees is delineated in table 7.2. The actual status of those employees on April 1, 1987, is given in table 7.3. Remarkably, almost twice as many elected to retire voluntarily than the reform plan projected. Critics of

Table 7.2. Projected status of former Japan National Railway employees, April 1987

Projected status	Number
To be employed in new railway firms	215,000
Voluntary retirements	20,000
To be assigned to Liquidation Enterprise	41,000
TOTAL	276,000

Table 7.3. Actual status of former Japan National Railway employees, April 1, 1987

Actual status	Number
Employed in new railway firms	200,650
Voluntary retirements	39,090
Employed in public sector	7,230
Regular retirements	6,390
Assigned to Liquidation Enterprise	23,660
TOTAL	277,020

privatization attribute this to the deterioration of worker morale caused by the anti-Kokurō campaign. But there was also a financial incentive. Each voluntary retiree received on average an allowance of about ¥ 12 million (the equivalent of ten months' full salary plus ¥ 2 million).

If the complete destruction of Kokurō was one of the hidden objectives of the reformers, they did not succeed. Because of the high number of voluntary retirements, most of the Kokurō unionists seeking employment in the new JR firms were hired. Only about five thousand of them were sent to the Liquidation Enterprise for retraining. Nevertheless, there have been many instances of discrimination against Kokurō members. Some have been given jobs that do not fit their skill levels, whereas others have been assigned to tasks unrelated to actual railway operations, such as manning noodle and confectionery stands. JR managers have even pressured employees in positions of responsibility to quit Kokurō. The union has responded by filing more than 180 complaints to the various labor commissions. Thus far, in four cases, the commissions have ruled totally in favor of the workers. About eighty railway employees have committed suicide largely because of cross-pressures about union affiliation.[9]

While Kokurō continues its struggle after privatization, Tetsudōrōren appears to be quite positive about the future. Matsuzaki, who is now chairman of the latter union for JR East, says that his ambition is to make the company the number one railway firm in the world. He wants to strengthen labor participation in the JR Management Council along the lines of West Germany's codetermination system. He hopes that the firm will prosper enough to offer stock options to workers in two years and substantial bonuses in five years.[10] Matsuzaki's journey from revolutionary Marxism (Kakumaru) to this form of "enlightened capitalism" symbolizes the dramatic transformation of the labor movement in the national railways.

Nippon Telephone and Telegraph

The Context of NTT Privatization

The labor movement among workers in Nippon Telephone and Telegraph has been much more cohesive than that in the national railway. Only one union has represented the telecommunications workers, and

9. Tateyama, *JR no hikari to kage*, 110–111, 131–135; and Onomichi, *Kore ga Rengō da!*, 188.

10. Interview with Matsuzaki Akira, April 15, 1988, in Tokyo.

Zendentsu now encompasses more than 99 percent of NTT's nonmanagerial employees.[11] By the early 1960s the Zendentsu leadership had skillfully purged the union of pro-Communist cadres. They did not follow Kokurō's practice (in JNR) of maintaining a balance between the anti-Communist Mindō and the pro-Communist Kakudō factions. When a small group affiliated with the radical Socialism Association of the JSP appeared within union ranks during the early 1970s, the leaders moved quickly to purge them from the organization. Compared to Kokurō, then, the executive leadership in Zendentsu enjoyed much greater autonomy and control over the union membership.

Given the rapid pace of technological innovation in the telecommunications sector, NTT executives stressed the need for good labor-management relations. Unlike their counterparts in JNR, they did not antagonize workers by launching a union-busting rationalization scheme like Marusei Undō. They instead chose to enlist union cooperation for rationalization programs through a mechanism of prior consultations (*jizen kyōgi sei*), which was first instituted during the 1950s. Zendentsu successfully persuaded management to promise not to dismiss employees or reduce the work force. NTT also committed itself to improving working conditions as rationalization progressed. Over time, the union achieved the shortest work hours and work week (thirty-seven hours per week) in the public sector.[12] In return, during the second half of the 1960s, NTT management was able to implement job transfers for 123,200 employees—about one-third of the work force.[13]

This tradition of cooperative industrial relations, however, did not mean that Zendentsu was any less militant than Kokurō in trying to secure the right to strike. In 1965, some 160,000 union members were disciplined for striking for the right to strike and wage increases. Zendentsu countered by initiating a massive lawsuit against the management. In 1974 the union staged an eight-day walkout. And one year later, Zendentsu was even more aggressive than the JNR unions during the coordinated ten-day strike for the right to strike. Whereas the Kokurō leadership wanted to stop the campaign midway after sensing defeat, the Zendentsu executives insisted on following through with the full strike plan. As in JNR, the union and managers in NTT engaged in a game of suits and countersuits regarding the dismissals and disciplinary actions that followed these work stoppages.

11. Technically, five other unions were representing NTT workers, but their memberships were so small that for all intents and purposes, NTT was a single-union enterprise.
12. "Information on Japan Telecommunications Workers' Union: Zendentsū" (Tokyo: Zendentsū, 1986), 35–37.
13. Kusahara Mitsuaki and Yamanaka Toshihiro, "NTT," in Makino Tomio, ed., *Nihon-teki rōshi kankei no henbō* [The transfiguration of Japanese-style labor-management relations] (Tokyo: Ōtsuki shoten, 1991), 210.

Although NTT was not plagued by staggering deficits like the national railways, it did suffer from low productivity in part because of the deals that had been worked out between Zendentsu and NTT management. In 1984 an NTT worker produced only ¥ 14.8 million for his company, compared to ¥ 40 million and ¥ 20 million per worker in the Japan Steel Corporation and private railroads, respectively. According to government auditors, the public corporation had about one hundred thousand redundant employees. During the Rinchō deliberations Dokō Toshio and other key commission members became concerned that NTT under these circumstances would not be able to compete effectively with foreign corporations like American Telephone and Telegraph as the telecommunications sector became more internationalized. They feared that without dramatic reform, NTT could go the way of JNR and burden the national treasury with debts.[14]

By spring 1982 the Rinchō subcommittee dealing with public corporations came around to supporting the privatization and breakup of NTT. The Ministry of Posts and Telecommunications and the telecommunications lobby in the LDP pressured Rinchō members against recommending such a radical course, but their appeals proved to be ineffective. In its July 1982 report Rinchō formally recommended the transformation of NTT into a special corporation with government-held shares under private management. The commission noted that despite the use of modern equipment and the implementation of direct dialing, personnel costs had increased, which, in turn, reduced NTT earnings. It also stated that NTT's working hours were shorter than those of large private corporations, and its labor-management agreements and work practices obstructed the rationalization of its management.[15]

Labor Participation in the Reform Process

During the formal Rinchō deliberations in 1981–1982, Zendentsu joined LDP and JSP politicians in opposing the radical restructuring plan (privatization, breakup, and work force reductions) proposed by commission members. Indeed, the union was gearing up for an intense mass struggle to block the reforms. But soon after the release of Rinchō's July 1982

14. Chalmers Johnson, "MITI, MPT, and the Telecom Wars: How Japan Makes Policy for High Technology," in Chalmers Johnson, Laura D'Andrea Tyson, and John Zysman, eds., *Politics and Productivity* (Cambridge, Mass.: Ballinger, 1989), 215–216.

15. Rinji gyōsei chōsakai OB kai, ed., *Rinchō to gyōkaku* [The SPCAR and administrative reform] (Tokyo: Bunshinsha, 1983), 343–344; and Katō Hiroshi and Sandō Yōichi, *Saisei no kōzu: Kokutetsu, Denden, Senbai* [The plan for rebirth: The railway, communications, and salt and tobacco monopolies] (Tokyo: Tōyō keizai shinpōsha, 1983), 154–157.

report, the union under Yamagishi Akira's leadership shifted gears and embraced the idea of privatization—even while NTT managers were still debating the merits of Rinchō's recommendations. One of the primary reasons for this abrupt turnaround was Yamagishi's frustration with the wage system in public corporations. He wanted to liberate the telecommunications workers from the low-wage schedule that linked NTT workers with employees of the deficit-ridden national railway. He felt that the current arrangement was unfair because NTT, unlike JNR, was a profit-making enterprise. Yamagishi calculated that privatization could raise NTT wages up to private-sector levels.[16]

Yamagishi also wanted to prevent the worst possible outcome: a breakup of NTT into regional companies that would effectively fragment Zendentsu into separate enterprise unions. Rather than assuming the complacent, uncompromising stance of Kokurō, he shrewdly decided to cooperate with the reform movement to engineer the best possible outcome for his union. Recognizing the limits of JSP parliamentary influence, the president of Zendentsu approached LDP leaders such as Kanemaru Shin (then chairman of the LDP Executive Council) and Tanaka Rokusuke (then LDP secretary-general) directly. In the end Kanemaru worked to amend the NTT reform legislation so as to put off the plan to divide the company. To apply pressure on the LDP, Zendentsu launched a petition campaign and succeeded in collecting more than ten million signatures. At a minimum, Yamagishi demanded that NTT workers gain the right to strike, that NTT managers and workers acquire the authority to make decisions independent of the state, and that conditions for fair competition be established.[17]

While Yamagishi promoted the interests of workers, reform-minded bureaucrats in the Ministry of Posts and Telecommunications (MPT) moved to overcome LDP resistance. MPT officials saw privatization as a way to increase their power over NTT management. With NTT as a private company, the ministry, rather than NTT executives, would be able to set telephone rates, establish product standards and certification procedures, and oversee telecommunications research. They argued that a privatized NTT would be freer to contribute funds to LDP politicians. Moreover, the sale of NTT stock would provide large amounts of money to cover a significant portion of the state budget deficit. These points were enough to convince the telecommunications lobby in the ruling party to end their obstructionist tactics.[18]

After the Diet approved the reform bills in December 1984, Zendentsu negotiated with NTT management for a new system of labor-management

16. Kikuchi Hisashi, *NTT rieki sammyaku* [NTT profit summits] (Tokyo: Kodansha, 1987), 46–47.
17. Kusahara and Yamanaka, "NTT," 212–213.
18. Johnson, "MITI, MPT, and the Telecom Wars," 217–218.

cooperation. The union was concerned that after privatization, employees would lose the protection of existing laws that proscribed layoffs, certain kinds of job transfers, and wage cuts. Zendentsu's leadership wanted to ensure that previous "social contracts" would remain operative by establishing a mechanism for worker participation in management. After a protracted bargaining process, the union and management agreed to create a Management Council (Kei'ei Kyōgikai) comprised of fourteen managerial and thirteen union representatives. The purpose of the council is to discuss all major management plans before they are formally considered by NTT directors and Zendentsu officers.[19]

Outcome of the Reform Process

In April 1985 NTT ended its status as a public enterprise and became a joint stock corporation. Three releases of stock took place between 1986 and 1988, and in 1992 a little more than one-third of the shares belong to private investors. Although NTT lost its monopoly over the telephone business, it still faces only minor competition from three long-distance carriers that together account for just 0.3 percent of total NTT sales. There are now more than 850 firms in the telecommunications sector, including those providing value-added networks (VANs), but NTT commands about 97 percent of the market. Because NTT gained the freedom to invest in other sectors, the company has created more than 170 subsidiaries employing former NTT workers in such businesses as health clubs and flower shops as well as high-technology fields.

On the whole, the outcome of privatization has been positive for Zendentsu and its members. The union has become the leading force for consolidating the labor movement, and Yamagishi was elected in November 1989 as the first chairman of the New Rengō, which encompasses both private- and public-sector unions. NTT employees continue to enjoy short working hours, and wages have caught up with those in the most profitable private firms. From 1986 through 1990 Zendentsu won larger pay increases for its members than unions in other major corporations. The one blemish in the union's postprivatization wage-hike campaigns is that despite the relatively large increases, pay scales have not kept up with per-person increases in NTT sales figures. With privatization, NTT employees acquired the right to strike on the condition that they give prior warning of more than ten days. Because NTT is legally considered a public-interest

19. Zenkoku denki tsūshin rōdō kumiai, ed., *Zendentsū rōdō undō shi: Kōsha seido kaikaku tōsō* [A history of the Zendentsū labor movement: The public company system reform struggle] (Tokyo: Zendentsū rōdō kumiai, 1988), 609–691.

enterprise (*kōeki jigyō*), however, the prime minister can still use an emergency order to stop a strike for a fifty-day period. In 1990 Zendentsu did exercise its right to strike by calling an 8.5-hour work stoppage—the first strike since 1978. As a result, NTT employees received a base-wage increase of 6.37 percent, compared with the average of 5.94 in other large enterprises.[20]

Despite the large number of redundant workers, no one has been laid off after the reforms because work force reductions have taken place only through voluntary retirements. At the time of privatization, NTT had 303,951 employees. By the end of fiscal year 1989 the number of workers had dropped to 266,017. According to the midterm management plan released in 1990, NTT wants to cut employment by another 36,000 by 1995. Zendentsu has agreed to cooperate with this plan under the understanding that there will be no forced layoffs and that new subsidiary companies will be created where workers can find jobs.[21]

From the perspective of the neoconservative reformers, however, NTT privatization has been a disappointment. The slow pace of internal restructuring has obstructed technological innovation, lowered the quality of service, and raised consumer costs. Consequently, members of the latest incarnation of the administrative reform commission are again pushing for a breakup of NTT into several regional corporations. This radical plan has won the support of LDP leader Mitsuzuka, the politician who guided the JNR reform plan through the ruling party. And in early March 1990 the Telecommunications Business Council, an advisory panel for MPT, recommended a more moderate division of NTT into two enterprises: one for local service, the other for long-distance service.

Zendentsu, of course, vehemently opposes any form of partition. Since the LDP lost control of the upper house of the Diet in July 1989, Zendentsu, through the JSP, should be able to block legislation calling for a breakup of NTT. Moreover, the union now has strong allies. Both NTT management and Keidanren have come out in favor of the status quo for the time being. Largely because of this resistance, Prime Minister Kaifu Toshiki announced in March 31, 1990, that the government would freeze the issue about dividing NTT until 1995.

Comparative Analysis

The privatization experiences of JNR and NTT share at least three important commonalities. First, they challenge the general statements about

20. Kusahara and Yamanaka, "NTT," 214, 216–220.
21. Ibid., 214, 220–222.

labor exclusion/weakness and conflict in public-sector industrial relations found in the literature on Japan. Despite a legal framework that restricted their actions, the militant JNR unions effectively used the PCNELR Commission and their strength at the workplace level to compel JNR managers to incorporate many of their demands. Over time, a pattern of labor-management exchange (what critics call collusion) developed at the cost of efficiency and flexibility. In the NTT case, the labor union cooperated with rationalization programs as long as worker interests were not sacrificed. Because of management's interests in smooth industrial relations, telecommunications workers achieved short working hours as well as job security. In many ways, the administrative reform movement provided a vehicle for those who wanted to transform this pattern of industrial relations. The outcome of NTT privatization demonstrates that the reformers were only partially successful.

Second, the two privatization cases call into question attempts to portray the Japanese administrative reform campaign of the 1980s as an example of neocorporatism. Rinchō's membership did, indeed, encompass representatives of the major interest groups, including labor federations. But labor's role in Rinchō's decision to recommend JNR and NTT privatization was limited. In the case of JNR, only after the basic reform plan became clear did the railway unions scramble to shape the specifics of the new order. Until then, the unions basically took an obstructionist stance, and the Rinchō member from Sohyo could do little to prevent the commission from coming out in favor of JNR's privatization and breakup. In the case of NTT, Zendentsu decided at a very early stage to cooperate with the government's privatization plan. But the union became involved in the reform process not through the formal Rinchō deliberations but through informal negotiations with LDP leaders after Rinchō issued its July 1982 report. In short, although labor unions can and do participate in the policy process, their participation still falls short of being formalized in a neocorporatist structure involving the summit organizations of functional interests.

Third, notwithstanding their neoconservative inspiration, both privatization processes were remarkably sensitive to worker interests. Despite all the discrimination and suicides and widely publicized cases of widows of railway employees being left out in the cold, JNR reform, as drastic as it was, appears strikingly humane when compared with comparable firings that took place in Reagan's America or Thatcher's Britain. Certainly, the old social contract in the national railway of secure lifetime employment and employee perks was rescinded. But very few workers were cut off abruptly. Voluntary retirees received sizable allowances, and the Liquidation Enterprise offered retraining and job placement for those not hired by the JR-related firms. NTT workers fared even better. Zendentsu managed to preserve its social contract with NTT even as the corporation underwent privatization. Not only have NTT workers enjoyed relatively good wage increases but they also continue to benefit from employment security even as NTT tries to scale back its work force.

Despite the noted common characteristics, the JNR and NTT privatization experiences diverge sharply in terms of both process and outcome. Whereas the JNR privatization process was highly conflictual, the NTT process was generally consensual. Whereas the major union in JNR, Kokurō, opposed privatization to the bitter end, Zendentsu supported privatization after initial opposition. Whereas the reform process in JNR led to a radical restructuring of labor organizations, Zendentsu remained intact and has continued to have almost an organizational monopoly among NTT employees. Finally, whereas JNR was broken up into multiple firms, NTT has yet to experience such a fate. How then can these differences be explained?

One possible set of explanations concerns the *economic status of the public enterprise*. The fact that JNR was suffering from a burgeoning debt while NTT was financially stable appears to account for much of the divergence between the two cases. A public enterprise facing a financial crisis is less likely to work out a labor-management accommodation during the privatization process than an enterprise in a relatively healthy financial situation because reformers are likely to insist on massive layoffs in the context of privatization. This appears to have been the case with JNR. The prospect of large layoffs probably hardened Kokurō's opposition to radical reform. The better financial situation of NTT made it easier to develop a more "voluntaristic" retirement and transfer system and, therefore, to preserve labor-management cooperation even while it reduced the work force. Moreover, NTT's profitability steered Yamagishi toward supporting privatization as a way to increase NTT wages relative to those at JNR. But this line of reasoning also presents a puzzle. The dire financial straights of JNR seem to suggest that privatization was inevitable, yet Kokurō failed to come up with a realistic response and remained confident until the final stages that drastic reform would be blocked. In other words, the financial condition of the public enterprise by itself cannot adequately explain the concrete response of labor unions to privatization.

One can also apply the economic variable to account for the divergent outcomes of privatization. Despite Rinchō's interest in breaking up NTT into multiple companies, the reformers did not push this notion as strongly as they did for JNR. Rinchō members were interested in observing the impact of the breakup of American Telephone and Telegraph in the United States before adopting a similar plan for NTT. Furthermore, many business leaders expressed concerns about how splitting NTT into regional firms might affect the competitiveness of the Japanese telecommunications industry at a time of internationalization.[22] These considerations strengthened Zendentsu's ability to block the partition proposal. By contrast, because the Japanese railway system was less exposed to international competition, those favoring a breakup of JNR were less restrained.

A second way to account for the divergence between JNR and NTT would be to turn to *sociological* factors such as the nature of the work force. One might argue that the relatively extreme reaction of the JNR workers to privatization derives from the fact that much of the work tends to be manual. Consequently, a greater sense of identity with the working class was likely and a greater commitment to defending a socialist agenda against a neoconservative reform campaign. NTT employees, on the other hand, may have had less identity with the traditional concept of the working class. Telephone operators and other service personnel were more likely to associate themselves with white-collar and clerical workers than with blue-collar and industrial workers. This weaker working-class identity would, then, explain why Zendentsu was much more moderate and pragmatic in its response to privatization than Kokurō. The difficulty with this explanation is that it fails to account for Zendentsu's behavior during the 1970s. Zendentsu was just as aggressive as Kokurō in seeking to win higher wage increases and the right to strike. The behavior of Dōrō, the union representing locomotive engineers, further confounds the sociological explanation. Although engineers generally require higher skill levels than other railway workers, Dōrō was the most radical union in JNR until 1986. In other words, the sociological factor is not a sufficient explanation of either union behavior or change in this behavior over time.

A third possible explanation of the differences between JNR and NTT privatization involves the *organizational characteristics of unions*. A union whose organization is highly centralized and whose leadership enjoys considerable autonomy from the rank and file is more likely to adapt successfully to environmental change and to reach an accommodation with management and the state that promotes labor interests. Union factionalism and the lack of leadership autonomy will complicate this adaptation and the negotiation of a positive accommodation. The JNR and NTT privatization cases appear to confirm this hypothesis. Kokurō was a factionalized union, and its leadership consisted of an uneasy balance between pro-Communist and pro-Socialist groups. The failure of Yamazaki's attempt in summer 1986 to steer Kokurō toward a more cooperative response to JNR reform clearly demonstrated his lack of leadership autonomy. By contrast, Yamagishi displayed his formidable power over the rank

---

22. Katō Hiroshi, *Taikenteki "Nihon kaikaku" ron* [A treatise on "Japanese reform" as personally experienced] (Tokyo: PHP Kenkyujō, 1990), 151–152.

and file of Zendentsu when he abruptly changed his union's policy toward privatization. Dōrō's response adds further credibility to the union organization thesis. Despite Dōrō's legacy of radicalism, Matsuzaki managed to shift gears rapidly when he saw that privatization was inevitable. Such an adroit response would have been impossible if the union had been factionalized and if Matsuzaki did not have autonomy vis à vis Dōrō members.

The fourth and final set of explanations for the divergence between the JNR and NTT cases concerns *political factors*. One possible hypothesis is that the presence of factions associated with the Japan Communist party and the Socialism Association (Shakaishugi Kyōkai) in a labor union will make it more difficult for that union to develop and sustain an accommodative labor strategy. The penetration of these leftist political forces will cause the union to assume a more ideological perspective and to be less pragmatic in responding to changing political circumstances. Zendentsu's pragmatic response to privatization supports this hypothesis. Zendentsu not only purged Communist activists from the union during the early postwar years but also successfully prevented the entry of cadres sympathetic to the Socialism Association. Despite the democratization movement of the 1950s, Kokurō, however, could not completely rid itself of Communist unionists. Moreover, by the 1970s, a sizable group of Socialism Association members emerged in the railway worker union. Both of these groups constrained Kokurō's ability to assume a more pragmatic approach to the privatization drive. Dōrō's behavior weakens somewhat this hypothesis because the union's radical Marxist-Leninist ideological line did not prevent it from adapting realistically to neoconservative reform. This suggests that the union organization variable may be a more powerful factor in shaping union behavior than the political variables of ideology and the presence of extreme left-wing factions.

Another "political factor" hypothesis is that state strategies and policies that are hostile or exclusive of labor unions will work against labor-management cooperation. Although never explicit, many reformers in the Rinchō deliberative process wanted to transform industrial relations in JNR by weakening, if not destroying, Kokurō. This hostile orientation reinforced Kokurō's hesitancy about accommodating with the proprivatization forces. On the other hand, the neoconservative reformers were less hostile toward Zendentsu. Although they wanted to promote NTT rationalization through work-force reductions as well as through privatization, they did not try to bust the union. If the privatizers had taken a more hostile approach, then Zendentsu's response might have been much less cooperative.

CHAPTER EIGHT

RENGŌ AND ITS

OSMOTIC NETWORKS

Yutaka Tsujinaka

A NEW PEAK LABOR ORGANIZATION, THE JAPANESE PRIVATE SECTOR Trade Union Federation, or Rengō, was founded on November 20, 1987. Rengō began as a national organization of unions in the private sector. But on November 21, 1989, Rengō absorbed Sohyo, a national center that had organized most public-sector workers and a considerable percentage of private-sector workers, thereby unifying public- and private-sector unions in one large organization. The new Rengō embraced seventy-eight industrial federations and 7.7 million members. Its membership comprised 9 percent of the nation's voters, 17 percent of all employees, and fully 65 percent of organized workers in Japan. The seventy-eight federations themselves had twelve thousand enterprise union affiliates. Rengō is, therefore, essentially a confederation of confederations.

Rengō has no formal authority or de facto power over the enterprise unions that are its members. At first glance such an organizational structure may seem weak and loose. It prompts three questions: Is Rengō strong or not? To what extent has Rengō succeeded in integrating its more than twelve thousand member unions? How does Rengō acquire effective bargaining power to use against business interests and public authorities?

Many foreign observers, including Chalmers Johnson, have noted that enterprise unions tend to be co-opted by the company's managerial logic and that employer control over personnel affairs easily penetrates union organizations. Consequently, "organized labor has no role or voice in politics."[1] Therefore, it has been argued that Rengō is a weak, poor, and

---

1. Chalmers Johnson, "Atarashii shihonshugi no hakken" [The discovery of a new type of capitalism], *Revaiasan*, no. 1 (1987): 119.

vulnerable national center. Leftist critics in Japan even use the phrases "rightist reorganization" and "cooperative with capital and government" to describe this character. Van Wolferen concluded that "no other major element of Japanese society has been so forcibly adjusted to the system as the post-war labor movement."[2] "Rengō, in fact, fits in very well with the expected wish of LDP [Liberal Democratic party] ideologues to expand the party's constituency to include the labor unions."[3] Therefore, he called Rengō "a union to end all unions."[4]

It is plausible that Rengō should appear weak. For example, its budget and staff are not centralized. In 1991 member unions had budgets that surpassed a total of ¥ 850 billion. Only ¥ 3.6 billion, however, were spent on Rengō staff, which numbered only one hundred, and other activities. In these respects, Rengō seems organizationally weaker than the former Sohyo.

Nonetheless, Rengō has a number of successes to its credit. First, it has achieved strong hegemony very rapidly within the labor movement. Rengō is the only labor center in the advanced industrial countries that has successfully integrated a national labor movement since the oil shock. Second, it plays an important part in highlighting labor issues and strengthening labor's position in the policy-making process. Third, Rengō, or its predecessors, has won favorable policy outputs during the age of reform in the 1980s, including the revision of several laws, such as the Employment Insurance Law (1984), the Accident Insurance Law (1986), and the Workers' Property Accumulation Law (1987). Rengō has also pressed for new laws, such as the Law for Employment Security for Workers in Specified Depressed Industries and Areas (1986), the Law for Human Resources Development Promotion (1985), and the Law for Employment Promotion of the Disabled (1987). Rengō has also prompted a new labor policy in microelectronics and proposed a variety of industrial policies. Fourth, Rengō demonstrated significant potential for power in the electoral process during the 1989 upper house election. These achievements confirm the discernible influence that Rengō enjoys in the Japanese polity.

Many interpretive models of Japanese politics have been advanced in recent years. All models confront the difficult challenge to explain both increasing pluralism, on the one hand, and effective crisis management by Japanese government (or by Japanese society) on the other. Some attribute the ability to manage crises to a skillful bureaucracy, others to salutary pluralistic interaction, and still others to LDP cleverness. But nearly all models ignore the role of labor unions.

2. Karel van Wolferen, *The Enigma of Japanese Power* (New York: Vintage Books, 1990), 65.
3. Ibid., 71.
4. Ibid., 72.

Only the corporatist model has seriously considered the relationship between pluralism and effective crisis management as it tries to account for the role of the labor movement in the political system. According to Peter Katzenstein, a fully corporatist system must fulfill three conditions. It must have an ideology of social partnership or social cooperation, a relatively centralized and concentrated system of interest groups, and voluntary and informal coordination of conflicting objectives through continuous political bargaining that involves interest groups, the state, and political parties.[5] This definition of corporatism is different from Schmitterian corporatism, which relies on mutually exclusive peak associations, and it seems to have gained more adherents recently.[6] Although Japan did not until recently fulfill the second condition, it did seem to meet the first and third. Japan's economic performance has also been very close to that of highly successful corporatist countries in Europe.[7] Does something in Japan serve as an analogue to the centralization of condition two? Along with Shimada, I believe that something does.[8]

I hypothesize that Rengō and its core members have developed osmotic networks that function on an intrasectoral and intersectoral basis. They also link Rengō to the government. By network I refer to netlike combinations of actors and units that are not necessarily based on legal or jurisdictional authorities. The links within networks are relatively weak and soft; they contrast with centralized, hierarchical patterns of authority that possess distinct boundaries and formal relationships.[9] The density of these osmotic networks, however, can function as an equivalent to the centralization that is achieved in corporatist countries by peak organizations, owing to the shared information and perspectives that they generate.

Rengō is able to enhance its influence as an osmotic network for two reasons. State and society in Japan have become an osmotic network system whose parallel structuring supports the functioning of Rengō and its

5. Peter Katzenstein, *Small States in World Markets* (Ithaca: Cornell University Press, 1985), 89.

6. Philippe C. Schmitter and Gerhard Lehmbruch, eds., *Trends toward Corporatist Intermediation* (Beverly Hills: Sage, 1979).

7. Ronald P. Dore, "Koporatizumu ni tsuite kangaeru" [Thinking about corporatism], *Revaiasan*, no. 4 (1989): 120–146; David Cameron, "Social Democracy, Corporatism, Labor Quiescence, and the Representation of Economic Interest in Advanced Capitalist Society," in John E. Goldthorpe, ed., *Order and Conflict in Contemporary Capitalism* (Oxford: Oxford University Press, 1984), 143–173; and Ikuo Kume, "Changing Relations among the Government, Labor, and Business in Japan after the Oil Crisis," *International Organization* 42 (1988): 659–689.

8. Haruo Shimada, "Wage Determination and Information Sharing: An Alternative Approach to Income's Policy?" *Journal of Industrial Relations* (June 1983): 177–200.

9. Aoki Masahiko, *Nihon kigyō no soshiki to jōhō* [Organization and information in the Japanese firm] (Tokyo: Tōyō keizai shinpōsha, 1989); and Jaeho Yeom, "A Bureaucratic Organization in a Network Setting: MITI and Japanese Industrial Policy for High Technology" (Ph.D. diss., Stanford University, 1989).

core members. Enterprise unions, the fundamental units of Rengō, have become information mediators for companies owing to the transformation into network companies.[10] In this light, Rengō has become an enlarged version of an enterprise union. It provides a node for the nationwide exchange of information among innumerable enterprise unions. Rengō then can negotiate with other actors by using the extensive information about the labor sectors that it controls. Consequently, Rengō has become a crucial element in the Japanese political system.

The Turning Point

The year 1964 was a turning point in the shift toward osmotic networks in Japan. At that time labor began to change from a vertical, hierarchical mode to a more diagonal, horizontal mode of organization.[11] A similar shift occurred in the mid-1960s in intracompany, intercompany, and bureaucratic arrangements, especially for industrial policy.[12] The mid-1960s was also an important period for the one-party dominance of the LDP.[13] Remarkable social mobilization between 1955 and 1965 along with high economic growth and urbanization changed Japanese society drastically and caused a change from class politics to status politics, to the age of the new middle mass.[14]

Three indicative events in 1964 had important implications for political governance. In July a research council for the revision of the constitution issued its report. Disputes between council members made it impossible to implement the report, which implied that the ruling coalition would, henceforth, have to give up its effort to recreate a centralized, statist approach to rearmament, strengthen police, and restore sovereignty to the emperor. In September of 1964 the First Special Administrative Reform

10. Aoki, *Nihon kigyō no soshiki to jōhō;* and Ken'ichi Imai, "The Corporate Network in Japan," *Japanese Economic Studies* 16 (Winter 1988): 3–37.

11. Shinoda Toru, *Seikimatsu no rōdō undō* [The labor movement at the end of the century] (Tokyo: Iwanami shoten, 1989).

12. Aoki, *Nihon kigyō no soshiki to jōhō;* Imai, "Corporate Network in Japan"; Yeom, "Bureaucratic Organization"; and Ōyama Kōsuke, "Gendai Nihon ni okeru gyōsei shidō no seiji kōzō" [The political structure of administrative guidance in contemporary Japan], *Shakai kagaku kenkyū* 40 (1989): 1–134.

13. Michio Muramatsu and Ellis Krauss, "The Conservative Policy Line and the Development of Patterned Pluralism," in Kozo Yamamura and Yasukichi Yasuba, eds., *The Political Economy of Japan*, vol. 1: *The Domestic Transformation* (Stanford: Stanford University Press, 1987), 516–554.

14. Imada Takatoshi, *Shakai kaisō to seiji* [Social stratification and politics] (Tokyo: Tōkyō daigaku shuppankai, 1989); and Murakami Yasusuke, *Shin chūkan taishū no jidai* [The age of the new middle mass] (Tokyo: Chūō kōron sha, 1984).

Council issued a report weakened by divisions on the committee created by vested interests and sectionalism within the Ministry of Finance.[15] Therefore, efforts by the council to strengthen prime ministerial powers were not implemented.

In June 1964, MITI also tried to win more centralized bureaucratic authority with the passage of a special act to promote industry (Tokushinhō). Even though the law was disguised to provide innocuous guidance for industrial restructuring, members of the ruling coalition and the opposition parties opposed passage. The LDP and other interest groups were not ready to accept a bureaucracy-led corporatist system.[16] The failure to implement these reports and laws signified rejection of the tendency toward a stronger state and more centralization.

Denied its intentions, the bureaucracy turned toward an osmotic network system that would enable it to develop more sophisticated and indirect means of control via the techniques of administrative guidance (gyōseishidō), flexible application of rules and law (un'yō), advisory councils (shingikai), nonstatutory administrative advisory committees (kondankai), public corporations, business associations, and a variety of personnel exchanges (especially amakudari and shukkō). Central ministries, thus, increasingly became networks where all subunits retained considerable autonomy but had osmotic relationships with other actors. This interaction produced the reciprocal consent that arises from sharing information and developing common perspectives.

Amakudari refers to the practice of having senior bureaucrats enter private and quasi-public corporations and associations after retirement. Such bureaucrats sometimes go to companies directly related to the ministries for which they formerly worked. But others enter unrelated firms or special corporations, public foundations, and trade associations.[17] Many public corporations were established in the 1950s and 1960s expressly to create "landing spots" for retired bureaucrats.[18] Former bureaucrats working in a wide variety of institutions mediate the interests of their former ministries. Therefore, amakudari is a phenomenon that fosters osmotic network formation between the bureaucracy and other institutions.

Shukkō is the seconding of personnel from official posts in government, usually central ministries, to other organizations and to private companies in keiretsu (affiliated enterprises). A cabinet decision on January 29, 1965, required all elite national bureaucrats to spend two years in other minis-

---

15. Akagi Suruki and Inakawa Shoji, *Seisaku kettei kikō to naikaku hojō bunkyoku* [Policy-making organizations and the cabinet staff divisions] (Tokyo: Gyōsei kanri kenkyū sentaa, 1983).

16. Ōyama, "Gendai Nihon," 1989.

17. Kyu Cheal Cho, "Nihon ni okeru amakudari no kōzō to kinō [The structure and function of descent from heaven in Japan], (Masters thesis, University of Tsukuba, 1991).

18. Tsujinaka Yutaka, *Rieki shūdan* [Interest groups] Tokyo: (Tōkyō daigaku shuppan-kai, 1988), 76.

tries, in local government, or in a public corporation to broaden their perspectives and to ameliorate sectionalism. As a consequence of this order,
the magnitude of shukkō doubled between 1968 and 1978. By the late
1980s, about three thousand bureaucrats were seconded to other ministries in one year, one thousand were sent to public corporations, and five
hundred were sent to local governments.[19]

Shukkō also seconds personnel from private companies into public entities. Although it is difficult to determine how many personnel are seconded "in reverse," in the late 1980s as many as 120 individuals may have
been working as temporary researchers and another 60 as temporary officials in public organizations.[20]

In addition to networking through personnel exchanges, the bureaucracy has also tried to use many advisory boards, nonstatutory advisory
committees, and joint study projects to communicate and to develop osmotic networks with other political actors. In 1965 272 advisory boards
served such purposes, although the number thereafter remained fairly stable. Instead, many subcommittees and innumerable nonstatutory boards
proliferated, thereby enabling ministries to extend their lines of influence.

Important changes in the mid-1960s altered patterns of relationship in
the private business sector. Businesses began to regroup along two lines:
through vertical subcontractor groups and through horizontal corporate
groups (*kigyō shūdan*). These changes occurred in response to trade liberalization in the early 1960s and to capital liberalization stimulated by
Japan's role in the International Monetary Fund (IMF).[21] The vertical and
horizontal groups are not centralized hierarchies but flexible, osmotic networks. Corporate groups are linked through associations of presidents,
mutual long-term shareholding, financing by core banks, and information
exchange through general trading firms.[22] Imai states that a corporate
group "can be considered as an intermediate institution that exists between the market and the organization."[23] Such groups form osmotic networks that parallel the functions of amakudari and shukkō in the public
sector. Vertical groups with subcontractors are also flexible because they
include many autonomous companies that maintain more than two lines
of relationships. Parent companies second their personnel to subcontractors and, thereby, expand networks. Even the quality circle (QC) movement within parent and related companies fosters expanded network
formation by involving enterprise unions with private management.

19. These figures are based on my analysis of Jinjiin, Nin'yō kyoku, *Shōwa X-nen ni okeru ippanshoku no kokka kōmuin no nin'yō jōkyō chōsa hōkoku* [Annual recruitment survey report of general public servants] (Tokyo: Jinjiin, various dates since 1954).

20. *Mainichi shinbun*, December 10, 1989, 2.

21. Tsuda Masumi, *Nihon-teki keiei no ronri* [The logic of Japanese-style management]
(Tokyo: Chūō keizai sha, 1977).

22. Imai, "Corporate Network in Japan."

23. Ibid., 18.

The one important body in Japan that did not properly adapt to the changes taking place in the mid-1960s was Sohyo. It simply misunderstood the emergence of osmotic networks as an attempt at centralization by state monopoly capitalism. Its socialist, public-sector bias was partly responsible for its position. When in December, 1964, the Japan Socialist party (JSP) adopted as its general principle "The way to socialism in Japan," it defined itself as a socialist party based on the principle of democratic centralization. Owing to its intimate links with the JSP, Sohyo, too, pursued a socialist line that prevented it from understanding how Ikeda Hayato's "new conservatism," in fact, abolished the ideal of a strong, hierarchical state.

In addition to Sohyo's own actions, two other important events in 1964 would have critical long-term effects on organized labor. In May the Japan Committee of the International Metalworkers Federation (IMF-JC) was established, and in November, a new national center based strongly on private-sector labor unions formed, Dōmei. In succeeding years the IMF-JC played a major role in promoting moderation within the private sector while Dōmei absorbed the great mass of new workers in private industry. Rengō emerged directly out of these developments with Dōmei and IMF-JC playing leading roles.

In the late 1950s it appeared that the JSP and Sohyo might follow a different path. Public resistance to the hierarchical, authoritarian path taken by the LDP and the government was strong at that time, and the JSP won increasing support.[24] In spite of a lot of strikes in the 1940s and 1950s, however, labor radicalism was terminated by two indicative events: the failure of the Mitsui-Miike strike in 1960 and the failure to establish strike authority by Tekkōrōren in 1962. The structural reform faction led by Eda Saburō seemed to have the potential to develop the kinds of osmotic networks that might have helped the JSP. However, Eda's vision for the party was defeated in 1962, and he was never able to win party leadership. His defeat spelled renewed support for leftist socialism. Thereafter, the absence of osmotic networks effectively connecting the JSP to other influential entities in Japanese society undercut the party's ability to govern. It was also unable to elicit support from the "new middle mass" identified by Murakami Yasusuke in the 1980s.[25]

In contrast with the JSP, the Liberal Democratic party (LDP) learned from its unpopular policies of the late 1950s and tried to change. It developed the Income Doubling Plan in 1960, a moderate labor policy that crystallized in the LDP Labor Charter of 1966, and a modernizing vision for the party promoted by Ishida Hirohide and Miki Takeo. As a result of

24. Ishikawa Masumi and Hirose Michisada, *Jimintō* [The Liberal Democratic party] (Tokyo: Iwanami shoten, 1989).
25. Murakami, *Shin chūkan taishū no jidai.*

these endeavors, the LDP succeeded in changing its relationships with the bureaucracy and business associations. Through an increasing proliferation of formal and informal bodies, the ruling party extended its alliance networks throughout society, especially among interest groups.[26]

The Networks of Rengō and Its Core Members

Rengō's networks manifest themselves at the microlevel in enterprises, at the mesolevel among industries, and at the macrolevel among national bodies. Its core members include fourteen major private-sector industrial federations that contain the major enterprise unions. The federations are organized in the electronics, auto-making, steel-making, shipbuilding, textile, electrical power, chemicals, commerce, metals, maritime shipping, life insurance, telecommunications, and transportation industries. The strength of these federations derives in turn from their constituent members, enterprise unions.

At the enterprise level are two bodies important to network building: the labor union and the joint consultation body. The latter originated in the 1950s and became more important in the 1960s as it participated more in consultations with management. Joint consultation bodies and enterprise unions are not incompatible; they are mutually supportive. In 1984, for example, nearly nine in ten companies with labor unions also had joint consultation bodies. In the 1990s in six of ten companies, consultations and labor negotiations are interrelated or mixed. When requested, nearly six in ten companies would be willing to provide classified information through the joint consultation mechanism.[27]

These practices lead to an intense, cooperative exchange of information in almost all private companies. The enterprise union becomes an indispensable partner to the employer, whose managers include some former labor union executives. In enterprise unions, all union officials continue to work as company employees. Even at the industrial federation level, more than half of the officials in the largest unions retain their status as company employees.[28] Aoki has even suggested that employees as a group have become indispensable network-specific assets.[29] Thus, in Rengō's core member unions, osmotic networks form through frequent consultation and the interpenetration of personnel.

26. Tsujinaka, *Rieki shūdan.*
27. Takashi Inagami, "Japanese Workplace Relations," *Japan Institute of Labor,* no. 14 (1988): 24–25.
28. Rengō, "Rengō soshiki hōshin sakusei ni muketa chūkan hōkoku" [Interim report on Rengō's organizational policy formation] *Rengō seisaku shiryō* 51 (1989): 1–8.
29. Aoki, *Nihon kigyō no soshiki to jōhō,* 4–5.

At the mesolevel Japan does not have the strong, suprafirm industrial unions that one finds in other advanced countries, such as the United Auto Workers in the United States and IG Metall in Germany. Enterprise unions instead strive to multiply their influence at the industrial level through two other mechanisms: industrial federations and informal alliances.

The approximately 250 industrial federations in Japan serve as formal bodies that consult with business associations and government ministries. Although most collective bargaining occurs at the enterprise level in Japan, a few industrial federations do undertake this task. For the most part, however, they engage in coordinated consultation and negotiation to mediate the interests of enterprise unions with other entities in the public and private sectors.[30]

Informal alliances that offer labor unions an opportunity to expand their influence across firms take many forms: joint-struggle groups pressing for wage increases, industry-specific policy organizations (such as the Labor Union Roundtable on Information Industry Policy), occupation-specific consultative bodies, comprehensive industry confederations such as the IMF-JC, bodies organized along common ideological lines, and many others.[31] In the absence of strong, formal industrial unions, industrial federations and many informal mechanisms facilitate union contact across firms, occupational categories, and industrial sectors.

At the national level, Rengō has been able to expand its influence by participating in formal consultative bodies, pursuing informal relationships, and establishing direct ties to specific ministries. Private and public employers, however, constrain labor influence.

Nitta Michio has identified five institutional networks among public and private employers that function especially to restrain wage demands. In an effort to minimize and stabilize transaction costs, a network of firms within corporate groups strives to check wage increases.[32] A second network arises between final producers and their subcontractors; both have a strong interest in keeping wages under control. A third network operates among regulated enterprises (such as electrical power firms), where government is able to maintain standards that conform to those in private industry. A fourth network arises within national, prefectural, and municipal governments. Wages for public employees are legally based on comparable salaries in the private sector, so governments have to follow the lead of private enterprises as they determine wage policies. Fifth, institutions in the nonprofit sector link their wage policies to those of the

30. Shinoda Toru, "Rengō jidai ni okeru seisaku sanka no genjō to tenbō" [Current conditions and the future of Rengō's participation in policy-making], *Nihon rōdō kenkyū zasshi*, no. 379 (June 1991): 48–60.

31. Shinoda, "Rengō jidai," 122–123.

32. Nitta Michio, "Shun'tō no yuku e" [The future of spring bargaining], *Nihon rōdō kenkyū zasshi*, no. 364 (January 1990): 84–85.

government. In all of these ways, the most powerful private firms are in a strong position to restrain wage increases across the economy because public and nonprofit entities essentially subordinate wage determination to private business interests.

In the face of such powerful institutional constraints, labor must work hard to ensure that its voice is heard. It participates in formal consultative bodies. In 1988, labor unions sent 185 members of a total of about 4,000 to seats on various *shingikai* (discussed more fully by Frank Schwartz in Chapter 9). Labor was represented on 63 of 214 bodies in that year. Although labor did not have representatives on boards dealing with justice, foreign affairs, education, or culture, it did have representatives on many advisory bodies that dealt with economic matters. In addition, labor participated in five of six of the most important advisory councils, Rinchō-gata shingikai (Rinchō-like advisory commissions), in the 1980s. Labor was also well represented in Sanrōkon (Tripartite Roundtable Conference on Industry and Labor Issues). Established in 1970, Sanrōkon had twelve labor representatives, twelve business representatives, and six others, including neutral intellectuals and some bureaucrats drawn from the Ministry of Labor and the Economic Planning Agency. Sanrōkon performed a very critical role in handling the crises of the mid-1970s after the oil shocks.

Labor tries to communicate its views by sending its delegates to a variety of informal bodies. In fact, labor representation at the semiformal, or informal, level is more important than that at the formal level. In the 1970s labor actually succeeded in entering many important subcommittees and nonstatutory advisory boards where substantial discussion occurs before consultation by the formal advisory body. For instance, in the Industrial Structure Council of the Ministry of International Trade and Industry (MITI) labor is represented on the International Economy Committee, Distribution Industry Committee, Steel Committee, Noniron Metal Committee, Information Industry Committee, and the Textile Committee. In addition, labor has participated in many study groups and roundtable meetings such as the Roundtable for A Future Vision of the Machine and Information Industry of the MITI in 1986 and the Study Group for a Future Vision of the Construction Industry in the Ministry of Construction (MOC) in 1984.[33]

Labor relies on direct consultation with central government ministries to get its views across. By the late 1980s, Rengō had ten standing committees, including three that dealt directly with MOF, MITI, and the Ministry of Health and Welfare (MHW). In contrast with Sohyo, which relied mainly on the Ministry of Labor (MOL) and direct, but ritual, contact

---

33. Shinoda, "Rengo jidai," 94–102.

with the prime minister, Rengō and its affiliates have created many direct channels of influence with many agencies and ministries. In fact, union officials now talk daily with directors and section chiefs (*kachō*) in the national bureaucracy and section chiefs draft bills and various policy papers as they deal with practical affairs.[34] In these ways, Rengō has greatly expanded its substantial ability to influence policy-making.

Rengō, its core members, and its affiliated enterprise unions operate in a society with dense, overlapping networks. Such networks assure wide consultation among the organizational elements within the labor movement itself, but they also facilitate contact with a wide range of private concerns and with many government entities. Contacts occur at all levels of the system, from relatively low-ranking section chiefs in national ministries to the prime minister himself. Such multifaceted relationships and intense interaction mark a sharp departure from the practices that Sohyo once employed. Rengō is far more deeply involved in affairs of state than its predecessors were.

The Effects of Rengō's Networks

The networks affiliated with Rengō help it mold shared perspectives with other actors in Japanese politics, broaden its contacts through responsible participation in political affairs, and strengthen its hegemony over the labor movement. In all of these ways Rengō's behavior contrasts sharply with that of Sohyo in the past.

As the networks of labor unions overlap with those of other actors and institutions, more interactions occur and more information can be shared across what become permeable boundaries. Actors begin to consider their partners indispensable and legitimate.[35] In an international survey of employees conducted in 1984, analysts revealed that "85 percent of regular employees working for large companies manufacturing steel, autos, or electrical machines (65 percent of them blue-collar workers) answered that their company's gains were more or less connected with their own."[36] This percentage was significantly higher than in the United States, the United Kingdom, and West Germany. In other surveys leaders of Rengō and its predecessors appeared more concerned about government policy for industry promotion, tax reform, and economic adjustment than about

34. Muramatsu Michio, *Sengo Nihon no kanryōsei* [Postwar Japan's bureaucratic system] (Tokyo: Tōyō keizai shinpōsha, 1981), 95–136.
35. Robert Presthus, *Elites in the Policy Process* (Cambridge: Harvard University Press, 1974).
36. Inagami, "Japanese Workplace Relations," 20.

government policy for job security or improvement of labor conditions. In industrial policy, they are especially interested in future plans, capital exports, and the hollowing of industry. Rengō chairperson Yamagishi Akira has said that "Japanese employees are more likely these days to think less like workers and more like company managers."[37]

Shared perspectives also emerge from cooperation with business firms and associations. In a 1989 Rengō survey 56 percent of the industry federations in Rengō were conducting cooperative consultation, and 38 percent of them were engaged in some kind of joint action with business associations. The latter included cooperation with Nikkeiren, Japan's major employers' association, to solve problems of company housing and with Keidanren on land and other structural reform issues.[38]

More responsible participation in public affairs takes many forms. Rengō is less likely than its predecessors to behave negatively or to exercise its veto power. Instead, it adopts a more positive approach to policymaking. It is oriented toward budgetary policies, it maintains close contact with higher administrators, it cooperates with the bureaucracy, it sends more members to advisory boards, and it is generally more favorable to the government than was Sohyo.[39] In contrast with all labor unions in previous decades, Rengō is far more likely to conduct regular meetings with business leaders, bureaucrats, and LDP politicians. It is, perhaps, joining the establishment.

The results from a comprehensive and comparative survey of Japan, the United States, and Germany clearly highlighted Rengō's distinctiveness as a national labor center. Using hierarchical statistical and spatial analysis, the survey analysts found that the "Japanese accommodationist approach" is based on fact.[40] The center of Japanese issue space is solidly occupied by "the most influential political, bureaucratic, business and labor actors."[41] The most impressive finding is that Rengō, the LDP, and the Ministry of Labor were all located in the center; they shared agreement on about fifty labor issues in the 1980s. In comparison with other national labor centers, Rengō is, thus, moderate and centrist.

The signs of Rengō's hegemony over the labor movement are numerous. First, it is the largest single labor federation in Japanese history. Its membership in the early 1990s was 70 percent larger than that of Sohyo at its

37. Peter Katzenstein, "Japan: Switzerland of the Far East?" in Takashi Inoguchi and Daniel Okimoto, eds., *The Political Economy of Japan*, vol. 2, *The Changing International Context* (Stanford: Stanford University Press, 1989), 288.

38. *Nihon keizai shinbun*, March 9, 1990, 1.

39. Muramatsu Michio, Itō Mitsutoshi, and Tsujinaka Yutaka, *Sengo Nihon no atsuryoku dantai* [Postwar Japan's pressure groups] (Tokyo: Tōyō keizai shinpōsha, 1986), 207–256.

40. David Knoke et al., "Issue Publics in the American, German, and Japanese National Labor Policy Domains," *Research in Politics and Society* 7 (1992): 15.

41. Ibid.

peak. Second, its membership encompasses the largest share of organized workers ever drawn under one umbrella, nearly two-thirds of the total. Third, it represents organized workers in private industry and public service alike. In 1989, 59 percent of the former and 86 percent of the latter were affiliated with Rengō. This kind of unity is significant because for most of the postwar period, public sector workers pursued their interests largely separate from private workers. Fourth, it is strongly represented in legislative bodies although it directly supported slightly fewer Diet members in the late 1980s than Sohyo formerly had. Rengō has intimate relations with four major opposition parties, not just one. Thus, Rengō supported significantly more legislators in prefectural and local assemblies (about sixteen hundred in 1990) than Sohyo ever did. Moreover, its influence on lawmakers and its ties to sympathetic members in the Diet have rapidly increased since the 1989 Upper House election.

When Sohyo was the nation's largest labor center between the early 1950s and the late 1980s, it behaved very differently from Rengō. Its behavior was, in part, attributable to the heavy presence of public-sector workers in its ranks. They drove Sohyo to engage in mass mobilization tactics, to emphasize a peace plank in its platform, and to maintain a constitutional protection movement. Sohyo was obliged to stress public awareness through mass mobilization. It did so with its "spring struggle" (Shun'tō) and through electoral campaigning for Socialist candidates.

Rengō has adopted very different tactics. One of its principal slogans is seisaku seido tōsō (the struggle for policy and institutional reform). To overcome labor's isolation in Japanese politics and society, Rengō and its predecessors have accentuated the cultivation and enlargement of osmotic networks that will penetrate the established policy process. To assist in these tasks, Rengō has developed its own think tank, a union leader education center, and a foundation for international networking and gained more and more success from its multidimensional networks. By the early 1990s, Rengō was approaching the central node of Japan's osmotic networks, the conservative establishment itself.

Models other than the osmotic network model do not account very well for Rengō's growing influence in Japanese politics. The bureaucracy-dominant model, which is popular in Europe and the United States, helps explain the efficiency of bureaucratic networks in Japan but does not adequately explain the significance of the horizontal relationships that characterize osmotic networks. The pluralist model helps explain the rise of LDP influence and the strength of interests in particular sectors, but it tends to neglect labor and to ignore the failure of the JSP. Cultural models help explain the broad factors that facilitate osmotic networks in the first place, but they do a poor job of illuminating the concrete mechanisms that facilitate osmotic networks, and they neglect the significance of the turning point around the mid-1960s. The corporatist model, as devised by European specialists, concentrates too much on centralized peak organizations. It, thus, neglects the often more informal networks in Japan that are a functional analog to peak organizations.

If Japan is becoming an information society, the osmotic network model offers a plausible explanation for Rengō's influence and it overcomes the deficiencies of other models. At the microlevel, osmotic networks enable enterprise unions to serve as important information mediators within private corporations. They adapt to and foster flexible corporate systems. At the mesolevel, Rengō's networks work well by stimulating those of other actors. And at the macrolevel, Rengō is learning to work effectively amid the establishment in a developing information society. Rengō's control over information generated in these ways both stabilizes the economic system and enhances Rengō's influence in it.

PART FOUR

SITES AND MODES
OF NEGOTIATION

MOST NATIONS HAVE CUSTOMARY SOCIAL MECHANISMS FOR AMELIORATING conflict and promoting consensus. American congressmen, for example, "twist arms in the cloakrooms" before controversial votes, preparing the groundwork for agreement before an official decision is made. In academic circles, faculty "work the halls" before departmental meetings to achieve the same ends. In undertaking such activities, Americans are trying to "get their ducks in a row," to find the grounds for agreement before conflict arises. One finds comparable practices in Japanese politics although the metaphors invoked to describe them are different. For example, root binding (the act of *nemawashi*) is one Japanese method of identifying and resolving differences among parties in an effort to draw them together on an issue. In fact, a specific institutional device was established expressly for root binding in national political affairs. It is called a *shingikai* (advisory body), and it is the subject of two chapters in this part of the volume.

Precursors to contemporary shingikai appeared in the late nineteenth century, but today's advisory bodies owe their format, functions, and composition in large part to reforms implemented after 1945 by the Allied occupation. Recently, shingikai have been numerous, and they have served equally numerous purposes as Frank Schwartz explains in Chapter 9. His close examination of two types of advisory bodies actively employed by Prime Minister Nakasone in the 1980s cautions against easy generalization concerning the purposes, powers, and effects of such bodies. His analysis also highlights the continuing diffusion of power in Japan's polity and the role that shingikai play in arresting chaos, nurturing consensus, and facilitating integration.

Hideo Otake focuses in Chapter 10 on one advisory body that studied land use policies, an especially controversial issue that promises to be endemic to Japanese politics for some time to come. With his penetrating analysis of a shingikai in action, Otake is able to fathom the countercurrents of ideological change during the years of conservative reform. He discovers a significant rift that arose within an apparently unified bloc of businessmen and reformers. This rift allowed bureaucratic and, in a loose sense, public interests to secure a discernible upper hand when writing a final report that was the basis for new land use legislation. Otake, thus, illustrates how, as McKean points out in Chapter 3, public interests can be served in Japan's negotiated polity even without the direct representation of consumer groups.

Shingikai are established in the early stages of the policy-making process to set agendas and to formulate policy options. After legislation has been passed, the same administrative organs that employed advisory bodies to promote the legislation are obliged to implement it. Frank Upham's chapter offers a unique and detailed account of how one influential ministry dealt with the insuperable problems posed by implementation of the Large-Scale Retail Stores Law. He indicates that bureaucrats are as willing to employ the principles of a negotiated polity in implementing legislation as they are in formulating it. By tracing the long-term evolution of MITI's implementation of this increasingly controversial law, Upham is also able to show how shifts in the balance of power among domestic actors and the intrusion of international pressure combine to create a process of legal implementation that evolves continuously. Such continuous evolution confirms the perduring importance of negotiated political practice long after a law has been passed in the Diet.

CHAPTER NINE

OF FAIRY CLOAKS AND FAMILIAR TALKS:
THE POLITICS OF CONSULTATION

Frank Schwartz

How can one best negotiate public and private interests? American pluralists such as Gabriel Almond recommend good "boundary maintenance": in the most developed political systems interest groups articulate the claims of society, parties aggregate those demands into a relatively small number of alternatives, and governments enact and implement laws. Dissenting from this orthodoxy, Harry Eckstein contends that parties integrate political opinions *too* well:

> Parties, in their very nature, tend to aggregate opinion on a very broad scale, rather infrequently, and for limited purposes, such as elections. . . . In attempting to win mass support, necessarily from a large variety of groups, they do not so much "aggregate" opinions [as Almond thinks] as reduce them to their lowest and vaguest denominators, sometimes distorting the perspectives and goals they seek to mobilize out of all recognition. One may doubt whether such systems could persist if groups did not have readily available outlets other than the parties through which to pursue their political goals.[1]

Because parties fall short in mediating between public and private interests, other supplementary channels have broadened, consultative councils among them. In the words of Léon Dion, consultative councils are "mechanisms of systemic interaction," "a bridge between the social system and the political system."[2]

1. Harry Eckstein, *Pressure Group Politics: The Case of the British Medical Association* (Stanford: Stanford University Press, 1960), 162.
2. Léon Dion, "The Politics of Consultation," *Government and Opposition* 8(1973): 332–353.

Students of Japanese politics appreciate the value of such councils. For Daniel Okimoto, the Japanese government's vaunted ability to harmonize interests arises in large part from the extensive interpenetration of the public and private spheres in that country. The maze of connections that link the two constitute an intermediate zone that comprises school and family ties, informal study groups, foundations, *amakudari* (bureaucratic retiree) connections, public corporations, industrial associations, and advisory councils.[3] In a similar vein, Tsujinaka Yutaka argues that consultative commissions, think tanks, and the like, inhabit a growing "region of intermediation," or "mingling" (*baikai*, or *kōsaku ryōiki*), that ties together polity and society, public and private.[4]

Japan's approximately two hundred and twenty consultative councils, or *shingikai*,[5] deliberate and report on every conceivable area of public policy from the narrow and mundane (e.g., the regulation of masseurs) to the sweeping and controversial (e.g., electoral reform).

Historical Background

The use of consultative councils has a long history in Japan: the forebearer of today's Council on the Legal System was established in 1893, and the five oldest commissions existing in 1962 could be traced back to 1900. But prewar councils differed from their postwar cousins in both membership and function. Although people from all walks of life now sit on shingikai, and the inclusion of incumbent bureaucrats is discouraged, the proportion of government personnel was relatively high in the past, and except for scholars and leading businesspeople (*zaikai*), few persons outside the government were consulted. Although contemporary shingikai play a variety of roles, prewar councils performed very limited functions. Under the prewar system of barely tempered bureaucratic absolutism, authorities generally restricted the recommendations of advisory bodies to a simple "yes" or "no" in response to officials' plans.

It was only after World War II that the Japanese government adopted a system of consultative councils that wielded an appreciable influence on policy-making ("was compelled to adopt" might be more accurate). Oc-

---

3. Daniel I. Okimoto, *Between MITI and the Market: Japanese Industrial Policy for High Technology* (Stanford: Stanford University Press, 1989), 152–160.

4. Tsujinaka Yutaka, "Shakai henyō to seisaku katei no taiō: Shiteki shimon kikan seiji no tenkai" [Social change and the response of the policy-making process: Evolution of the politics of private consultative bodies], *Kitakyūshū daigaku hōsei ronshū* 13(1985): 1–69.

5. Consultative councils go by such names as *shinsakai*, *chōsakai*, *iinkai*, *kyōgikai*, and *kaigi* as well as *shingikai*. *Kai* translates as meeting or assembly; the other words mean deliberation, investigation, or committee. In this chapter I do not distinguish among the different Japanese labels but subsume them under the single term *shingikai*.

cupation authorities introduced a system of statutory advisory bodies to restrain administrative arbitrariness and to encourage participatory democracy as much as to introduce new perspectives. The National Administrative Organization Act first authorized the creation of consultative councils, and ministries began to establish shingikai on the cabinet-minister, bureau-chief, and section-chief levels with implementation of this law in 1949.

The Prime Minister's Office (PMO) experienced an especially rapid growth in number of councils owing to the diversity of policy areas under its jurisdiction (see fig. 9.1). Agencies dealing with large, influential interest groups also created numerous commissions: while the Ministries of International Trade and Industry (MITI) and Agriculture, Forestry, and Fisheries (MAFF) consulted a variety of nongovernmental actors, such ministries as Justice (MOJ) and Foreign Affairs (MFA) felt little need to include such groups in their decision making and, consequently, witnessed little increase in their councils.

Although subjected to repeated cutbacks, shingikai tended to "multiply like bacteria," in the words of one critic. When the Ad Hoc Commission on Administrative Reform (Rinji Gyōsei Chōsakai, or First Rinchō)—itself a PMO advisory body—investigated the entirety of administrative operations in the early 1960s, it recommended that the government follow the principle of "scrap and build" to simplify bureaucratic organization and heighten efficiency. In accordance with this principle, the government managed to override bureaucratic opposition and reduce the number of statutory consultative councils from their 1966 peak of 277 to 212 by 1978, and by 1986 that figure had increased by a mere two. (In all fairness, one must note that, to some extent, these reforms succeeded only in shifting the expansion of the shingikai system from statutory to unofficial, or private, councils.)

Membership Composition and Deliberations

Although shingikai are attached to and appointed by administrative agencies, bureaucrats do not enjoy the freedom to appoint whomever they please. Some council members serve ex officio. In other cases, nominations require the consent of both houses of the Diet, cabinet approval, or the recommendation of concerned parties. Although the head of a parent agency most often has discretion to appoint members freely from among those persons meeting fixed criteria, the specified qualifications can be quite detailed. More importantly, the establishment of a council attracts public attention, and parent agencies must consider how their appointments will affect perceptions of that council's legitimacy and, thus, its

Figure 9.1 Number of *shingikai* by ministry, 1949–1985

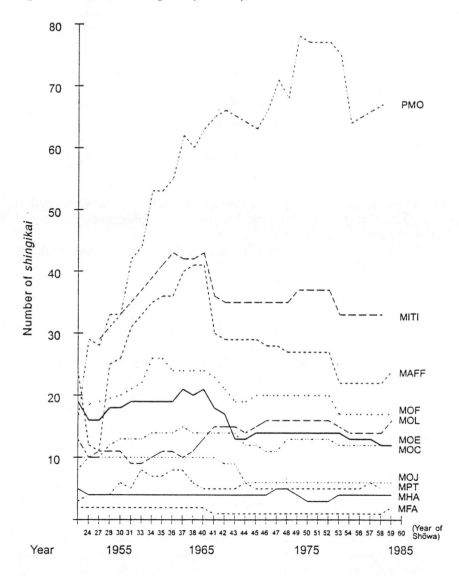

authority. Even a lack of formal restraints should not be confused with a free hand on the part of authorities because they never operate in a political vacuum. Where the law stipulates that a shingikai include representatives of a specific interest, such members will generally come from the largest organization of the interest concerned, regardless of whether or not they are sympathetic to the positions of the parent agency and the ruling

Table 9.1. Social groups represented on *shingikai*, 1973 and 1983

Social group	1973	1983
University	85[a]	89
Business and agriculture	78	79
Other *tokushu hōjin*[b]	60	54
Mass media (including NHK)	49	55
Government bureaucrats	43	21
Subnational governments	30	31
Labor	21	30
Public corporations and national enterprises	17	7
Lawyers	12	17
Women	10	11
Diet members	6	3

Source: Ehud Harari, *Policy Concertation in Japan*, Social and Economic Research on Modern Japan Occasional Papers no. 58/59 (Berlin: Verlag Ute Schiller, 1986), 8–9.

[a]Numbers given are the percentage of total active *shingikai* on which the social group is represented.

[b]Semigovernmental organizations other than public corporations and national enterprises.

coalition. The consensual nature of Japanese politics is easily exaggerated, but the conservative establishment is clearly sensitive to the need, at least, to consult minority views.

In recent years, the trend has been toward the appointment of more councilors who, explicitly or implicitly, represent identifiable interest groups, and the great majority of shingikai now contain such members. However prevalent the practice, the Japanese are not unanimous about its advisability. For private actors to participate formally in public decisions on matters of personal concern to them is fraught with danger in the eyes of some observers. The Recruit scandal that rocked Japan in 1988 highlighted the conflict-of-interest issue: Prime Minister Nakasone Yasuhiro was accused of using his position to help appoint the chairman of the Recruit Cosmos corporation to commissions considering matters with a direct bearing on the company's employment and information businesses. Nevertheless, growing diversity inevitably follows in the wake of economic development, and councils have come to reflect this. Doctors, lawyers, and stockbrokers, local governments and public corporations, women, consumers, and environmentalists—the scope of representation in the shingikai system is very wide, if sometimes of questionable fairness. Today's controversies have less to do with the legitimacy of their participation than with the relative influence granted different groups (see tables 9.1–9.3).

Given the economic orientation of postwar Japanese policy and its close ties to the ruling Liberal Democratic party (LDP) and the bureaucracy,

Table 9.2. Relative numerical weight of participants in *shingikai*, 1973 and 1983 (percentage)

	Mode		>50 percent		<33 percent		<10 percent	
	1973	1983	1973	1983	1973	1983	1973	1983
University	85	83	6	8	88	81	28	17
Business and agriculture	100	100	22	13	54	60	15	14
Other *tokushu hōjin*	33	43	—	—	100	99	58	62
Government bureaucrats	75	71	5	9	72	66	26	18
Subnational governments	59	35	1	9	91	98	56	68
Labor	35	33	—	—	98	100	52	59
Public corporations and national enterprises	15	11	—	—	100	100	91	93
Lawyers	45	47	—	—	86	91	50	56
Women	15	29	—	—	100	100	87	91
Mass media (including NHK)	30	29	—	—	100	100	76	71

Source: Same as table 9.1.
Note: In 1983, 83 percent was the greatest proportion of seats that university professors occupied in any council; they constituted a majority in 8 percent of the councils on which they sat; made up one-third or less of the members in 81 percent of the councils on which they sat; and so on.

Table 9.3. Distribution of *shingikai* by membership and ministry, 1984 (according to official regulations)

Representation	PMO	MOJ	MFA	MOF	MOE	MHW	MAFF	MITI	MOT	MPT	MOL	MOC	MHA	Total	Percentage
Diet members included	9	0	0	0	0	0	0	0	1	0	0	0	0	10	4.7
Tripartite[a]	0	0	0	0	0	2	0	0	0	0	5	0	0	7	3.3
Knowledgeable persons and bureaucrats	9	1	1	4	1	2	0	3	2	1	0	3	1	28	13.1
Knowledgeable persons alone	25	2	1	10	8	9	16	21	6	2	4	4	2	110	51.4
Knowledgeable persons and interest group representatives	0	1	0	2	4	8	2	1	0	1	5	1	0	25	11.7
Knowledgeable persons, bureaucrats, and interest group representatives	1	0	0	1	1	0	1	1	1	0	0	0	1	7	3.3
Others	2	2	0	0	0	0	0	0	0	0	0	1	0	5	2.3
No appointed members	2	0	0	0	3	0	2	1	1	0	0	0	0	9	4.2
Not stipulated	2	1	0	0	0	1	1	6	1	1	0	0	0	13	6.1
TOTAL	50	7	2	17	17	22	22	33	12	5	14	9	4	214	100
Percentage	23.4	3.3	9.3	7.9	7.9	10.3	10.3	15.4	5.6	2.3	6.5	4.2	1.9	100	

Source: Sone Yasunori et al., *Shingikai no kiso kenkyū: Kinō, taiyō ni tsuite no bunseki* [Basic research on *shingikai*: An analysis of their function and conditions] (Tokyo: Keiō University, 1985), 11.

[a]Opposing interest groups and public interest (*kōeki*) representatives.

business has enjoyed wider representation within the shingikai system than any other interest group. Although it has easy access to the ruling party, participation in consultative councils offers several advantages to industry. As noted, party-political considerations extraneous to groups' concerns inevitably intrude when interest groups work through parties. The LDP's support coalition includes diverse groups. Neither the business community nor any fraction thereof enjoys the party's undivided attention, and precisely because the party enjoys the support of all industries, it is loath to favor any one sector over another. Shingikai, however, provide a forum where contending parties can confront one another directly; delegates to consultative councils are more representative of particular interests than are Diet members. The fact that companies leave themselves open to requests for political donations when they ask for help also deters them from approaching the LDP. Businesses, therefore, prefer to contact the party only on fundamental issues, working through the ministries and their commissions on more detailed matters.

The privileged position of the business community has attracted the attention of Marxists, needless to say. Satō Hidetake, for example, asserted that "monopoly capital sends representatives in some form to every shingikai." Contending that economic commissions constitute "the core" of the system, Satō examined eleven important economic councils and found zaikai occupying 56 percent of their seats in 1976. In MITI's Industrial Structure Council, the "champion" of economic commissions, zaikai and the representatives of individual firms held 64 percent of the 1,411 subcommittee member and specialist member positions between 1972 and 1977. In an extreme example like the Steel Subcommittee, a whopping 98 percent of the members were business representatives. Satō considered zaikai domination of councils to be "watertight," and he concluded: "In the sense that most shingikai can reflect the views of zaikai and particular classes without necessarily reflecting the views of the masses of the people, especially workers, one has no choice but to say that they have been transformed into an anti-democratic institution of monopoly capitalism."[6]

This kind of research is tendentious, focusing on consultative councils that may well be important but are not representative of the shingikai system as a whole. Producer interests held a majority of seats on only 22 percent of all shingikai in 1973, and this figure had declined to 13 percent ten years later (see table 9.3). Even taken at face value, nothing is particularly surprising about Satō's figures if (as I argue) one of the main functions of these commissions is to adjust the competing claims of interest groups and administrative authorities. It is necessary to disaggregate these statistics in

6. Satō Hidetake, "Shingikai seido kaikaku no kokuminteki kadai: Kokka dokusen shihonshugi to rippō, gyōsei kikan" [The national task of reform of the *shingikai* system: State monopoly capitalism, law, and administrative bodies], *Keizai* 174 (1978): 123–150.

any case. Business interests are represented on several levels: by individual firms; by *gyōkai* (industry associations); and by the four peak associations, whose memberships include practically all industries (e.g., the Japan Federation of Employers' Associations, Nikkeiren). In 1983, 34 percent of those shingikai including members from business or agriculture contained representatives of zaikai, gyōkai, and firms; 33 percent gyōkai and firms; 16 percent gyōkai only; and 16 percent firms only. Furthermore, big business sends only a fraction of those councilors representing individual firms: in 1974, 20 percent of the business representatives in policy-making councils came from Japan's one hundred largest corporations, 25 percent from large corporations listed on the Tokyo Stock Exchange, and 55 percent from smaller firms.[7] Considering this multiplicity of organizations, the structure of business representation appears to be fairly pluralist, and it is safe to assume that business councilors spend more time seeking to coordinate their interests with the ministries and one another than trying to impose the wishes of monopoly capital on the government.

The conservative coalition's second major partner, agriculture, is more tightly organized than business: cooperatives embrace 99 percent of Japan's farmers, and the Association of Agricultural Cooperatives (Nōkyō) actively lobbies for legislative and bureaucratic decisions favorable to farmers on the national level. Although this might lead one to expect consultative councils dealing with agriculture to play an especially weighty role as vehicles of corporatist interest intermediation (cf. Swedish *kommitte*), that is not the case. The issue area of agriculture is highly politicized in both senses of the word: politicians routinely intervene and policy-making is often conflictual. Unlike much industrial policy, connections are obvious between agricultural policy and elections, and many LDP Diet members dependent on farmers' votes press for greater support of their constituents than the administration is willing to give. Direct negotiations between the party and the ministries thus tend to overshadow the recommendations of councils dealing with agricultural issues.

Critics of the shingikai system have long charged that the government often excludes labor unions from councils in whose activities they are vitally interested, and that they are inequitably represented on those councils to which they do have access. These accusations are not entirely unfounded; although unions can make their presence felt in individual commissions, labor influence within the shingikai system as a whole is unquestionably weaker than that of business groups. If that proportion of councils to which unions sent representatives rose from 21 to 30 percent in the decade before 1983, this widening scope of labor representation across commissions was not matched by a commensurate increase in labor's

7. Ehud Harari, *Policy Concertation in Japan,* Social and Economic Research on Modern Japan Occasional Papers nos. 58 and 59 (Berlin: Verlag Ute Schiller, 1986), 15–19.

relative weight within them. In no council did labor members constitute more than one-third of the total in 1983, and in 59 percent of the councils to which unions sent representatives, they held no more than 10 percent of the seats (see tables 9.2 and 9.3).

Unions do have a powerful incentive to participate in shingikai nonetheless. Workers normally achieve their aims through direct negotiations with management, through the Diet, or through the bureaucracy. The prevalence of enterprise unions and the attendant strength of corporate, as opposed to class or occupational, consciousness have limited the scope and influence of labor agreements in Japan, and working conditions have been adversely affected by problems like the oil crises and structural change that call for national solutions. In addition, labor has not spoken with a single voice in the Diet since the Democratic Socialist party split from the Japan Socialist party in 1960, and even together the two parties cannot begin to match the political resources and parliamentary strength of the probusiness LDP. Participation in consultative councils is, thus, important to unions if government policy is to reflect their demands. This is by no means to suggest that shingikai are always the most important avenue for labor influence, of course. They supplement, not supplant, collective bargaining and parliamentary deliberations.

Political elites in Japan have not accorded labor the same recognition it receives in other advanced industrial democracies; this is undeniable. Recent trends do favor a more inclusionary policy-making process, however. Divided for decades among four national centers, Japan's labor movement has been handicapped by its lack of a unified peak organization, but by the end of 1989, Sohyo, Dōmei, Chūritsu Rōren, and Shinsanbetsu had all disbanded to join the new national center, Rengō. Rengō embraces 65 percent of Japan's 12.3 million organized workers and ranks as the third-largest union federation in the non-Communist world. Because it follows a moderate line in industrial relations and permits its constituent unions to support whichever party they please, the LDP and the bureaucracy actually encouraged the establishment of Rengō, and its birth set the stage for a much more active dialogue with the government. Labor's voice in policy-making will likely grow, and this should be reflected in heightened union participation in the shingikai system.

State actors participate in shingikai both directly, through the appointment of Diet members or bureaucrats as councilors, and indirectly, through the appointment of "neutral" members and the management of council operations. Indirect participation is more effective for a number of reasons.

The inclusion of Diet members has always engendered controversy. On the one hand, their appointment to councils is arguably a violation of the principle of separation of powers: it involves the intervention of the legislative branch in administrative bodies. Legislators' participation, however, is motivated primarily by pork barrel politics: many of the shingikai that include Diet members deal with public works and construction projects, and their Diet members are prominent in the ruling party. The cabinet has repeatedly resolved "in principle" not to appoint national legislators to councils, and if these resolutions have not always been observed, the number of commissions containing Diet members has declined significantly, falling from twenty in 1974 to only ten (of 214) in 1984 (see tables 9.2 and 9.3).

Incumbent bureaucrats occupy far more council seats than do legislators, and their participation is no less controversial. Ideally, officials would avail other members of their knowledge and experience in a disinterested manner. But they cannot avoid the suspicion of promoting bureaucratic interests, of guiding deliberations toward conclusions convenient to their agencies (*temori shingikai-ka,* the "help yourself-ization of councils"). Cabinet resolutions have repeatedly recommended that, "in principle," administrative staff should confine their participation to shingikai secretariats and not receive membership appointments, and progress has, in fact, been made. Between 1973 and 1983, the proportion of councils containing bureaucrats fell from 43 percent to 21 percent, and the numerical weight of bureaucrats' membership was high in only a small minority of cases. If anything, these numbers overestimate administrative influence because the single category "bureaucrat" suggests a monolith that does not exist. The category must be unpacked. As the severe sectionalism that characterizes Japanese administration would lead one to predict, bureaucratic councilors sitting in the same shingikai tend to come from different ministries or from different bureaus within the same ministry. Their presence, thus, suggests the felt need for inter- (and intra-) ministerial coordination as much as a bid for bureaucratic domination.

The appointment of retired bureaucrats, or OB (from the Japanese-English "old boys," alumni), raises questions, too. Retired officials are clearly important shingikai members, occupying about one-fifth of all council seats in 1984. Like incumbent officials, OBs ostensibly participate as specialists in areas within their former ministry's jurisdiction. Like incumbent officials, however, they, too, are widely suspected of acting on the instructions of ministries, or at least of being chosen by virtue of their shared bureaucratic values and policy positions. The role of OBs is by no means clear, though. Not all of these retired officials return to service in commissions attached to their former ministries, which would certainly mitigate any feelings of loyalty to that commission's parent agency. Furthermore, upon retirement OBs normally assume new positions outside the bureaucracy with new roles to affect their perspectives. Finally, most OBs called on to serve on a council have retired from one of the higher ranks of the civil service, so the officials alledgedly controlling OBs are often their former subordinates. In such a situation, officials might well expect sympathy but not obedience. It cannot be assumed that OBs will uniformly defend administrative views, and even when they do, it goes without saying that the views defended will often be those of competing agencies and not of some mythical, undifferentiated "establishment."

A more subtle means of representing governmental views is through the appointment of "disinterested" persons. When the law sets criteria for council membership, the most common qualification is that a councilor be "a person of learning and experience" (*gakushiki keikensha*). Such members are also referred to as "neutral" (*chūritsu*) or "public interest" (*kōeki*) representatives in commissions with a tripartite composition. These members may be journalists, lawyers, staffers at research organizations, or bureaucratic OBs, but they are most often scholars. Unlike other formal qualifications, "person of learning and experience" is extremely vague, allowing parent agencies to select councilors likely to sympathize with their positions. Bureaucratic discretion is constrained in councils that include the representatives of interest groups, however. Precisely because a careful selection of "public interest" members could tip the balance in a particular direction, interest groups are attentive to the appointment of supposedly neutral members, and because the participation of these interest groups is both voluntary and often necessary to ensure the legitimacy of proceedings, they can sometimes wield a de facto veto over ministerial choices.

The most effective means of governmental participation in shingikai is through their secretariats. With very few exceptions (e.g., the First Rinchō), a council's parent agency will manage its affairs, and this involvement in the deliberation process goes beyond responsibility for mere clerical duties.

> A shingikai will first hear the government's explanation of the draft it submitted for deliberation [*shimon'an*]. There will follow questions and answers, an airing of views with respect to a concrete plan if one is presented, or a discussion of how to take up the points at issue when there's an abstract proposal or none at all. Here, too, it is normal for the government to present a plan [*gen'an*]. In continuation of this, or parallel to it, the government will describe the existing state of affairs, and for this reason, a great amount of data is submitted [by the parent agency]. . . . Members rather frequently question relevant government officials at this time, too. In our country, it may resemble the Diet on this point, with more give and take between the members and the government than among the members. Be that as it may, with a lot of give and take between members and government in this way, it turns out that the shingikai view will strongly reflect government inclina-

tions. In shingikai which include concerned parties in an explicit way, on the other hand, there will ordinarily be heated arguments among those groups.[8]

Finally, councilors most often entrust the composition of their reports to the secretariat, only reviewing and revising the bureaucrats' draft. Thus, through the selection of members, the assignment of a council's task, the provision of reference materials, and the drafting of the final report, the government has ample, sometimes excessive, opportunity to have its views reflected in consultative councils.

The Functions of Shingikai

In its 1964 report the First Rinchō distinguished between consultative (shimon) shingikai, which deliberate on policies, and examining (sanyō) shingikai, which ensure the fair application of laws through active participation in administrative decision making. The consultative type of commission is far and away the more common of the two, and I concentrate here on shimon bodies alone.

As noted, the original purposes of the shingikai system were to introduce new ideas and to pluralize governmental decision making. Like all occupation reforms, however, it inevitably underwent a process of naturalization, and consultative councils not only perform these duties in ways unforeseen by reformers but also function in ways downright inimical to their idealistic intentions.

Of the many functions attributed to advisory bodies, the most straightforward is the provision of outsiders' advice. A high level of technical expertise is a necessity in every branch of today's administration. The very proposition that councils do provide special insights has come under attack, however, with critics alleging that the value of consulting outsiders has declined because it is in the bureaucracy itself that expert knowledge tends to accumulate. It would be a mistake, however, to downplay the expertise of qualified members, even vis-à-vis trained administrators. Max Weber made a useful distinction between two *kinds* of specialist knowledge: technical knowledge (*Fachwissen*) and a knowledge of the conduct of an office (*Dienstwissen*). As supremely professionalized as Japan's bureaucrats may be, officials are, on the whole, generalists rather than specialists (as exemplified by the predominance of graduates of faculties of law), and their authority rests more on a knowledge of their duties than

8. Ogita Tamotsu, "Shingikai no jittai" [The realities of advisory commissions], *Nenpō gyōsei kenkyū* 7(1969): 21–71.

on their technical knowledge. Furthermore, because individual section or bureau chiefs rotate through a variety of posts, they must often reach out to private individuals when they lack necessary technical knowledge, and this dependence has only increased over time. Shingikai routinize such consultation.

The council system is still a force for democracy in the eyes of some. Such faith is misplaced, however. Because the Anglo-American procedure of public hearings is not widely used in Japan, the forums shingikai provide do help forestall arbitrariness or complacency on the part of bureaucrats. And unlike administrative investigations, the establishment, deliberations, and reports of commissions do usually attract press coverage, thus focusing citizens' attention on governmental concerns. But if councils were to reflect, and not merely consider, the "popular will," representatives chosen by citizens themselves would have to constitute the core of councilors. They do not. Although some advocates of grassroots democracy look forward to the day when shingikai might become the means for institutionalizing direct citizen participation in policy-making, the pluralizing influence of advisory bodies remains limited because parent agencies *appoint* their members. The democratization of administration will continue to rest on its obligation to respect the will of the people as it is reflected through electoral politics, and it is a dangerous mistake to exaggerate the significance of consultative councils in this regard.

In part because of such misunderstandings, critics of the shingikai system are legion. Commissions are often portrayed as helpless or willing tools of their parent agencies, and they have been referred to as ministries' "robots" (*robotto*), "cheering sections" (*ōendan*), "backers" (*ato oshi*), "tunnel organizations" (*tonneru kikan*, a concealed channel of influence), "sham bodyguards" (*shin'eitai magai*), and "ornaments" (*kazarimono*). The most common unflattering epithets for councils are *goyō kikan* (kept, or government-controlled, body), and *kakuremino* (an invisibility-granting fairy cloak, i.e., a means of parrying criticism or obscuring bureaucratic responsibility). In this view, the ostensible reasons for establishing shingikai are no more than a pretense: "The most prevalent way in which the council is put to use is as a supporting device for the government," charged one influential commentator.[9]

Consultative councils may support their parent agencies in a variety of ways. In goyō kikan dominated by members sympathetic to government aims, the referral of a problem to a shingikai may be no more than a stratagem to authorize a predetermined policy with the imprimatur of seemingly disinterested citizens. Councils can be good public relations. Shingikai sometimes allow ministers to shift the blame for unpopular de-

---

9. Yung Ho Park, "The Governmental Advisory Commission System in Japan," *Journal of Comparative Administration* 3(1972): 435–467.

cisions onto "neutral" advisors, of whose motives the public is less suspicious. Commissions can justify bureaucratic *inaction* as well as action, of course, either by prolonging deliberations or by defending the status quo outright. Within the government, councils may defend one bureaucratic unit's claims against those of another in inter- (or intra-) ministerial confrontations, an increasingly common phenomenon now that budgets have become tighter and the expansion of administrative functions has raised more and more issues that simply do not fit traditional divisions of jurisdiction.

Epithets like *goyō kikan* or *kakuremino* are fitting—in certain cases. But the fact that some, perhaps many, councils do little to contribute expert advice or democratize administration does not preclude other councils from doing so. More to the point, the *official* purposes of the shingikai system do not exhaust its actual functions.

Many observers credit commissions with enhancing the fairness and rationality of administrative decision making. In the prewar era, officialdom claimed to embody a neutral, public interest distinguished from private interests, which were ipso facto illegitimate. In the postwar era, though, the assertion of private interests has gained a measure of legitimacy, and they are vigorously and publicly pressed, often in confrontation with a bureaucracy whose fairness is increasingly questioned. With the decline in officials' authority has come a need for the review of administrative decisions by neutral specialists, that is, by consultative councils.

Most relevant here, shingikai are a means of adjusting all kinds of conflicting interests. The diversification of Japanese society has occasioned a marked increase in the need for the coordination of both competing private interests and private and public interests. Despite the postwar doctrine of parliamentary supremacy, it is a commonplace that the Diet is not the pivot of political integration, and however much information and technical ability the administration possesses, it alone cannot bear the burden of interest adjustment in a mass society, either.

Consultative councils perform this function in a variety of ways. Ideally, shingikai that include representatives of opposed interests will arrive at mutually acceptable policies. Even when they themselves do not resolve a conflict, council deliberations accurately reflect contending points of view and oblige participants to clarify and justify their respective positions. By allowing interested parties to express their opinions, commissions serve the government as useful listening posts: rather than imposing policies from above, Japanese ministries will typically sound out concerned parties (*sebumi o suru*, "find out the depth of water by wading in it") and lay the groundwork for new initiatives (*nemawashi o suru*, "dig around the root of a tree," as before transplanting). Conversely, shingikai offer their members' parent organizations a valuable means for learning the views and plans of agencies and of other interest groups with which they commonly interact. Finally, consultation facilitates implementation: as the price for formal, prior representation of their views, interest groups necessarily share some measure of responsibility for the success of policies they helped frame.

What need is there for commissions when interest groups are in continuous, direct contact with the ministries? Shingikai are especially useful to those interests that lie outside an agency's everyday constituency. Whether unionists on a council considering industrial policy or insurance companies on a council deliberating on securities markets, it is these "outsiders" that are too distant from some policymakers to merit continuous attention but too important to be ignored who probably derive the greatest benefit from shingikai. They do not necessarily wield much influence over deliberations, but without representation in consultative councils, their opinions might get no hearing at all.

From the government's point of view, shingikai help screen policymakers from the particularistic and, thus, disintegrative pressures to which direct lobbying exposes them. Because the unmediated collision of competing groups within government leads to sectionalism or to compromises worked out without regard to policy coherence, it is necessary to shield decision-making bodies from disputes among conflicting interests. The ruling LDP has its Policy Affairs Research Council to help soften and mediate interest group confrontations before they reach more authoritative party organs; within the administration, shingikai play that role.

The significance of consultative councils is frequently underrated because the discussions held at shingikai meetings themselves tend to be ceremonial. Actual negotiations among ministry bureaucrats and private interests generally occur "under the table" so that council meetings often end up formalizing agreements reached elsewhere. It must be kept in mind, however, that participation in shingikai and direct talks among concerned parties are complementary, not independent. Ministries use councils to designate those actors whose views they are willing to consider and to provide a framework for both the official and unofficial consultation of those views. The formal talks and the substantive talks advance in parallel; they are like two wheels of a cart.

Muramatsu Michio has collected survey data on political actors' perceptions of shingikai performance (see table 9.4). Although opposition parliamentarians predictably emphasized the likelihood of government manipulation, bureaucrats and ruling party politicians stressed the positive contributions that councils make to the policy process.

I have distinguished among shingikai roles for analytical reasons; this is not to suggest that existing councils each perform only a single function, of course. A commission may simultaneously play a variety of roles, and it

Table 9.4. The role most often played by *shingikai* (percentage)

Role	Bureaucrats (n = 251)	LDP Diet Members (n = 50)	Opposition Diet Members (n = 51)	Total (n = 352)
To enhance the fairness of policies	30	34	22	29
To adjust societal interests	29	20	12	26
To obtain specialists' views	25	30	27	26
To authorize administrative decisions	15	12	25	16
Other	1	4	14	3

Source: Muramatsu Michio, *Sengo nihon no kanryōsei* [Postwar Japan's bureaucratic system] (Tokyo: Tōyō keizai shinpōsha, 1981), 125. These responses are based on survey data collected in 1978.

may fill different functions over time as its environment and the needs of its parent agency change.

Shingikai in the 1980s

The 1980s witnessed a surge of interest in consultative councils as shin-gikai seemed to be converted from auxiliary organs of administration to political actors on the highest levels of state affairs. So many commissions participated in the formulation of such important policies that commentators began speaking of "brain (adviser) politics" and wondering whether shingikai were turning into an alternative, appointed legislative branch. This is a far cry from "fairy cloaks." What accounts for this dramatic rise in prominence of consultative councils?

Prime Minister Nakasone Yasuhiro was largely responsible for this change. What was noteworthy about Nakasone's political style was not the *number* but the *types* of councils he created and the uses to which he put them. Nakasone established several Rinchō-type shingikai on the model of the Second Provisional Commission on Administrative Reform and a variety of "private" advisory bodies that, although outwardly in-distinguishable from shingikai, were not formally grounded in law. Both the Rinchō-type and the private councils were used in (ultimately unsuc-cessful) attempts to implement major policy shifts, the first attacking the vested interests that had entrenched themselves during the years of rapid economic growth, the second promoting a highly conservative ideological agenda on a number of sensitive issues.[10]

Rinchō politics cannot be understood apart from the fiscal crisis that gripped Japan in the wake of the oil crisis. When the expansion of its econ-omy was leading the world, so was its expansion of government expendi-tures: the general accounts budget for 1974 was over ten times that of 1960 (in nominal terms). High growth came to be expected as a matter of course, and spending controls became lax. The Ministry of Finance (MOF) gradually lost much of its control over budget making, and "fiscal rigidification" (*zaisei kōchok-ka*) set in.

In Japan, as in the United States, fiscal rigidity was and remains a prod-uct of vested interests buttressed by deep-rooted, compartmentalized power relationships. These relationships have been conceptualized in the form of "iron triangles" or "subgovernments"—networks of politicians,

10. Sone Yasunori et al., *Shingikai no kiso kenkyū: Kinō, taiyō ni tsuite no bunseki* [Ba-sic research on advisory commissions: An analysis of their functions and conditions] (Tokyo: Keio University, 1985), passim.

interest groups, and bureaucrats that coalesce around particular policies. The LDP regime has traditionally courted electoral support by channeling public expenditures to its constituencies, and its increasingly profession- alized Diet members have taken to clustering in issue-specific "tribes" (*zoku*) whose expertise and contacts are nearly unassailable in their re- spective fields. Ministries that administer government programs naturally cultivate close ties with both the parliamentarians that authorize spending and the clienteles that benefit from it.

It took the first oil shock to bring home the costs of politics as usual. Whereas the real growth rate of Japan's gross national product (GNP) had averaged almost 11 percent in the 1960s, it plunged to a level of 3 to 5 percent in the years following 1973. Tax revenues fell sharply just as spending for social welfare was taking off. Slow to respond, the govern- ment rapidly accumulated a gargantuan national debt that was spiraling out of control. Borrowing financed more than one-third of the general ac- counts budget in 1979 and 1980. Close to losing its parliamentay majority, the ruling LDP lacked the resolve either to impose new taxes or to rein in spending. Raising taxes was strenuously opposed by business, and the beneficiaries of government spending naturally resisted any attempt to re- duce expenditures.

When the LDP regained a secure parliamentary majority in 1980, Prime Minister Suzuki Zenkō elevated administrative reform (*gyōsei kaikaku*, or *gyōkaku*) to his primary goal. Because it was difficult to ex- pect the Diet and administrative organs to reform themselves, gyōkaku was entrusted to a third-party, a shingikai, and the Second Provisional Commission on Administrative Reform, or Second Rinchō, was inaugu- rated in 1981. The second Rinchō addressed a wide array of issues. Among other things, it proposed that the government: restrain, then re- verse, budget growth across the board and end its dependence on deficit financing; reduce national contributions to the health insurance system, slash subsidies, and put several costly public works projects on hold; freeze public servants' salaries, trim the civil service, and streamline the entire bureaucratic apparatus; revamp certification and authorization procedures, privatize public corporations—and not raise taxes. Although Suzuki resigned in 1982, Nakasone, who succeeded him as prime minister, vowed to carry through the reform process.

Results were apparent even before the commission disbanded in 1983. In 1982 alone, legislation abolished or revised 355 laws concerning li- censes and permits and the government rejected the recommended pay hike for civil servants for the first time in thirty-three years. Whereas gen- eral account expenditures had expanded at an annual rate of about 14 per- cent until fiscal 1979, they rose only 1.8 percent in fiscal 1982, the lowest rate of increase since 1955. The Administrative Management Agency was combined with the PMO to form the Management and Coordination Agency (MCA), reducing the number of agencies in the central government for the first time in the postwar period, and Nakasone eventually succeeded in denationalizing not only the deficit-ridden Japan National Railway, but also the highly profitable Nippon Telephone and Telegraph and Japan Monopoly Corporation.

These were impressive achievements. What accounts for them? Besides Chairman Dokō Toshio, one of the most famous and influential industrialists in the country, the Second Rinchō included two businesspeople, two union officials, two retired bureaucrats, one journalist, and one academic, all clearly chosen for the balance of groups they could represent and for their extremely high status. Alone among recent shingikai, the Second Rinchō reported to the Diet through the prime minister, and both Suzuki and Nakasone were unusually closely involved in the work of the commission. When the Second Rinchō was first getting underway in 1981, Suzuki publicly staked his career on the success of administrative reform, and as prime minister, Nakasone compared Rinchō reports to Supreme Court rulings.

The Second Rinchō conducted intensive nemawashi with important politicians and bureaucrats and strove to soften the resistance of interest groups that stood to lose by reform. Although some labor leaders and their political allies assumed an antagonistic stance toward the commission, organized labor in general remained cooperative, and the opposition never got beyond challenging separate items to mount sharp attacks on the Second Rinchō itself. The commission was lent authority by the crisis atmosphere of the time, an atmosphere that the commission consciously fostered to the point of building a groundswell of public enthusiasm for austerity.

The Second Rinchō was nicknamed "another government" and "the Privy council"; to some observers, it threatened to eclipse the Diet. In the end, however, the commission passed from the scene, and few of its successes proved unqualified. The *rate* of growth of public expenditures may have slowed, but the national debt continued to climb. The Diet's passage of a new sales tax in 1988 buried once and for all the Second Rinchō's cardinal principle of "fiscal rehabilitation without new taxation." Personnel cutbacks never went beyond what administrative agencies could achieve through attrition and voluntary departures, and besides creating the MCA, the commission barely tampered with the bureaucratic apparatus. No fewer than ten thousand businesses were still required by law or ordinance to obtain government authorization after the Second Rinchō disbanded.

Everyone acknowledged that action was necessary—except in one's own bailiwick. "Approve the principle, oppose the specifics" (*sōron sansei, kakuron hantai*), as the Japanese phrase puts it. Because a cohesive elite consensus never developed in support of administrative reform, the commission's ambitions were frustrated by the same subgovernments whose actions had precipitated the fiscal crisis in the first place. Administrative reform roused insurmountable opposition among private interests, bureaucrats, and conservative politicians.

Big business was the commission's only real constituency among interest groups; powerful LDP constituencies like rice farmers and the construction industry actively opposed such Rinchō initiatives as the reduction of agricultural subsidies and a slowdown in public works spending. Jealous of their autonomy and desirous of maintaining their close links to clientele groups, the ministries had a conservative interest in the status quo. Diet members—LDP backbenchers in particular—were incensed by the attribution of authority to the Second Rinchō. After all, it was the Diet, and not the commission, whose members had won a mandate to govern from the people in free and open elections. What right had a mere shingikai to encroach on parliamentary prerogatives? "In the final analysis, the council was sustained by the prime minister's will; it was a vehicle of prime ministerial politics,"[11] and both Suzuki and Nakasone often found advocacy of a vaguely defined movement to be more expedient than commitment to specific measures.

These qualifications aside, the Second Rinchō represented a noteworthy innovation in the politics of consultation. The commission may not have solved the problem of fiscal rigidity, but it did wield unprecedented authority for a council. Gathering influential persons and possessed of a measure of representativeness, it led public opinion and gave direction to Diet deliberations when it did not overshadow them outright. People's expectations concerning shingikai grew immeasurably as a result of the Second Rinchō.

Private (nonstatutory) advisory bodies (*kondankai*) have in recent years played a role in no way inferior to that of Rinchō-type shingikai.[12] Private councils have dealt with some of the most controversial issues of public policy: the Peace Problem Study Group reexamined the 1976 cabinet decision to limit defense expenditures to 1 percent of GNP; the Roundtable on the Problem of Cabinet Worship at Yasukuni Shrine explored the separation of church and state; and the 1986 "Maekawa Report" of the Study Group on Economic Structural Adjustment for International

---

11. Michio Muramatsu, "Administrative Reform in a Pluralist Political System," *Japan Echo* 10(1983): 30–39.

12. Private advisory bodies go by such names as "roundtable conference" (*kondankai* or *konwakai*, "a gathering for a familiar talk"), "study group" (*kenkyūkai* or *benkyōkai*), or "preliminary conference" (*uchiawasekai*), all of them falling under the catchall category of "private consultative body" (*shiteki shimon kikan*). For convenience, in this chapter I refer to them collectively as *kondankai*.

Harmony, one of the most famous and influential proposals ever issued by a Japanese consultative council, advocated sweeping changes in the country's political economy.

The difference between public commissions and their private cousins is vague. In truth, the term *private advisory body* is a misnomer. Participants are remunerated with public funds, parent agencies provide their kondankai with secretariats staffed by civil servants, and the government often chooses to publicize their reports. The only real difference between the two is that creation of a kondankai instead of a shingikai permits the government to ignore the legal niceties pertaining to an explicitly public body.

Although the use of such bodies long predates the 1980s—the Showa Study Group of 1933–1940 was one of the largest bodies ever to conduct research on public policy in Japan's modern history, and private advisory bodies have been an integral part of the political landscape since the 1960s, at least—the proliferation of kondankai stood out as a signal characteristic of former Prime Minister Nakasone's political style. Because the MCA frowns on the establishment of private councils, ministries do not publish lists of kondankai, and no one knows exactly how many are in existence at any one time, but there were references to 298 kondankai in the press between January 1984 and September 1985.[13]

Nakasone had a weak factional base within the LDP, so his policy initiatives would never have seen the light of day had he followed the normal procedure of acting with the approval of the party's Policy Affairs and Executive councils. And considering the party discipline to which MPs are subjected, there was little chance of Nakasone's drumming up bipartisan support on a case-by-case basis in the Diet. This was especially true in light of his political agenda. Nakasone called for "a final settlement of accounts of postwar politics," which involved nothing less than a recasting of state administration and finance, the national railway, social security, defense, and education. These ambitious plans were not only broad in scope but highly ideological in tone. Nakasone had always stood on the most conservative fringe of the LDP, and many observers suspected that his ultimate aim was to revise the country's constitution, to complete the "reverse course" that had nullified many of the occupation's most progressive reforms.

Skirting the LDP and Diet, in which he was weak, Nakasone appealed directly to public opinion by playing an active role on the world stage and by mustering prominent people in Rinchō-type shingikai. He established the Administrative Reform Promotion Council, the Committee to Supervise the Rehabilitation of the Japan National Railway, and the Ad Hoc

13. Tsujinaka Yutaka, "Shiteki shimon kikan no yakuwari to Yasukunikon" [The role of private consultative bodies and the Yasukuni roundtable], *Jurisuto* 848 (1985): 67–76; and Tsujinaka, "Shakai henyō to seisaku katei no taiō," 23.

Commission on Education on the model of the Second Rinchō. The most convenient way for him to maintain his freedom of action vis-à-vis the LDP and Diet, however, was through the frequent use of kondankai. This strategy took the form of gathering respected private citizens into ostensibly nonpartisan advisory bodies, using them to transmute the prime minister's personal ideas into official-looking reports, publicizing these reports in the mass media, then acting on the public opinion thus aroused. Kondankai could reflect Nakasone's positions more forcefully than could Rinchō-type shingikai or an activist foreign policy (or the LDP's own Policy Affairs Research Council, which was a stronghold of the prime minister's intraparty opposition); because informal bodies lie outside the ambit of legal regulation, their establishment, personnel, and reports are easily manipulated. Nakasone disingenuously portrayed himself as a willing tool of the citizenry when, in truth, private commissions served as the prime minister's tools, useful levers with which he attempted to bend people and party to his will.

Japan's parliamentary democracy legally operates in the following way: the people elect the Diet, the Diet forms a cabinet and oversees the bureaucracy, and officialdom is advised by shingikai that derive once again from the people. Nakasone rescrambled this formula: the prime minister created Rinchō-type and private councils that were intended to sway the people and, through them, the Diet and bureaucracy. His advisory-body politics were, in essence, an attempt to assert the predominance of a prime minister–centered executive branch. Functions of the Diet, which represents the nation, were increasingly encroached upon by independent, informal advisory bodies, each of which claimed to embody a specialized representativeness in its respective field.

Continued popularity among voters failed to convince Nakasone's own party to retain him as its president much beyond the two-term limit stipulated by LDP bylaws, and his successors appear to be unable or unwilling to engage in his brand of "one-man" politics, yet kondankai continue to proliferate nonetheless. Prime Minister Nakasone's deliberately eyecatching politics drew attention away from more mundane, potentially more profound developments within the bureaucracy. Contrary to the impression given by media coverage, the fact is that kondankai directly linked to Nakasone and, more generally, those with a strong political coloring, always occupied an extremely limited proportion of all private advisory bodies. Between January 1984 and September 1985, only 2 percent of the kondankai, the subject of whose deliberations could be identified, dealt with explicitly political themes (see table 9.5).

Private commissions are just as convenient a tool of persuasion for bureaucrats as for politicians. In establishing kondankai, bureaucrats are free to dispense with all of the bothersome rules and regulations that normally

Table 9.5. Focus of private advisory body deliberations, January 1984–September 1985

Focus	Percentage of Total
High technology / postindustrialism	34
Administrative reform / low growth	11
International / diplomatic	9
Regional development	5
Aging society	2
Political	2
Other	37

Source: Tsujinaka Yutaka, "Shiteki shimon kikan no yakuwari to Yasukunikon" [The role of private consultative bodies and the Yasukuni roundtable], *Jurisuto* no. 848 (1985): 72.

constrain them. Compared to shingikai, kondankai are, thus, all the more likely to become "fairy cloaks." There is another, more fundamental, cause for the recent spread of kondankai, however. With Japan's social structure growing more complicated and change accelerating, administration would become unmanageable without the input of private actors, and ministries have established a considerable number of kondankai to collect information, grasp new interest configurations, and draft necessary policies. Shingikai alone cannot fill the need: the administrative reform movement consolidated many old councils and curtailed the creation of new ones. So long as agencies maintain the pretense that their kondankai are no more than informal study groups, though, they can go on establishing them freely.

Besides helping to cope with transformations in society at large, kondankai have been useful to ministries in coping with the transformation of their own task-related environments. Recent developments have shaken the bureaucracy's traditional predominance in policy-making. Administrative reform and liberalization curtailed the ministries' use of such traditional policy instruments as the granting of licenses, and deficit financing has restrained their spending. The growing policy-making expertise of the LDP also threatens ministries' prerogatives. To regain the initiative in policy-making, it has become more necessary than ever for ministries to fight with their heads, as it were, and they have responded by turning to private councils to come up with new policies.

Dion distinguished among consultations that are "optional" (when the consulting authority is not obliged to ask for advice), "compulsory" (when the consulting authority is obliged to seek advice but is not obliged to act on it), and "executive" (when the consulting authority is obliged to seek advice and must act on it).[14] Consultations of (shimon-type) shingi-kai are either optional or compulsory; they are never executive. Parent agencies are generally expected to have an obligation and, frequently, a legal duty, to "respect" (*sonchō suru*) council reports, but "respect" is not unambiguous, and to attribute decision-making authority to shingikai is both constitutionally untenable and politically naive. Whether council recommendations are adopted in toto, partially implemented, or simply shelved is entirely up to the government. Policymakers must consider a variety of factors comprehensively, and a shingikai report constitutes only one of those factors.

The significance of consultative councils does not lie in their handing down authoritative decisions, however. They encourage the expression and reconciliation of public and private interests. Although the proliferation of commissions became especially marked, and remarked upon, during the Nakasone administration, their spread throughout the government cannot be accounted for by the machinations of one vulnerable and ambitious politician. They have come to mediate between state and society, and they will continue to do so—to an increasing degree—whoever happens to occupy the prime ministry in the future.

14. Dion, "Politics of Consultation," 337–338.

CHAPTER TEN

THE RISE AND RETREAT OF A

NEOLIBERAL REFORM:

CONTROVERSIES OVER LAND USE POLICY

Hideo Otake

JAPANESE POLITICS OF THE 1980S WERE CHARACTERIZED BY THE "POLI-tics of ideas."[1] The central ideology was laissez-faire liberalism as mani-fested in *small government, deregulation,* and *privatization,* basically the same ideas that guided the Reagan and Thatcher administrations.[2] In Ja-pan, this policy package was commonly called, somewhat misleadingly, administrative reform. The Nakasone Cabinet reflected this ideological current by deregulating land use and by inviting private capital into pub-lic works projects (the Minkatsu policy) in the early eighties.

The first challenge to administrative reform began with the spectacular rise of land prices in metropolitan Tokyo and environs in 1985, which spread to all major cities in Japan. Rising land prices shattered the dreams of urban salaried workers to possess their own homes and rapidly exacer-bated inequalities in property ownership. Land price increases became a serious obstacle to improvements in social infrastructure and distorted Ja-pan's economic activities. They also led to strong U.S. demands in the Structural Impediments Initiative (SII) talks to resolve the problem. Many came to believe that the deregulatory and Minkatsu (*minkan katsuryoku*

This chapter is based primarily on reportage drawn from the *Mainichi* and *Yomiuri* news-papers, which appear daily in Japanese. The analyses of the reports and power structure of Land Rinchō are based largely on interviews with participants in the Land Rinchō that I conducted in 1989 and 1990.

1. Martha Derthick and Paul Quark, *The Politics of Deregulation* (Washington, D.C.: Brookings Institution, 1985).

2. Otake Hideo, "Nakasone seiji no ideorogii to sono kokunai seijiteki haikei" [The ide-ology of Nakasone's politics and their domestic political background], *Revaiasan,* no. 1 (1987): 73–91.

no katsuyō, mobilization of private-sector vitality) policies were primarily responsible for land price hikes and that a fundamental reexamination of previous policies was needed.

During the late 1980s, the land problem together with tax reform became one of the most controversial political issues in Japan, triggering the reexamination and, at least temporarily, the retreat of the strongly promoted neoliberal reform line. Disputes in this policy area, thus, changed greatly the ideological configurations in Japanese politics. My aim in this chapter is to bring into focus the ideological currents of the 1980s and to scrutinize their shifts through the lens of land use policies.

The Rise and Development of Land Use
Deregulation Policy

With administrative reform as its banner, the new Nakasone administration in November 1982 held fast to zero budget ceilings for fiscal reconstruction, the privatization of the national railway and the Japan Telephone and Telegraph Corporation, and the relaxation of various industrial and commercial regulations. It introduced deregulation measures for intensive land use to stimulate investments in the construction industry, and it attempted to invite private capital and entrepreneurial initiative into public works projects under the umbrella of Minkatsu.

Deregulation and Minkatsu policies for land and construction began when the prime minister issued direct instructions immediately after the inauguration of the cabinet. Thereafter, this policy was initiated and pushed energetically by the prime minister himself, with ideas supplied by his private advisory organs and private advisors.

At the end of February 1983, three months after the inauguration of the Nakasone cabinet, the prime minister instructed Administrative Vice-Minister Maruyama of the Ministry of Construction (MOC) to begin a ministry study of drastic (*omoikitta*) easing of house zoning and other deregulatory measures that would promote the construction of high-rise buildings in the Tokyo metropolitan area. The MOC immediately established a Committee to Promote Urban Development, with Maruyama as chairman, and initiated studies in several subcommittees.

On assuming office Nakasone incurred strong public criticism for hawkish, pro-U.S. statements about defense policy, to wit, that Japan was an unsinkable aircraft carrier and constitutional revision was needed. He tried, therefore, to revise his image by emphasizing domestic politics. From mid-February Nakasone invited officials from all sixteen ministries and agencies, including Vice-Minister Maruyama, for thirty-minute briefings and instructions on major policy issues. Nakasone unmistakably had the April local elections and the June Upper House election in mind.

The first instructions to the MOC, then, were for deregulation. In the preceding two weeks the MOC had already decided to deregulate building construction in commercial areas by relaxing limits on the total floor space index (*yosekiritsu*) up to 1.75 times, if green areas were provided. Although the measure would promote intensive land use, it would also contribute to city green space. In September of the previous year, the Ministry of Construction had, in order to increase the land available for building and urban redevelopment, instructed all the prefectural governments to review boundaries between the commercial, or Urbanization Promotion Areas, and residential, or Urbanization Control Areas. On the day Nakasone issued directions, the MOC decided to promote the construction of high-rise buildings. For this purpose it established a Study Committee to Promote Private Redevelopment that included private developers and examined measures for a revised tax system, deregulation, and coordination of interests. Because deregulation policy had already begun within the MOC, in contrast to other ministries that failed to prepare immediate deregulation proposals, the MOC was able to respond quickly to Nakasone's instructions.

At the end of March the prime minister gave Vice-Minister Maruyama further instructions for deregulation that would make it possible to construct buildings above five stories anywhere within the Yamanote Line (the core area of Tokyo). The relaxation of limits on building heights, which was also on the list of twenty-two items for the stimulation of the economy proposed by the MOC in mid-March may have been a response to demands by large developers who had problems finding land for buildings in the inner city. The real estate and construction industries were in severe recession and had requested that the MOC (and the prime minister) promote deregulation to stimulate their business activities.

On April 5, the government's Council on Economic Measures decided on an eleven-point business countermeasures policy. These countermeasures reflected strong LDP preelection pressure and aimed to increase domestic demand for business recovery. To promote private investment through deregulation, the council recommended the promotion of urban redevelopment by means of appropriate revisions in the First Residential Zone (building code) to intensify land use in metropolitan areas. Based on this recommendation, the MOC decided to push for a change in zoning; First Residential Zone areas with building heights restricted to ten meters were rezoned to allow taller buildings.

In early May, the MOC decided to revise part of the Enforcement Ordinance for the City Planning Law in order to reduce the minimum size of housing developments in noncommercial areas from twenty hectares to five. Then, in early July, to promote the construction of high-rise buildings within Tokyo's Seventh Loop Highway, the MOC issued two more revisions: one eased restrictions on buildings facing the street, and the other gave preferential treatment to transaction taxes. On July 14 the MOC's Committee to Promote Urban Development completed the report, "Promotion Measures for Urban Development through Deregulation," with the aim of intensifying land use, and presented it to Nakasone. A final draft was presented to the LDP's Construction Committee on July 21 and was approved. This sequence reversed the normal policy-making style in Japan and confirms that the deregulation policy was initiated by the prime minister, rather than by the LDP *zoku* (policy specialist groups).

Objections were raised to this deregulation policy within the Ministry of Construction. Such deregulatory measures implied a shift from previous MOC policies introduced during the Tanaka cabinet (1972–1974) to cope with rapid increases in land prices and regulatory policies for sunshine rights and environmental protection demanded by residents. The heated debate within the MOC until just before the July 14 decision on promotional policy[3] reflected the fact that calls for planning and arguments against disorderly development were still powerful within the ministry.

Two currents of opinion competed within the MOC regarding the resolution of land problems.[4] One argument emphasized increasing available land for buildings through market incentives and demanded deregulation in land use. Neoliberal economists used the same argument, in their prominent role in the administrative reform movement during the Suzuki and Nakasone cabinets. I call proponents of this opinion "deregulators." "Urban planners," or "regulators," comprised the mainstream officials in charge of the MOC's land use policy from the late 1960s.[5] Regulators around Kono Shozo (then the section chief of housing lot development) led the MOC's policy on land use, establishing the system of publicizing land prices and arguing for the absorption of windfall profits (the return to the public of any increase in the value of real estate arising from government action, or *kaihatsu rieki no shakai kangen*). But in the 1980s, with the rise of economic liberalism, they were forced onto the defensive. Yet the regulatory group within the MOC remained influential despite deregulatory policy currents. Undoubtedly, the prime minister's "direct instructions" decisively influenced attempts to overcome resistance within the ministry against deregulation.

3. *Mainichi shinbun*, July 15, 1983.
4. Interview with officials in the Ministry of Construction. Tokyo, July 23, 1989.
5. The deregulatory group and the planners do not imply the existence of factional groupings or factional strife. The terms refer only to loosely held ideological positions.

Local governments, not the MOC, however, had the final authority to change land use regulations. Hence, on August 8, the ministry sent a memorandum, "Outline of Building Lot Development Guidance," to all prefectural governments, requesting that "excessive" regulatory measures be abolished. The ministry strongly requested that certain areas within the Seventh Loop Highway in metropolitan Tokyo, then designated as the First Residential Area, be redesignated as the Second Residential Area, thus allowing the construction of high-rise buildings. But the Tokyo city government stubbornly opposed the change. Most other local governments also refused to follow MOC's instructions, and deregulatory measures were largely unrealized.[6]

Some MOC bureaucrats opposed the ministry's official policy and slowed deregulation policy progress.[7] For the regulators, who were mostly in charge of implementing deregulation, it had been a "bitter experience" to be forced to accept what they considered improper policy. More importantly, however, MOC officials in charge, as well as local government officials, hesitated to implement deregulatory measures because they thought them impractical, or worse, disastrous. For example, even if the limit of the total floor space index were increased, the construction of high-rise buildings was impossible without simultaneously expanding road capacity. In other words, without constructing adequate infrastructure and without adequate city planning, the supply of land for high-rises was judged to be impractical. Administrative rationality thus prevailed against the political will of the prime minister.

The Rise and Development of Nakasone's Minkatsu

From the beginning, deregulation policy, which was supposed to be implemented simultaneously with the policy to use the vitality of the private sector, was given the role of countercyclical fiscal policy. Nakasone, himself, conducted public relations on this policy and said that deregulation would bring an increase in domestic demand of ¥ 1 to 2 trillion. Mere deregulation, however, could not spur the expansion of private demand, especially if most local government and MOC officials were obstructing the implementation of deregulation. Therefore, an active promotional policy of private investment, to be introduced through fiscal and taxation policies, was needed. This new policy was advertised as Minkatsu.

6. *Mainichi shinbun*, April 7 and July 12, 1984.
7. "Sabotage" was the frank word that participants employed in interviews with the author.

Minkatsu originated in the context of continuing fiscal austerity. Public works were reduced; the MOC was pressed to find a way out; and Nakasone was compelled to initiate an active policy before the elections. Yet, as might be expected, given the Nakasone cabinet's emphasis on administrative and fiscal reform as its central policy, it was not able to adopt an expansive fiscal policy. Thus, the stimulation of private investment and private initiative through the "Minkatsu line" was undertaken as a last resort in early 1983 (at the same time as deregulation began).

At the end of February 1983, the MOC had already announced the establishment of the Study Committee to Promote Private Redevelopment, a committee dominated by the private sector. Five months later, the Committee to Examine Private Sector Vitality was established within the ministry, with the vice-minister as chair. This was nothing more than the previous Urban Policy Promotion Committee reorganized and expanded. When the major points for the next year's budget were decided in August, the promotion of urban redevelopment was given central importance. The MOC wanted to stimulate urban redevelopment by means of deregulation, government grants, and preferential tax treatment. The central importance once accorded to the construction and leasing of public housing was abandoned, and emphasis was shifted toward the encouragement of construction of private housing with government grants.

While these changes were occurring at the MOC, the LDP, in July, established the Special Investigatory Commission for the Introduction of Private Sector Vitality, with Sakurauchi Yoshio as chairman. This commission was unexpectedly popular among LDP Diet members. After a rush of applicants, it became an "exceptional" commission with seventy members.[8] It established three subcommittees to study land use and redevelopment and presented its report on October 18 to Prime Minister Nakasone. One key proposal was to allow the private sector to use publicly owned lands.

On October 24, the Japan Committee for Economic Development (Keizai Doyukai) announced through its Urban Problems Development Committee (chaired by Mitsui Real Estate Company President Tsuboi, who later became a member of Land Rinchō) a proposal, "Promoting the Efficient Solution of Urban Problems through the Mobilization of Private Sector Vitality." Its central aim was to promote the participation of the private sector in public development projects.

At this same time another facet of Nakasone's land use policy, the sale of government lands (including, among others, those held by the Japan National Railway) went into effect. In August 1983 the prime minister

8. *Yomiuri shinbun*, August 28, 1983.

had the Ministry of Finance (MOF) establish the Public Servant Housing Problems Committee as an advisory council. The council urged that superannuated public servant housing be made into high rises and that open land be sold to the private sector for redevelopment. The research council, composed mostly of private developers, compiled a report within one month. Using this report, fifty-six developers established the Shinjuku-Nishitoyama Development Corporation in December. The inauguration of Nojima Yoshiro as the president of the joint corporation was severely criticized by the mass media and by the Japan Communist party in the Diet in March 1985 because Nojima was a major contributor to Nakasone's campaign funds. The public found these developers very self-serving.

Meanwhile, the Ministry of Transportation (MOT) and Japan National Railway began investigations into the sale of national railway lands. Proposals were advanced to use them for urban redevelopment in conjunction with JNR privatization. In March 1984 the freight-handling area of Shinagawa station was sold (at three times the price of surrounding areas) to the Kowa Real Estate Corporation. Nakasone called such urban redevelopment an "urban renaissance" and worked to promulgate it as an important domestic policy of his cabinet. These policy decisions before the end of 1983 were meant above all to enhance the LDP positions in the April local elections, the June Upper House election, and the December Lower House election in the coming year.

As 1984 began, debate over the mobilization of private-sector vitality became more spirited. In the fall of 1984 one more feature was added to Minkatsu policy—the introduction of private capital and private entrepreneurship to large-scale public projects. The model was the Trans-Tokyo Bay Highway proposal. Once dormant, the proposal came up again during the fall 1984 LDP presidential election when the Economic Policy Council, a private advisory council to Nakasone, suggested it to Nakasone (as a presidential candidate) as one example of Minkatsu. Nakasone strongly promoted this idea and restrained the opposition of the MOC and the LDP construction zoku.[9] When the Kansai International Airport Corporation Bill was outlined within the government in February 1984, Nakasone forcefully intervened in the decision making to demonstrate how the private-sector vitality model could be an example of public work done by private initiative.[10]

Most giant projects, such as the Trans-Tokyo Bay Highway and the New Tokyo Loop Highway projects, were shelved in the 1970s because of antipollution movements and the oil shock. Many returned with Nakasone's Minkatsu. In July 1985, Nakasone made clear that he wanted

9. *Asahi shinbun*, February 21, 1986.
10. *Mainichi shinbun*, February 23 and February 28, 1984.

construction of three major projects, the Trans-Tokyo Bay Highway, the Capital Beltway, and the Akashi Straits Bridge, to begin in the next fiscal year under Minkatsu auspices. However, the MOC and LDP construction zoku, who had nurtured those projects, insisted that a semipublic administrative organ, the Public Road Corporation, be made the nucleus. In contrast, the Ministry of Finance supported the Nakasone proposal because of financial considerations. It took some time to achieve consensus among these political actors, but owing to the strong will of Nakasone, the third-sector model (joint enterprise by the private and public sector) was adopted at the end.

The prominent activities of the Japan Project Industry Council (JAPIC) were clearly behind the increase in such large-scale projects. This organization was originally formed in 1979 as a cooperative organ of the construction industry and the steel industry (as a construction materials industry). At that time the construction industry was in dire straits owing to the shortage of public works. Demand for the steel industry also stalled, and the industry was structurally depressed. The construction and steel industries set up a cooperative organ to examine new ways to exploit demand and groped for pressure-group activities to expand public works. With the rise of Minkatsu, this cooperative venture was expanded in April 1983 and reorganized to include major business associations. JAPIC became so large that many called it a second Keidanren.[11] As the central representative of the Minkatsu line in the private sector, it proposed in April 1984 specific measures to use private-sector vitality, and it played a central role in promoting large-scale projects such as the Trans-Tokyo Bay Highway.

This movement toward Minkatsu indicates the shift in the mainstream business world, which had previously advocated financial restraint for the purpose of fiscal reconstruction. During budget preparations in summer 1987 for the fiscal year 1988 the New Council to Promote Administrative Reform (Shin Gyōkakushin) proposed an increase in public spending to expand domestic demand and a special exemption from minus ceilings for the public works budget. The participants in Minkatsu policy now included not just the real estate and construction industries, which are nonprestigious groups in Japanese business, but also the mainstream business community.

The growing influence behind Minkatsu policies bore fruit as the Minkatsu Package Bill and Comprehensive Economic Measures. The contents of the bill, which included preferential measures for taxes and generous public loans, were decided at a cabinet meeting on March 7, 1986,

11. Tanaka Tateo, "Daini Keidanren: JAPIC no sugao to omowaku" [The second Keidanren: JAPIC's appearance and intentions], *Shūkan economisuto* (December 13, 1983): 16–19.

presented to the Diet, and passed in May. The Comprehensive Economic Measures aimed to expand domestic demand and stimulate the economy. It was confirmed on April 8 by the government's Council on Economic Measures just before Nakasone's visit to the United States and the Tokyo Summit. The redevelopment of downtown areas by deregulation was considered the most important comprehensive countermeasure. It pulled together all previously proposed land deregulation measures.

The 1983 to 1986 deregulation and Minkatsu policies in land use and construction policy areas attracted many new actors, giving rise to a string of new policies.

Implications of Land Use Deregulation and Minkatsu Policy for the Shift in Policy Currents

Nakasone's deregulation and Minkatsu, roughly divided, consisted of three categories: deregulation in land use and construction, sale of state-held land, and large-scale projects. All of them, viewed ideologically, were parts of the administrative reform movement directed by the powerful advisory organ, the Second Provisional Commission for Administrative Reform (Rinchō). They appealed to public opinion that supported neoliberal reform. Arising as they did amid admiration for privatization and deregulation, it was difficult to oppose them. Inherent in the Minkatsu line, however, were partisan and economic policy considerations that concealed crucial differences with the dominant Rinchō line.

The administration recognized the necessity to promote an active domestic policy before the coming local and Upper House elections. Nakasone had espoused a passive, or "curative," policy of fiscal reconstruction. To regain popularity, he had to shift toward an active policy in the midst of severe financial conditions. The idea of mobilizing private capital and entrepreneurship to achieve social investment was very attractive; two birds could be killed with one stone. For Nakasone the promotion of investment in construction also assured access to the large political resources of the real estate, construction, and steel industries.

Minkatsu policy would stimulate economic activity through investment in construction and thus answer strong American pressure for expansion of domestic demand. The Rinchō line was financially restrictive and, clearly, had a negative impact on domestic demand. In contrast, deregulatory policy meshed nicely with U.S. demands for liberalization of the Japanese market. Reformers assumed that domestic demand would expand over the long run as private enterprise flourished. Urban redevelopment especially would have immediate economic effects.[12] Once private projects were promoted and combined with deregulation quick expansion would be ensured. Given the prospects for economic stimulus and political contributions, it was only natural that emphasis was placed on large-scale private projects.

Behind the call for Minkatsu policy, however, was another broader change. The antidevelopment movement, provoked by the antipollution and environmental protection movements of the late 1960s and the early 1970s, began to recede near the end of the 1970s. In the 1980s popular support for redevelopment reappeared.[13] Consequently, rising popular expectations and private-sector desire for an increased chance to make profits eased the way for Minkatsu policy acceptance.

Although the Minkatsu line was justified by Rinchō's ideology of economic liberalism and was accepted as the trend of the times, it is clear from the above analysis that it was not merely a policy of neoliberalism as small government, privatization, and deregulation. It included something different. From the government's perspective it was a new method for realizing the policy goal of short-term expansion of domestic demand and public facilities. For the private sector it provided a chance to participate in public works. And, as mentioned, for the ruling party it was a chance to capture interests by means of new subsidies, a practice that was severely criticized by Rinchō. For this reason Minkatsu was often criticized as nothing but a reorganization of Japanese-style iron triangles, or the creation of a new dependence on government, precisely what neoliberals were attempting to dismantle through deregulation and privatization.[14] It is undeniable that Minkatsu did embody a strong expectation toward "big government."

As long as Minkatsu was implemented by deregulatory policy, however, it also had aspects of neoliberalism. Particularly in urban redevelopment, private enterprise would be allowed free rein, which meant a denial of the previous policy of orderly development promoted by the MOC. Essentially, the MOC, which favored implementation of state projects through uniform plans, was opposed to the implementation of private-sector initiatives based on the priority of profitability. The MOC feared that private initiative would delay local public works in peripheral areas, resulting in

12. Kamagata Kiyo, *Minkatsu to wa nan darō* [What is Minkatsu?] (Tokyo: Kyōikusha, 1986).

13. Akizuki Kengo, "Hi-rutin gata seisaku to seifu kan kankei" [Nonroutine policymaking and intragovernmental relations], *Hōgaku ronsō* 124 (1988): 1–15; and *Asahi shinbun*, Chiba shikyoku, *Tsuiseki wangan kaihatsu* [Tracking shoreline developments] (Tokyo: Asahi shinbunsha, 1987).

14. Ono Takao, *Tenki ni tatsu toshi to kokudo* [Cities and land at the turning point] (Tokyo: Shin Nihon shuppansha, 1986).

further excessive concentration of wealth and power in Tokyo (or other metropolitan areas). Owing to previous deregulatory and Minkatsu policy, the core political groups in the LDP-style big government, particularly MOC officials and construction zoku, were forced onto the defensive. More precisely, they were tossed about by Nakasone, who had been an outsider to the iron triangle on public works projects. Their position remained ambivalent because although they feared Nakasone's intervention and were opposed to his proposal for third-sector implementation, they could not avoid being attracted by the new opportunities to expand areas of government activity (and partisan intervention) offered by the Minkatsu policy.

The new networks that the Minkatsu line provided to the party, administration, and private sector were not simply the revival of old political ties (or at least that was not intended). As Sakakibara Eisuke notes, the Japanese economy has coexisting structures: the private (large corporation) sector and the public sector. The latter consists of local governments and central ministries as entrepreneurs.[15] Minkatsu policy, by fusing both sectors, tried to introduce the capital and enterpreneurship of the private sector (private sector vitality) to works in the public sector. This is the reverse of the traditional fusion—introducing public capital and public control to the private sector. In other words, Minkatsu entailed a qualitatively different reorganization of public-private relations. In this context the MOC attempted to transform itself from a mere implementation organ into an "idea ministry" (policy agency). The decision to reject the idea to make the Public Road Corporation a principal agent in constructing projects such as the Trans-Tokyo Bay Highway was made against the strong wishes of the MOC and LDP construction zoku.[16]

In the Minkatsu line from the first, the two ideologies of small government and big government were, thus, in conflict. Moreover, within big government were two political currents: the planners and bureaucratic regulators on one side and the pork barrel politicians of the LDP construction zoku on the other. The sharp rise in land prices in the late eighties brought this ideological conflict to the surface, drastically changing the power balance among these actors.

15. Sakakibara Eisuke, *Shihonshugi o koeta Nihon* [Supracapitalist Japan] (Tokyo: Tōyō keizai shinpōsha, 1990).

16. The extent to which third sector work projects were really led by private enterprise is unclear. With regard to the Trans-Tokyo Bay Highway, the private sector complains that new companies are merely conduits for collecting money from the private sector. Conversely, the Public Road Corporation is critical that construction is done by the private sector, whereas the corporation is responsible for difficult tasks such as compensating the fishing industry, troublesome negotiating over environmental assessments, and bearing the risks of disasters and debts. (See the *Asahi shinbun* for January 26 and February 22, 1986.) Hence, it is necessary to examine both the intentions of policymakers and the real activities of the so-called third sector.

The Establishment of Land Rinchō and Its Reports

As the last year of the Nakasone administration began in 1987, deregulation and Minkatsu policy faced the need for serious reconsideration. In 1986 the land price problem had become a political issue as prices escalated in Tokyo. These events caused a partial comeback of the Socialist groups that had played a merely secondary, or worse, defensive, role in land-use policy (as well as in administrative reform in general). The Socialist resurgence altered the lines of ideological conflict.

The direct cause of land price problems was the sharp increase in demand for office space in the center of Tokyo that accompanied internationalization. The excessive supply of money from a large trade surplus triggered speculative investments in property, spreading price increases to the residential areas surrounding Tokyo. These price increases were considered, at least in part, to be the outcome of Nakasone's administrative reform: promotion of construction investment by Minkatsu policy, deregulation, and the sale of government land. Nakasone was also severely criticized because such policies as financial liberalization encouraged extreme concentration of business activities in Tokyo, thereby arresting the development of peripheral regions.

The Nakasone cabinet, however, maintained the position that if the supply of land were encouraged by land sales and deregulation, land prices would stabilize and decrease. Thus, the cabinet continued to oppose regulatory policies begun by Tokyo and other local governments. When land price increases showed no signs of stopping, however, the administration was forced in 1987 to regulate real estate finances through the Ministry of Finance (MOF), to postpone the sale of government land, and to apply "area supervision" by the National Land Agency (with the cooperation of local governments). In January 1987 Takeshita, LDP secretary-general, was the first to begin debate on constitutional rights of land use, announcing that drastic reforms including restriction of private property rights on land were necessary.

Faced with these dilemmas, Nakasone in July 1987, urged an influential blue ribbon advisory council, the New Council to Promote Administrative Reform, to set up a special committee to explore possible measures to stem the sharp rise in metropolitan land prices, especially in Tokyo. The council was a second follow-up organ of Rinchō, which had been a driving force for administrative reform during the early eighties. Otsuki Bunpei, the council chairman, was to chair the new Special Study Committee on Land Problems, commonly known as Land Rinchō. This body confirmed how important the council thought land problems were. The Land Rinchō implied a need for fundamental reexamination of Nakasone's Minkatsu and the administrative reform line in general. Ironically, the very council that had promoted administrative reforms in the first place was now subjecting reform to renewed scrutiny. Ideological conflict over economic liberalism thus resurfaced over a new issue. Henceforth, economic liberalism was on the defensive.

Land Rinchō was set up in August 1987. In October it made an emergency interim report on "Countermeasures for Land Prices for the Time Being" to cope with extraordinary land price increases resulting from speculative land transactions. In June 1988 the committee submitted a final report to the government on land problems including land prices. Land Rinchō proposed strengthening regulations in the emergency report and emphasized the necessity of planning and regulating land use in the final report. By pushing the concept that land is a public good, Land Rinchō gave the impression of a dramatic shift away from the ideology of economic liberalism advocated by the previous Rinchō. The council's debate was characterized by severe confrontation, however, and the contents of its reports were, thus, ideologically cloudy. Nonetheless, when compared with the heyday of neoliberalism, the revival of planning and regulation was undeniable.

The interim report of October 1987 called for tighter controls on speculative land transactions using every measure provided by such existing laws as the National Land Utilization and Planning Law. Specifically, it urged the central and local governments to use a surveillance system for land transactions in specially designated surveillance areas and to begin designating restricted areas in which all land transactions would be authorized by the local government. It also called for tighter supervision and instruction of real estate agents and financial firms and a temporary freeze on the sale of state and public lands in high-priced areas. These regulatory measures were all offered as emergency safety measures. Nonetheless, it was stated in the preface that "land is a limited resource for the people (in general), and . . . 'public welfare' is to be given priority." In the main text "the public and social character" of land was emphasized.

Relying on this report, the cabinet approved an order for "Emergency Land Measures Essential Points," and instructed all ministries and agencies to implement them without delay. Ironically, land prices had already begun to stabilize. Yet it was generally thought that government regulation caused the decline and that a more long-term solution was needed.

In these circumstances, the final report presented eight months later aimed not only for the short-term goals of stabilization and lowered land prices but also for a long-term goal concerning general land policy. The public philosophy of the committee (and the parent council) was more fully manifested in these recommendations. The committee accepted the basic concept that land, unlike other goods, was to some extent a public property owing to its special public and social characteristics. The report noted that the following five principles should guide future policy:

1. Land ownership is accompanied by the responsibility of land use;
2. In the use of land, public welfare is given priority;
3. Land use must be planned;
4. Part of development profits (windfall profits) must be returned to society to assure social fairness; and
5. In accordance with land use and the benefits derived from it, the social burden must be borne equitably.

These claims are completely different from those of a liberal economic view; in fact, they are expressions of its opposite. This point is underscored by the report's targeting the supply of housing as a social policy objective, in place of business oriented large projects. It is only natural that all of the leftist opposition parties, except the Japan Communist party, gave this report a more or less positive evaluation.

In the specific proposals of the final report, however, ideological implications were less clear. Reflecting the conflict of opinions in the committee, the report was the product of compromise. For example, three groups had conflicting claims for large-scale development: one for planned development (demands for balance between business and housing development), one for free development (by means of deregulated business development), and one against any large-scale developments on principle (an opinion advocated by a leftist member, a representative of the General Council of Trade Unions). The free developers (in contrast to the Left) had no objections to public support of the large-scale development advocated by the planners. The planner group argued for the public supply of privately owned individual houses and housing lots or public support of housing by the private sector, whereas the Left emphasized construction of public housing for lease (public apartments). Both the planners and the leftists agreed that development profits should be returned to society, privileged buying rights should be given to the development project by local governments, and the priority rights of public corporations to acquire government and public land should be respected.

Generally, the planned development group (moderate regulators) were dominant throughout committee deliberations. Yet strong opposition from the whole-hearted deregulators, mostly respresentatives of the real estate business, forced the moderates to retreat. At the final stage of debate, representatives of the real estate business argued strongly for deregulation, for supporting the private sector's excellent projects, and for strengthening public support measures. Public aspects incorporated in the original draft were eliminated or reversed in the final report.[17] As a result, the committee rejected some of the provisions in the draft prepared by government officials and modified others.

17. Hara Takafumi, "Tochi Rinchō shimatsuki" [An accounting of the Land Rinchō], *This Is* 5(July 1988): 20–29.

Nonetheless, Nakasone's Minkatsu line was forced to change. As a matter of principle, the committee rejected the purchase and use of government land by the private sector and changed the direction of planned public use. Emphasis shifted from business-oriented urban redevelopment to the supply of family housing and then to the public supply of housing. It judged deregulatory policy regarding land use a failure and requested a policy change. The planners did not obtain an undiluted victory on the third point. Altering slightly the Nakasone era's unplanned, uniform deregulation, the committee opined in their report that the incentives of the market would be manipulated by selective deregulation. For example, to promote the supply of housing, the so-called planned introduction of deregulation (based on the careful calculation and forecasting of policy results) was needed. Successful deregulation would require solidification and clarification of authority (as Masaru Mabuchi notes in Chapter 5), and a possible increase in land taxes.

Discussions within Land Rinchō and Its Power Structure

Land Rinchō was instituted by means of Nakasone's strong will. Its twenty-two members included six former vice-ministers, representatives of academics, the mass media, labor, and business, and the vice-governor of Tokyo. From the standpoint of composition and operation Land Rinchō was an extension of other Rinchō-related advisory committees. In other words, the recruitment of members and the distribution of influence did not change the administrative reform line. Sejima Ryuzo, the central figure of Nakasone's brain trust who had managed Rinchō, played the decisive role in the creation and operation of Land Rinchō. Sejima at first expected to assume the post of Land Rinchō chairman, but owing to personal opposition from Miyazaki Kagayaki, this plan failed, and Otsuki, the chairman of Shin Gyōkakushin, Land Rinchō's parent council, was appointed. Because Sejima, however, was the only one who could manage Land Rinchō with the support of other Nakasone advisers as well as Nakasone himself, he assumed real leadership. As the Nakasone cabinet struggled with sharp increases in land prices, Sejima, responding to Nakasone's desire, tried to overcome this crisis with some kind of proposal or countermeasure.

Sejima called Iijima Kiyoshi, Kato Hiroshi, Sando Yoichi, Tsuboi Higashi, and Yayama Taro and organized the Shadow (Ura) Land Rinchō. Except for Tsuboi, the Mitsui Real Estate chairman who was close to Nakasone personally, all of these men had acted as Nakasone's brain trusts in the old Rinchō. This group excluded other members and decided to manage the general framework and direction of the committee's deliberations by itself.

It did not occur to this group that owing to the land problem the neoliberal political trend, which had been dominant since the introduction of administrative reform, would shift. They still believed that even if some regulation were unavoidable, direct regulation should, as a basic principle, be kept to a minimum. They concluded that the necessity to regulate land use derives from treating land as a commodity and conceded, therefore, that public regulation should be imposed. They did not retreat from a basic commitment to the principle of economic liberalism. Until Rinchō group members participated in Land Rinchō, they did not realize how deficient planning for Japan's land use was nor how disorderly urban redevelopments had been under the Nakasone Minkatsu line. When they learned about actual developments, they became more cautious toward land use deregulation although, as a matter of principle, they really approved of it. Therefore, even though the report reflected shifts in political trends, this group did not take the initiative on deliberations within Land Rinchō. It was the political comeback of MOC's planners that decisively influenced the report contents.

As with other Rinchō-related advisory organs, the General Affairs Agency oversaw the secretariat of Land Rinchō, providing secretarial assistance. The secretariat was composed of seconded officials from ten ministries and agencies related to land policy. Most of them were unfamiliar with land problems, so bureaucrats seconded from the MOC and the National Land Agency (most officials of which, in turn, were seconded from the MOC), with expertise on land problems, led the secretariat. They played a decisive role in deliberations in the council and in the arrangement and provision of technical data and analysis. Kamemoto Kazuo, a specialist on land use policy in the MOC, was assigned to write the first draft of the final report and was occasionally asked to explain problems and comment on concrete proposals throughout the committee's discussions.

The secretariat of a government deliberation council generally exercises great influence as it collects materials and prepares rough drafts of reports. Because few Land Rinchō members were specialists on land problems, construction bureaucrats exercised considerable power, and Land Rinchō became an exception to most Rinchō-related committees in which formal committee members were often quite influential.

As stated, although the planners within the MOC were willing to correct regulation excesses, they were up against the indiscriminate deregulatory policy of the Nakasone cabinet. The MOC officials seconded to Land Rinchō belonged to the planners group and found themselves with an opportunity to reverse the trend of Nakasone's earlier land use policy.

In contrast to the period when deregulation was introduced in 1983, public opinion now supported them. Within the MOC itself, conviction was growing that the previous uniform deregulation of the Nakasone cabinet was a failure. The "rough draft of the draft" (sōan no sōan) for the final report was prepared in this secretariat. Not surprisingly, it emphasized urban planning and strengthened regulations.

The members of the draft committee, who examined the report, consisted of the core members of the Shadow Land Rinchō, Iijima, Kato, Tsuboi, and Yayama, joined by Chairman Otsuki, Miyazaki, Hayashi Shuzo (a legal specialist), and Professor Ishihara Shunsuke. The officials of the secretariat also participated in the debate on an equal footing. A severe clash of opinions arose within the drafting committee, which took more than one month to deliberate the final draft, debating heatedly almost every day.

Miyazaki and Tsuboi, who requested complete deregulation, expressed dissatisfaction that most of their opinions were not incorporated in the rough draft and severely criticized the proposal by the secretariat. Kato and others of the Rinchō group protested that regulatory and planning ideas were too strong. The Rinchō group, however, did not argue solely for deregulation because they did not debate only on the basis of fixed ideological principles or as representatives of concrete interests. For example, Yayama said that because new housing demands arose from new business developments, each business undertaking would require a housing development. He, thus, supported the long-standing demands of the construction bureaucrats. The Rinchō group further urged preparation of a broad administrative master plan for orderly urban planning. Nonetheless, the demands of the Rinchō group and the representatives of the real estate business revised the overall report toward liberalization.

Kato, Yayama, and other neoliberals, who had played a major role as Nakasone's brain trust in promoting administrative reforms, were not familiar with land problems in Japan. The construction bureaucrats persuaded them that the land problem was a specialized issue that could not be solved with a liberal economic philosophy alone. Their persuasion seems to have been successful.

The person who consistently supported the planners from the MOC throughout this debate was urban planning specialist Professor Ishihara Shunsuke. In the Land Rinchō, which had few specialists on land and construction problems, his views carried great weight and the necessity for urban planning was written into part 5 of the report.

Meanwhile, in support of a Yomiuri newspaper editor, Hara Takafumi, who represented the mass media in Land Rinchō, the Yomiuri shinbun continued to conduct an active press campaign on land problems that backed up the regulators and planners. Yomiuri had previously shown a strong interest in land problems and had set up a land problems investigation committee within the company. In May 1985, as the result of three years of research, it presented a proposal entitled "For the Establishment of a Land Policy That Will Support Japan in the Twenty-First Century." Hara brought this report into Land Rinchō, and supported the argument of MOC planners.

Otsuki Bunpei, council chairman and former chairman of Nikkeiren, Japan's major employers' association, was a top business leader who specialized in labor relations. He strongly believed that it was the dream of salaried workers to own their own homes that drove hardworking Japanese employees. He was very critical of policies that rendered such aspirations impossible. His opinion that land should be a public property derived from this background. As chairman of the Housing and Housing Lot Deliberation Council, he stressed the importance of housing supply and is said to have gone around persuading business (*zaikai*) leaders behind the scenes. Otsuki, however, who was weak in theoretical debates, is said to have entrusted real leadership in the deliberations to Sejima and Kato and himself commented little in the council.

Within Japan's business community, a lineage resists Keidanren's mainstream of economic liberalism and incorporates the trend toward revised capitalism.[18] Kikawada Kazutaka, one-time chairman of Keizai doyukai and a close advisor to former Prime Minister Miki, represented those business leaders during the early seventies. With the rise of Rinchō, this group receded into the background, but its points of view never entirely disappeared. Therefore, as political trends altered in the late eighties, at least part of the big business community began to emphasize the social and public responsibilities of business corporations.

Those who advocated further deregulation were the representatives of real estate companies and corporations with huge land assets (like Miyazaki, president of Asahi Chemical Textile). This position, however, was subjected to severe public criticism. The sharp rise in land prices had largely nullified their persuasiveness. Public criticism was particularly severe against the real estate business, which had profited greatly through the manipulative resale of land. Outright deregulators, such as Tsuboi, whose arguments seemed to represent their own business interests, thus lost the trust of Nakasone confidants like Kato and Yayama. A rupture occurred between the representatives of the business world because some continued to advocate complete deregulation while others promoted planned development.

18. Hideo Otake, "The Zaikai under the Occupation: The Formation and Transformation of Managerial Councils," in Robert E. Ward and Sakamoto Yoshikazu, eds., *Democratizing Japan: The Allied Occupation* (Honolulu: University of Hawaii Press, 1987), 366–391.

Two men represented the interests of organized labor on Land Rinchō: Homma Yoshito and Kakinuma Yasunori. Homma, the journalist who represented the General Council of Trade Unions, was a *Mainichi shinbun* reporter and a specialist on land problems. The staff of the General Council of Trade Unions had no specialists on land problems. Moreover, because land was a problem that had no direct relation to the interests of trade union organizations, they selected candidates to the committee who were not labor leaders. Homma basically advocated restraining land prices through strict regulation, and he emphasized the necessity of increased construction of public housing (instead of the public supply of private housing or public support of private supply). The Rengō Policy Bureau chief, Kakinuma Yasunori, who was selected as a representative of Dōmei (the moderate peak labor union), was not a land problem specialist. He supported the appeals of Otsuki for homeownership for salaried workers, and he helped Homma by trying to represent laborers' interests.

These two men (according to Kakinuma) were of the same mind on policy, but they were a tiny minority in the committee. Rather than conducting the intimate prior consultations that characterized the Rinchō group, they merely supported one another in debates within the committee. (The Japanese labor movement was in the midst of forming a grand coalition, and, hence, the alliance of Homma and Kakinuma had a wider political implication.) They were opposed to deregulation and favored urban redevelopment shaped by urban planning. In the midst of fears that environmental problems would become more severe, they felt that regulation should be strengthened rather than relaxed. When they tried to express their opposition to the draft prepared by the secretariat and the Shadow Land Rinchō, they confronted much resistance. Homma dared to overcome it with defiance, an attitude that was quite uncommon in the deliberation council.

By stressing that planning and regulation were necessary, Homma's position was, thus, close to the construction bureaucrats. However, in deliberations he clashed severely with the deregulation group and also with the MOC officicals so that he was isolated. He clashed with the latter, in part, because of his opposition-partylike distrust of the government and government officials. From a policy perspective, however, there may have been a difference in judgment with regard to the implementability of public regulations. The construction bureaucrats, for example, were negative toward Homma's appeals for the designation of regulatory areas in which all land transactions would have to be authorized by the local government. They knew the limits of state power in the regulation of economic activities.

MOC officials saw land price increases as mostly the result of excessive fluidity (excessive money supplies caused by Japan's huge trade surplus). They felt that the part wrought by deregulation was marginal. Therefore, they concluded that the effect of strengthened regulation on land prices was extremely limited. They also believed that a powerful drug like the designation of regulatory areas (the suspension of free economic activities) could only be administered temporarily. Despite a popular image to the contrary, Japan's economic bureaucrats, who are supposed to be in charge of regulation and planning, have a basic commitment to the free market. This is true of MOC and MITI bureaucrats, who are seen as synonymous with planning bureaucrats.[19]

Local government officals were also very negative toward direct regulation. They did not think that rising land prices were bad. Far from it. Some felt that their land prices should not be behind those in Tokyo, and land prices were seen as a barometer of a city's economic power. They expected increased revenue from real estate taxes, and to cope with sharp land price increases, designating supervisory and regulatory areas meant restricting regional economic activities. Like MOC officials, local government officials were also averse to suspending all regional land transactions. For these reasons, local governments opposed the Land Agency's attempt to extend supervisory areas or introduce regulatory areas. The MOC was influenced by the judgment of these "street-level bureaucrats."

The MOC regulators, then, rejected the kind of strong regulations and planning requested by Homma. They also acceded to a partial acceptance of the neoliberal opinions of the Rinchō group. Compromise was achieved between two mainstream groups, and the final report reflected its character.

Proceeding in parallel with deliberations on Land Rinchō, a Basic Land Act was drafted by the opposition parties and presented to the Diet in May 1988. After Land Rinchō presented its final report, the LDP government drafted its own Basic Land Act, presented it to the Diet, and had it passed in November 1989. Thereafter, the land problem continued to be a heated political debate over land taxes. As this issue evolved, it is no exaggeration to say that Land Rinchō functioned to shift the ideological current. From a wider perspective that takes into account the Recruit scandal and the introduction of the consumption tax, the land problem presented a grave challenge to the administrative reform line that had led to stable LDP dominance during the first half of the eighties. The great success of the JSP in the July 1989 Upper House election undoubtedly owed to the shifts in the political current identified.

The development of land policy in the 1980s can be seen as a process of the rise, transformation, and retreat of an ideological reform. It began with the introduction of reform attempts under the concepts of small

19. Otake Hideo, *Gendai Nihon no seiji kenryoku keizai kenryoku* [Political and economic power in contemporary Japan] (Tokyo: San'ichi shobō, 1979).

government, deregulation, and mobilization of private sector vitality. These ideas were rampant and popular. They materialized in concrete policy outcomes with the privatization of the national railway, budget cuts in welfare programs, and deregulation in government-industry relations, to mention only a few. Without due consideration of the unique conditions of land problems in Japan or careful preparation, simpleminded reform was introduced in this field largely because of political considerations on the part of the prime minister. Shortly thereafter, neoliberal reform became entangled with various political and economic considerations of other political actors foreign to liberal ideology. This result was most clearly manifested when giant public projects were resumed. The subsequent policy outcomes soon caused soaring land prices and forced reform attempts to retreat altogether.

It is commonly acknowledged that land as public property should not be left to the mercy of the market and that public restrictions and intervention are needed to control land use. It does not seem, however, that the retreat of neoliberal ideology on the land problem spilled over in a clearcut way into other policy areas and strengthened regulation and planning. Nor does it seem that the retreat went far enough toward social democratic ideas even in land policy. It is, at least, clear that the planners did not achieve an unambiguous victory. After winning success with crisis management of rapid land price increases, two groups, the deregulators and the regulators, began a tug-of-war over such issues as the enactment of the Basic Land Law, examination of land taxes, and U.S.-Japan Structural Impediments Initiative talks. As a result, the Japanese government returned in the late eighties to the normal pattern of Japanese-style land use policy, patchwork regulations without comprehensive planning.

Japanese land use policy has long been an interesting puzzle for Japan specialists. The Japanese state, which is commonly regarded as a strong state, seems almost powerless to regulate private landowners. Land property rights are respected to an extent unthinkable in most European nations. The difference is manifestly clear when compared with the attitude in Germany, the nation sometimes referred to as an ideal *Marktwirtschaft* (market economy), where public authorities, nevertheless, have imposed very strict regulations and introduced comprehensive city planning.[20] In contrast, the history of Japanese city planning is nothing but a series of frustrations.[21] Behind this powerlessness of the Japanese state, apparently, lies a traditonal (agrarian) political culture not unlike French-style individualism. The Japanese people adhere to land like traditional farmers do.

20. Fujita Tokiyasu, *Nihon no tochi hō to Nishi Doitsu no tochi hō* [Japanese land law and West German land law] (Tokyo: Sōbunsha, 1988).
21. Kent E. Calder, *Crisis and Compensation: Public Policy and Political Stability in Japan, 1949–1986* (Princeton: Princeton University Press, 1988).

They are mistrustful of government intervention into property rights, preferring the individual provision of future securities to the public provision of welfare. Land, along with savings, is considered an important means for securing individual welfare.[22]

Neoliberal ideology seems to have deepened popular mistrust of government. It strengthened people's adherence to land, and it contributed to the increase in demand for land, thereby escalating prices. When the Recruit scandal broke, mistrust of governing elites soared. By touching the delicate nerve of the masses, neoliberal reforms caused an unexpected explosion.

22. On the preference of the Japanese masses for the private provision of welfare, see Kabashima Ikuo, "Yūkensha no hōkaku ideorogii to Nakasone seiji" [The conservative ideology of voters and Nakasone's politics], *Revaiasan,* no. 2 (1988): 23–52. This individualistic culture of self-help undoubtedly contributed to the success of the administrative reform movement, including the reduction in outlays for pensions and health care in the 1980s.

CHAPTER ELEVEN

PRIVATIZING REGULATION:

THE IMPLEMENTATION OF THE

LARGE-SCALE RETAIL STORES LAW

Frank Upham

IN THIS CHAPTER I USE THE STRUCTURE AND IMPLEMENTATION OF THE Large-Scale Retail Stores Law (LSRSL)[1] to explore interest intermediation in contemporary Japan. One focus is on the policy embodied by the law itself, which in many ways is typical of postwar Japanese regulatory statutes. The political compromise that determined its content and the way in which local and central politicians have influenced enforcement policy are further evidence of the importance of the political process in Japanese economic regulation. What makes the story of the LSRSL distinctive, however, is less the process of its creation than its case-by-case application to specific circumstances. Although the statute itself may be adequately explained by conventional theories of pluralist politics, the manner in which the Ministry of International Trade and Industry (MITI) and local governments have cooperated with local merchants in its enforcement provides a different perspective on Japanese interest intermediation. Instead of applying the statute in each particular instance in a manner consistent with the political compromise that created it, MITI throughout the 1980s delegated its power under the law to the large and small retailers themselves. Although scarcely unique in Japanese bureaucratic practice, MITI's behavior in this instance challenges prevailing paradigms of interaction among the state, political parties, and businesses and of the nature of regulation itself.

---

1. *Daikibo kouri tenpo ni okeru kourigyō no jigyō katsudō no chōsei ni kansuru hōritsu* [The law concerning the adjustment of retail business operations in large-scale retail stores], Law no. 109, October 1, 1973. For a full text of the law, see Iwanami shoten, comp., *Roppō zensho* [Compendium of the six law codes] (Tokyo: Iwanami shoten, 1987), 2097.

The State of the Japanese Retail Industry

Whatever its long-term social and economic contribution to Japanese social welfare, Japan's distribution system in the 1980s was woefully inefficient by conventional economic measures and was often labeled so by
foreign and domestic critics alike.[2] In its "Cost of Living '88" report, for
example, the Economic Planning Agency (EPA) estimated that the cost of
living in Tokyo was 97 percent higher than in New York and traced part
of the cause to the distribution system generally and to the LSRSL
specifically.[3] The EPA also estimated that 40 percent of the retail price of
domestic goods and 59 percent of imported goods were attributable to distribution costs[4] and that 30 percent of the savings theoretically achievable
by the rise of the value of the yen in the two years between October 1985
and December 1987 was absorbed by the distribution sector rather than
passed on to the consumer.[5]

Part of this inefficiency was produced by a complex wholesale network.
In the early 1980s, for example, the number of employees per wholesale
store was the lowest in surveyed countries[6] and in one EPA survey the

2. By some individual measures, the Japanese distribution system is more efficient than
those of other Organization for Economic Cooperation and Development (OECD) countries. In value added per employee, for example, the United Kingdom is less efficient. See
1987/1988 OECD Economic Surveys: Japan (Paris: OECD, 1989), 80 (hereafter cited as
1987/1988 OECD); in the mix of large and small retailers, both Italy and France are even
more dominated by small stores than Japan. See Tsūshō sangyō shō, *Daitenhō kankei shiryō*
[Materials concerning the large stores law] (Tokyo: Tsūshō sangyō shō, 1988), 16 (hereafter
cited as MITI Materials); and *1987/1988 OECD*, 80. But in any overall comparison, the
Japanese distribution system appears to be the least efficient of the OECD countries to which
it is most commonly compared. It is important to note that these measures are premised on
a narrow definition of efficiency that excludes the external costs and benefits of small and
large stores. An accurate appraisal of the efficiency of the distribution industry would have
to include such benefits of small and family-owned retail units as social stability, neighborhood cohesion, retirement security, effect on family structure, employment security, and so
forth. See, for example, Hugh T. Patrick and Thomas P. Rohlen, "Small-scale Family Enterprises," in Kozo Yamamura and Yasukichi Yasuba, eds., *The Political Economy of Japan*,
vol. 1: *The Domestic Transformation* (Stanford: Stanford University Press, 1987), 331.

3. *Nihon keizai shinbun*, October 21, 1988, 1.

4. Keizai kikaku chō, *Kaihō-gata ryūtsū shisutemu no kōchiku ni mukete* [Toward the
construction of a liberalized retail system] (Tokyo: Shōji hōmu kenkyūkai, 1988), 53 (hereafter cited as *EPA Report*).

5. Quoted in A. E. Cullison, "Japan Mission to Study Distribution in U.S.," *Journal of
Commerce*, October 25, 1988, 1; and in Tsūshō sangyō shō, *Wagakuni no ryūtsūgyō ryūtsū
kōzō nado ni tsuite (sankō shiryō)* [Concerning Japanese retailing industry and structure
(documents)] (Tokyo: Tsūshō sangyō shō, 1988), 13. For a detailed report on price trends for
imports and for domestic products that compete with imports see *EPA Report*, 30–31, especially the charts and graphs on 51–60. A close reading of these two sources demonstrates
that much of the savings are passed on to consumers rather quickly in sectors where domestic
competition is vigorous. It is in the areas, such as European luxury goods, where competition
is weak that little or no decrease in retail prices is realized.

6. *1987/1988 OECD*, 80.

ratio of the value of wholesale to retail sales was more than double that of any other country.[7] These figures portray a wholesale industry dominated by large numbers of small firms, each of which added to the product's price while adding little to its value.[8]

But high distribution costs were also attributable to the inefficiency of Japanese retailing. In 1982, for example, the number of retail stores per capita was 75 percent higher in Japan than in the United States, the next highest country, and the value added per employee was 28 percent less.[9] Stores with only one or two employees accounted for 60 percent of all stores, yet generated less than 14 percent of all sales. Conversely, the 1,754 largest stores, with less than four hundred thousand employees, sold 40 percent as much as the almost 1.5 million smallest stores and their more than three million employees.[10] The annual sales per employee in the largest stores was more than four times that of those in the smallest.[11]

Many factors contributed to the structure of Japanese distribution networks. Historically, Japanese manufacturers had been heavily involved in all levels of the distribution chain and had been able to dominate a system that has often been described according to production estimates more than consumer desires.[12] Manufacturers guaranteed their distributors' margins and, in turn, received price stability. The result was a system largely organized along *keiretsu* (affiliated enterprises) lines in which long-term relationships and uniform and inflexible pricing reduced bargaining and other transaction costs and provided an effective barrier to both non-keiretsu consumer goods and new entrants into the industry, including foreign entrants. One reason this system worked, one is told, is that Japanese consumers emphasized quality and service more than price in consumption decisions. Uniform prices, therefore, were not a major source of

7. *EPA Report,* 74, table 12. The ratio was 4.21 for Japan, 1.87 for the United States, 2.03 for the United Kingdom, 1.57 for France, and 1.67 for West Germany.

8. Ibid., 80; tables 20 and 21 for the prices charged by wholesalers as a percentage of ultimate retail price.

9. *1987/1988 OECD,* 80, table 27. The value-added per-employee figure is for the distribution industry as a whole.

10. JETRO, *Retailing in the Japanese Consumer Market,* JETRO Marketing Series no. 5 (1985): 28, especially exhibit no. 13 (hereafter cited as JETRO Marketing Series no. 5). There is no date for the statistics, but they appear to be from the early 1980s.

11. Ibid. The one economic criterion by which small stores are more efficient than large ones is sales per square meter. Stores with two or fewer employees had sales of ¥ 4.2 million per square meter, whereas those with more than fifty employees had sales of ¥ 1.03 million per square meter. This advantage was present only for the smallest stores. Those with three to four employees had sales of only ¥ 0.74 million per square meter.

12. See Miyazawa Ken'ichi, "Endaka keizaika de hen'yō suru ryūtsū kikō" [Changing structure of distribution under the high-yen economy], *Ekonomisuto,* September 13, 1988, 53 (hereafter cited as Miyazawa). Miyazawa is an economics professor and former president of Hitotsubashi University who served as the chair of a recent Economic Planning Agency report on the distribution industry.

concern.[13] Another reason, however, was the effectiveness of government intervention to favor both manufacturers and merchants more than consumers, as represented by the Large-Scale Retail Stores Law and its predecessors dating back to the 1930s.

In the late 1980s, however, much of this arrangement had begun to crumble. As more Japanese traveled abroad and learned that they did not need to pay premium prices for brand name products, they began to emphasize price and style more in consumption decisions at home. Simultaneously, new modes of importing developed to complement and compete with the exclusive import agents, general trading companies, and foreign subsidiaries that had historically dominated importing. In addition, as Japanese manufacturers began to import their own goods produced overseas, they began breaking down the distinctions between manufacturer, wholesaler, and retailer. At times they skipped the wholesaler and took orders directly from retailers, and at other times they performed both wholesale and retail functions. Retailers, conversely, began moving upstream, using their superior information about consumer demand to initiate their own designs and even produce their own products.

Adding to these economic forces was a shift in government policy occasioned by foreign pressure both to liberalize the distribution system and to shift to a demand-pull economy. In the late 1980s, the American government put the distribution system on the trade agenda as part of the Structural Impediments Initiative (SII) round of bilateral trade negotiations, and Prime Minister Takeshita promised reform of the distribution industry in June 1988. Despite the plausible argument that the LSRSL system greatly hindered the entry of foreign retail chains into Japan, American pressure initially focused on barriers to entry within the domestic market rather than barriers to foreign direct investment. Buttressed by the EPA's statistics that showed an almost 50 percent higher markup on imported over domestic goods, the U.S. government argued that large Japanese stores sold more imported goods proportionately than did small stores and that deregulation would increase both the absolute level of consumer spending and the proportion going to imports. When American retailers, particularly Toys "R" Us, expressed a strong interest in direct participation in the Japanese industry, however, the focus expanded to include easier entry for foreign retailers into the domestic market.

In this instance the Americans enjoyed many Japanese allies, including the Keidanren (Federation of Economic Organizations), the Economic Planning Agency, and the Fair Trade Commission (FTC), who believed that liberalization was necessary to fulfill Japan's assumed macroeconomic role as driving world demand and to improve the standard of living

13. Ibid.

for Japanese consumers.[14] The American spotlight on the issue also resulted in a series of articles in the popular media about the injustice and corruption engendered by the way MITI implemented the law.[15] Stories of ten-year delays in the opening of stores, of extravagant payoffs to local power brokers, of the sellout of some local merchants by others, and of a general abuse of the statutory procedures convinced many of a wide gap between the original content and purpose of the law and the reality of its operation.

By the end of the decade, the coalition of American trade negotiators and their domestic allies had made reform inevitable. In May 1990, MITI announced a series of steps to lower barriers to entry in the distribution industry and to reform the implementation of the LSRSL, and by one year later the Diet had passed a series of amendments that included doubling the minimum size of a "large-scale" store covered by the law. Results were immediate in both the number of store openings and foreign access. The number of stores approved leaped in the second half of 1990, and a Toys "R" Us became the first foreign retail store to open under the LSRSL. Reform in the implementation process was less dramatic, but by the end of 1990 it was clear not only that there had been a fundamental change in the mode of implementation of the LSRSL but also that protection of small independent retailers in the 1990s would take place within a very different framework.

The History and Structure of the Large-Scale Retail Stores Law

The Large-Scale Retail Stores Law had its origins in the 1920s when department stores began to expand beyond luxury and high-priced goods into a broader range of merchandise intended to reach the mass of Japanese consumers. As competition from department stores increased and exacerbated the general effects of the Great Depression, small and medium-sized retailers began to call for protective legislation. By the 1930s both the Seiyūkai and the Minseitō, the two conservative political parties, had filed draft legislation, and in 1937 the Ministry of Commerce and Industry, the

14. See, for example, Keizai Koho Center, "Deregulating Distribution: Keidanren Proposals for Transport, Trade, Retailing, and Farming and Food Processing," *KKC Brief No. 48* (Tokyo: Japan Institute for Social and Economic Affairs, 1988) (hereafter cited as Keidanren Proposals).

15. See, for example, "Gekishin ima, ryūtsū ga kawaru" [Severe earthquake now, distribution changes], *Shūkan tōyō keizai* (August 6, 1988): 8 (hereafter cited as Gekishin). See also the articles appearing in a special edition of *Ekonomisuto* entitled "Daitenhō no kyojitsu o tsuku" [Exposing the truth and falsehoods of the large stores law], *Ekonomisuto*, December 13, 1988.

predecessor of the current MITI, after consultation with the Japan Chamber of Commerce and Industry (Nihon shōkōkaigisho), submitted a draft to the Imperial Diet in March. The language of the resulting Department Store Law (Hyakkatenhō), passed that August, states well the basic premise of Japanese retail regulation:

> On the one hand, it goes without saying that department stores contribute to the rationalization of the retail system and to the interests of consumers. On the other hand, however, they are managed on a large scale and operate with abundant capital and huge amounts of credit, and their rapid advance inevitably results in a substantial impact on numerous small and medium-sized retail enterprises.[16]

The law required a permit for the opening or expansion of any department store, which was defined as any single retail store dealing in a variety of goods that contained more than fifteen hundred square meters of floor space.

The 1937 Department Store Law (DSL) was repealed in 1947 as inconsistent with the newly enacted Antimonopoly Law. As economic recovery in the 1950s brought renewed competition in the retail sector, however, small retailers' groups again began calling for protection. Both the Japan Socialist party (JSP) and the Democratic Socialist party (DSP) filed members' bills in the Diet, but it was a MITI-sponsored bill drafted in consultation with the Industrial Rationalization Council (Sangyō gōrika shingikai) that passed in May 1956. The new Department Store Law followed the pattern of the old one, retaining the permit system and the definition of department stores as single retail units of more than fifteen hundred square meters of floor space.

For the next fifteen years the Department Store Law helped structure Japanese retailing to serve the interests of department stores and small retailers alike. The permit system cartelized the department stores by preventing new entrants and guaranteeing the territory of existing branches. Meanwhile, the restrictions on new department stores protected small merchants outside the established commercial centers from high-volume, high-status competitors.

By the late 1960s, however, the system was breaking down. One factor was demographic. Suburbs grew in previously rural areas where there had been little commercial activity. Increased discretionary income and heightened interest in consumer protection led to a change in consumer behavior that made changes in the industry structure possible. Most important, however, was the ability of new forms of retailing, particularly superstore (*suupaa*) chains, to take advantage of these opportunities. Superstores were mass merchandisers offering a mix of clothing, household goods,

16. Quoted in MITI Materials, 1.

and food similar to that of department stores but without the latter's fashionable image. They developed in the 1960s independently of the preexisting retail groups, generally as small food or clothing stores in Tokyo or Ōsaka. They expanded rapidly in the 1970s by exploiting the niche between department stores and small neighborhood retailers. By 1981 six of the ten largest retailers in Japan were superstores (the remaining four were department stores), and the superstores led by firms like Daiei and Ito-Yokado held a 53 percent share of the retail sales handled by the two hundred largest retailers.[17]

Superstore chains were able to build large stores in new areas because of the clever exploitation of a loophole in the Department Store Law. The law defined department stores as *single units* of more than fifteen hundred square meters. Superstores, on the other hand, consisted of several legally separate entities, each less than fifteen hundred square meters, operating under a common corporate identity on different floors of the same building. The new corporate form rendered the DSL ineffective in protecting either department stores or small retailers, and by the late 1960s both were lobbying for its revision. Department stores wanted superstores included in a more relaxed regulatory regime. Small retailers also wanted superstores included but with strengthened statutory restrictions. The superstores were satisfied with the status quo. The resulting compromise is the Large-Scale Retail Stores Law of 1973.

There were three significant differences between the Large-Scale Retail Stores Law and its predecessor. It added the protection of consumer interests to the purposes of the act. It replaced the direct regulation of the permit system with a notification and adjustment system. Under the DSL, department stores could not operate without explicit approval from an administrative agency; under the LSRSL no approval was necessary, but large stores had to notify MITI of their plans and participate in an adjustment process. The LSRSL shifted the target of regulation from the type of store, that is, department stores, to the volume of retail activity by focusing on the amount of retail floor space in a single building and disregarding the legal nature of the store or stores within it.

Although its passage might be adequately explained as the result of a political struggle among department stores, small and medium retailers, and superstores, official MITI commentaries on the LSRSL invariably cited strengthened consumer protection and industry rationalization as statutory goals.[18] Besides guaranteeing small merchants an enterprise op-

17. JETRO Marketing series 5, 25 and 16, respectively. The top six superstores in 1982 were Daiei, Ito Yokado, Seiyu, Jusco, Nichii, and Unii. They were still the top six, in the same order, in 1988. *Yomiuri shinbun*, October 20, 1988, New York ed., 6.

18. See Arima Jun, "Ima gyōsei wa rigai no tairitsu suru daitenhō ni do torikunde iru ka" [How will the bureaucracy deal with the large stores law as it is now the object of interest

portunity, Articles 1 and 11 of the law specifically required due consideration to the interests of consumers and to the well-being of the retail industry as a whole, which contributed to a generally positive initial appraisal of the law by economists and large retailers.[19]

The procedural requirements of the LSRSL were simple and straightforward.[20] Persons wishing to construct a building (Article 3) with more than fifteen hundred square meters of retail space and prospective retailers (Article 5) within the building had to notify MITI of their plans. If MITI determined (Article 7) that the operation of the new store would have a significant impact on local small and medium retailers, it had four months to issue a recommendation (*kankoku*) that the prospective retailer delay the proposed opening date, decrease the floor space, or otherwise modify its plans.

During these four months, MITI had to solicit the opinion of two tripartite deliberative councils made up of merchants, consumers, and representatives of the public interest: the Large-Scale Retail Stores Deliberative Council at the regional level and the Commercial Activities Adjustment Board established within the local chamber of commerce. The latter was to investigate local conditions, negotiate with the prospective large retailer regarding possible changes in its plans, and report to the regional council, which, in turn, gave its opinion to MITI. Acceptance of a recommendation was voluntary, but Article 8 of the law gave MITI the power to order compliance if necessary to prevent severe injury to the interests of local merchants. The statute contemplated that the entire process would normally take no more than eight months.

Commercial Adjustment under the Large Stores Law

From the first, however, implementation under the LSRSL was only loosely related to its formal structure. The shift from the permit system of the Department Store Law to the notification system of the LSRSL

conflict?], *Shōgyōkai* 41 (April 1988): 146. Arima was then a MITI official involved in policy-making in the retail sector. See also MITI Materials, 3.

19. Tsuruta Toshimasa, "Kokusaika jidai no daitenhō wa dō arubeki ka" [What should the LSL be like in the age of internationalization?], *Ekonomisuto*, December 13, 1988, 47 (hereafter cited as Tsuruta).

20. Article 2 of the law distinguishes between class one stores, those over fifteen hundred square meters, and class two stores, those between fifteen hundred square meters and five hundred square meters. For simplicity, the following description deals primarily with the construction and operation of a new class one retail outlet. The main difference in treatment of classes one and two is that the former comes under the initial jurisdiction of the regional office of MITI and the latter under the prefectural governor's office. The adjustment process

ostensibly meant that government intervention would be the exception rather than the rule, and an emphasis on free market principles played a role in convincing large retailers and others to support the law. The insertion of the goals of consumer protection and industry modernization into a law intended to protect small business may, however, have created a contradiction that doomed the statute to incoherence. At the same time that it was extolling free market competition to the large retailers, for example, MITI and the Liberal Democratic party were promising small and medium retailers that the notification system would operate "just like a permit system."[21] In the subsequent fifteen years MITI more than fulfilled this promise and oversaw the creation of a system that erected barriers to entry into the retail industry far surpassing those of the Department Store Law in everything but formal legal authority.

Although MITI's creative interpretation of the draft legislation may have helped the LDP pass it, it was not successful in preventing criticism thereafter. In the first five years of operation, almost fifteen hundred new large stores were opened under the law, approximately doubling the number existing before 1974, and many chain retailers began avoiding the law altogether by shifting to stores of just under fifteen hundred square meters.[22] In response, local governments passed ordinances and administrative guidance restricting stores of less than fifteen hundred square meters, and independent retailers began pushing hard for extended coverage and tighter restrictions on new entrants into the industry.[23] By 1977 the Diet had passed a resolution urging action to protect small retailers, and MITI had established a series of study commissions on the "retail problem."[24] In 1978 the Diet extended the LSRSL's coverage from stores of more than fifteen hundred square meters to all stores of more than five hundred square meters. The former became "class one" stores under the

also applies to renovations of existing stores and changes in operating conditions (floor space, hours, monthly and annual days of operation) that bring the store's operations under the law's purview.

21. Gekishin, 9. ("Kagirinaku kyōkasei ni chikai todokede-sei ni suru" is the Japanese phraseology.)

22. Tsuruta, 49. In Tokyo, for example, both the prefecture and each ward have separate sets of administrative guidance in addition to the LSL. See Tōkyō to kouri shōgyō chōsei ni kansuru yōkō [Tokyo Prefecture outline guidance concerning the adjustment of retailing] (April 22, 1985), and, for example, Suginami-ku chūkibo kouri tenpo shutten ni kansuru shidō yōkō [Suginami Ward outline guidance concerning the opening of medium-scale retail stores] (July 1, 1986). Both are typescripts on file with the author. The Nihon keizai shinbun estimated that more than 60 percent of local entities have some form of locally created restriction on the opening of medium-scale retailers, which generally includes all stores of less than five hundred square meters. Nihon keizai shinbun, September 29, 1988, 2.

23. Tsūshō sangyō shō, ed., "Shin daikibo kouri tenpohō no kaisetsu" [(New) explanation of the large-scale retail stores law] (Typescript, Tokyo, n.d.), 3.

24. Ibid.

direct jurisdiction of MITI; the latter became "class two" stores under local government jurisdiction. In addition, in 1979, MITI issued administrative guidance that required Article 3 notification thirteen months before the proposed opening date rather than the statutory seven months.

When 1979 and 1980 saw both an increasing number of store openings and sluggish consumer expenditures, however, small retailers began to call for a return to the permit approach of the DSL and a reorientation to regulate stores on the type of retail activity as well as floor space. The latter was necessary to protect independent stores from yet another new competitive threat, the convenience store chains, which competed not on the basis of size but on price and hours.[25]

Any attempt to pass legislation that favored small retailers would have elicited substantial opposition, but, as it turned out, recourse to the Diet was unnecessary. In January 1982 MITI issued guidance entitled "Interim Measures concerning the Notification of Large-Scale Retail Stores" that accomplished the small retailers' goals without legislative action. One set of measures modified the statutory adjustment process by requiring builders of class one outlets and their primary tenants to "explain" their plans to local merchants *before* notification under Article 3 of the law. Previously, Article 3 notification had been the initial step in the adjustment process. Similarly, it moved the adjustment process, which statutorily was to commence after each retailer had completed notification under Article 5, to commence before that notification. These new requirements became known as "prenotification explanation" and "prenotification adjustment," respectively.

This guidance frontloaded the adjustment process so that contact between prospective retailers and local merchants was to begin before any steps were taken under the statute and be completed before the individual retailers had even filed their formal plans. As a result, official adjustment after Article 5 notification was to be a mere formal endorsement of the prenotification adjustment results. These changes did not necessarily mean a complete transformation of the system, however. The thirteen-month time limit of the 1979 administrative guidance remained, and the prenotification adjustment was still to be carried out by the Commercial Activities Adjustment Board, which had to include consumer and public interest representatives as well as local merchants.[26]

These administrative measures took the implementation of the LSRSL some distance from its statutory framework. Actual practice under the

25. See Miyazawa, 58–59; and *Nihon keizai shinbun*, October 24, 1988.
26. MITI did not rely entirely on changes in the notification and adjustment process, however. It also addressed the problem more directly by calling on large retailers to exercise self-restraint in opening new class one stores in areas it designated as restricted zones. MITI also established annual allotments for increases in total floor space for certain specified retail companies.

law, however, was removed even farther from the original intent, so far removed, in fact, that in many instances it was inconsistent with both the statutory requirements and even the administrative guidance itself. Local variations make generalizations dangerous, but one consistent feature was the removal of real power under the LSRSL from the regional MITI bureaus and their statutory advisory councils to local merchants operating under the umbrella of local chambers of commerce. Beginning in 1979 and accelerating in the 1980s, MITI refused to accept Article 3 notification unless the builder appended a document setting forth the terms under which local merchants unanimously agreed to the new store's opening.[27] As a result, even the prenotification adjustment process envisioned by the 1982 administrative guidance before Article 5 notification became a meaningless formality, replaced by an even more informal process known as "pre-prenotification adjustment."

At this stage, before any formal steps had been taken under the law at all, the large-store and local merchants entered negotiations on the four items generally covered by adjustment: opening date, floor space, daily hours, and annual days of operation. Sometimes these negotiations were carried out by the members of the formal Adjustment Board but more frequently by local merchants themselves in a Large-Store Countermeasures Task Force or Large-Scale Retail Stores Policy Subcommittee loosely affiliated with the local chamber of commerce.

This distortion of the statutory procedure and the general withdrawal of MITI from its statutory role as final decision maker corrupted the implementation of the Large-Scale Retail Stores Law. Instead of the contemplated seven to eight months between initial notification and opening, it became common for negotiations to take seven to eight years, and delays of ten years were not unheard of. The resulting agreements clearly reflected the veto power given to local merchants. They covered not only the four statutory items but also frequently extended to matters wholly unrelated to the legitimate concerns of the LSRSL itself. They included, for example, requirements that the new store include specified local merchants as subtenants on favorable terms; make large "donations" to local merchant groups; and maintain prices or services at the same level as surrounding merchants.[28]

The Legal Nature of the Adjustment Process

Given the gap between the goals of the Large-Scale Retail Stores Law and the actuality of its operation, one might expect that one or more of the

27. Tsuruta, 48.
28. Seifu kisei nado to kyōsō seisaku ni kansuru kenkyūkai, *Kisei kanwa no suishin ni tsuite* [In regard to the promotion of deregulation] (Tokyo: Kōsei torihiki iinkai, 1989) (here-

many individuals and groups injured by the process would have convinced the courts to force MITI to implement the statute in accord with its content and intent. As in the United States, if a Japanese plaintiff can show that a government act violates the statute on which it is based, a court will nullify it, and a common way to demonstrate illegality is to show that the government agency has used the wrong criteria or followed incorrect procedures in making a decision. Why no one successfully brought such an action against the implementation of the LSRSL can be explained by the litigation that grew out of the opening of a store in Iwate Prefecture.[29]

On March 20, 1979, the Etsurigo Shopping Center Cooperative notified MITI of its plan to build a three-story, 23,904 square meter shopping complex in Etsurigo Village. The superstore, Jusco, was to occupy 14,000 square meters and local merchants 6,000 square meters. The Etsurigo Commercial Activities Adjustment Board met six times between May 18 and July 23 and recommended that Jusco's space be reduced to 7,500 square meters and that of the local tenants remain at 6,000 square meters. Jusco accepted this recommendation, and on September 12, 1979, Jusco and the prospective local tenants filed their Article 5 notification.

The Adjustment Board reconvened on October 19. Ten days later, at its eighth meeting, the board adopted, over two dissents, a resolution accepting the stores' Article 5 notification and forwarded it to the regional Tohoku Large Stores Council. The council, in turn, submitted its opinion to MITI on November 27, recommending a further 15-percent reduction of total space. MITI then issued a recommendation to Jusco calling for the reduction suggested by the council and for certain reductions in operating hours, which Jusco accepted. The whole process took less than nine months.

In January 1981, 117 local merchants sued for the nullification of MITI's recommendation. The plaintiffs claimed that the recommendation was too lenient to Jusco because it did not give local small merchants the enterprise opportunity provided by Article 1 of the LSRSL and that the process by which the recommendation was formed violated both the statute and the detailed administrative guidance issued by MITI stipulating how the adjustment process was to be conducted. Specifically, they alleged that President Takahashi of the Etsurigo Chamber of Commerce, whose

---

after cited as *FTC Report*). This research committee is a creation of the Fair Trade Commission. Its report contains several case studies of the operation of the LSRSL. See also *Nihon keizai shinbun,* September 29, 1988; and Tsuruta, 49.

29. For background on the litigation, see Matsumoto Tadashi, "Meikaku ni sareta daitenhō no fubi" [The clear defects of the large stores law], *Hanrei taimuzu,* no. 463 (May 1, 1982): 71. See also Judgment of the Tokyo District Court of March 16, 1982, 1035 *Hanrei jihō* 17; and Judgment of the Tokyo High Court of June 24, 1985, 1156 *Hanrei jihō* 37. The abuse of the Adjustment Board to promote, rather than restrict, the opening of large stores apparently occurred more frequently between 1974 and 1979 than later. The important point is that the informality of the process allowed abuse in either direction.

son was the president of the Etsurigo Shopping Center Cooperative, had had a direct conflict of interest and had selected members of the regional board solely on their proshopping center views as demonstrated by the fact that the spouses of three of the members were to become tenants in the complex. They argued that the participation of these persons in the board's deliberations violated both Article 1 of the LSRSL and MITI's own administrative guidance requiring the president of the local chamber of commerce to appoint members who will "represent the views of all local small-scale retailers."

Even if the blatant conflict of interest of the board members did not in itself invalidate its action, the plaintiffs further alleged that the board's investigation and deliberations were insufficient. They argued that the board had failed to consider the current condition of small-scale retail operations in the area, local retailers' prospects for modernization, consumer convenience, and the extent of the detrimental impact on existing retailers and that it had not followed the detailed computation formulas provided in MITI's guidance and handbooks. Nor had the regional MITI bureau supervised the board's deliberations as required by ministry rules. The MITI representative failed to attend a single meeting despite repeated requests by local merchants to investigate improprieties in the composition and activities of the board. Plaintiffs pointed to parts of the Diet debates on the LSRSL for proof of the importance of adequate governmental supervision to proper implementation of the law and argued that the failure of the local MITI office to exercise such supervision rendered the board's process unfair and illegal. Because MITI did not conduct its own investigation and based its eventual action solely on the board's findings, the plaintiffs argued that it, too, was illegal.

Journalistic reports and practices elsewhere under the LSRSL leave little doubt that the plaintiffs' factual claims were largely accurate and that the facts amounted to a blatant conflict of interest on the part of Takahashi and the board members and a clear abdication of its statutory duties by MITI. Such procedural irregularities would probably have been enough to convince the courts to declare the whole process illegal. Because the doctrines of Japanese administrative law so restrict judicial review of government action, however, it made little difference what improprieties the plaintiffs might have been able to prove. And in the end, the district and high courts had little trouble either rejecting the local merchants as proper plaintiffs or finding that the MITI recommendation to Jusco was not the type of administrative act that could be challenged in court.[30]

30. The district court opinion dealt directly only with the question of whether the plaintiffs had standing to bring this action. It concluded that they did not, so there was no need to inquire whether a plaintiff with standing could challenge a recommendation. The high court confirmed the district court's conclusion of no standing but went on, nonetheless, to

Under Article 3 of the Administrative Case Litigation Law (ACLL), which governs judicial review of bureaucratic action in Japan, a plaintiff must show that the allegedly illegal act is an "administrative disposition or other exercise of public power," which the Supreme Court has interpreted narrowly to include only "official conduct which forms rights and duties in citizens or confirms their scope"[31]. To be actionable, in other words, bureaucratic action must either deny citizens a previously existing legal right or compel them to perform a new legal duty, and the effect must be immediate and directed at the plaintiff specifically. Actions that affect one's economic interests, as opposed to legal rights, are considered too informal to be judicially cognizable. In the *Etsurigo* case the challenged act was the MITI recommendation based on Article 7 of the LSRSL. The plaintiffs argued that such a recommendation was, in practice, the equivalent of a permit to operate and as such gave the shopping center a right that it did not previously have. It followed that the opening of the shopping center would infringe the rights of local merchants to be protected from such competition unless proper procedures were followed and a legally valid recommendation issued.

Japanese courts interpreting the ACLL, however, are generally uninterested in the substance of government actions or their practical effect on citizens. They are centrally concerned with the legal nature of the action, however, and the recommendation in *Etsurigo* changed no one's legally enforceable rights or duties. Unlike in an Article 8 order, Jusco had no legal duty to abide by the recommendation; technically, it was completely free to ignore it. Similarly, it gave Jusco no right it did not have before because it was legally free to open its store without any action by MITI whatsoever. Because the recommendation gave Jusco no new right, indeed had no legal effect at all beyond providing the basis for a possible order to follow, it could not possibly have legally affected the plaintiffs.

Furthermore, even if the recommendation had created a right or duty in Jusco, it would have made no difference in the ultimate result because the courts also found that the merchants did not have the standing to bring the action. ACLL Article 9 limits standing in administrative actions to persons with a "legal interest" in the administrative disposition. Japanese courts have interpreted this provision narrowly: "Legal interests are created by provisions vesting an administrative agency with the duty of protecting

---

decide that a recommendation was not in the nature of an administrative disposition and, therefore, could not be the subject of administrative litigation under the Administrative Case Litigation Law, Law no. 139 of 1962. For a fuller discussion of doctrines governing judicial review of administrative action in Japan, see Frank K. Upham, "After Minamata: Current Prospects and Problems in Japanese Environmental Legislation," *Ecology Law Quarterly* 8 (1979): 213.

31. Decision of February 24, 1955.

some personal interest. But where an agency is to act for the general public interest, personal interests affected by the action are only reflex interests. A plaintiff with only a reflex interest does not have standing to sue."[32] A legal interest, therefore, requires injury to an individualized interest that the agency is specifically charged to protect under the relevant statute.

In the *Etsurigo* opinions, the courts concluded that the goal of "enterprise opportunities" for local merchants set forth in Article 1 of the LSRSL was not enough to give any individual merchant more than a reflex interest in the adjustment process. Nor did the whole of the 117 plaintiffs' interests amount to more than the sum of their individual interests. Had the situation been reversed and consumers been suing MITI on the ground that the 6,390 square meters allotted to Jusco in the recommendation was too small to serve their interests, the result would have been the same. Neither regional consumers nor merchants have the individualized interest under the LSRSL to grant them standing to challenge MITI action.

The only potential plaintiffs under the LSRSL would have been prospective large retailers dissatisfied with the amount of space given them through the adjustment process. Even then, the retailers could not have sued on the basis of a MITI recommendation because they would not have had any legal obligation to follow it. They would have had to defy the recommendation and wait until MITI issued a legally binding order under Article 8. At that point the retailer would have lost the right to open a store under any terms other than those of the order and would have had the right to challenge the order for illegality, including grounds such as those alleged by the *Etsurigo* plaintiffs.

The problem is that MITI rarely, if ever, resorted to a formal order in the implementation of the LSRSL.[33] The large retailer invariably either reached a compromise with local merchants, waited it out, or gave up. According to the pre-prenotification procedures in effect during most of the 1980s, MITI did not even accept Article 3 notifications from retailers without an appended agreement with local merchants. Under these circumstances, MITI was not formally involved until the deal had been cut and had no reason even to issue a recommendation, much less an order.

Theoretically, a large retailer could have attempted to notify MITI without appending the required agreement with local merchants and, when MITI refused to accept the notification, sued to force MITI action. Its argument would have been that requiring such an agreement with local merchants was an illegal delegation of MITI's public duty to implement the statute to private parties.[34] Precedent exists for such a suit, and MITI subsequently admitted that its blanket refusal to accept notifications dur-

32. Quoted in Upham, "After Minamata," 239.
33. I have not found a single instance of MITI issuing an Article 8 order under the LSL.
34. See, for example, the Judgment of the Osaka High Court of July 30, 1979.

ing the 1980s had been illegal, but victory at this stage would only have gotten the plaintiff the right to proceed with the formal adjustment process as provided for in the statute. Although the formal process might have been more sympathetic to the interests of the retailer and consumers, it would have been time consuming and, given MITI's great discretion under the statute, might easily have resulted in an eventual order no better than what the retailer could get from the merchants directly. If MITI eventually did issue an order, the retailer would finally be able to challenge it directly, but by that point any victory would have been pyrrhic indeed.

The Structural Effect of the Large-Scale Retail Stores Law

The courts' tolerance of this regulatory approach meant that MITI could implement the LSRSL to respond freely to changing circumstances. Consequently, by the early 1980s barriers to entry into the retail market were stricter under the free-market principles of the LSRSL than they had been under the explicit government intervention of the DSL. The number of class one stores making notifications under the law dropped from a high of 576 in 1979 to 132 in 1982 and 125 in 1983. Thereafter, it remained below 200 until the late 1980s. By November 1990, six months after Japan's promise to the United States to relax restrictions, it had rebounded to a pace of more than one thousand openings per year.

These figures demonstrate MITI's ability to respond to political pressure and its effectiveness in preventing specific commercial activity without recourse to formal legal measures. After independent merchants were successful in convincing the LDP and cabinet to tighten restrictions on new stores in the late 1970s, MITI was able to cut the number of notifications by 75 percent in three years and then hold it steady at a slightly increased level thereafter. Then when the political pressure reversed and it became necessary to demonstrate good will to the Americans, the number increased severalfold in the space of months. To accomplish these shifts, MITI relied solely on administrative guidance and negotiations with the leading chains.

Flexible response to the prevailing political winds, however, was not one the statutory goals of the LSRSL, and it is debatable whether the law was effective in doing more than that. It seems highly unlikely that the law succeeded in protecting the interests of consumers, no matter how those interests might be defined. Nor is it plausible to argue that the law contributed significantly to the healthy development of the retail industry as a whole. It is clear from the rush of new stores once implementation was relaxed in 1990 that previous modes of implementation had substantially distorted the growth of the Japanese retailing industry. Furthermore, the influence was haphazard at best, following the vagaries of international and domestic politics rather than any overall plan of MITI or of the industry.

Only the very naive, however, would have expected MITI's management of the LSRSL to contribute to either consumer interests or the healthy, in the sense of market-conforming, development of general retailing. The real test of the law and of MITI's management is whether it protected the small and independent merchants whose political clout helped pass it in 1973 and convinced the Diet and MITI to strengthen it in the late 1970s. By this standard the results were mixed. Certainly, the small retailers who were included as tenants in new retail complexes or received direct payoffs benefited from the law. Those small retailers in areas where new stores were excluded entirely or were forced into price or merchandise cartels with local merchants also benefited, at least in the short run. But the overall effect of the law does not seem to have been to ensure "enterprise opportunities" for small independents in general. In fact, the number of small retailers began to decline for the first time in Japanese history between 1982 and 1985, a period of very tight restrictions under the LSRSL. During this period, stores with less than three employees declined 9.3 percent and stores with three or four employees declined 1.1 percent. In the meantime, the number of stores in every other category increased with that of the largest (more than one hundred employees) increasing 4.5 percent.[35]

Despite its apparent failure to accomplish any of its statutory purposes, however, few of those directly involved were dissatisfied with the LSRSL during the 1980s. Small merchants certainly complained about its inability to protect them from a decline in absolute numbers, but they vigorously defended the law when it came under attack. Nor did large retailers, as a rule, oppose the law or call for its repeal. Besides its disguised shift of wealth from consumers to retailers, the law had helped large retailers form an effective cartel.[36] During the late 1970s, a period of relatively lax enforcement of the LSRSL, competition had been intense for territory and reduced profits. By August 1988, however, the superstores had registered their highest profits in history, and large retailers generally had made a comeback.[37] The reasons were complex, chief among them the increased

35. The original statistics are quoted in *EPA Report*, 66–67.
36. On the cartelization of large retailing, see Miyazawa, 60; Gekishin, 11–12; Tsuruta, 51; *Nihon keizai shinbun*, October 21, 1988; and *Nihon keizai shinbun*, November 28, 1988.
37. *Yomiuri shinbun*, October 20, 1988. The top six superstores were Daiei, Ito Yokado, Seiyu, Jusco, Nichii, and Unii.

margins made possible by the yen's rise, but it seems likely that the cartelization of retailing engendered by the LSRSL had contributed to improved profits. It is interesting to note in this context that the ranking of the largest retailers remained essentially stable through the decade, arguably because the cartel effect of the LSRSL stifled competition.[38]

But cartelization was far from complete. As they had under the Department Store Law, competition and change continued, and entrepreneurs created new forms of retailing such as specialty stores, discount stores, franchise chains, and electronic marketing that effectively bypassed the restrictions of the LSRSL. But the forces that most visibly restructured the distribution industry in the 1980s were the massive leisure complexes and the convenience stores. On the one hand, retailers moved out to the suburbs and built huge retail, sports, and entertainment centers on former factory sites.[39] On the other hand, they "downsized" their stores below the LSRSL level and opened "24-hour" convenience stores. Between 1982 and 1985, the same period in which the smallest independents were decreasing in number by 9.3 percent, the sales of convenience stores rose by 84 percent, faster than any other form of retailing.[40]

Many economists and business observers, on the other hand, argued that the LSRSL had fundamentally weakened the industry's ability to adapt and innovate. One Economic Planning Agency official remarked that, just as the Department Store Law had made the department stores vulnerable to the superstores, both department and superstores had by the end of the decade forgotten how to open new stores in a competitive environment—instead they had become specialists in determining "how much money to give to which local boss."[41] Similarly small and medium retailers had come to rely on political expertise, the ability to mobilize power and articulate opposition to particular store openings, rather than business acumen. To these observers the long-term health of Japanese retailing required a fundamental reform of the Large-Scale Retail Stores Law, and they became natural allies of the Americans.

The Process of Change

Given the LSRSL's cartel effect, it is not surprising that large retailers were not eager to introduce unrestricted competition. As President Asami of Eidensha, a large regional appliance retailer, candidly phrased it in 1988,

38. Miyazawa, 60.
39. *Nihon keizai shinbun*, October 3, 1988.
40. Unpublished EPA materials on file with the author.
41. Gekishin, 10.

"The level [of restriction] is just about right now. Any looser and rivals could come in. Any stricter and we couldn't expand out." One unnamed superstore official elaborated, "To put it bluntly, the LSRSL is like a depression cartel for superstores. If we didn't have it and were forced to compete freely, there would be a major restructuring among the major companies via mergers and acquisitions."[42]

Most large retailers spoke in more measured tones, especially when speaking for attribution. President Nakauchi of Daiei, the largest superstore, for example, made a perfunctory nod toward free competition but was clearly satisfied with the way the law had protected his store's status: "I approve [of retail liberalization] in both general theory and in the particulars. It is, however, not necessary to repeal the LSRSL. That would be unacceptable—before you knew it, there would a Sears opening next door! It would be fine if the Commercial Activities Adjustment Board would just discuss matters correctly. Not even getting a foot in the door is inappropriate, but if it was done according to the language of the statute, it would be fine."[43] President Nishikawa of Unii, which had seen a steadily rising market share frozen in sixth place by the strengthening of the LSRSL in the mid-1980s, said when asked whether the LSRSL protected the superstores, "No. No. If we fall into a protectionist mentality, our industry is finished. We grew because we made it our practice to always be looking for opportunities for new stores, new locations, and new products. If a company is protected by the law and fixates on controlling its own dominant territory, it will be ruined. . . . We don't need it. We don't need it. Under the restrictions [of the law], all is serene and peaceful, but if it all becomes vested rights, then those with influence are strengthened, and that's a problem."[44]

One informed source summarized the large retailers' attitudes: "To repeal the LSRSL and go to free competition would threaten earnings, and the big superstores are most afraid of that. The fundamental consensus is that the LSRSL should be applied in a way more advantageous to the superstores. Without mincing words, they would like a shift from 'restricted competition under the leadership of small retailers' to 'managed competition under the leadership of the superstores.' "[45]

Attitudes shifted subtly among the smaller retailers, also. Their decline during the period of the LSRSL's strictest enforcement convinced many that they could not survive on their own and that competition with the new forms of retailing required a revitalization of established commercial areas that could only be accomplished with the cooperation of large retailers. But their ambivalence did not extend to the repeal of the LSRSL or

42. Ibid., 11.
43. Ibid., 12.
44. Ibid., 11–12.
45. Ibid., 12.

its substantial relaxation. They wanted to retain control so that they could invite or exclude large stores into their areas as circumstances dictated. To ensure their continuing ability to do so, many small merchants wanted the formal statutory power of the LSRSL strengthened: "It's a rule under the LSRSL that large stores must talk with the local merchants before opening, but the authority is in various forms of administrative guidance. If this rule were to disappear, it would be like a kite whose string has been cut. We need the authority to conduct adjustment transferred to the local governments."[46] Representatives of small merchants even used the inefficiencies fostered by the LSRSL as a reason to retain it: "There are only 69 persons for each retail store in Japan as opposed to 136 in the United States, 240 in the United Kingdom, and 166 in West Germany, but you do not need to cite such statistics to realize that there is excessive competition in the Japanese distribution industry. How can we possibly consider relaxation now?"[47]

Despite the retailers' general satisfaction with the LSRSL, some level of reform became inevitable in the late 1980s. Foreign pressure was a major impetus for reform, but domestic pressure was equally strong and not entirely directed toward appeasing the Americans. In 1988–1989 the *Nihon Keizai Shinbun*,[48] the Keidanren,[49] the Economic Planning Agency,[50] the Fair Trade Commission,[51] and the Second Provisional Commission on Administrative Reform (Rinchō)[52] all called for varying degrees of relaxation. Perspectives varied, but all cited the heavy toll on Japanese consumers, especially the gap between dropping import prices and high retail prices, and the unfairness and anti-import bias inherent in the implementation of the law.

Although most critics made only vague appeals for more flexibility or increases in permissible operating hours for large retailers, the EPA and the FTC both called for the eventual repeal of the LSRSL and total liberalization of the retail industry. By November 1988 Rinchō recommended a series of bureaucratic measures that together meant a thorough reform of MITI implementation of the LSRSL.

1. Consistent with the original intent, the requirement that builders explain their plans to local merchants as a prerequisite to MITI's acceptance of their Article Three notification should require only explanation, not negotiation.

46. *Nihon keizai shinbun*, October 21, 1988.
47. Gekishin, 10–11.
48. See "Reform Distribution Now," an editorial in the *Japan Economic Journal*, March 25, 1989.
49. See Keidanren Proposals.
50. See *EPA Report*.
51. See *FTC Report*.
52. Summarized in *Nihon keizai shinbun*, November 13, 1988, 3.

2. Return the actual adjustment process to the Commercial Activities Adjustment Board so that consumer and public interest representatives' opinions will be reflected in the final recommendation to MITI.
3. Take concrete steps to shorten the adjustment process such as establishing a certain period by which it must be completed and eliminating the requirement of unanimity among Board members. If the process is not completed within the set period, it should move to the next step in the statutory procedure.
4. Allow stores to make minor increases in operating hours, floor space, etc., easily in order to respond to changes in the lifestyle and needs of Japanese consumers, including the needs of households with two working spouses.
5. Reevaluate MITI's 1982 administrative guidance requiring large retailers to exercise "self-restraint" in certain designated areas.
6. Eliminate over-regulation by local governments.[53]

To make the adjustment process more accountable to the public, the EPA also suggested that the law be amended to make board members quasi-public servants so that they would be subject to criminal prosecution for bribery and that the record of the adjustment process be made public.

As the direct target of the small retailers' displeasure, MITI's views were, naturally, somewhat different. In a December 1988 interview, Takahashi Michinao, MITI's councillor for commercial distribution, responded to American criticism by pointing to the rising share of imports in the total retail sales of superstores and department stores and by reiterating the special circumstances that made the current rate of about two hundred new large stores per year appropriate for Japan: "Japanese retailing is characterized by many stores of extremely small scale densely packed into small land areas. If you look at it from this perspective, some adjustment of commercial interests is necessary within each area and the LSRSL is one way to accomplish that. If large stores were completely free to open, it would plunge local business into chaos."[54]

Even Takahashi, however, recognized that the delays and conflicts currently caused by the LSRSL were excessive and that some reforms were necessary. Although avoiding any commitments to specific measures, he noted that the November Rinchō report had called for an elimination of excessive variation in local rules and regulations and implied that reforms of the adjustment process and some relaxation of hours were under consideration. Although it seemed clear that some degree of bureaucratic reform had become acceptable to MITI, he took pains to stress that

---

53. *Nihon keizai shinbun*, November 13, 1988, 1.
54. Takahashi Michinao, "Un'yō no 'kaizen' de daitenhō wa sonzoku suru" [With "reform" in implementation, the large stores law will continue], *Ekonomisuto*, December 13, 1988, 56.

complete deregulation was premature: "On the one hand, many people talk about the benefits and convenience to consumers [of 24-hour convenience stores]. Closing times are one example. If you have to go to work or something and return to find the stores all closed, there's nothing you can do. It's very inconvenient. So, complete liberalization would be great, they say. But you cannot forget the perspective of the really small merchants caught in this kind of competition. How much protection do you give them? From this perspective the framework [of the LSRSL] is necessary."[55]

On May 24, 1990, however, MITI announced a package of short- and long-term reforms pursuant to the Structural Impediments Initiative talks with the United States. First, immediate steps would be taken under current law to make opening a large store quicker and easier. Second, MITI would submit to the 1991 regular session of the Diet amendments to the LSRSL that would further streamline the process. Third, MITI pledged to reevaluate fundamentally its policy toward the retail industry within three years, including consideration of total liberalization.

The immediate measures meant substantial changes in the operation of the law. MITI announced that it would accept all notifications regardless of the area, an implicit acknowledgment of the illegality of its former system of "restricted zones," where authorities had refused to accept any notifications whatsoever. The fundamental nature of the process of commercial adjustment was changed. The first step was still to be the explanation by the prospective retailer before Article 3 notification of its plans to local merchants, but the new rules limited this stage to four months and eliminated the requirement of the local merchants' consent. If they remained dissatisfied, the formal process moved to the next stage regardless. The entire process from initial announcement of intention by the large retailer to the final decision was to take no more than eighteen months.

In addition to the measures relating directly to the process of commercial adjustment, MITI also increased immediately the permissible hours and days of operation for large stores and exempted retail space devoted to imports from the law in certain circumstances. It also initiated measures to increase the "transparency" of the process by requiring quarterly reports on the status of pending notifications, establishing a bureau within MITI to answer inquiries regarding notifications, and providing for limited disclosure of the results of meetings of the various entities involved in the adjustment process.

MITI explained these measures to the Americans as the maximum change possible under the LSRSL.[56] They were not. Not only was the

---

55. Ibid., 57.
56. MITI's exact language from its English-language explanation was "These are the maximum measures which are legally possible under the current Large Scale Retail Stores Law."

eighteen-month deadline almost double the maximum time anticipated by the statute itself, but the liberalized hours and days of operation were well short of what MITI could have established by simply revising its ministerial order. Furthermore, true transparency remained impossible as long as the informal and nonstatutory prenotification explanation meetings were a significant part of the process. If MITI had simply decided to follow the formal process delineated by the law, the degree of liberalization would have been much greater, but to do so would have meant an immediate and substantial loss of control of the speed of reform.

Despite the lack of change in the nature of LSRSL implementation, the results changed dramatically. In the first six months following the measures, more than nine hundred prospective new large stores were announced, more than double that of the previous year and more than nine times the rate during 1982–1985.[57] The American toy retailer, Toys "R" Us, became the first foreign store to be allowed to open under the LSRSL and announced that it planned one hundred stores by the end of the decade. Large Japanese retailers also reported that the adjustment process had become easier.[58] Small merchants and local governments accelerated the trend toward using large stores as the nucleus for the revitalization of established areas, and trade associations for small and medium retailers began to lobby on the national level for various forms of subsidies to replace the declining protection of the law.

In December 1990 MITI, through a joint report by subcommittees of the Industrial Structure Council and the Small and Medium Enterprise Policy Council, announced the shape of the proposed amendment of the LSRSL to be submitted to the Diet in 1991. The eighteen-month period for store opening established in May was to be further shortened to one year and increases in floor space devoted to import goods further liberalized. To streamline the process, prenotification explanation, which had taken up to ten years in the mid-1980s, was to be eliminated entirely by starting the process with the Article 3 notification by the builders/owners of new retail spaces. After notification, they would be required to explain their plans for the buildings to local merchants, which could not take longer than four months. The next step was to be the Article 5 notification by the retailers who planned to open in the new building and an eight-month period for commercial adjustment, that is, to decide whether the proposed retail complex should be allowed to open as planned or whether changes should be recommended by MITI.

Crucial to the shortening of the period in the proposed amendment was the elimination of the Commercial Activities Adjustment Boards. Instead, initial deliberation on the impact on local retailers and consideration of

57. *Yomiuri shinbun*, December 6, 1990, New York edition, 6.
58. Ibid., 1.

reductions in size or operating conditions was to be performed by the Large Stores Council. It was hoped that the regional rather than local nature of the council and the status of its members as quasi-public servants, which made them subject to criminal liability for bribery or self-dealing, would eliminate the corruption and deliberate delay that had marked the history of the boards.

In May 1991 the Diet passed a series of bills effective in 1992 that largely carried out MITI's proposals.[59] If implemented in accord with their spirit, these amendments meant a fundamental change in the nature of retail regulation in Japan. The replacement of the boards and the elimination of the prenotification stage would require MITI and the Large Store Council to make the substantive decisions required by the statute. Instead of forcing large retailers to negotiate with their competitors, both sides would present their cases to a supposedly neutral decision-making body in a process that would be considerably more open and accountable than its predecessor. In themselves, these changes would not necessarily mean a greater number of large store openings or any substantive change in the results of the process. In practice, however, the procedural regularity and the clear deadlines for action would likely mean that the retailing industry would develop in closer conformity with the natural demands of the market than under the LSRSL as it operated until 1990. Supporting this interpretation was MITI's concurrent reiteration of the strong possibility that the LSRSL would be repealed by 1994.

Reform and even repeal of the law did not mean abandonment of small retailers, however. Simultaneously with its announcement regarding the future of the law, MITI stated its intention to introduce further legislation that would provide a wide range of subsidies to small merchants and would integrate protection of small merchants' interests into the city planning process. Consistent with the strategy already adopted by many small retailers and local entities, the proposed law would aim at the "coexistence and coprosperity" of individually owned stores and large-scale retail stores within the framework of large integrated shopping centers complete with parking lots and other facilities necessary to revitalize the surrounding commercial area. The law would require each local municipality to draft a shopping zone plan under the City Planning Law, which when approved by the governor and the Ministries of International Trade and Industry, Construction, and Local Autonomy would entitle participating merchants to a wide range of financial subsidies and tax relief. The goal for the first decade after implementation of the law was to be one hundred such shopping zones throughout Japan.

59. *Yomiuri shinbun*, May 9, 1991, 2.

Public Power and Private Interests

Tamura Masanori, professor of law at Kobe University, has identified four characteristics of LSRSL practice in the 1980s that reflect what he calls the underlying ideology of Japanese economic regulation.[60] The first is a closed economy. It was not a coincidence, according to Tamura and others, that the LSRSL was passed just as Japan was contemplating financial liberalization and the domestic retail industry feared a tide of foreign investment in Japanese distribution. To take his argument seriously, one need only note that no foreign-owned or managed retail store opened under the LSRSL until the 1990s,[61] but the goal of a closed economy relates not only to foreign entry but also to uncontrolled entry by any outsiders.

Tamura suggests a second characteristic, development egalitarianism, which he sums up with the Japanese aphorism, "The nail that sticks up gets hammered in." He considers both the expansion of the Department Store Law to cover superstores and the measures taken by local governments to restrict convenience stores as responsive to the ideal that all parties should act within the same frame of reference. He identifies a third characteristic as coexistence and coprosperity, which rejects the market principle that only those who are able to compete should survive. In the LSRSL context it meant that the large stores could survive and even prosper to the degree that they exercised management effort and expertise and that the small stores could survive regardless of their competitive abilities.

He describes a fourth characteristic as regionalism and the desire of each locality to fashion the adjustment process to meet its own economic, social, and political circumstances. Thus, the opening of large stores was controlled not by centrally, or even regionally, determined policy but by the particular circumstances pertaining in each neighborhood. As a result, the concept of a national retail market was replaced by the reality of many fragmented and isolated markets, each of which was relatively easily manipulated by the players in the LSRSL process.

The natural vehicle for economic regulation with these characteristics is cartelization, and the implementation of the LSRSL in the 1980s fostered cartels on the national, regional, and local levels.[62] Cartels by definition

60. *Nihon keizai shinbun*, October 24, 1988, 3.
61. Tsuruta, 45; Miyazawa, 57.
62. For prewar practices in retailing see Suzuki Yasuaki, *Shōwa shoki no kourishō mondai* [Problems among retailers in the early Shōwa era] (Tokyo: Nihon keizai shinbunsha, 1980). For complementary interpretations of contemporary Japan, see Chalmers Johnson, *MITI and the Japanese Miracle: The Growth of Industrial Policy, 1925–1975* (Stanford: Stanford University Press, 1982); and Richard Samuels, *The Business of the Japanese State* (Ithaca: Cornell University Press, 1987). For postwar practice, see the citations above and Michael Young, "Judicial Review of Administrative Guidance: Governmentally Encouraged Consensual Dispute Resolution in Japan," *Columbia Law Review* 84 (1987): 923–983 (on

require barriers to entry, and the history of retailing regulation and legislation from the prewar Department Store Law through the 1978 amendment of the LSRSL is, perhaps, best interpreted as repeated attempts by established retailers to deal with either new entrants or new forms of retailing. Cartels are also ideal vehicles for Tamura's development egalitarianism and coexistence and coprosperity characteristics because they are dominated by a convoy mentality that both attempts to keep everyone in business and enables the most efficient to reap additional profits, as Yasunori Sone illustrates at greater length in his concluding chapter.[63] Finally, cartels are well suited to regional and local solutions to general problems. Once it was clear that the LSRSL was going to be implemented by groups of self-appointed local merchants unfettered by centrally developed criteria, the pace and nature of change in the retailing industry could be tailored to meet the peculiar requirements of each commercial neighborhood.

MITI's formal role under the LSRSL was to enforce the cartel in accordance with its statutory standards, and the manner in which MITI chose to exercise this role is, perhaps, the most striking aspect of the LSRSL story. Instead of developing a national plan for the retail industry that balanced the interests of consumers, large retailers, and small independents and then basing the criteria for local application on the goals and rationale of the plan in consultation with the Commercial Activities Adjustment Boards and the Large Stores Councils, it simply delegated its power to the retailers themselves.

In doing so, MITI effectively substituted the private interests of local merchants for the public interests embodied in the statute. By inserting in Article 1 of the LSRSL the goals of consumer welfare and the healthy development of the retail industry, the Diet was not merely adding boilerplate to a fundamentally protectionistic statute. Neither the first nor the second Department Store Law contained language about consumers' interests or the retail sector in general. The language was inserted as statutory goals by the Diet because the political power of the small merchants was insufficient to keep them out. The insertion of consumer protection and the shift from a permit to a notification system were concessions to

---

land use planning); Frank K. Upham, "Ten Years of Affirmative Action for Japanese Burakumin: A Preliminary Report on the Law on Special Measures for *dōwa* Projects," *Law in Japan: An Annual* 13 (1980): 39–73 (on welfare programs); Frank K. Upham, "The Legal Framework of Japanese Declining Industries Policy: The Problem of Transparency in Administrative Processes," *Harvard International Law Journal* 27 (1986): 425–465 (on declining industries); and Akinori Uesugi, "Japan's Cartel System and Its Impact on International Trade," *Harvard International Law Journal* 27 (1986): 389–424 (on cartels generally).

63. Masaru Mabuchi describes a similar situation in the financial industry in Chapter 5 of this volume.

the large retailers and others who wanted a more efficient distribution industry and a clear departure from the direct regulation of the Department Store Law.

The decision by MITI to delegate the process of adjustment entirely to a group of local merchants operating outside the tripartite structure of the Adjustment Boards, therefore, was a decision to gut the statute of much of its original meaning. The further decision to require unanimous consent among local merchants essentially granted each such merchant a property right in the competitive status quo; it completed the transformation of the LSRSL from an instrument of public policy to a tool of a limited number of private parties to use in their own self-interest with no reference whatsoever to the original political compromise that had shaped the statute.

There were several advantages to MITI in this course of action. In the first place, it was easy. To implement the statute as written would have required MITI to exercise its discretion based on its own investigation and the critical evaluation of the investigation and conclusions of the advisory councils. This, in turn, would have required both additional budget and personnel. One of the most telling aspects of the May 1990 reform of the LSRSL was MITI's immediate request for forty additional staff to carry out the reform. As Mabuchi discusses in Chapter 5 in regard to declining administrative resources available to the Ministry of Finance, government regulation consistent with the wishes of those to be regulated requires few personnel. When the administration moves against those wishes, however, the call on resources is much greater. Although sold to the Americans and others as deregulation, the reforms actually meant that for the first time in one decade MITI would have to regulate the retail industry contrary to the wishes of an important segment of its members.

More important than the administrative burden of regulation, however, was the potential political cost if MITI had chosen to make the decisions itself. Whereas the political compromise at the level of the national Diet had included the other interests, the political calculus at the local level where the statute had to be applied was heavily weighted toward the protection of local merchants. Although the top level of the Liberal Democratic party had the political leeway to refuse to pursue the interests of small merchants exclusively, the rank and file frequently did not. They needed the support of local chambers of commerce and their members to be reelected, and the recitation of the value of market discipline meant little to local merchants faced with the loss of their livelihoods. In the 1970s MITI had learned the political cost of ignoring this reality and saw no reason to make the same mistake twice. The satisfaction of large retailers with their increased profits in the 1980s meant that simply nothing was to be gained by playing an active role.

Finally, there was an unexpected cost to offending local interests. It could be personally very unpleasant. Local merchants and their families had demonstrated in their battles with large retailers and their local allies, especially those who leased land to the proposed new stores, that they were willing to use violence and harassment to gain their goals. There was no reason to suspect, should MITI act inimically to their interests, that local merchants would have treated them any differently. Indeed, MITI bureaucrats ruefully noted that it was always easy to identify the desk of a regional official involved in an LSRSL conflict: it was the one dented by the iron rods and baseball bats wielded by irate merchants determined to get their points across.

As Rosenbluth points out in Chapter 4 regarding the Ministry of Finance, ease of regulation can at times be a more important bureaucratic goal than the expansion of budget, personnel, or even jurisdiction. In the LSRSL context, MITI had jurisdiction over the retail industry, but during the 1980s it chose not to exercise the direct power that jurisdiction gave it. Instead, by granting local merchants a veto power over new stores in their neighborhoods, MITI created an informal framework within which private parties worked out their own accommodations. Its refusal to accept an Article 3 notification without the appended agreement of the local merchants forced large retailers into open-ended bargaining with their competitors. Whether or not the store opened and, hence, the direction and pace of change in the retail industry, depended not on MITI's regulation of the industry but on the results of private negotiations. These could turn on factors as idiosyncratic as whether the prospective new entrant correctly identified the bosses within the local merchant community.

Whatever else one might say about this scheme, it is not what one would expect of an elite bureaucracy regulating the market in the national interest. Indeed, if one defines "regulation" as government intervention in the operation of the market, it is difficult to describe the implementation of the LSRSL as government intervention at all. Beyond setting the original entitlements, that is, granting veto power to local merchants, the government was rarely involved. Although MITI in the 1980s implemented the statute as a permit system in the political sense meant by then MITI minister Nakasone in his 1973 pledge to small retailers, it did not do so according to the dictates of an interstate commerce commission or a bureau of motor vehicles: it did not grant or withhold entry into a market or grant a license based on facts submitted by applicants in accordance with a set of stated criteria. Instead, it delegated the permit decisions to a system of private ordering.

This system of private ordering operated like a market: to open a store, the large retailer had to purchase the right from the small retailers in the area just as it had to purchase or lease land or any other factor of production. As with every other market, it was created by the government giving rights to potential players in accordance with political decisions and then stepping back and allowing the final allocation of resources to be

determined by private ordering. In this instance the Diet initially decided
that small merchants were to receive some degree of protection through
the LSRSL, and MITI subsequently defined the degree of protection as a
veto power over new entrants.

Regulation by market creation or other forms of private ordering is
common in Japanese economic policy. Many towns and cities have created
similar markets in development rights by granting neighbors of proposed
highrise buildings some form of veto over the construction. Unless the developer can reach some accommodation with the local residents, the municipal government will refuse to grant necessary services for the new
building such as access to public water or sewage systems.[64] The result has
often been the same style of private ordering as that in the LSRSL case.
Similarly, the Ministry of Posts and Telecommunications (MPT) does not
allocate new television channels by deciding among a number of rival applicants as anticipated by relevant statutes and as is common in the United
States and elsewhere. Instead, the MPT announces to all parties that it will
entertain only one application. The rivals are then forced to negotiate
among themselves with the result that either a joint venture incorporating
all parties is formed or a rotation system similar to the *dangō* (preliminary
consultation) system in government construction contracts emerges.[65]

This form of regulation requires relatively few bureaucrats because it
does not obligate the government agency to investigate or evaluate applications. It is also invisible: as long as the bureaucracy makes no decision,
it bears no responsibility. It is not accountable legally or, at least on a microlevel, politically. It carries an implication for the operation of the free
market envisioned by economists. The general lack of criteria for entry
into the market and for setting conditions on entry or operation after entry implies a relative lack of concern for efficiency or market discipline on
the part of the regulator who has created the framework within which the
private ordering occurs. The mode of implementation—large stores buy
out small ones, efficient developers buy out neighboring residents, and so
forth—does not *stop* the market as a more conventional licensing regime
or a quota system might.

The LSRSL and Trends in Regulatory Style

Although the LSRSL experience is scarcely evidence of a strong state in the
sense of an elite bureaucracy pursuing national interests aloof from par-

---

64. See Young, "Judicial Review."
65. See Jonathan Weinberg, "Broadcasting and the Administrative Process in Japan and
the United States," *Buffalo Law Review* 39 (1991): 615–735.

tisan strife, neither is it evidence of a weak or irrelevant bureauracy. Once the politicians set policy on the macro level, as they did in 1973, 1977–1979, and the late 1980s, it was left almost entirely up to MITI to determine what this policy would look like at the microlevel. As Muramatsu points out in his reconsideration of patterned pluralism in Chapter 2, it is the bureaucrats who are engaged in the complex, troublesome, and sometimes political work of accommodating varying interests. In the first period of its implementation of the LSRSL and then again after May 1990, MITI regulated directly; in the 1980s it allowed private parties to operate freely within the framework it had created. In both circumstances, MITI was responding to political and international pressure on the macro level, but the speed and ease with which it responded and manipulated the number of store openings demonstrate the autonomy and power of the ministry to operate within its jurisdiction.

Although achieved with equal facility, the dramatic decrease in openings in the early 1980s and the equally remarkable increase in 1990–1991 occurred within quite different political and international contexts and at different points in the evolution of postwar economic regulation. By the late 1980s the international pressure that had earlier contributed to the partial deregulation of other sectors had reached retailing, and the policy changes of 1990 are at least superficially consistent with the hypothesis of a decline in bureaucratic resources and concomitant economic liberalization identified by Muramatsu, Tsujinaka, Mabuchi, Rosenbluth, and others in this volume.

Muramatsu divides the development of regulatory administration in the postwar period into three phases, each characterized by a specific bureaucratic instrument: the control period (1945–1960) when ministries such as MITI had direct legal power over the economy; the administrative guidance period of decreasing legal power and increasing party and industry power (1960–1980) when the government was forced to rely more on administrative guidance and relationships with trade associations and other institutions within their jurisdiction; and the period of deregulation or soft administration after 1981. The progression from the Department Store Law (1956–1973) through the Large-Scale Retail Stores Law (1973–1990) to the LSRSL's amendment and the passage of legislation integrating retail regulation into urban planning in 1991 initially appears to fit this periodization well.

Closer inspection, however, reveals some twists and turns within the pattern that give depth to the meaning of the different periods. A comparison of the licensing provisions of the DSL with the notification and administrative guidance of the LSRSL fits Muramatsu's control and administrative guidance phases well, but this apparent decline in legal power did not mean a decline in MITI's practical power at the micro level. Article

8 of the LSRSL gave MITI a measure of legal power greater than many other economic statutes.[66] MITI's virtually unconstrained ability to raise or lower the number of store openings without recourse to formal legal measures demonstrates that caution is necessary in equating legal power under regulatory statutes with actual effectiveness in the implementation of statutory policy.

The DSL prevented department stores from opening without MITI's permission, but its jurisdiction was too narrow for MITI to prevent the emergence of the superstores. The broader jurisdiction of the LSRSL and MITI's willingness to police a cartel that benefited all sectors of the industry meant that its administrative guidance was more effective in restricting retail expansion in the 1980s than its formal legal power had been in the 1960s. Whether the policy shifts and legislation of 1990 and 1991 toward protection for small merchants through subsidies and promotion rather than restrictions on market entry represent economic liberalization, therefore, may depend as much on international and domestic political forces as on the nature of the regulatory tools at MITI's disposal.

66. See Frank K. Upham, "The Man Who Would Import: A Cautionary Tale about Bucking the System in Japan," *Journal of Japanese Studies* 17 (Summer 1991): 323, for a discussion of the problems MITI had in enforcing its policy under the Petroleum Industry Law. That law, unlike the LSRSL, did not have any legal sanctions to back up the ministry's administrative guidance. In the end, MITI was able to enforce its policies, but the difficulty it encountered may be evidence of the importance of Article 8 of the LSRSL.

CONCLUSION

STRUCTURING POLITICAL BARGAINS:

GOVERNMENT, *GYŌKAI*, AND MARKETS

Yasunori Sone

POLITICAL AND ECONOMIC CHANGE HAPPENS FAST IN JAPAN. THIS WAS
certainly true in the 1980s when administrative reform, a speculative economic bubble, and the country's rapidly expanding influence on the international economy all stimulated thoroughgoing changes. In the
chapters in this volume one captures a sense of these changes in a variety
of political arenas and from a variety of perspectives.

Our efforts to apprehend such changes resonated with two very different efforts to comprehend Japan that took place during the period when
we were carrying out our studies. One effort arose under the auspices of
the Structural Impediments Initiative (SII) talks between Japan and the
United States. By sheer coincidence our second meeting at Airlie House
was also one site for those talks. Undertaken as intergovernmental negotiations to explore structural problems in the Japanese-American relationship, the SII talks treated many subjects examined in these chapters. A
second effort to understand Japan was led by the revisionists. This group
included the Japan scholar, Chalmers Johnson, and journalists and con-
sultants such as James Fallows, Clyde Prestowitz, and Karel van Wolferen.
The revisionists attracted considerable attention to Japan through the
mass media with their acute critique of prior scholarship on Japan.
Whereas the SII talks focused on economic sources of binational tensions
and normal governmental solutions to them, the revisionists directed a
multifaceted critique at Japan's entire system of government, administration, and economics.

Our concerns in this volume mirror, in part, issues raised by the SII
talks and topics scrutinized by the revisionists. These shared concerns

include the relationships between politics and economics, between government and the market, and between government and industry. From my perspective as a scholar in Japan who studies political theory and public administration, I try in this conclusion to show how our work can help clarify these controversial issues. In particular, I suggest how we can use the notion of *gyōkai,* or policy clienteles, to illuminate the distinctively Japanese structures in which negotiations over public and private economic interests take place.

Government and Markets

There are many views of the relationship between politics and economics in Japan. One view frames the issue as a problem of state-society relations. The very breadth of this problem, however, creates analytical difficulties. Another possibility is to frame the issue in two abstractions, the government and the market. Economists employing the tools of macroanalysis can work fruitfully with such abstractions, but political scientists benefit by asking more pragmatic questions. Precisely how does the government intervene in markets? Is the government a central actor in economic markets? Is it the core of the economy and the market just an appendage? What means does the government have at its disposal when executing policies? Just how does one define the relationships between government and the market in a complex, capitalist society like Japan?

To discuss such relations, one must be alert to the cultural overtones embodied in common terms. Both Japan and the United States have market economies. In Japan, however, it is generally held that government intervenes in the market to promote rationality, whereas in the United States it is commonly felt that the government's proper role is to stay out of the market. To assume that Japan and the United States are both capitalist market economies is to recognize that Japanese and Americans embrace different views of the same concept, in this case, the market. (The same is true of a concept such as fairness.) Nonetheless, one must tolerate some ambiguity when using such terms in cross-national analyses.

I posit a simple model. Imagine an economy with a government and no market and another with a market but no government. In figure C.1 the X axis spans the spectrum between the two extremes. In classical, liberal economic thought, the market was more important than the role of government. An economy operating under these principles would appear on the right side of the X axis. In contrast, a command or socialist economy directed by a government where only a black market existed would appear on the left side of the X axis.

Figure C.1 Hypothesizing government-market relations

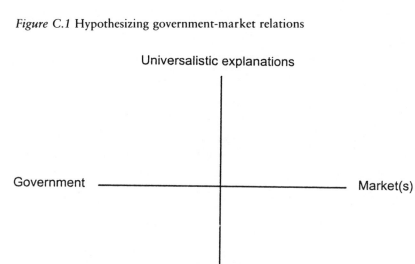

One can posit a similar dichotomy for the Y axis. One can imagine an economy that operates according to nearly universal principles. One can also imagine a country with a pattern of economic relations based on its particular culture and history. To cite an extreme case, one could claim that Japan's economic growth is a result of its unique culture and the studiousness of the Japanese people. This claim would put Japan at the lower end of the Y axis as a special case to be explained by particular, not universal, considerations. In contrast, an exemplary universal case would be one in which geography, history and culture have no influence on the economy. The deterministic assertion that socialist revolution was inevitable fits this universalistic model.

In figure C.2 I have arrayed explanations for Japan's economic success to show how they might fit on this two-dimensional grid. Particularistic explanations that stress factors nearly unique to Japan appear near the bottom while approaches that emphasize factors common to most advanced industrial countries appear near the top. Likewise, approaches stressing the importance of governmental actions appear toward the left while explanations giving weight to more purely market factors under an open international trade system appear on the right.

Without engaging in a detailed review of the literature (something that Margaret McKean has already done in Chapter 3), I note two things. First,

Figure C.2 Specifying government-market relations

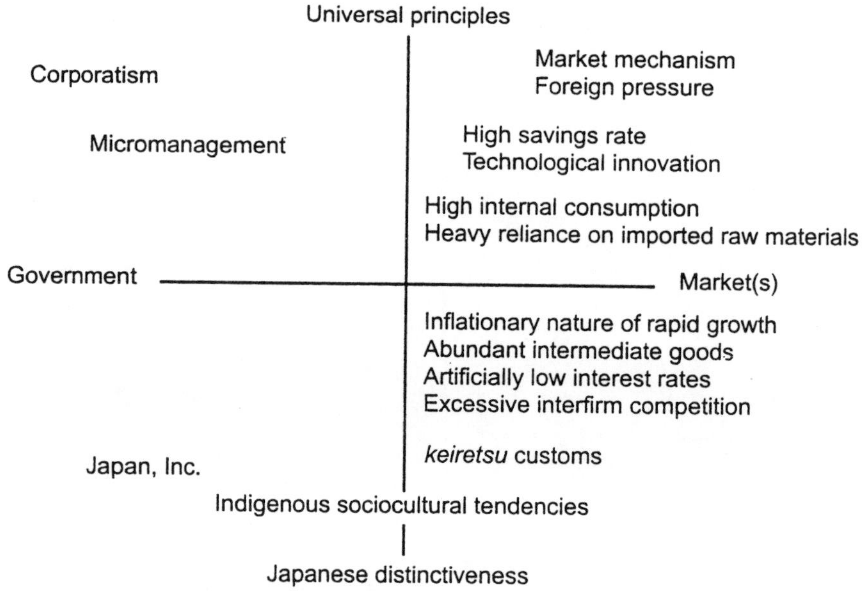

```
                    Universal principles
                            |
                            |        Market mechanism
   Corporatism              |        Foreign pressure
                            |
                            |     High savings rate
   Micromanagement          |     Technological innovation
                            |
                            |  High internal consumption
                            |  Heavy reliance on imported raw materials
                            |
Government ─────────────────┼──────────────────────── Market(s)
                            |
                            | Inflationary nature of rapid growth
                            | Abundant intermediate goods
                            | Artificially low interest rates
                            | Excessive interfirm competition
                            |
                            |  keiretsu customs
   Japan, Inc.              |
                Indigenous sociocultural tendencies
                            |
                    Japanese distinctiveness
```

figure C.2 helps one to appreciate that the relations between the government and the market can and do change over time. In several of the preceding chapters Michio Muramatsu, Masaru Mabuchi, Hideo Otake, and Frank Upham have indicated how direct government intervention in Japanese markets declined during the 1980s owing to resource constraints on the part of the government. Similarly, foreign pressure in the 1990s aimed at ensuring unrestricted access to Japanese markets from abroad has posed a challenge to the particularistic emphasis on *keiretsu* (affiliated enterprises) barriers to trade.

Second, explanations for the success of the Japanese economy have changed over time. An explanation stressing Japan, Inc., might have possessed more than a grain of truth for the late 1950s; such an explanation seems less well suited to the 1980s, given the increasing autonomy of Japanese corporations remarked in many chapters in this volume. To cite another example, an emphasis on artificially low domestic interest rates may have explained high levels of corporate investment in the 1960s, but the very different combination of financial arrangements of the late 1980s would require alternative explanations.

Despite the past emphasis on the role of the government in Japan's economic success, very little evidence affirms that the government has been the central actor in the market. The paucity of government-owned enterprises in Japan, especially when compared with European nations, supports this claim. Privatization arose in Japan during the 1980s just as it did in other advanced industrial countries, and by the end of the 1980s Japan had even fewer nationally owned enterprises than Great Britain. The privatization of the three major national corporations (the railway, the telephone and telegraph services, and the salt and tobacco monopoly) was symbolic of Japan's retreat from public enterprise management. In comparative international terms, the importance of public enterprises has always been relatively low in Japan.

Other measures of government size and intervention, however, are not based on nationalization or the management of public enterprises. What do they indicate about Japan's government-market relations? If one uses five measures of government size developed by Richard Rose, one finds that Japan does not have a very large government.[1] Although the size of the government sector of the economy began to expand in the late 1980s, compared to other advanced industrial countries Japan's governmental spending still remained relatively low. For example, government expenditures as a percentage of gross national product (GNP) were 33 percent in Japan in the mid-1980s, whereas they were 48 percent in West Germany and Great Britain and 53 percent in France.[2] Comparing the number of (civilian) public employees for every one thousand citizens about 1980, one finds that Japan had only forty-two while West Germany had sixty-five, France seventy-four, and England one hundred.[3] The number of laws passed in Japan, normally fewer than one hundred per year, is also relatively low. And, finally, the number of government agencies and the number of public projects are also relatively low. According to all these measures, Japan has had a small government.

The role of the Japanese government is revealed not only in such numerical data but by examining its real influence with qualitative measures as well. For example, one can identify differences according to strength or weakness, hardness or softness (as Masaru Mabuchi does in Chapter 5), or wisdom or foolishness (as Margaret McKean does in Chapter 3). One can appreciate these distinctions by considering the large, strong, and hard—but foolish—government of the Stalinist Soviet Union.

Is Japan's state strong, even though it is small? Is it strong according to its legal powers or the force of its authority? Excessive use of administrative guidance (*gyōsei shidō*) casts doubt on the strength of government as Michio Muramatsu suggests in Chapter 2. Moreover, legal powers can

---

1. Richard Rose, *Big Government: The Programme Approach* (London: Sage Publications, 1984).
2. Itō Motoshige, Kiyono Kazuharu, Okuno Masahiro, and Suzuki Kōtarō, eds., *Sangyō seisaku no keizai bunseki* [An economic analysis of industrial policy] (Tokyo: Tōkyō daigaku shuppankai, 1988), 112.
3. Ibid.

differ considerably among ministries. MITI seems to have steadily lost power during the postwar era while the Ministry of Finance (MOF) has preserved its legal powers as Masaru Mabuchi demonstrates in Chapter 5. This returns to a question raised by the advocates of a pluralist aproach to Japanese politics: How great is the influence exercised through governmental roles? In many cases, one can only answer this question by examining specific policies. Conceding this, one is obliged to assess government influence in each policy area.

To summarize government-market relations in Japan: the government has not been an adversary of market mechanisms or the central actor in the market; government enterprises have been a relatively small part of the economy; in comparison with other advanced industrial countries, general account expenditures of the government as a percentage of the GNP have been relatively low; and the Japanese government has engaged in the market more as a coach than as a player. Opinions of its role as a coach are widely divided. Some say the government has been successful (both owing to MITI and in spite of MITI), whereas others say it has experienced many failures. In making these judgments, observers have generally employed the concept of industrial policy (sangyō seisaku) to provide an overly abstract description of the relationship between the government and private markets. I suggest that a slightly different perspective that relies on gyōkai policy offers a more fitting approach to reality.

Gyōkai as an Intervening Variable

Ordinarily gyōkai is used to refer to the formal associations that represent the interests of an industrial sector, such as auto makers or steel producers. I use the term in this sense but also in a somewhat broader sense to refer to all of the entities (firms, enterprises, and trade associations) that fall under the legal jurisdiction of a particular ministry. In this broader sense, the gyōkai under MITI jurisdiction refers to all manufacturing firms (large, medium, and small) as well as to the industry-specific manufacturing trade associations. To cite another example, the gyōkai under MOF jurisdiction includes banks, insurance companies, and securities firms, as well as the various trade associations that represent their interests. In the broader sense in which I use the term, therefore, we can think of gyōkai as policy clienteles, in contrast with trade associations.

The Japanese government did not deal with the market by employing abstract macrolevel policies. Policies took concrete form at the level of gyōkai. Recognizing this, one can speak about different histories among different gyōkai and use gyōkai as an intevening variable central to an analysis. Of course, one cannot deny the importance of four economic associations: Keidanren, the Keizai dōyūkai (Japan Committee for Economic Development), Nikkeiren (Japan Federation of Employers' Associations), and the Japan Chamber of Commerce and Industry. Each trade association belongs to one or more of these bodies. Most concrete policies that affect a particular industrial sector, however, are made by the government for implementation at the level of a gyōkai.

Gyōkai arise as a consequence of the jurisdictional boundaries of ministries and agencies. Jurisdictional boundaries prevail whether events affect a gyōkai constituent engaged in activities inside or outside Japan. A manufacturing firm in Indonesia, for example, would still fall under MITI jurisdiction not that of the Ministry of Foreign Affairs. Policy takes concrete form through its execution at the gyōkai level. The more concrete policies become, the more important it is to consider the role of firms and associations among the various gyōkai. Actual policies differ among gyōkai because, in general, two contradictory phenomena are at play: the keen competition that exists among individual Japanese enterprises and the internal stability of the gyōkai themselves. The role of the government, acting through its ministries and agencies (especially at the level of the section, or *ka*), is to deal with actual conditions on a gyōkai by gyōkai basis.

Different conditions obtain among gyōkai. Harmonious relations and a cartel-like nature characterize the iron and steel industry. By comparison, the auto industry is internally competitive. The consumer electronics industry is even more competitive: unity is difficult and consensus lacking. Moreover, stability within a gyōkai is never fixed. Sumitomo Metals and its defiance of MITI directives concerning investment in new plant is a well-known case in point. The auto industry offers another example. MITI wanted to organize two or three large firms to make automobiles to compete with America's "big three." But Honda and other firms entered the industry, and in 1992 ten vehicle manufacturers compete against each other. Government ministries have not always been able to compartmentalize (*shikiri*) and supervise industry as they wished.

Contradictory tendencies exist among gyōkai and between gyōkai and government ministries. They may have cartel-like qualities, but by no means always. Competition among enterprises is keen, but the Japanese market is not merely the product of fierce interfirm competition. When describing the relations between gyōkai and ministries, contradictory perspectives also emerge. Ministries can regard competitive enterprises as troublesome and, therefore, undeserving of attention at the same time that they feel protective toward noncompetitive enterprises. In general, ministries tend to want to eliminate excessive competition.

There is some commonality in the way that different gyōkai deal with government ministries. Declining industries, such as agriculture and coal, entreat ministries for assistance. In contrast, competitive enterprises and industries hope for autonomy. Government ministries however, tend to set rules and deal with different gyōkai on the standard set by the weakest enterprises. Some claim that the government creates protective convoys (*gosō sendan*) in which no one moves any faster than the weakest member, which does not allocate resources within gyōkai efficiently. Others—especially those from abroad—criticize the high entry barriers for new firms. But government policy that protects weak firms creates entry barriers for prospective Japanese firms, too. Consequently, an administration that nourishes gyōkai tends to protect vested interests.

Japanese administrations have not favored only designated industries for development. They have tried to be fair across the full spectrum of the industrial sector when making industrial policies. Thus, some consistency exists between MITI's visions for expanding industries and the realities of the market. Toyota and Matsushita did not become first in their fields because of support from MITI, but in the financial sector small enterprises *were* sustained by MOF policies that regulated interest rates and set fees to ensure their survival, however economically irrational such policies might have seemed. Under this regime, fairness ensured that nearly everyone made some profit while the largest firms made the greatest profits. Differences have arisen between Japan and the United States owing to this distinctive definition of fairness. To the Japanese fairness in this sense means an unwillingness to grant special favor to a specific firm within a gyōkai, even a foreign one, but Americans tend to see the issue differently.

The conditions of specific gyōkai are described in many chapters in this book. Margaret McKean, in Chapter 3, examines how the state engages gyōkai in a broad context. Michio Muramatsu, in Chapter 2, characterizes the pattern of relations between a number of ministries and gyōkai. Frank Schwartz, in Chapter 9, and Hideo Otake, in Chapter 10, both illuminate the role of gyōkai in the policy process by focusing on their representational activities and influence on advisory commissions (*shingikai*). And the concrete nature of specific gyōkai in finance, coal and steel, and the small retail sector is described in Chapters 4, 5, 6, and 11, respectively. In these chapters analysts provide clear evidence of the sometimes competitive and sometimes protective character of government-gyōkai relations and how they can—and do—change over time. Ferment and dynamism seem to be constant features of the Japanese political economy despite the superficial appearance of stability.

In contemporary Japan the most solid structural system is the enterprise society, an entity consisting of management and labor. Sometimes this system is called *Nihon-teki keiei* (Japanese-style enterprise management) and sometimes, as the Toyota *kanban* ("just-in-time") technique suggests, it is characterized by an emphasis on production-line efficiency. An enterprise society is a very secure system in which the corporate value placed on loyalty and growth has been widely diffused and internalized by all the individuals involved. Such values are the foundation on which interfirm competition rests and imply why such competition can be so intense. These attitudes facilitate the exclusive trade customs that easily develop when *keiretsu* arise. When Americans during the SII talks pointed to the effects of Japanese-style enterprise management on trade problems, they were not far off the mark.

Most commentators on the so-called Japanese-style enterprise management are referring to that common in the efficient, large-scale manufacturing sector. This part of the economy, however, is actually shrinking, and for more than one decade has comprised less than 20 percent of the GNP. Therefore, one can go too far in trying to reify explanations based on such phenomena as the "lean system" or the "just-in-time" technique. It is important to acknowledge the full range and diversity of the Japanese economy. This perspective would take into account the productivity of a service sector that comprises nearly 60 percent of the economy and would consider the internationally gigantic banks, insurance companies, and securities firms with their large white-collar work forces. Finally, an encompassing view of the Japanese economy would take into account the less competitive agricultural sector and small and medium-sized enterprises. It would be especially difficult to understand Japanese politics without appreciating the Liberal Democratic party's (LDP) reliance on votes from the inefficient agricultural and small-enterprise sectors.

The durable and indestructible Japanese enterprise system is the basic unit of behavior in the political economy. Its energies are aggregated in the gyōkai that mediate political relations with the government and administrative entities. More so than the concept of an abstract market, the notion of gyōkai offers an effective and realistic vehicle for understanding Japan's contemporary political economy.

Iron Triangles, Corporatism, and Labor's Distinctive Position

The manner in which government ministries and agencies compartmentalize society is reflected not just in gyōkai but elsewhere as well. Committees in the Diet, policy bodies in the LDP and other parties, and many shingikai, too, all basically conform with the principles of ministerial compartmentalization. There was once an attempt to organize the Diet according to issue areas or problem areas, but in the early postwar period the ministry-agency pattern of organization was restored. In particular, section-level engagement with gyōkai became a basic feature of administration. This explains, in part, why the *zoku giin* (legislators who specialize in specific policy areas) arose; they often seek results through separate ministries at the section level. In this way Japan's particular pattern of interest representation and reconciliation has also evolved. Thus, administration, political parties, and the legislature all easily adopt policies that conform with the gyōkai pattern.

Labor is one institution that does not conform well with the notion of the gyōkai. One might think that if private enterprises were organized according to the gyōkai principle, then labor unions would be, too. In fact, however, labor unions have found it far more difficult to achieve consensus at a federated level than have unions in other countries. The high incidence of enterprise unions in the private sector has inhibited the collective strength of organized labor. But labor entities *have* been organized at the industry or gyōkai level. Most people, however, have given them little credence, regarding them only as weak agents trying to coordinate strong unions rooted in separate enterprises, such as those of Nissan or Toyota in the auto industry labor federation.

Another factor inhibiting the influence of organized labor has been its problematic relationship to government ministries. The Ministry of Labor (MOL), historically politically weak, embraces all workers under its jurisdiction whether they are organized or not. In keeping with the administrative preference for fairness, MOL attends to broad issues such as working conditions and labor standards. The MOL, therefore, is not a strong advocate for organized labor as a gyōkai in its own right. Even though organized labor in heavy industry might have expected MITI to advocate on its behalf, MITI has preferred to view labor problems in the firms under its jurisdiction as the private concerns of the firms themselves. This position both reflects and affirms the importance of the enterprise society. But as a consequence, both MITI and MOL eschew administrative representation of organized labor's interests thereby leaving organized labor largely to fend for itself.

Organized labor has been plagued with difficulties as it tries to strengthen itself at industry and national levels. The lack of a dominant, single national center, before Rengō emerged in the late 1980s, obviously hampered labor's ability to participate in a fully corporatist polity. A kind of corporatism, however, has functioned—not at the national level—but on a microlevel within firms. It has not embraced a tripartite combination of government, management, and labor. Instead, microcorporatism has brought together management, labor, and shareholders. As is well known, shareholders play a minor role and exert little influence in Japan's distinctive style of enterprise management. Therefore, microcorporatism binds management and labor in a strong embrace at the firm level. This pattern of relations produces not "corporatism without labor" but corporatism without government.[4]

If one excludes government from the concept and reality of corporatism, what then emerges? The outcome is not a polity in which government, management, and labor function as relatively equivalent, collective forces at the national level (see the introductory chapter and Chapters 6, 7, and 8). What emerges is a polity in which gyōkai serve as influential political mediators for many sectors of society, but labor is an exception to this rule. Excluded by jurisdictional difficulties and ministerial biases and hampered by higher-level organizational impediments, organized labor has had to accept a subordinate position within the polity. Nonetheless, as the authors argue in Chapters 6, 7, and 8, labor has been able to overcome its apparently weak position in the larger polity to achieve on a microcorporatist field of action the objectives it values most highly.

In this light, how should one interpret Rengō? Rengō is a peak organization, but it did not come about by destroying the enterprise unions on which it is based. Instead, as Yutaka Tsujinaka argues in Chapter 8, Rengō depends heavily on the enterprise-level networks of its constituents. Rengō also tries to take advantage of the networks formed by its industry-level federations. And Rengō does function in some ways to represent organized labor as a peak organization in national affairs. Its ability to do this, however, is restricted by the fact that it represents only 25 percent of the entire labor force and a relatively small share of workers in the large and growing service sector. Rengō is also operating with a weak legacy of labor participation in national affairs as Yutaka Tsujinaka notes in his discussion of Sohyo's pattern of political actions during the 1960s and 1970s. Organized labor's influence, therefore, is concentrated at the enterprise level and to a lesser extent at the level of industry groups and has been relatively weak at the center.

I have argued that to understand how the government in Japan has intervened in the market one must appreciate how government policies have been conceived and executed at the level of the gyōkai. This perspective offers explanations for many key features of Japan's contemporary polity, including the effects of sectoral and industrial policies, the relations among bureaucrats, politicians, and legislators, the pattern of contacts between government and the private sector, and even the emergence of *seisaku zoku* (informal groups of legislators who specialize in specific policy

4. This is the title of a germinal essay on the role of organized labor in Japanese politics by T. J. Pempel and Keiichi Tsunekawa, "Corporatism without Labor? The Japanese Anomaly," in Philippe C. Schmitter and Gerhard Lehmbruch, eds., *Trends toward Corporatist Intermediation* (Beverly Hills: Sage Publications, 1979), 231–270.

areas). The notion of gyōkai helps to account for the political competition that produced the financial reforms treated in Chapters 4 and 5, and it illuminates how the shingikai discussed in Chapters 9 and 10 represent and reconcile political interests. A gyōkai perspective also helps to explain, in part, the structurally distinctive political role of organized labor detailed in Chapters 6, 7, and 8. The gyōkai notion does not, however, explicate the position of consumers in the polity because they do not possess a gyōkai-like vehicle to aggregate their interests. Sections within ministries that directly supervise and deal with consumers are both weak and few. From this perspective, it is correct to say that Japan has a producer-oriented structure.

Japanese industry, however, is internally extremely competitive, and such market competition did not come about by ignoring the consumer. Margaret McKean suggests in Chapter 3 how politicians pursuing their own self-interests have, nonetheless, (possibly unintentionally) promoted the public interest in a general way. Business firms pursuing their self-interests in competitive markets have (perhaps unintentionally) satisfied consumer interests, too. Markets have, thus, been one important cause of growth in Japan, but the government has played a role by complementing those markets. Through administrative rather than legal or adversarial processes the Japanese government has preserved market order and modulated excessive competition. The government has also used both political and administrative means to extend relatively generous protection and assistance to weak and declining industries.

Highly competitive sectors and foreign firms have regarded government intervention as meddlesome, whereas declining sectors have probably seen it as benevolent. These contradictions highlight the fact that Japanese administration can and does simultaneously embrace and reject intervention, depending on the conditions of the gyōkai at issue. In a Japan where the roles of officials and the people, along with public and private interests, are becoming increasingly commingled, political analysts must be prepared to accept this kind of ambiguity and to expect such contradictions.

INDEX

administrative case law, 274–279
administrative reform (*gyōsei kaikaku*),
    4–5, 41–42, 61, 182–184, 234–237,
    250, 256
affluence, 8–9, 19–22, 121–122
amakudari (descent from heaven), 3, 28–
    30, 82, 204, 227–228
Anchordoguy, Marie, 84
Aoki, Masahiko, 207
auto industry, 85

Banking Act of 1982, 113–114
Banking Bureau. *See* Ministry of Finance
Bank of Japan, 136, 146
banks, 109–114, 137–138, 141–142
Basic Land Act, 261
big business, 4, 41–44, 81–88, 224–225,
    237, 247–250, 256–259, 282–283
Broadbent, Jeffrey, 78–79
bureaucrats: administrative styles of, 132–
    134, 148–152, 270–274, 284–287,
    292–294; persisting influence of, 45–
    47, 255–256; political roles of, 58–60,
    76, 115–116; representation of, on *shin-
    gikai,* 226–228; waning influence of,
    8–9, 63–68, 80–88. *See also entries for
    specific ministries; amakudari; shukkō*

Calder, Kent, 83, 137
Campbell, John, 46, 87
capacity constraints, 12–13, 60–61,
    279–287
citizenship. *See* economic citizenship

clarification, 135–136, 150–152
coal industry, 86, 159–168, 177–179
collective action theory, 90–94, 99–102
collusion, 99–104, 196
Commercial Activities Adjustment
    Board(s), 271–279, 282, 284, 286–
    287, 290
commercial paper, 113–114
compensating balances, 110–113
computer industry, 84, 101–102
constitutional reform, 203
consumers, 96–99, 102–104, 111–114,
    120–125, 265–268, 279–281, 306
consumption tax, 35, 60–61
convenience stores, 281
corporate bonds, 111–113
corporatism, 94–96, 100–104, 202, 212–
    213, 303–305
corruption, 35. *See also* Recruit scandal
courts, 80, 117–118, 274–279
Curtis, Gerald, 79

declining industries, 83–84, 165–168,
    301–302
democracy, 103–104
Department Store Law(s), 268–271
deregulation, 85–88, 139–142,
    243–246
disclosure rules, 119–120, 151–152
Doi, Takako, 31–35, 51–53, 126
Dokō, Toshio, 41–42, 192
Dōmei (Confederation of Japanese Labor
    Unions), 181, 206

Library of Congress Cataloging-in-Publication Data

Political dynamics in contemporary Japan /edited by Gary D. Allinson
   and Yasunori Sone.
      p.   cm.
   Includes bibliographical references and index.
   ISBN 0-8014-2852-1 (cloth : alk. paper).—ISBN 0-8014-8096-5
(pbk. : alk. paper)
   1. Japan—Economic conditions—1945– 2. Japan—Politics and
government—1945– 3. Japan—Economic policy—1945– I. Allinson,
Gary D.   II. Sone, Yasunori.
HC462.9.P56 1993
338.952—dc20   92-56777